KENILWORTH SCHOOL
LIBRARY

WITHDRAWN

C000060664

9000153999

Portrait of a Decade
1910-19

TREVOR FISHER

B.T. Batsford Ltd, London

Contents

The original idea for the Portrait of a Decade series was conceived by Trevor Fisher.

© Trevor Fisher 1991
First published 1991

All rights reserved. No part of this publication may be reproduced in any form or by any means without permission from the Publisher.

Typeset by Tek-Art Ltd Kent
and printed in Great Britain by
Hillman Printers (Frome) Ltd,
Frome, Somerset
for the publishers
B.T. Batsford Ltd
4 Fitzhardinge Street
London W1H 0AH

A CIP catalogue record for this book is available from the British Library

ISBN 0 7134 6071 7

Frontispiece: War work. The First World War brought women into Britain's factories to do jobs previously undertaken by men.

Introduction 3

1910
Victoria's Grandchildren 6
World news 8
Sport and the arts 10
Science and technology 11

1911
The *Panther* Crisis 12
World news 14
Sport and the arts 16
Science and technology 17

1912
Titanic! 18
World news 20
Sport and the arts 22
Science and technology 23

1913
The Armory Show 24
World news 26
Sport and the arts 28
Science and technology 29

1914
Death in Sarajevo 30
World news 32
Sport and the arts 34
Science and technology 35

1915
The *Lusitania* Mystery 36
World news 38
Sport and the arts 40
Science and technology 41

1916
The man who could
have lost the war 42
World news 44
Sport and the arts 46
Science and technology 47

1917
Russian Revolution 48
World news 50
Sport and the arts 52
Science and technology 53

1918
All Quiet on the Western Front 54
World news 56
Sport and the arts 58
Science and technology 59

1919
Making the Peace 60
World news 62
Sport and the arts 64
Science and technology 65

Time chart 66
Key figures of the decade 68
Acknowledgments 70
Books for further reading 71
Index 71

Introduction

The world scene

The world in 1910 was dominated by European countries. The most important were the 'big five', consisting of Britain, France, Germany, Austria-Hungary and Russia. Outside Europe, only the USA and Japan counted as important countries. By 1910, bitter arguments had divided up the European countries, and war seemed very likely. The countries lined up in two 'camps' – Germany, Austria-Hungary and Italy forming the 'Triple Alliance', with France and Russia forming the 'Dual Alliance'. All these countries were pledged to fight with their allies against the others – although in 1914 Italy broke its promise.

Britain was lined up with France and Russia in the Triple Entente – friendly agreements made in 1904 and 1907. However, while Britain was friends with these two countries, it had no alliance – so legally was not compelled to fight with them. But the naval race with Germany meant that it was very likely that Britain would fight with the French against their old enemy, Germany. The Germans had been building a large navy, and Britain had retaliated by building Dreadnought battleships, the most powerful afloat. Germany started building their own, and in 1909 a race had started to see which country could build the most.

Outside Europe, each country tried to build empires. Britain was the most successful, and by 1910 the British could boast that 'the sun never sets on the British Empire'. Other Great Powers tried to do the same, France having colonies mainly in Asia and Africa, Germany a few in Africa and the Pacific, while Russia and America set their sights on expansion in the Pacific. The Russians found themselves quarrelling with the Japanese over China, and after they had been defeated by the Japanese, turned back to try to expand in the Balkans. There they were opposed by the Austrians who were backed by their German allies. In 1910 Russia had just suffered humiliation when the Austrians took over the Serbian provinces of Bosnia and Herzegovina. The Serbs had called on Russia to help them but Russia had not dared risk war against Germany.

British news

Britain seemed to be a prosperous and successful trading country, and most people thought this would continue. Though the experts were worried about Germany, which was producing more goods than the British, Britain continued to expand its output of goods and seemed able to sell them. Few British people saw problems ahead, though widespread poverty and bad housing was causing increasing discontent among the working classes and helping the Labour Party gain support. Nevertheless many people felt anxious about the growth of the German navy. Britons had long boasted that 'Britannia rules the waves' and it had been over a century since any country had been able to threaten the British navy.

In politics, the two main parties were the Conservatives and the Liberals. These two parties had been going so long that very few people could remember a time when politics was not a two-horse race between these two.

Kaiser and King: still on friendly terms for George V's visit to Germany in 1913.

A new kind of warship: the Dreadnought. *Developments in naval technology accelerated the arms race between Britain and Germany in the years before World War I.*

Introduction

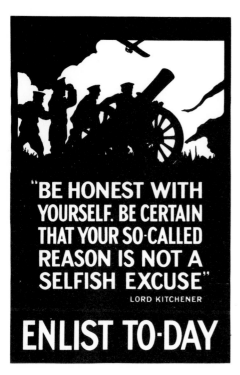

'Be honest with yourself . . .': A British recruitment poster during World War I.

Dramatist and critic George Bernard Shaw: a towering figure but very different from the Modernist writers who were to emerge in the years before 1914.

The Irish Nationalists represented the Catholic people of Ireland, but were too few to make any real difference. A fourth party – the Labour Party – was steadily growing but had even fewer MPs in 1910 than the Irish Nationalists.

Exciting developments in technology and science

By 1910, advances in travel were becoming front page news. On land, the railway was being challenged by the motor car, which was replacing horse-drawn transport on the roads. Previously only rich people had been able to afford automobiles, but in 1909 Henry Ford produced the first Model T Ford, mass producing cars on conveyor belts so that the price dropped to a level that middle-class people could afford.

This was also the age of the steam ship. Steam had long since replaced sail for long-distance sea travel, and steam turbine engines meant faster and more powerful ships. In 1907 the Cunard liners *Mauretania* and *Lusitania* had been fitted with turbines, and promptly broke all records on the trip from Europe to New York. In 1909 the *Mauretania* completed the journey in four and a half days. The rival White Star line decided it could not compete in terms of speed, but planned two ships set to meet new standards of size and luxury – the *Olympic* and the *Titanic*.

Rumours that the Americans had made the age-old dream of flight come true had been confirmed in 1908 when Orville and Wilbur Wright had flown publicly in the USA and France. In 1909 Louis Bleriot confirmed that the aircraft was a practical means of travel by flying across the English channel. It was the age of daring young men in flying machines.

In pure science, especially physics, it was an exciting time. The discovery of x-rays which could 'see' through flesh and bone had set scientists investigating other mysterious rays and particles. Pierre and Marie Curie had discovered radium and radio activity, while Ernest Rutherford had discovered that radium gave off alpha rays and Paul Villard had discovered gamma rays. While scientists struggled to understand their discoveries, Albert Einstein had given physics a new and controversial theory in 1905 with his ideas about relativity.

Experiments in art

All branches of art were undergoing experiment in 1910, but none more so than painting. In France the group known as 'Les Fauves' led by Matisse, Derain and Vlaminck used colour to describe their feelings, not what they saw, and had enormous influence. Even less 'realistic' were the Cubists, led by the followers of Frenchman Paul Cezanne. The Spanish cubist, Pablo Picasso, said, 'I paint objects as I think them, not as I see them'. Music was equally undergoing experiment with composers such as Schoenberg and Stravinsky abandoning conventional sounds and rhythms. In 1909 Diaghilev's Ballets Russes had arrived in Paris from Russia and both Picasso and Stravinsky were to find a home for their experiments in the ballet.

Introduction

Even in poetry experiment was starting to affect a very conventional art form. In 1907 the Scots banker Henry Simpson had formed The Poets Club in London. In 1909 this had published a pamphlet containing poems by T.E. Hulme, who then broke away from the Club and set up his own group in the Soho Café, Tour d'Eiffel. This group was to become known as the Imagist group.

In sport, the Olympic Games had become well established following the first modern games in 1896, and a successful Olympics had been held in London in 1908 with another planned, on the old four-year schedule, in 1912. In December 1908 Jack Johnson had become the first black heavyweight champion of the world, a sign both that the USA was becoming more important in world sport, and that non-European races were becoming significant in the world of athletics.

The coming of flight: Louis Bleriot had been the first to fly the channel in 1909.

1910 Victoria's

Edward VII dies

ON 6 MAY 1910 the English King, Edward VII, was suddenly struck down by an attack of heart asthma, and died within a few hours. His death brought to an end the Edwardian era in British history, a fairly peaceful and prosperous era in the eyes of most British people. Edward's son became George V, King of England.

Europe in 1910.

The Grandmother of Europe

THE CORONATION of George V brought home to people across Europe how much the monarchies of the major countries had become linked through marriage into a great family business. Of the five Great Powers, four still had Royal Families – only France was a republic. Three – Britain, Russia and Germany – had Royal Families connected to the descendants of the old English Queen, Victoria. George V, in fact, counted the German Kaiser Wilhelm II, as his first cousin on his father's side, and the Russian Tsar, Nicholas II, as his first cousin on his mother's side.

No real power

BUT WHILE THEY REIGNED, did they rule? Kings and Queens were not as powerful as they used to be. Only in Russia did the King run the country in his own right, and in Russia opposition to the Tsar's power was widespread and often violent. In 1881, Nicholas's grandfather, Alexander II, had been killed by a bomb, and Nicholas II had only survived after a revolution in 1905 by giving the Russian people a parliament. The parliament had no power, however: Nicholas had no desire to become like his British and German cousins.

His British cousin, George V, had no real power at all. Parliament ran the country, and the violent demonstrations of the suffragettes were aimed not at the King but at parliament and the Prime Minister. The Prime Minister ran day-to-day government, responsible to parliament. This was a compromise between the French system (a republic, where there was a parliament but no king at all) and the Russian system, where there was a king and a parliament with no real power.

Germany and Austria were more like Russia than Britain. In both countries, there was a parliament which had some power but not much, while the king and his advisors took most of the government decisions. Wilhelm II in Berlin, Emperor Franz Joseph in Vienna, and Nicholas II in St Petersburg, all had considerable power in 1910. Yet within eight years they had been swept away, and each of their countries had become a republic like France.

Grandchildren

Cousins: George V and Kaiser Wilhelm II.

A final gathering

WHEN THE CROWNED HEADS of Europe and their relations assembled in London for the funeral of Edward VII and the coronation of George V, therefore, they were not just witnessing the start of the reign of a new English king. They were gathering for the last time as the ruling families of Europe and, for Queen Victoria's descendants, the last family occasion of its kind. It is unlikely any of them had the slightest idea of the fate that lay in store for most of them.

Departure of the German Emperor

The German Emperor left London yesterday afternoon . . . . His departure was witnessed by a number of spectators, who uncovered and silently waved hats and handkerchiefs as the carriage passed. Their Majesties, bowing their acknowledgments, drove bare-headed through the lines of onlookers . . . . The way from the Palace to Victoria, along Buckingham Palace Road, was guarded by policemen and fringed with sightseers, the lines being in places three or four lines deep.

The *Times* 24 May

World News

Calm before the storm

AT THE START of the second decade of the twentieth century, the world seemed unusually peaceful. No wars were going on anywhere in Europe, little more than colonial skirmishes disturbed the peace outside Europe, and trade was flourishing. However, the world was enjoying little more than the calm before the storm.

On the continent, the four major powers lined up against each other, France against Germany, Russia against Austria, with Germany backing Austria against the Russians. The famous Schlieffen plan for a German attack on France via Belgium had been adopted in 1905, and the building of railway platforms on the German side of the Belgium border showed what was planned. Nevertheless, relations between Britain and Germany were particularly good in 1910 and France feared that the entente with the British might not last. The German Chancellor Bülow, whom the British disliked, had been replaced in July 1909 by Bethmann Hollweg, and relations between the two countries improved. The Kaiser created a good impression when he attended the funeral of his uncle, Edward VII, in May 1910, and in July Britain and Germany started negotiations aimed at limiting the naval arms race. These went on till May 1911, but came to nothing. The Germans wanted the British to abandon their ententes with France and Russia, and make an entente with them. Britain was happy to make an entente with Germany, but not if this meant abandoning France and Russia. Britain was aware that any agreement with Germany over warships could be broken – and if it was, it would be useless to try to get back friendly relations with France and Russia. Britain could be left without any friends at all. She continued her Dreadnought building programme even while the negotiations went on.

Trouble brewing in the East

MEANWHILE, IN EASTERN EUROPE, the calm was also deceptive. In 1908 and 1909, the Great Powers of Russia, Austria and Germany had almost gone to war over the crumbling Turkish Empire. Everyone could see that the Turks in Constantinople were losing control of the Balkans. Four small Christian nations – Bulgaria, Rumania, Serbia and Greece – had broken free. Austria and Russia had planned to take over remaining Turkish areas together, but Austria had jumped the gun in 1908 and taken over the province of Bosnia. Russia had thought of going to war with Austria as the Russians had gained nothing, but in early 1909 the Germans warned Russia that in an Austro-Russian war, she would join in on the side of Austria.

This action ruined any remaining trust between Russia and Germany, and ended any hope that in a war between France and Germany, Russia would remain neutral. Moreover, the events of 1908 and 1909 tied Russia more firmly to Serbia. Serbia had hoped to take over Bosnia herself when the Turks went, because the people in Bosnia spoke Serbian and were next-door neighbours. The Serbs had been furious when Austria took over Bosnia, but were too small a country to do anything about it. Russia was determined they would not let down their friends in Serbia if there were a second quarrel with Austria.

The Liberals call an election . . .

In 1906 the Liberal Party had won the general election, gaining 377 seats in the House of Commons. The Tories had gained only 157, and even if the 29 Labour MPs and 83 Irish Nationalists allied with the Tories, the Liberals still had a majority. Most members of the non-elected House of Lords, however, were Conservatives, and the Tories decided to use the votes of the Lords to prevent the Liberals from passing Acts of Parliament. This was unfair but not illegal. In 1909, the Lords had gone a stage further. They voted against the government budget when the Chancellor, Lloyd George, tried to make the landlords pay taxes on their land. If the budget did not become law, the government would not have the legal right to collect taxes. Facing bankruptcy, the Liberals decided to call an election to gain the backing of the electors.

The election was held in January 1910, and though the Liberals lost seats, they held on as the government. They gained 275 seats, the Tories 273, Irish Nationalists 83, and Labour 40. Since the Irish and Labour voted with the Liberals, the Liberals had enough MPs to vote through what they wanted. If the Lords continued to obstruct them, they assumed the King would support them, and create enough Liberal Peers to outvote the Tories (as only the King could make new Lords).

The Peers versus the People

BY 1910, the normal business of government in Britain was in danger of grinding to a halt because of a quarrel about who made the major decisions in politics. Until 1906, all parties had accepted that the House of Commons, which was elected – although only men could vote – made the decisions, and the House of Lords only advised the Commons and corrected mistakes. Whichever party won the election to the Commons and had the most MPs in the House, ran the government.

In fact the King demanded that the Liberals win *two* elections before he would create new peers and allow the Liberals to control the House of Lords.

H.H. Asquith.

. . . and another

BY NOW, THE LORDS had allowed the budget to pass, because the whole issue of who should control politics was now the main concern. The Liberals brought out the Parliament Bill, which gave the House of Commons the sole right to decide Acts of Parliament. The House of Lords naturally opposed this, and refused to pass the Bill. The Liberals knew they had to win an election if they were to get the King to honour his promise, and called an election for December. The result was very close to that of January. The Liberals and Tories tied on 272, Labour gained 42, the Irish 84. The Liberals now argued that as Labour and the Irish backed them, the question was now settled. As the year closed, they looked forward to the King keeping his promise.

Churchill speaks out against Landlordism

HERE WINSTON CHURCHILL explains the Liberals' objections to the fact that landlords did not have to pay taxes on their land:

The landlord who happened to own a plot of land on the outskirts or at the centre of one of our great cities . . . sits still and does nothing. Roads are made, streets are made, railway services are improved, electric light turns night into day, electric trams glide swiftly to and fro, water is brought from reservoirs . . . and all the while the landlord sits still . . . To not one of these improvements does the land monopolist as a land monopolist contribute. He renders no service to the community, he contributes nothing to the general welfare. Quoted in Donald Read, *Edwardian England*

Sport and the Arts

An international phenomenon

SPORT AT THE START of the second decade of the twentieth century was beginning to become a more truly international phenomenon. Football was joining the Olympics as an internationally organized entity. England had joined the Federation Internationale de Football Association (FIFA, formed in 1904) in 1906, and in 1910 the Scots, Welsh and Irish Football Associations followed them into the world's governing football body.

In 1910 came a clear indication of the growing strength of sport outside Europe and America. The first rugby tour of South Africa since 1891 by a British side took place. In 1891 an English and Scots team had won all their games. In 1910 the touring side lost 8 out of 24 matches, including 2 of the 3 tests. The view of sport as a pasttime for rich amateurs who did not take it seriously also suffered in cricket from the success of Kent, who won the County Championship in 1906, 1909 and 1910, and were to win it again in 1913, feats directly resulting from forming a Tonbridge 'nursery' in 1897 which supplied them with a flow of professional talent.

Books and Music of 1910

The Frenchman Claude Debussy completed the first of his two books of *Préludes*, Englishman Edward Elgar wrote his violin concerto, and the Russian Igor Stravinsky wrote the controversial *Firebird Suite*.

Arnold Bennett published his book *Clayhanger*, H.G. Wells *The History of Mr Polly* and E.M. Forster *Howard's End*.

Joseph Conrad began work on his novel *Chance* for the *New York Times*, and George Bernard Shaw staged the play *Misalliance*.

From Fauvism to Futurism

THE VISUAL ARTS continued to produce work of great richness. Braque and Picasso continued to develop the style of analytical cubism they had begun the previous year, Picasso painting the portraits of Vollard and Kahnweiler in this controversial style. Expressionism was a style, influenced by the Fauves, which in the years after 1905 achieved an exciting form of art, especially in Germany. Meanwhile in Italy the movement known as Futurism, formed by artists such as Marinetti, Boccioni, and Severini in 1909 to produce an art based on things produced by machines, was among the most interesting developments taking place in 1910.

Jack Johnson, the World Heavyweight boxing champion.

Challenging tradition

HOWEVER THE REALITY of competitive sport in modern times still failed to make inroads in all areas. In Wimbledon tennis, the authorities still held to the ridiculous rule that the previous year's champion was not required to play any match other than the final itself, which meant he could play fresh against an opponent who had played all the challenge rounds. A.F. Wilding, who won the first of his four championships in 1910 (and was champion in 1911, 1912 and 1913) was to plead in vain to be allowed to play the challenge rounds. Such hidebound attitudes could not protect sport as the preserve of rich, white amateurs – especially in the most working-class of all sports, boxing, where Jack Johnson had broken through the race barrier in 1908 by winning the world heavyweight boxing championship – the first black man to do so – and retaining the title till 1915. In 1910, Johnson beat the white heavyweight Jim Jeffries to retain his title.

The plane comes of age

BY 1910, THE AEROPLANE had come of age in both Britain and the USA. After Bleriot had flown the English Channel in 1909, no one could be in any doubt that the aircraft was a reliable and important means of transport, not just a toy. 1910 was a year when the rapidly increasing range of the aeroplane was headline news. In April, the Frenchman Louis Paulhan won the Dail Mail's £10,000 prize for the first flight between London and Manchester. He beat the Englishman, Claude Graham-White (both men flew planes built by the French designer, Henry Farman) but the Englishman put his name in the record books by making the first night flight in Europe between two stops on 28 March. Graham-White later won the Gordon-Bennett speed contest at the Belmont Park meeting in the USA with an average speed of 61 mph. Though planes had to be taken across the Atlantic in ships, flying was an international business. Flights across the English Channel were becoming common, and on 2 June C.S. Rolls made a double crossing without landing in France.

Radium is an element

IN PHYSICS, arguments had been going on since 1906 about radium – was it really an element? In 1910 Marie Curie proved once and for all that radium was a genuine element, by producing it pure as a metal, and later that same year summarized all the existing work on radioactivity in a book – *A Treatise on Radioactivity* – which ran to over 1000 pages. Given that nothing had been known of the subject when she began to research it in 1897, she could be regarded as the founder of the subject of radioactivity.

The military take an interest

IN AMERICA, the Wright brothers were beginning to be outshone by Glenn Curtiss, whose standard bi-plane was now winning prizes. On 31 May, Curtiss himself won $10,000 with the first flight from Albany to New York City. On 13 June C.K. Hamilton flew one of his planes from New York to Philadelphia and back. Curtiss was able to interest the military in the potential of the airplane for war, on 30 June becoming the first man to carry out bombing tests when he dropped dummy bombs on the shape of a battle ship marked out by flagged buoys on Lake Keuka, USA. Then, at the end of the year, a Curtiss bi-plane piloted by Eugene Ely successfully took off from the American cruiser *Birmingham*, which had an 83-foot platform built on the foredeck, making it the first aircraft carrier.

Early Marconi radio apparatus, as shown on a contemporary cigarette card.

The significance of aeroplane altitude records

With a rapidity which has astonished experts, the aeroplane has progressed from one altitude to another, until now the *maximum* height attained stands at over 4,100ft. Judging by the rate of improvement which within a year has altered the record from 300ft. to 4,100ft., it can be safely surmised that flying machines will very soon be capable of soaring to the height of a mile, and that not a few but many aeroplanes will possess this power. This development opens up new prospects for the employment of the aeroplane for warlike purposes, or, to be more correct, it commands with more insistence the immediate consideration of the aeroplane for such purposes.
The *Times*, 29 March 1910

Dr Crippen arrested by radio

DR CRIPPEN, suspected of poisoning his wife, was sensationally arrested despite trying to escape across the Atlantic by boat. He fled from England with his girlfriend Ethel Le Neve on the liner *SS Montrose*. Once aboard Crippen thought he was safe. He was unaware that the ship's captain had secretly informed the police by radio that he was on board and that Inspector Dew had left England in pursuit on the faster liner *Laurentic*. When the *Montrose* arrived in Canada on 31 July, the Inspector and two Canadian policemen boarded the ship in international waters, dressed as sailors. They arrested both Crippen and his girlfriend: Crippen was convicted of murder later that year and hanged. The value of the radio telegraph had been dramatically revealed.

1911

The *Panther*

A fatal step

BRITAIN AND GERMANY were quite friendly at the start of 1911. They stayed on good terms until June 1911, when Germany took a step which permanently damaged relations with Britain. That step became known as the Panther incident.

No sign of trouble could be seen in the spring, when Kaiser Wilhelm visited London for the unveiling of the Queen Victoria memorial. When his son came to the coronation of George V in June, all seemed set fair. Behind the scenes, however, a furious row was brewing. In April the French had sent troops to the Moroccan town of Fez to protect the Sultan against a rebellion. Germany took this to mean that France was taking over Morocco, and felt that nothing was to be gained from talking to the French. At the end of June, the Germans sent a gunboat, the *Panther*, to take over the Moroccan port of Agadir.

German Chancellor Bethmann Hollweg said:

The condition of peaceableness is strength. The old saying still holds good that the weak will be the prey of the strong. When a people will not or cannot continue to spend enough on its armaments to be able to make its way in the world, then it falls back into the second rank . . . There will always be another and a stronger there who is ready to take the place in the world which it has vacated.
Quoted in Donald Read, *Edwardian England*.

Friends for the moment: the Kaiser.

Britain prepared to go to war

WHEN THE *PANTHER* sailed into Agadir on 1 July, the British were infuriated. On 4 May Sir Edward Grey, the British Foreign Secretary, told the German Ambassador that the British wanted to be involved in any talks over Morocco. The British were afraid the Germans would build a naval base at Agadir, and threaten British ships in the Eastern Atlantic. The Germans did not reply. On 21 July Grey saw the Ambassador again, who said that he had heard nothing from Berlin. That night Lloyd George, Chancellor of the Exchequer, who was felt to be one of the most peace-minded members of the cabinet, made a speech at the Mansion House.

After consulting Grey and the Prime Minister, Asquith, he made a powerful warning that if Germany continued to try to force concessions out of France, then Britain would be prepared to go to war:

If a situation were to be forced upon us in which peace could only be preserved by the surrender of the great position Britain has won by centuries of heroism and achievement, by allowing Britain to be treated as if she were of no account in the Cabinet of nations, then I say emphatically that peace at that price would be a humiliation intolerable for a great country like ours to endure.
(Lloyd George, 21 July, quoted in Winston Churchill, *The World Crisis, 1923*)

Crisis

Sir Edward Grey.

Fleet prepares to set out

THE SPEECH CAUSED A SENSATION. Britain had heard that Germany was trying to force France to give them land in the Congo and trading rights in Morocco. Britain was not concerned about the Congo, but feared a German take-over of an area close to the British base at Gibraltar. To underline how seriously they felt, they prepared to send out a fleet strong enough to sink the entire German navy. The Germans immediately claimed they had no interest in the coast of Morocco, but still claimed 'compensation' for the French 'take-over' of Morocco, in the form of land in the French Congo. Talks between France and Germany proved difficult, as the French would not give Germany the land they wanted.

Treaty signed

BY LATE AUGUST, the negotiations deadlocked, and on 1 September talks were postponed. Only after a war panic swept German businessmen did talks come to a conclusion. On 11 October, France and Germany signed a treaty guaranteeing French control of Morocco against German interference. In exchange, France gave Germany land in the Congo. The *Panther* was withdrawn shortly afterwards.

An inglorious charade

THE EFFECTS OF THE CRISIS in Africa were small. Germany gained a piece of land in the Congo, Morocco was placed more firmly under French control. But the effects on opinion in Germany and Britain were dramatic. Germany felt that she had been forced out of Morocco by the actions of the British, and Prince von Bülow, the German politician, commented

Like a damp squib, it startled, then amused the world, and ended by making us look ridiculous. After the leap of the *Panther* on Agadir there was a fanfare which, on Lloyd George's speech, died down in the most inglorious charade.

Germany was now convinced that Britain would back France come what may, and this led to her relying even more firmly on her one true friend – Austria. The British, indeed, became even more suspicious of Germany, and friendly with France. Some British people were now convinced that Germany could not be trusted, and was bound to go to war sooner or later.

Italy declares war on Turkey

THE ITALIANS had long wanted to build an empire in Africa. In 1896 they had sent an army to Abyssinia (Ethiopia) but the attempt failed when the Abyssinians wiped out the Italian army at Adowa. The Italians then turned their attention towards Tripoli (now called Libya) across the Mediterranean from Italy.

Turkey controlled Tripoli, and realizing the Italians' intentions obstructed Italian traders and bankers trying to set up in Tripoli. The long-awaited show-down came in September 1911, when Germany and France were both tied up in the Agadir crisis and unable to intervene in Tripoli themselves. The Italians felt they could defeat the Turks and on the 24 September made a complaint to the Turks about the treatment of their bankers and traders. They claimed to be unhappy with the Turkish reply, and declared war on 25 September.

Mutual incompetence

THE ITALIAN NAVY took over the ports easily, but the Italian army advanced into the interior only with difficulty. On 23 October, a crack Italian regiment fighting the Turkish army found itself attacked by local Arabs who had decided to back the Turks, and had to be rescued. The Italian attack ground to a halt. The incompetence of the Turkish army was worse, however, giving the Balkan nations a chance to beat the Turks, which they did in 1912.

The Chinese Nationalist leader, Dr Sun Yatsen.

Revolution in China

AT THE OTHER SIDE of the globe, the impact of imperialist intervention was stirring a revolt in an ancient country: China. China had long resented the growing interference of Europeans and Americans and in 1900 with the Boxer rebellion had tried to expel their influence. This had been a disastrous failure and had weakened the already unpopular Manchu government. In 1898 Dr Sun Yat-sen had attempted a revolution in Canton. Forced to flee when it failed, he spent 15 years in exile and formed a secret society to overthrow the Manchu dynasty. Many army officers joined the society, and in 1909 and 1910 there were four attempted revolutions in Canton. Finally on 12 October 1911 the army rebelled in Wuhan province. The rebellion spread, and on 25 December Sun Yat-sen returned, landing in Shanghai. He was elected as provisional president of a new republic. As the year closed, it was clear the Manchu government was on its last legs.

Tory Die Hards

AFTER WINNING the two general elections of 1910, the Liberals expected the King's backing to get the Parliament Bill through the House of Lords. On 15 May the Commons passed the Bill by 121 votes and sent it to the Lords. The Peers first tried to amend it to give their House more powers, but the Liberals refused to accept any changes to their plans.

This led to the emergence of a 'no surrender' movement among the Tory Lords, who became known as the 'Die Hards'. Lloyd George told the Tories that the King had finally agreed to create enough Liberal Peers to vote the Bill through if the Lords voted against it, but the Die Hards remained firm. They even ignored an instruction from Tory leader A.J. Balfour to let the Bill go through. The Bill allowed the Peers to delay future laws for two years, and Balfour preferred to accept this and keep Tory control of the Lords, rather than let the King create a Liberal majority.

A step towards votes for women

MEANWHILE, THE 'VOTES FOR WOMEN' movement was becoming important. In 1911 the supporters of the suffragettes suggested a 'Conciliation Bill' designed to win support from MPs of all parties. This would give the vote to a limited number of wealthy women. Since this would mainly benefit the Tories, Labour and Liberal MPs could not vote for it. Nevertheless the need for some move towards giving women the vote was widely accepted, and a modified Bill was passed by 167 votes. The Liberals promised to find time to complete passing the Bill in 1912.

A wave of strikes

THE LABOUR PARTY, however, was falling back. At the elections of 1910 the number of working-class MPs had dropped from 53 to 40. As the courts had ruled in 1909 that it was illegal for unions to pay money for political ends, the Party was in financial difficulties. Trade unionists lost faith in the ability of the Labour Party to get benefits for them, and turned to strike action. In June the seamen won an important victory, and in August the dockers came out on strike. Two dockers were shot dead by troops in Liverpool, and on 19 August Lloyd George arranged a settlement. There was a lull until December, when a lock-out left 126,000 weavers out of work.

An historic debate

THE LIBERALS could only count on 75 votes from the 250 peers, and expected to lose. The King prepared to create the Peers needed to vote down the Die Hards – but he did not need to do so. On 10 August amid great drama, the Bill was narrowly passed by 131 votes to 114. Twenty-nine Tories voted for the Bill, together with both archbishops and 11 of the bishops. The Liberals had won.

After an historic debate . . . the House of Lords last night passed the Parliament Bill by a majority of 17 . . . It was evident long before the House got to business yesterday, the attendance being again great, that the sitting would be one of unexampled interest for many years. Everywhere on the Opposition benches there were conferences and discussions . . . and the air was full of electricity . . .
The *Times*, 11 August

Poetry

IN 1911 THE IMAGIST MOVEMENT in poetry, which had largely been dormant since the collapse of the Tour d'Eiffel group at the end of 1909, saw developments which were to bear fruit. T.E. Hulme, the original leader, stopped writing poetry, but a new leader, the American Ezra Pound, came forward. Pound had produced three books of conventional poetry, when he became secretary to writer Ford Madox Ford. Ford helped Pound develop a new style, and by the autumn of 1911 they began to meet with a group of writers at the home of Brigit Patmore who later became known as the Imagist group.

Arts News of the Year

Gordon Craig, an Englishman, wrote a highly provocative book on theatrical production, in which he argued that the director was to be the main figure in producing a play, not the actors. It was called *On the Art of the Theatre*.

Death in Venice by Thomas Mann was published, as were *The New Machiavelli*, by H.G. Wells and *Hilda Lessways* by Arnold Bennett.

Stravinsky wrote *Petrushka* for the Ballets Russes.

Germany leads the way

A NEW GROUP OF PAINTERS, known as Der Blaue Reiter (the Blue Rider) group, emerged in Germany, led by the artist Wassily Kandinsky. Painters like Franz Marc, August Macke and Paul Klee produced mystical and increasingly abstract paintings. Germany also led

The American poet Ezra Pound.

the way in architecture, where Peter Behrens and his pupil Walter Gropius worked to create a new, functional approach to buildings. Behrens, working for the electrical company AEG from 1901 to 1907, produced a large machine assembly hall in Berlin, which influenced Gropius in designing the Fagus Factory at Alfeld an der Leine in 1911.

Gentlemen versus players

THE YEAR ALSO SAW the famous E.A. Murrow cartoon, which the international C.B. Fry included in his magazine, showing John Bull speaking to a white-flannelled and presumably professional cricketer, saying:

Yes, my dear fellow, I expect you to go to Australia for half a year to uphold my prestige in cricket. It will cost you £250, I will allow you £70 . . . You lose half a year's income . . . I fear I cannot help that, you must stand the loss. The Australian clubs and the MCC will no doubt make several thousands profit . . . there it is!
Quoted in Brian Dodds, *Edwardians at Play*

With attitudes like these around, it is not surprising that the 'gentlemen versus players' issue remained strong in sport, with the professionals (the 'players') treated as second-class citizens.

Unofficial apartheid

THE INTERNATIONAL SCENE in sport provided some sad examples of hypocrisy and prejudice. The South Africans toured Australia in 1910-11 and though apartheid was not yet official, showed blatant prejudice. There was only one black player in the team, C.B. Llewellyn, who had played for Hampshire in England. He was so badly treated that he had to lock himself in hotel lavatories to escape his white companions.

Long-distance flying

IN FLYING, although technical progress was slow, the first long-distance flights took place, the airplane was used in war for the first time, and there were innovations in flying techniques. Notable achievements in long-distance flying began when on 12 April Pierre Prier flew non-stop from London to Paris, covering the 250 miles in four hours. Races popularized these achievements, and there was one from Paris to Rome, Paris to Madrid, and the first European circuit race of 1000 miles, from Paris and back via Brussels, London and Amiens. In America, McCurdy flew 90 miles across water from Key West to Havana, Atwood flew from St Louis to New York via Chicago, and C.P. Rodgers flew across America from Long Island (New York) to Long Beach (California), crashing 19 times on the way.

Birth of the seaplane

IN JANUARY, Glenn Curtiss introduced the first practical seaplane in history, putting floats under the central section and wings of a standard Curtiss land plane. It first flew in San Diego, California, and on 25 February Curtiss took up the first passenger to fly in a seaplane. As far as sea war went, more significant was the first take off and landing from a ship at sea, by Ely in January. In the same month the first live bomb test was made by the US army. In France, the first 'Concours Militaire' took place in October and November to display aircraft that could be used in war, and on 22 October an aircraft was first used in war, when an Italian, Captain Piazza, made a reconnaissance flight from Tripoli to observe the Turkish positions.

Unsinkable ship launched

FOR INTERCONTINENTAL TRAVEL, however, the ocean liner remained unrivalled. The year saw the *Olympic*, second biggest liner in the world, enter service, while the even bigger and more modern *Titanic* was launched. It had a revolutionary design:

In the event of an accident, or at any time when it may be considered desirable, the captain can, simply by moving an electric switch, instantly close the doors throughout, making the ship practically unsinkable.
Irish News and Belfast Morning News, 1 June

Marie Curie.

Marie Curie hounded by press

IN PURE SCIENCE, the activities of scientists were now front page news. The fame of the Curies led to a major controversy when Madame Curie attempted to become elected to the French Academie des Sciences. This would have been public recognition of her achievements as a scientist and laid to rest the rumour that she had done little of the work herself, many spiteful people believing that the discovery of radium had been made by her dead husband. No woman had ever been elected to the Academie, and there was a good deal of anti-female feeling – especially as she stood against a respected French male scientist for the vacant post.

On 23 January, the scientists voted by 28 to 30 against Madame Curie. It was a close thing, but decisive. Madame Curie was deeply hurt. She was even more deeply hurt on 4 November when a Paris paper published a story alleging that she had caused the breakdown of the marriage of a male scientist, Paul Langevin. The press was viewing scientists in the way that pop stars and movie stars would be viewed later in the century. Even the news, which Madame Curie received on 8 November, that she had won the Nobel Prize for Chemistry (making her the first person, let alone the first woman, to win two Nobel Prizes) hardly compensated for the intrusion into her personal life.

1912

Titanic!

An age of wonders

IN THE YEARS before World War One, there was enormous confidence in science and technology. For as long as most people could remember, inventors had produced one wonder after another, and there seemed no reason why this should not go on for ever. Then, in 1912, came a disaster which shook this confidence – the sinking of the *Titanic*.

The unsinkable ship

THE *TITANIC* WAS LAUNCHED as the largest and most modern ship in the world. It could displace 66,000 tons, and was 882.5 feet (269 m) long. It could carry 3000 people, although it only had enough lifeboats for 1178. No one worried about this, because the ship had the most up-to-date safety devices including doors that could divide the ship into watertight compartments. The ship could float with a hole in the side and two or three compartments flooded. No one could imagine a hole so big it would flood more compartments.

On 10 April 1912, the *Titanic* left Southampton on her maiden voyage to New York. She carried millionaires, noblemen, tourists, immigrants and crew to a total of 2154 people. No one could imagine a disaster happening. As Mrs Albert Caldwell came on board, she asked a deck hand, 'Is this ship really unsinkable?' 'Yes, lady', he replied, 'God himself couldn't sink this ship'.

The Titanic: *an artist's impression of the ship's last moments.*

Disaster strikes

THE CRUISE ACROSS the Atlantic was uneventful until 14 April, when the ship sailed into floating ice. A nearby ship, the *Californian*, radioed a message to the *Titanic* saying 'Large icebergs five miles south'. The *Titanic* was then 40 miles away and heading for the ice, but did not slow down.

The night was completely calm and clear, with plenty of stars but no moon. There was no wind – which meant there were no small waves which would have helped show up icebergs in the darkness. At 11.40 p.m. lookout Frederick Fleet suddenly saw an iceberg, dead ahead and growing larger every second. He rang the bell three times – the warning of danger ahead – and phoned the bridge. For half a minute the ship did not turn, then the bow began to swing to port. It looked as though the ship might miss the berg. Then a deep grinding sound indicated the *Titanic* had run alongside the ice.

Abandon ship!

THE CAPTAIN rushed to the bridge, and ordered the designer, Thomas Andrews, to check the damage. The news was grim. The berg had ripped open five compartments and water was rushing in. With five compartments flooded, the weight of water would pull the bow below sea level and the ship must sink. Captain Smith had no choice: he gave the order to abandon ship.

Unwritten rule ignored

THE UNWRITTEN RULE ON BOARD SHIP was 'women and children first'. On the *Titanic*, it did not work that way. Some of the men loading the boats played by the rule – the officer loading boat Number Six only allowed one man on, a yachtsman with useful experience – but lifeboat Number One, which could take 40 people, only carried 12. These included Sir Cosmo Duff Gordon, his wife and Lady Gordon's secretary, who were the only women on board. The richer you were, the better your chances were of being saved. All five children from the first class were saved, and all 24 children in the second class, but 53 children in the third class died. Fifty-eight male passengers from the first class survived, but 101 women from the third class died. It was clear that the idea that gentlemen would always behave nobly had been ignored.

Bravery of the crew

THE CREW, HOWEVER, was very brave. The band played on until the water was over their feet and played a hymn as the ship went down. The engineers kept the engines going to keep the lights on until the last three minutes. All 36 were drowned. The stokehold watch, 84 men, went down to keep the boilers stoked. Only eight were saved. Of the crew as a whole, 875 men and 23 women, 686 men drowned and 2 women. When news of the disaster reached New York, the city was stunned. It took time to realize that on its first voyage, the 'unsinkable' ship had sunk.

The news breaks

The terrible news about the *Titanic* reached New York about 11 o'clock last night, and the scene on Broadway was awful. Crowds of people were coming out of the theater, cafes were going full tilt, when the newsboys began to cry 'Extra! Extra! Titanic sunk with 1800 on board!'. You can't imagine the effect of those words on the crowd . . . The excitement was almost enough to cause a panic in the theaters. Women began to faint and weep and scores of people in evening clothes jumped into cabs and taxis and rushed to the offices of the White Star Line where they remained all night waiting for news.

Letter from Alexander Macomb, to his mother, 16 April 1912, quoted in Walter Lord, *The Night Lives On*

News of the Titanic's *sinking reaches London.*

The struggle continues in China

IN CHINA, the new Republic struggled to establish itself in 1912. Sun Yat-sen had been elected as provisional president, but not until 12 February did the Manchu dynasty give up the throne. The abdication was arranged by the leading General, Yuan Shih-kai, who allowed the child Emperor to retain the summer palace to live in. The day after the abdication, Sun Yat-sen resigned as president and on 15 February Yuan was elected in his place. Yuan had agreed to move the capital to Nanking, away from the Emperor in Peking. On 25 February Republicans arrived to escort Yuan to Nanking. However, four days later soldiers in Peking mutinied, and Yuan stopped the mutiny because he was the leading general. After that he stayed in Peking, claiming that only he could prevent a second mutiny.

Young Turks resign

AS TURKEY STRUGGLED to defend Tripoli against the Italians, restlessness at home increased. In June the Albanians rebelled, and as the rebellion spread through the Balkans the Young Turk government resigned on 17 July. The troubles affecting the Turks were a sign to the Christian nations that it was a good time to attack and force the Turks out of the Balkans for good. Bulgaria signed treaties with Serbia and Greece. On 30 September the allies mobilized their armies and declared war. The Turks lost battle after battle and fell back to defend their capital, Constantinople. There the Turks beat off two Bulgarian attacks, and an armistice (ceasefire) was agreed.

Ulster volunteer force organized

THE GREAT ISSUE which dominated British politics in 1912 was Irish Home Rule and the resistance of the Ulster Protestants. In the autumn of 1911, Sir Edward Carson, the Ulster Protestant leader, had held a meeting of his supporters, 100,000 strong, at Craigavon, declaring total opposition to Home Rule. To back this up, on 5 January 1912 Carson applied for and got permission from local magistrates to organize a volunteer force – an unofficial army. 80,000 men marched before Carson and the new Tory leader, Bonar Law.

Ulster Covenant signed

DESPITE ALL THIS, the Home Rule Bill passed the House of Commons on 9 May. The Bill failed to pass the Lords, however, because the Tories still had a majority there. Following the Parliament Bill, the new Act would still become law, but only after two years. In September 1912, as the Home Rule Bill began the two year delay period, Carson got his supporters to sign the Ulster Covenant, pledging resistance to Irish Home Rule.

Ulster's Solemn League and covenant

Being convinced in our consciences that Home Rule would be disastrous to the material well-being of Ulster as well as of the whole of Ireland, subversive of our civil and religious freedom, destructive of our citizenship and perilous to the unity of the Empire, we ... men of Ulster, loyal subjects of his Gracious Majesty King George V ... do hereby pledge ourselves in solemn Covenant throughout this our time of

Britain and France more closely allied

BACK IN EUROPE, there was alarm in Britain over the threat of war with Germany after the events of 1911. At the end of 1911 the British had suggested to the Germans that the British lead in battleships be lowered from a ratio of 2:1 to 16:10. Haldane, Secretary for War, went to Berlin, but found little interest there in forming better relations with Britain. Admiral Tirpitz had persuaded the German Parliament to pass a Navy Law to increase the size of the German navy. Moreover, Haldane found Germany demanding British neutrality if a war between France and Germany broke out. Even if the Entente had not existed, Britain could not accept this – it would mean the German fleet could capture the ports facing Britain without Britain being able to do anything. Instead, Britain made a firmer commitment to defend the French ports if this was attempted, although this did not constitute a firm alliance in the eventuality of war, as the British Foreign Secretary formally agreed in a letter to the French Ambassador:

My dear Ambassador,

From time to time in recent years the French and British naval and military experts have consulted together. It has always been understood that such consultation does not restrict the freedom of either Government to decide at any future time whether or not to assist the other by armed force. We have agreed that consultation between experts is not, and ought not to be regarded as an engagement that commits either Government to action in a contingency that has arisen and may not arise. The disposition, for instance, of the French and British fleets respectively at the present moment is not based upon an engagement to co-operate in war.

(Extract from letter from E. Grey, 22 November)

Opponent of Home Rule Sir Edward Carson addressing an anti-Home Rule rally.

threatened calamity to stand by one another in defending for ourselves and our children our cherished position of equal citizenship in the United Kingdom and in using all means which may be found necessary to defeat the present conspiracy to set up a Home Rule Parliament in Ireland . . . And in the event of such a Parliament being forced upon us we further solemnly . . . . pledge ourselves to refuse to recognize its authority . . .
Ulster Day, Saturday 28 September

Campaign by arson

ON THE MAINLAND, both women's suffrage and trades unionism entered new periods of militancy. This exasperated MPs, and the moderate Women's Suffrage Bill introduced in 1911 failed in March 1912 by 14 votes. The government then brought in a bill to give all men the vote, which could be amended to include women. The suffragettes decided to keep the pressure on the government, and began a campaign of arson.

Strike wave continues

MEANWHILE THE STRIKE WAVE continued. A miners' strike began on 1 March. The Liberal government brought in a bill to set minimum wages in the industry, and this settled the dispute. It was followed by a second dock strike, over a foreman working as a docker. The dockers argued only dockers could do dockers' work, and 100,000 men struck in the London docks. The employers recruited men to do dock work from among the unemployed, and the strike collapsed. This ended the strike wave.

Olympic Games held in Sweden

THE MAJOR SPORTING EVENT of 1912 was the fifth Olympic Games, held in Stockholm, Sweden. De Coubertin, founder of the modern Olympics, had argued in 1909 that 'the Games must be kept more purely athletic; they must be more dignified, more discreet; more in accordance with classic and artistic refinements; more intimate, and, above all, less expensive' – but he had then advised the Swedes to award medals for events such as mountain ascents, and aeronautics. These games were the first to have an official medals table, with America coming top, scoring 80 points, Sweden coming second with 30, Finland third with 29, and Britain well down the list with 15. There was an outcry in Britain – the Olympics were no longer just games, but a measure of national pride.

Nijinsky joins the Ballets Russes

THE LEADING BALLET COMPANY of the time, Diaghilev's Ballets Russes, appointed the greatest male dancer of the age, Vaslav Nijinsky as choreographer. The dancer produced a successful ballet to Debussy's *Prélude à l'après-midi d'un Faune*, which caused a mild scandal over an alleged obscene pose – but nothing like the storm that Nijinsky and the composer Stravinsky were to cause later in 1913.

Arts news

Schoenberg composed his *Pierrot Lunaire*, a work written for reciter and chamber ensemble.

George Bernard Shaw's *Androcles and the Lion* had its premier.

One of the first classic films was produced in France: George Melie's *A la Conquete du Pole*, which was one of the earliest monster films.

D.H. Lawrence published one of his first books, *The Trespasser*.

Jim Thorpe up at bat for the New York Giants.

Hero of the hour

THE GAMES SAW A TRIPLE gold medallist in Finland's Kolehmainen, who won the 5000 metres, 10,000 metres, and 8000 metres cross-country, but the star of the Games was the phenomenal half-Indian American, Jim Thorpe. Thorpe, who was said to do virtually no training, won the decathlon and the pentathlon without turning a hair. Fifty years later, his points total would still have placed him first in the British decathlon ratings. He returned home a hero, but in 1913 it was revealed he had once played baseball at $25 a week. This violated his amateur status, and he was ordered to return his medals. The US committee apologized, saying that:

The reason he himself did not give notice of his acts, is explained by him on grounds of ignorance. In some justification of his position, it should be noted that Mr Thorpe is an Indian of limited experience and education in the ways of other than his own people.

This offensive nonsense was compounded by the Olympic Committee, which tried to award the Golds to the second placed athletes, Bie of Norway and Wieslander of Sweden. Both refused, pointing out they had been beaten fair and square. Thorpe went on to become one of America's greatest ever professional athletes.

Lesson from *Titanic* disaster

THE *TITANIC* DISASTER emphasized both the achievements and the limitations of science and technology. The role of radio in the tragedy had been especially sad. The *Titanic* had been warned by radio that it was sailing into an icefield, but ignored the warning. Even worse, the ship that had sent the warning, the *Californian*, radioed to the *Titanic* at 23.00 a message saying 'We are stopped and completely surrounded by ice'. The *Titanic*'s radio operator, overworked, radioed back the fatal message 'Keep Out'. *Californian*'s radio operator took the hint and went to bed. When the *Titanic* radioed for help an hour later, the nearest ship to respond was 68 miles away and arrived after the *Titanic* had sunk. *Californian*, which was far nearer, switched on its radio at 7.30 to learn with horror that while it slept, just over the horizon the *Titanic* had sunk. After that, regulations were drafted that ocean-going ships must keep their radios on at all times.

Antarctic expedition

ON 9 MARCH 1912, the *Times* recorded that the South Pole had been reached on 14 December the previous year by the Norwegian explorer, Captain Amundsen. Amundsen spent three days at the pole making observations to confirm he had really arrived at his target. The *Times* noted that 'We have still to hear the story of Captain Scott's expedition during the Antarctic summer, and it is . . . possible that he reached the Pole before December 14th'.

Wilbur Wright dies

THE SADDEST EVENT in aviation history, however, was the death of Wilbur Wright in May from typhoid fever. 'A short life, full of consequences', wrote his father; 'An unfailing intellect, imperturbable temper, great self-reliance, and as great modesty; seeing the right clearly, pursuing it steadily, he lived and died'. The historian Charles H. Gibbs-Smith described him as 'the greatest man in aviation'. The *Times* included the following obituary:

He was indeed an extraordinary person: no one could forecast what he would do in any particular circumstances. The only thing that one could count on was the truth of any positive statement that he made; but then he never made a positive statement if he could help it . . . His love of solitude (and his machine) led him to sleep on two or three planks laid across the roof beams of his aeroplane shed, and if the crowd went home hungry after a blank day he was merely sorry, but no less deliberate in his movements on the next day. His mind was too full of scientific problems to concern itself with the spectacular side of the affair.
The *Times* 31 May

Wilbur Wright.

Royal Flying Corps formed

THE MILITARY WERE TAKING more and more interest in aircraft. In Britain the Royal Flying Corps (later the RAF) was formed in April, and in September a military and naval review took place at Hendon. In the same month France used aircraft in military manoeuvres at Poitou, and the Germans set up a military flying school.

Marie Curie gravely ill

IN PHYSICS, it was a year of steady progress rather than spectacular developments. The American scientist Lee de Forrest discovered the oscillating properties of the audion tube for radio. In France, Madame Curie, suffering badly from nervous exhaustion caused by scandal and the strain of receiving the Nobel Prize, became so gravely ill that her children were not allowed to see her. Not until 17 October was she able to settle to work again, though from 7 October 1911 to 3 December 1912 she could not continue her work on radium standards. In her absence, a standard measure of radium was prepared and accepted by the International Bureau of Weights and Measures.

1913 The Armory

The cream of European art

IN FEBRUARY AND MARCH 1913, New York art lovers came in their thousands to visit one of the most important and controversial art shows of the age – the Armory Show. The show startled the American public, as it brought together and exposed for the first time the cream of the new painting being produced in Europe.

The exhibition was put on by a new group of artists in America, the Association of American Painters and Sculptors. Formed at the start of 1912, the main purpose of the Association was to exhibit new American art, but the Armory Show did much more than that. The Chair of the Association, Arthur Brown, came across the catalogue of the 1912 Cologne Sonderbund show, which displayed much of the finest European art of the time. Brown showed the catalogue to painter Walt Kuhn, who visited the Cologne exhibition and was convinced that the Americans should see these new artists. Kuhn arranged with dealers and artists to lend the work they owned, and the Armory Show was born.

What the critics said

THE EXHIBITION had three sections – Modern American, Historical, and Current European – and it was the last section which attracted controversy. The exhibition was widely talked about, and in the month it was open between 62,000 and 75,000 people paid to go in. Among the visitors were millionaire banker Morgan, society wife Mrs Astor, former President Teddy Roosevelt, and singer Enrico Caruso.

What attracted the crowds was largely the new abstract European art – especially Duchamp's *Nude Descending a Staircase*. This experimental attempt to paint movement attracted ridicule. It was described as 'a lot of disused golf clubs and bags' and 'a dynamited suit of Japanese armour'. Brancusi's abstract *Mlle Pogany* was described as 'a hardboiled egg balanced on a cube of sugar'. Other comments were not so humorous. Matisse, according to art critic F.J. Mather:

[takes] the ugliest models, poses them in the most grotesque and indecent poses, and draws them as would a savage or depraved child.

Other critics attacked the art not just because it was unconventional. One argued:

The propaganda of the cubist, futurist and post-impressionist painters is not only a menace to art but a grave danger to public morals.

There were plenty of people who thought that art could influence behaviour. Some critics defended the exhibition. Alfred Steiglitz wrote:

The dry bones of a dead art are rattling as they have never rattled before. The hopeful birth of a new art that is intensely alive is doing it.

He was one of a small minority, however.

A powerful force

DESPITE THE PROTESTS and criticism, however, the Armory Show was a key event in twentieth-century art. Not only did it bring together a great number of artists to public view, and create a vast amount of interest in new art in the USA, but it brought to public attention the fact that a new and experimental type of art was flourishing. No matter how much the conventional critics might disapprove, the tide of new art was flowing too strongly to reverse. The Armory Show demonstrated how powerful it was.

National Guard to the rescue

BROWN AND KUHN managed to get hold of work from the best contemporary artists of the day – painters like Duchamp, Matisse, Brancusi, Dufy, Braque, Picasso and others – and painters of the older generation such as Cezanne, Degas and Renoir. The organizers needed a large building to house the exhibition – which had 1300 exhibits – and eventually decided to hire the armoury of the 69th Regiment of the National Guard on Lexington Avenue. This gave the show its rather strange name.

Show

Nude Descending a Staircase *by Marcel Duchamp*.

Femme á la Mendoline *by Pablo Picasso.*

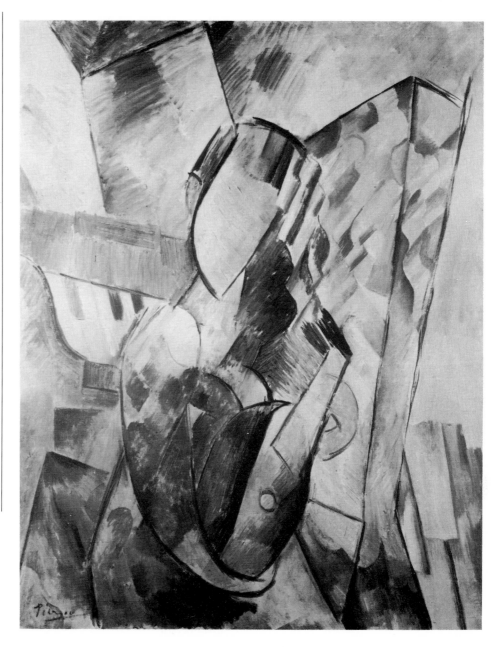

The Balkans bubble up

THE PEACE CONFERENCE held in London at the start of the year was the last attempt before the First World War to settle the problems of the area. Turkey had now been pushed right out of the Balkans apart from a small – but vital – area around their capital, Constantinople. The three Christian nations who had beaten the Turks wished to divide up the old Turkish area between themselves. Austria-Hungary objected to this, claiming that the area on the coast was Albanian, and should not be divided up between Greece and Serbia. The real reason was that Austria did not want the Serbians gaining ports on the coast. The Serbs living inside the Austrian Empire wanted to break away to join Serbia, and Austria did not want the Serbs to gain ports from which they or the Serbs'

Russian allies could launch a naval attack if war broke out.

The Austrians won the argument, and Albania was set up as a new nation. This led to quarrels among the Christians. Serbia and Greece demanded that instead of Albania they should get parts of Macedonia which had been given to Bulgaria. Bulgaria refused, and Serbia and Greece threatened war. Bulgaria decided to attack first, and went to war on 30 June. At this point Rumania, to the north, decided to attack Bulgaria's defence-less northern border. Bulgaria could not fight three countries at once, and was forced to sign a peace treaty at Bucharest on 10 August. Bulgaria lost land to Serbia, Greece and Rumania, and came to hate its neighbours.

Germany prepares for war

AUSTRIA WAS FURIOUS at Serbia's new success, and just before the Treaty of Bucharest was signed secretly proposed to her allies, Germany and Italy, that Serbia be attacked. The Italians refused, and the plan was dropped. However the Germans seemed to have concluded by January 1913 that war was inevitable. In March they published plans to increase the intake of con-scripts to the army from 280,000 to 343,000, and increase army supplies. The Germans decided to raise an extra 1000 million marks (£50,000,000 – a huge sum for 1913) in taxes, and many concluded they were planning war for the summer of 1914, when Germany would still be stronger than her continental enemies. The Russian army was growing stronger and might be more powerful than the German army by 1917.

Naval arms race continues

DESPITE FEARS OF WAR, the ambassadors' conference in London closed in August, removing the one forum where the powers could meet. In November the Turks appointed the German General Liman von Sanders to become Inspector General of the Turkish army. Churchill, meanwhile, had failed in an attempt to slow the naval arms race. On 26 March he suggested that as Britain was due to start building four new battleships in 1914, and Germany two, both should postpone their construction. He repeated the offer on 18 October, but the Germans turned him down.

Home Rule talks fail

THE ULSTER ISSUE continued to cause storms. In September Tory leaders Bonar Law and Lord Landsdowne called on the King to dismiss Asquith as Prime Minister and force a General Election on the Home Rule issue. The King rejected the idea, but arranged talks between Churchill (for the Liberals) and Bonar Law, and then Asquith and Bonar Law. Bonar Law demanded the exclusion of the four Protestant counties and perhaps Tyrone and one other county with a large Protestant minority (in 1922 six were excluded from Ulster to form Northern Ireland). Asquith turned him down.

On 28 November, Bonar Law called on the army to disobey orders – i.e. to mutiny – while the director of Military Operations, Sir Henry Wilson, who advised Carson's Ulster Volunteers, advised army officers to refuse to serve in Ulster. He also betrayed state secrets to Bonar Law. Given this open incite-ment to illegal actions by leading Tory politicians, it is not surprising that on 25 November the Catholics formed the Irish Volunteers. The Liberal Govern-ment immediately banned the import of weapons into Ireland – which, the Catholics pointed out, they had not done when the Ulster Volunteers had been formed.

Cat and Mouse Act

MEANWHILE THE SUFFRAGETTE arson campaign was raising the level of emotions among its supporters. Letters in pillar boxes were set on fire. Empty houses, and other buildings, were burned, pictures were slashed and monuments attacked. A number of women were imprisoned, and then went on hunger strike in jail. They had to be force fed, which caused outrage, and in the middle of the year the Home

Corruption alleged

ROWS BETWEEN LIBERALS AND TORIES became more bitter. The previous year rumours spread that the Liberal Post-Master General had awarded a contract to the Marconi radio company because other ministers with Marconi shares had influenced him. A government inquiry cleared the minister, Samuel, but three other ministers were shown to have shares in the American Marconi Company. This was not the same as the British Marconi Company, so no corruption was involved, but the ministers should have made their connection clear. In June 1913 they admitted a lack of judgement and apologized. The Tories then voted for their resignation, which the Liberals defeated. Only corruption could justify the resignation call. It was a sign of how much the Tories hated the Liberals.

A Suffragette poster attacking the Liberal Government's 'Cat and Mouse' Act.

Emily Davison.

Secretary, McKenna, passed the 'Cat and Mouse' Act. This act allowed the authorities to release women from prison so they would not die, then arrest them when they had recovered so they could complete their sentence. Above all, the suffragettes mourned their first martyr in 1913. At the Derby in June, a suffragette supporter, Emily Davison, protesting against the Government, ran onto the course during the race and collided with the King's horse. She suffered injuries from which she later died.

Row over 'Rite of Spring'

ON 29 MARCH 1913, the world of ballet was shaken by the storm over the first performance of Stravinsky's *The Rite of Spring*. Diaghilev brought together the composer, Stravinsky and the dancer Nijinsky, who choreographed the ballet. The curtain in the Paris theatre rose on a scene in a Russian forest where pagan rites were imitated by mass movements of dancers. There were no soloists, and no ordinary dancing at all. Laughter greeted the opening, which quickly turned to catcalls and shouts of opposition from lovers of conventional ballet. Supporters of the avant-garde began to shout back in defence. Soon the theatre was in uproar, the orchestra playing on unheard and the dancers performing to Nijinsky's shouted counting.

The problem was partly the unfamiliar way of dancing Nijinsky had devised. Dancers had to move with bent knees, feet placed flat on the ground, keeping their heads in profile while making their bodies face the audience. It was an attempt to recreate ritual dancing, but it was difficult and appeared clumsy. Stravinsky's music was even more complex, with its unusual harmonies and fierce syncopated rhythms. This later became accepted, but in 1913 it was deeply shocking. That night in Paris, the whole audience knew they were watching a break with tradition.

In composing the 'Rite', I had imagined the spectacular part of the performance as a series of rhythmic mass movements of the greatest simplicity which would have an instantaneous effect on the audience . . . The music of the dance, clear and well defined, demanded a corresponding choreography – simple and easy to understand. But . . . although he had grasped the dramatic significance of the dance, Nijinsky . . . complicated it either by clumsiness or lack of understanding.
Stravinsky on *The Rite of Spring*.

The sensation of the ballet world: Nijinsky.

Literary highlights

D.H. Lawrence's first major novel, *Sons and Lovers*, was published. Dealing with the struggle of a young man to discover himself, it was the first of Lawrence's novels to express his deepest feelings successfully.

G.B. Shaw also produced a major exploration of inner feelings with his popular story of a working-class girl educated to become a society hostess, *Pygmalion*.

Thomas Mann's *Death in Venice* was published, and Proust produced the first volume, *Swann's Way*, of his work *Remembrance of Things Past*.

Golden Age of Physics

BY 1913, PHYSICS was enjoying a golden age of discovery, especially in the study of radio-activity. That autumn, Madame Curie attended Birmingham University to accept an honorary doctorate. She took the opportunity to praise Ernest Rutherford, saying

Dr Rutherford is the one man living who promises to confer some inestimable boon on mankind as a result of the discovery of radium. I would advise England to watch Dr Rutherford; his work in radio-activity has surprised me greatly. Great developments are likely to transpire shortly, to which the discovery of radium is only a preliminary.
Quoted in *Marie Curie*, by Robert Reid

Rutherford was not alone, however. In 1913 Danish Physicist Neils Bohr made a great leap forward for physics by devising a mathematical formula to explain the workings of the atom using Max Planck's quantum theory. Discoveries such as those of radium showed that the atom did not follow the rules of 'classical' physics. In 1900 Planck revealed the quantum theory, that energy comes in packets called 'photons'. This enabled the young physicist Albert Einstein to show that the reason why electrons – minute parts of an atom – did not follow the old rules was because of quantum theory. Einstein's mathematical work in 1905 enabled Bohr, in 1913, to announce an entirely new theory of how the atom works. Bohr's theory is today the basis of modern atomic physics.

Experimental use of radium

1913 ALSO SAW THE FIRST experimental use of radium, only ten years after its discovery. Hungarian physicist George Charles de Heresy, working in the Vienna Institute for Radium, used the radio-activity given off by Radium D – an isotope of lead – to study the solubility of lead sulphate in water. It was the first practical use of radio-activity.

Flying soars ahead

IN FLYING, FRENCH HISTORIANS refer to 1913 as 'La Glorieuse Année', as it was a memorable year. A milestone was passed on 20 August when the Russian Nesterov performed the first loop the loop. The day before, Frenchman Adolphe Pegoud had performed the first parachute jump from an aeroplane, and in September he perfected the basic tricks of aerobatics. It was also a year for long-distance flying, including the first non-stop flight across the Mediterranean, from St Raphael in France to Bizerta in Tunisia. The air speed record was broken three times by Frenchman Prevost on a Deperdussin, ending at 126.67 mph. In Russia, Igor Sikorski designed and flew on 13 May the first four-engined aircraft, the Bolshoi. However, the honours went to France. A Seguin won the record for distance over a closed circuit (634.54 miles) while Legagneux pushed the height record up to 20,079 feet.

Scott of the Antarctic

ON 11 FEBRUARY 1913 the *Times* reported that news had reached London the previous night of the tragic end of Captain Scott's expedition to the South Pole, which had perished in the intense cold of the Antarctic. The expedition had been missing for over a year, and hope of finding anyone alive had been slim. Search parties had been sent out from base camp at the end of the Antarctic winter, on 30 October 1912, and on 12 November Scott's tent had been found. The details of the tragedy were revealed in the expedition diary. Scott's party had reached the South Pole on 18 January 1912 to find that the Norwegian Amundsen had beaten them by over a month. Then on the way back, the seaman Edgar Evans died of concussion in February, and on 17 March Captain Oates, seriously ill, had dragged himself away from the party to die. On 29 March the other three party members, Scott, Wilson and Bowers, froze to death in a blizzard. When the news reached London, the *Times* commented:

One has to go a long way back in the history of British exploring enterprise to find any disaster of like magnitude . . . The loss to British exploring enterprise can hardly have been greater.
The *Times* 11 February

Death in

Archduke to visit Bosnia

SERBIA'S VICTORY in the Balkan wars of 1912-13 increased the pressure among Serbs in both Serbia and Bosnia to unite. The Austrians, having taken over Bosnia in 1908 were in no mood to compromise with the Serbs and the more extreme Serbian nationalists turned to violence. Between 1910 and 1914 there were six attempts to kill members of the ruling Austrian Royal Family. Nevertheless, the Austrian authorities were remarkably complacent when the heir to the Austrian throne, Archduke Franz Ferdinand, decided to visit the Bosnian capital of Sarajevo in June 1914.

The Archduke, the Inspector General of the Austro-Hungarian armed forces, planned to visit army exercises in Bosnia. Reports that Serb nationalists were plotting to murder the Archduke were known to the police, yet no real precautions were taken to guard him. When his father had visited the town in 1910, a double cordon of soldiers had lined the streets and nationalists were placed under house arrest. In 1914, only 120 police were on duty to cover the four mile route from the railway station to the Town Hall.

Gavrilo Princip is hustled into custody after his assassination of Archduke Franz Ferdinand in Sarajevo, June 1914.

Nationalists attempt assassination

WHEN FRANZ FERDINAND arrived on the 28 June, members of a secret Serbian nationalist group, the Black Hand, were mingling with the crowd. As the six-car procession passed down a riverside road called Appel Quay, it passed two conspirators who were too frightened to do anything. A third, Nedjelko Caprionovic, was bolder, asking a policeman first to point out the Archduke's car, then knocking the cap off a hand grenade and throwing it at the Archduke. Franz Ferdinand saw it coming and with great courage beat it away. It exploded and injured twenty people. The party was then driven to the Town Hall at speed and the rest of the tour cancelled.

Archduke and wife shot dead

THE ARCHDUKE still had to get back to the railway station for the trip home. He asked General Potiorek, Military Governor of Bosnia, if it would be safe to drive back. Potiorek replied, 'Your Imperial Highness, you can travel quite happily. I will take the responsibility.' The party decided to change the advertised route back to the station, but no one told the driver.

The car started back down Appel Quay, but at Franz Joseph Street the driver turned right. He should have gone straight on, so Potiorek shouted, 'What is this? Stop! You are going the

Sarajevo

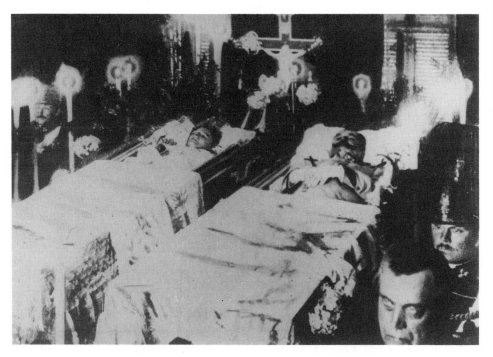

Lying in State: the bodies of the Archduke and Duchess.

wrong way! The driver stepped on the brake and pulled up. On the pavement by the car was another Serbian nationalist, Gavrilo Princip. Princip was armed with a revolver, and fired at point blank range, hitting both the Archduke and his wife. Within minutes, both were dead.

The war begins

THE MURDERS GAVE the Austrians the motive they had long wanted to crush Serbia. Though it was never proved that the Serbian government was involved in the murders, Serbian Secret Servicemen were suspected of being involved, and it was undeniable that Serbia stood to gain from the murders. However, the Austrians knew that a war with Serbia might bring in Serbia's powerful ally, Russia. Austria could not face Russia alone, so they turned to their German ally. Would Germany back Austria? The Germans hesitated, then agreed.

On 23 July, Austria-Hungary sent Serbia an ultimatum demanding virtually total control of Serbia. The Serbians rejected this, but offered to let an international conference decide what should be done about the murders. Austria rejected this, and declared war on 28 July 1914. That afternoon Austrian guns opened fire on Belgrade. The war had begun.

Declaration of War

Official text published in Vienna, 28 July

The Royal Government of Servia not having given a satisfactory reply to the Note presented to it by the Austro-Hungarian Minister in Belgrade on July 23, 1914, the Imperial and Royal Government of Austria Hungary finds it necessary itself to safeguard its rights and interests and to have recourse for this purpose to force of arms. Austria-Hungary therefore considers itself from this moment in a state of war with Servia.
The *Times* 29 July

An unanswered question

REVIEWING THE AUTOBIOGRAPHY of an Austrian Countess, the *Graphic* magazine commented:

The immediate topical interest in the Countess Zanardi Landi's life story . . . is to be found in the pages which divert from the main theme . . . the Countess suspects that there was more behind the crime at Sarajevo on 28 June than has come out, and that Servia should not bear all the blame . . . 'It cannot be doubted that the removal of Franz Ferdinand and his wife came as a relief to many. The court as a whole watched with apprehension the way in which the old Emperor was harassed by the two parties, the adherents and the enemies of the late heir apparent, and from its point of view the future looks more peaceful now'.
Graphic, 19 September

Did the Austrian court welcome the murder of the Archduke? The question has never been answered.

Preparations for war

ALL THE GREAT POWERS had been preparing for war before 1914, but the most elaborate preparations had been those of Germany. Following the alliance of France and Russia in 1894, Germany faced the prospect of being attacked from east and west at the same time. Dividing the German army into two to meet these attacks was highly dangerous. The German commanders were confident they could beat either France or Russia, but could they defeat both at once? The generals decided it was too dangerous to try.

The Schlieffen Plan

IN DECEMBER 1905 the German Commander, Count von Schlieffen, invented his famous Plan. It depended on a lightning attack by the whole German army against France, a speedy victory in six weeks, then turning the German army round to fight Russia. The Plan involved two gambles – firstly that the Germans could beat France in six weeks, secondly that the Russian army could not attack in that six weeks.

In 1905, Schlieffen gambled on a surprise attack through Belgium, which all the great powers had agreed would be neutral back in 1839. The French did not expect the Germans to break the treaty, so made no plans to defend the Belgian border. The Germans knew this, and expected to sweep into Northern France and capture Paris. The Germans knew the British might fight to defend Belgium, but gambled that they could defeat France before Britain could land her army.

Chain of events

WHEN AUSTRIA DECLARED WAR on Serbia on 28 July, one step led to another. Russia went to war to defend Serbia, Germany went to war with Russia to defend Austria, France went to war to defend Russia, and Britain went to war to defend Belgium.

A scrap of paper

The step taken by Britain because of our infringement of the neutrality of Belgium was terrible to a degree. Just for a word, neutrality; just for a scrap of paper, Great Britain is going to make war on a kindred nation which desired nothing better than to be friends with her. It is unthinkable. It was like striking a man from behind while he is fighting for his life against two assailants.
(The German Chancellor to the British Ambassador to Germany, 4 August 1914)

Failure of the Schlieffen Plan

BY 20 AUGUST THE GERMANS had captured the Belgian capital, Brussels, and the new German Commander, Moltke, was convinced the plan could work. But though the German army was in northern France by the first week in September, the troops were exhausted from marching in the heat. The French were able to rush their army to the north of Paris and counter-attack. From 6-11 September the French flung their troops into battle using 250 Paris taxis. Though the Germans could see the Eiffel Tower in the distance, they could not advance. On 11 September the Germans decided to retreat. The Schlieffen Plan had failed.

Battles in the East

BATTLES IN THE EAST helped defeat the Plan. The Russians attacked more quickly than expected, and the Germans had to send troops to fight them. Though they beat the Russians at the battles of Tannenberg and the Masurian Lakes, the German army fighting the battle of the Marne was weakened. The Germans had machine guns, which the Russians did not have. Back in France, the machine gun was proving so dangerous that the soldiers had to dig trenches in the ground to hide from the bullets. By the end of 1914 the trenches stretched from the English Channel to the Swiss Alps, and soldiers could only attack with great difficulty. There was deadlock on the Western Front.

Trouble brewing in Ireland

UNTIL THE WAR BROKE OUT, the biggest story in Britain was the crisis in Ulster. The Home Rule Bill had been passed in 1912, and was due to come into operation in 1914. The Tories decided to take serious action to stop the Liberal Government's plans. The government ordered Sir Arthur Paget, Commander of the army in Ireland, to move troops from Dublin to Ulster in case of trouble.

Paget knew that many of his fellow officers were Ulster Protestants who did not want to have to fight fellow Protestants if Ulster revolted. He announced that those officers who did not wish to serve in Ulster could resign. Fifty-seven of the 70 officers of the 3rd Cavalry Brigade said they would resign on 20 March, together with many infantry officers. Government supporters were furious at what they regarded as mutiny – refusal to obey orders – but Seely, the Minister of War, gave the officers led by General Gough a written assurance that 'they would

'It'll be over by Christmas'. A recruiting office, August 1914.

War breaks out

ONCE GERMANY INVADED BELGIUM, most people backed the government in declaring war on Germany. The British army was tiny – seven divisions against the 57 divisions the Germans sent to fight France – and the whole force was sent to France as the British Expeditionary Force. Most people had thought the war would be over by Christmas, but even in August Lord Kitchener, appointed Secretary for War, predicted it would last three years and aimed to raise an army of 70 divisions.

The Warlords: German Generals Hindenberg, von Falkenhayn and Ludendorff pore over maps of the front.

not be called on to enforce the present Home Rule Bill on Ulster'.

This provoked a major row. The government would not allow officers to decide which orders to obey, and Seely had to resign. Asquith himself took over as Minister for War. However, he took no action against the officers, and it seemed likely that if trouble broke out in Ulster the army could not be relied on to carry out orders. Trouble built up in Ulster. On 24 April the Ulster Volunteers landed 30,000 rifles and 3 million bullets illegally. This provoked the Catholic National Volunteers to bring in weapons at Howth, near Dublin. Troops were called out but failed to stop the gun runners. However they opened fire on crowds stoning them at Batchelors Walk, killing three and wounding 38. The Catholics were furious, pointing out the failure of the government to take action against the Protestants. Though the Catholic Irish leaders backed Britain when the war broke out – the Home Rule Bill was suspended till the war ended – the bitterness remained.

Thousands volunteer

THIS WAS TO BE RAISED by voluntary recruitment, and the appeal for recruits was enormously successful. 100,000 volunteers had been expected – 175,000 volunteered in the week ending 5 September alone. By the end of September 750,000 had joined up, and by the time conscription was imposed in March 1916 two and a half million men had volunteered. It was this volunteer army which did the fighting up to and including the Battle of the Somme.

Sport and the Arts

Soccer

SOCCER IN BRITAIN saw the conclusion of a chapter in sport's long running amateur versus professional battle. In 1906 the Amateur Old Boys' Club in London broke away from the London Football Association, and in 1907 this became a national split when the Amateur Football Association broke away from the Football Association. However, the international football body FIFA refused to accept the AFA and even in the amateur world of the Olympics, the British Olympic Committee called on the Football Association and not the Amateurs to help organize the 1908 Olympics. In February 1912 negotiations began to heal the absurd split, and in February 1914 the rebels returned to the parent body. The reconciliation was marked by a mock duet in C.B. Fry's magazine for March 1914, where the two leaders were supposed to have sung:

Imagists, Futurists and Vorticists

IN POETRY, THE IMAGIST movement led by Ezra Pound broke up in 1914. In 1913 Pound had collected a number of poems together for an anthology, but could not get it printed. The collection, titled *Des Imagistes*, appeared in 1914. It included poems by James Joyce – who published his novel *The Dubliners* in 1914 – Ford Madox Ford and Amy Lowell. Pound had annoyed the other Imagist poets by his arrogance, however, and in the late summer of 1914 Lowell came from America to London and took over the leadership of the Imagists. Rejected by the Imagists, Pound found a new interest in the Vorticist movement, a movement of painters led by Wyndham Lewis. The first edition of Lewis's Vorticist magazine *Blast* appeared in June 1914. Lewis linked together developments in British painting and poetry with

C. Wreford-Brown (AFA) (sotto voce)

I repent, and sink upon my knees,
To crave forgiveness, Mr Clegg
Take me back, and I'll work hard to please,
And never try to pull your leg,
I've been wrong, made blunders by the
    score,
And your indulgence I must beg,
I won't be a bad boy any more,
So try to love me, Mr Clegg!

J.C. Clegg (FA) (through a megaphone)

I am King! The FA is my throne,
O'er bags of gold I hold my sway,
Sir, how dare you call your soul your own,
And try to go your own sweet way?
Bring your men, let them be bought and sold
(and prices are not going down).
Come and hide your face within the fold,
For I forgive you, Wreford-Brown.
Quoted in Brian Dobbs, *Edwardians at Play*

The poet Rupert Brooke.

European experiments. He was particularly interested in a group of Italian painters called the Futurists. The leader of this group, Marinetti, published an article in June 1914 on 'Vital English Art' which claimed that Lewis was a Futurist.

Patriotic poetry

NEVERTHELESS, THE EXPERIMENTS affected very few people. Popular art was still very conventional, and the poetry most people read was still similar to that of the Victorian period. A patriotic war poet such as Rupert Brooke, who welcomed the war, reached millions of people with poems like *1914*.

Now, God be thanked who has matched us
    with His hour
And caught our youth, and wakened us from
    sleeping,
With hand made sure, clear eye, and
    sharpened power,
To turn, as swimmers into cleanness
    leaping,
Glad from a world grown old and cold and
    weary,
Leave the sick hearts that honour could not
    move,
And half-men, and their dirty songs and
    dreary,
And all the little emptiness of love!

Oh! we, who have known shame, we have
    found release there,
Where there's no ill, no grief, but sleep
    has mending,
Naught broken save this body, lost but
    breath;
Nothing to shake the laughing heart's long
    peace there,
But only agony, and that has ending;
And the worst friend and enemy is but
    Death.

Film comes of age

IN 1914, A 'NEW' ART FORM reached maturity, when in February Charlie Chaplin made his first film, *Making a Living*. In the same month his first 'tramp' film was released, and in November Chaplin made the first full-length six-reel feature film – a reel in 1914 lasted ten minutes, and previous films had been one or two reels at most. Chaplin's six-reel film was *Tillie's Punctured Romance*, and with it the film came of age.

One of the first Sikorski four-engined biplanes.

Curie Institute opens

MADAME CURIE IN 1914 saw her world fame reap a practical reward when she opened her own scientific institute. In 1912 the Pasteur Institute had offered to build a laboratory to be run by Madame Curie and be devoted to radio-activity. The Pasteur Foundation and University of Paris had reached an agreement that half the new laboratory would be devoted to research in physics and chemistry, run by Madame Curie, and the other half devoted to medical research. On this basis the Institute was built, opening in July 1914. A month later it was deserted – all the workers had gone to the war.

Progress in the air

IN 1914, THE TECHNICAL PROGRESS of the plane slowed down. However, Sikorski in Russia started productive flying with the second of his famous four-engined cabin planes, the Ilia Mouriametz, which first flew in January 1914. On 11

X-rays on the move

TEN DAYS AFTER THE WAR started, Madame Curie received a request from the French Minister of War to equip operators for radiographic work. The use of X-rays to detect injuries in the body had already started. Marie Curie found ways to equip cars with the X-ray machines to go where the fighting was. By October Marie with her daughter and an operator were at work converting a car into an X-ray van. On 1 November radiological car E was ready and rolled into action.

February it took up 16 people and in June flew from St Petersburg to Kiev and back – 1590 miles. This inspired Count Zeppelin to start making large aeroplanes as well as balloons. In America the first scheduled airline in history was opened, over 22 miles in Florida. A converted Sopwith Tabloid on floats raised the speed record for sea planes to 92 mph and won the second Schneider trophy speed contest.

At the start of the war, the Allies had 208 airplanes on the Western Front and the Germans about 180. These were employed in scouting and, after radio was fitted, for artillery spotting. Fighters were unknown in 1914 as pilots could not shoot forward without hitting their own propellors, but planes with propellors at the rear, and a gunner at the front, were flying. They were too slow to use as fighters but could be used as bombers by simply tossing bombs over the side by hand.

1915

The Lusitania

Dangers of war-time travel

ON 15 MAY 1915, the Cunard liner *Lusitania*, the fastest ship on the Atlantic route, was returning from a voyage to New York with over 1250 passengers. The sea around Britain had been declared a war zone by Germany, and German U-boats (submarines) had already been sinking British ships in the area. The German Embassy in New York had issued a notice on 22 April warning US passengers intending to travel on British ships of the dangers.

NOTICE!

TRAVELLERS intending to embark on the Atlantic voyage are reminded that a state of war exists between Germany and her allies and Great Britain and her allies; that the zone of war includes the waters adjacent to the British Isles; that, in accordance with formal notice given by the Imperial German Government, vessels flying the flag of Great Britain, or of any of her allies, are liable to destruction in those waters and that travellers sailing in the war zone on ships of Great Britain or her allies do so at their own risk.

IMPERIAL GERMAN EMBASSY
WASHINGTON, D. C., APRIL 22, 1915.

Notice to Travellers posted at the Imperial German Embassy, Washington DC, 1915.

Lusitania torpedoed

OFFICIALLY, HOWEVER, NO ONE expected the U-boats to sink a British liner carrying Americans (*Lusitania* carried 159 US citizens). The USA was neutral in the war and was the most powerful country in the world. Drowning any of her citizens would anger Americans, and might bring the USA into the war against Germany. Yet at 2.10 p.m. on 7 May, when the ship was ten miles off the Irish coast, the German U-boat U20 fired a torpedo into the ship without warning. There were two explosions and the ship sank in 20 minutes. 1201 people were drowned.

'An act of piracy'?

THERE WAS AN IMMEDIATE outcry in both Britain and the USA. In Britain the sinking was described as an act of murder of innocent men, women and children. British newspapers called the sinking a 'foul crime' and 'an act of piracy' (*Daily Express*). In the USA there was strong feeling over the deaths of Americans, including millionaire Alfred Vanderbilt. The US ambassadors in Britain and Germany expected their country to go to war with Germany. This did not happen straight away, but the sinking of *Lusitania* was a turning point, playing a major part in turning America against Germany.

Remember the *Lusitania*

The jury's verdict says: 'We find that the said deceased died from their prolonged immersion and exhaustion in the sea eight miles south-south-west of the Old Head of Kinsale on Friday, May 7th, 1915, owing to the sinking of the R.M.S. *Lusitania* by a torpedo fired without warning from a German submarine.'

'That this appalling crime was contrary to international law and the conventions of all civilized nations, and we therefore charge the officers of the said submarine and the Emperor and Government of Germany, under whose orders they acted, with the crime of wilful and wholesale murder before the tribunal of the civilized world.'

It is your duty to take up the sword of justice to avenge this devil's work. ENLIST TODAY. Recruiting poster issued before conscription was introduced in Britain.

Or a legitimate act of war?

BUT WAS THE SINKING an act of murder and piracy? The Germans claimed it was a legitimate act of war within international law, because the *Lusitania* was not simply a passenger ship. The German government argued with the US that the *Lusitania* was an armed auxiliary ship of the Royal Navy, that the U20 could not surface and warn the *Lusitania* because the British had ordered merchant vessels to ram and sink German submarines, and that the *Lusitania* carried munitions, other war goods, and had been used to carry Canadian troops. If these points were true, it meant *Lusitania* was a ship of war and the U20 was justified in sinking it.

The Americans refused to investigate the German claims, accepting British denials. The semi-official British naval history published after the war did admit the *Lusitania* carried some munitions, however, but that this

Mystery

The Lusitania: *a contemporary artist's impression of the liner's last moments.*

did not matter. By then the affair was history.

The Germans justified their act on the plea that she carried some 5000 cases of small arm ammunition and shrapnel. This was true. But even so by every accepted canon it would not warrant the destruction of a ship whose chief freight was non-combatant (i.e. non-war T.F.) passengers, and least of all her destruction without warning. In further defence of the indefensible, the Germans asserted she was armed as a cruiser. This was not true. She was not even armed defensively.

Quoted in *Naval Operations*, Vol. 2, Sir Julian S. Corbett

The suspicion remains

THE SINKING OF THE *LUSITANIA* had an immediate effect – the Germans stopped their submarines operating in the Atlantic for fear of killing more Americans and bringing the US into the war. The questions about the *Lusitania* still remain. A US diver who visited the wreck in 1962 claimed to have seen a gun barrel. Was the ship armed? Could the U20 have given warnings? Though the British denied it, they had ordered their merchant ships to ram U-boats which surfaced. Was it carrying more war goods than even the British later admitted? The ship sank in 20 minutes, and eye-witnesses reported two explosions. The *Titanic*, though badly holed in 1912, had stayed afloat for two hours. No torpedo could have made a hole big enough for this – but high explosive could have ripped the ship apart.

Even more seriously, was the *Lusitania* deliberately sacrificed? The British Admiralty could read German radio messages and knew U20 was in the area. Yet naval escorts were ordered back into harbour while no orders were given to the *Lusitania* to head for safety in Queenstown. Was the ship deliberately allowed to sail to destruction in order to bring the USA into the war against Germany? The suspicion remains.

The Western Front

ON THE WESTERN FRONT the machine gun and artillery could pour such a massive hail of bullets across the battlefield that soldiers had to live in trenches to avoid being shot. An eyewitness described the strange sight of the apparently deserted countryside.

One can look for miles and see no human being. But in those miles of country lurk (like moles or rats it seems) thousands even hundreds of thousands of men, planning against each other perpetually some new device of death. Never showing themselves, they launch at each other bullet, bomb, aerial torpedo and shell. And yet the landscape shows nothing of all this, nothing but a few shattered trees and three or four lines of earth and sandbags; these and the ruins of towns and villages are the only signs of war anywhere visible.
Quoted in Lobban, *The First World War*

The Generals tried to break through by launching thousands of men in great battles, but these were held up by barbed wire – and while they tried to cut the wire, they were shot down. The French attacked in the Champagne region from January to March 1915, but lost 90,000 casualties to gain only five miles. The British attacked at Neuve Chapelle on 10 March but gained only a square mile for the loss of 12,000 men. Further battles showed the same result – little land gained, massive casualty lists, no breakthrough. The Germans did gain a breakthrough in their one attack on the Western front in 1915, by using poison gas. The gas killed so many British that the Germans could walk through the trenches at Ypres – but then they ran into their own gas and had to retreat.

Trench warfare: the grim reality.

The Eastern Front

THE GERMANS DID LITTLE FIGHTING on the Western Front in 1915, concentrating on helping the Austrians fight the Russians. Using their railways, the Central Powers grouped their forces and by May were ready to attack. There were few trenches on the Eastern Front because the huge distances meant the troops were spread thinly. The Central Powers had better equipment than the Russians and drove them back 200 miles. Two million Russians were killed, wounded or taken prisoner.

Gallipoli

AS THE ARMIES COULD NOT attack on the Western Front, and there was no way round the trenches north or south, Churchill decided that the best plan was to knock out Germany's ally Turkey, send supplies to help the Russians, and force Germany to pull troops from the Western Front. In March a naval force tried to break through the Dardanelle Straits to attack the Turkish capital Instanbul, but three ships were sunk by mines and the force withdrew. In April troops were landed on the Gallipoli beaches, but the Turks were ready and trapped the soldiers by the sea. The troops spent months in trenches, then after attempts to break into the mountains and force the Turks back had failed, the army was withdrawn in January 1916. Russia remained cut off from the Western Allies.

Women at war

THE MOBILIZATION of millions of men for the armed forces left so many jobs vacant at home that they could only be filled by employing women. The suffragettes, who had been attacking the government, swung round and demanded the right to serve the war effort. Before the war women had worked in only a very small number of occupations, mainly as servants, and had been told they were not strong enough to work in factories, or bright enough to work with their brains or even vote. Now they were given all sorts of jobs to do, and astonished men by how well they worked. Particular praise went to women working in the high explosive sections of munitions factories. One commentator said:

The women who undertake this work are doing a very gallant service. Theirs is the highest courage, for many of them are nervous. The writer has seen a little group of new workers in tears because, although they had undertaken to work in the danger houses, they were scared when the moment came to go there. It is all the more to their honour that they were insisting through their tears that they 'would be perfectly safe if they were careful'.
Quoted in Lobban, *The First World War*

Control on social life

ON 8 AUGUST 1914 the government had passed the Defence of the Realm Act (DORA) which gave it sweeping powers to control the lives of the British people. Censorship of letters and newspapers was brought in, and it soon became impossible to obtain accurate information about the war. All aspects of life were affected by the war, but among the most long-lasting effects were the changes in the licensing laws. Before 1915 pubs could stay open all day until midnight. Drunkenness was widespread, but the brewers were too influential to be restricted. When drunkenness affected war production, however, the government acted, only allowing pubs to open at lunchtime and in the evening.

The munitions crisis

BY THE SPRING OF 1915, the failure of the army in France was causing fierce debate. The newspapers picked up a story that the army was short of shells, and though the generals knew it was not true, it was a convenient excuse. There was indeed a shortage of weapons like machine guns and basic supplies like great coats. The 'Shell Crisis' scandal forced the Liberal government to take action, appointing Lloyd George – Chancellor of the Exchequer – to be Minister of Munitions. The Tories argued that at a time of national crisis they should be part of the government, and a coalition was formed with Asquith staying on as Prime Minister. Thus the last purely Liberal government came to an end.

War work. With men sent to the front, women were employed to keep the wheels of industry turning.

Experiments in art continue

DESPITE THE WAR, the experimentation in European art continued, though at a slower pace, and with the artists confined to the lands of either the Allies or the Central Powers. The Imagist poets separated, Amy Lowell going back to Boston, Richard Aldington joining the army and being posted to the Western Front. D.H. Lawrence and his German wife, both of whom opposed the war, went to Cornwall. Lawrence published one of his greatest novels, *The Rainbow*, in 1915.

Vorticism remained strong, and the Vorticist painters held their first exhibition in 1915. Wyndham Lewis wrote a note about the exhibition making it clear that the magazine *Blast* 'was started principally as a vehicle for the propagation of their ideas'. Only two editions appeared, the second in July 1915, in time to record the death in battle of the Vorticist sculptor Gaudier-Brzeska, one of many artists to die in the war.

Artists and the war

ATTITUDES AMONG ARTISTS to the war varied considerably. Rupert Brooke represented one extreme, welcoming the conflict, as did the Futurists, especially Apollinaire, who one critic said 'accepted the war joyfully as a magnificent manifestation of modern beauty'. Probably more typical was Aldington's attitude. He served with distinction, but reluctantly and with a sense of the futility of the Western Front expressed in his poem *Battlefield*:

The wind is piercing chill
And blows fine grains of snow
Over this shell rent ground;
Every house in sight
Is smashed and desolate
But in this fruitless land,
Thorny with wire
And foul with rotting clothes and sacks
The crosses flourish –
Ci-git, ci-git, ci-git . . .
'Ci-git i soldat Allemand,
Priez pour lui'.

Film reaches the heights

MEANWHILE, IN THE NEUTRAL USA, the film industry was developing at a great pace. The most popular artist was undoubtedly Charlie Chaplin. In January he moved from Mack Sennett's studio to that of Essanay. Sennett could not afford the $750 a week which Chaplin demanded, and Chaplin accepted the enormous sum (for 1915) of $1,250 per week. Chaplin made 14 films in his year at Essanay, and developed his 'tramp' character into a fully-fledged portrait of genius. The most important film of his Essanay period was *The Tramp*, released on 11 April 1915, including for the first time pathos and an unhappy ending. Chaplin was becoming more than just a comedy star.

Long Live the Vortex!

Long live the great art vortex sprung up in the centre of this town !

We stand for the Reality of the Present—not for the sentimental Future, or the sacripant Past.

We want to leave Nature and Men alone.

We do not want to make people wear Futurist Patches, or fuss men to take to pink and sky-blue trousers.

We are not their wives or tailors.

The only way Humanity can help artists is to remain independent and work unconsciously.

WE NEED THE UNCONSCIOUSNESS OF HUMANITY—their stupidity, animalism and dreams.

We believe in no perfectibility except our own.

A page from Blast

The first epic

MEANWHILE THE US CINEMA was producing another genius, the director D.W. Griffith. Griffith had been making films since 1908. In 1913 he had made a four reel film, violating the company rule that the maximum was two reels, and left Biograph as a result. Between July and October 1914 he shot a film called *The Clansman*, which renamed *The Birth of a Nation* opened in New York in March to a sensation. Though cut, it lasted for 165 minutes – the first epic movie. Though the cost was $110,000 to make, it took $18,000,000 at the box office and technically it was the most advanced film yet made. It shot Lillian Gish to stardom overnight.

Air power. An early Vickers fighter, with front-mounted machine gun and rear-mounted propeller.

The Curies at war

MARIE CURIE AND HER 17 year-old daughter Irene spent 1915 touring the battlefields in their radiological car, using X-rays to probe the bodies of injured soldiers. The most serious problem she faced was the lack of trained staff, for trained radiologists were scarce and the armed forces were recruiting or conscripting scientists without thought for the loss of technical skill. Marie Curie's favourite Polish co-worker, Jan Danysz, was killed in 1915 serving as a captain of artillery. The same year Henry Rutherford mourned the loss of a brilliant young physicist, Harry Moseley, 'shot clean through the head' in the Gallipoli campaign. War was being stripped of its glamour. Marie Curie later wrote:

I never could forget the terrible impression of all that destruction of human life and health. To hate the very idea of war, ought to be sufficient to see what I have seen so many times, all over those years; men and boys brought to the advanced ambulance in a mixture of mud and blood, many of them dying of their injuries and many others recovering but slowly, in the space of months, with pain and suffering.

Aircraft

THE COMING OF THE WAR gave a great stimulus to the development of aircraft. Each side strove to improve their aircraft to beat those of the other, but neither side could get ahead for long. Planes were used for observation early in the war, but only two-seater planes could carry guns, because the pilot of a single seater could only fire ahead – and could not do this without hitting the propellor. Then, on 1 April 1915, the Frenchman Roland Garros 'opened the era of true fighter aircraft' when he shot down a German plane by firing a machine gun through his propeller. After five successful dog-fights, Garros crashed and was captured. The Germans studied his plane, and Fokker produced an improved method of firing through the propellor, using a gear system to ensure that the bullet always fired into the empty space between the propeller blades. The first Allied plane was shot down by this on 1 August, and it was so good that until the Allies came up with a similar device their pilots considered themselves 'Fokker Fodder'.

Not until January 1916 was an Allied rival produced. For more peaceful purposes, the thick section cantilever wing, which Hugo Junkers had patented in 1910, without external bracing with struts or wires, was finally used for an all-metal monoplane, powered by a 120 hp Mercedes engine, in December 1915. It was an 'epoch-making invention'.

A new weapon

THE YEAR SAW THE FIRST use of a new and terrible weapon – poison gas. The Germans, realizing that normal infantry and cavalry attacks could not break through the trenches, decided to release clouds of the gas. They hoped that this would kill the enemy soldiers who inhaled it, allowing their soldiers to advance. In fact, gas did kill many of the enemy, but proved unreliable, as it often blew back into the faces of those who used it.

The man who

U-boat war

AT THE START OF 1916, the navies of Britain and Germany faced each other across the North Sea in very different moods. The British looked back on a successful eighteen months. They had a larger navy than the Germans. With minefields in the English Channel, the British Grand Fleet could bottle up the German High Seas Fleet in the North Sea from its Orkney Islands base of Scapa Flow. The British navy stopped the German merchant fleet operating, while British merchant ships could sail the Seven Seas. It was a satisfactory start to the war.

The German navy, on the other hand, was deeply frustrated. Although the battlecruisers made hit-and-run raids on the East Coast of England, these were pin pricks. The great naval battle like Trafalgar which both sides looked forward to did not take place – the Germans could not risk it with the odds against them. The German plan of using submarines to sail under water into the Atlantic and sink British shipping had proved very successful till the sinking of the *Lusitania*. After that, the Germans had to limit their U-boats to ships which did not carry Americans, which meant they were virtually useless.

The plan

THE GERMANS DECIDED they had to use their surface ships, but without risking a full-scale battle between the Grand Fleet and the High Seas Fleet. The Germans knew the British fleet was partly split, with the battleships at Scapa Flow and the battlecruisers at Rosyth, 200 miles further south. The Germans calculated that if they could lure the battlecruisers into battle using their own battlecruisers, then trap Beatty's battlecruisers into a fight with the more powerful German Dreadnoughts (battleships), then the Germans could destroy the battlecruisers before the British Dreadnoughts could arrive from Scapa Flow.

On 31 May 1916 the plan was put into action. The German battlecruisers under Admiral Hipper were sent to lure out Beatty's ships, with the Dreadnoughts under Admiral Scheer following behind. What Scheer did not know was that the Russians had captured a German code book, and passed it to the British. The British could read the German radio signals, and knew the German Dreadnoughts had left harbour. Immediately the British Dreadnoughts left Scapa Flow and sailed south.

Jutland

THE BRITISH COMMANDER, Admiral Jellicoe, carried a heavy responsibility. Churchill later said, 'He was the one man who could lose the war in a single afternoon'. By this he meant that while the Germans could lose the battle and not be threatened, if the British lost they could then be open to invasion.

Jellicoe knew this, and could not risk an all-out fight. When the battle started, he played a cautious game. The battlecruisers came together in the

early afternoon, with the Germans coming off best. When the German Dreadnoughts came into the battle, Scheer felt he was on the brink of a stunning victory. Then, to his horror, the British Grand Fleet sailed over the horizon and as the evening drew on, shells from Jellicoe's Dreadnoughts began to hit his ships.

Scheer could not risk a full-scale

could have lost the war

battle with the Grand Fleet, and he had to break off the fight. Sending part of his battle fleet on a suicide attack to divert the British, he turned his ships round and fled for home. The night fell and covered his escape. In the gathering darkness, Jellicoe decided to take no risks and called off the chase. For this he was later accused of cowardice, but in fact he had no choice. When dawn broke next morning, the Grand Fleet found itself alone. The Germans had escaped.

Following the battle, the Germans claimed victory, saying they had sunk more British ships and killed more British sailors. This was true. The British lost 14 ships, a total of 112,000 tons, and the Germans 11 ships, totalling 62,000 tons. The British lost

The Battle of Jutland – an artist's impression after the event.

6000 sailors, the Germans 3000. But the morning after the battle saw the Grand Fleet in charge of the North Sea, and the High Seas Fleet never again came out to fight. The British command of the oceans remained intact.

Over the top. British troops advancing into No Man's Land, during the Battle of the Somme.

The Western Front

IN 1916 BOTH THE ALLIES and the Germans launched great battles on the Western Front. The Germans decided that since they could not break through, they would aim to 'bleed the French dry' – kill so many French soldiers that the French could not fight any more. The Germans could plan this because they had a larger army than the French. The German strategy was to attack the fort of Verdun, one of the historic fortresses of France. They knew the French would defend this to the last man. The battle started in February, and when it ended in the autumn the French had suffered 315,000 casualties, but 280,000 Germans had also become victims.

The battle of Verdun forced the British to bring forward their own plan for a massive attack, in the valley of the River Somme. The British Commander, Haig, believed he could break through with a big bombardment. For five days 2000 British guns shelled the Germans. The Germans simply retired into deep bunkers where the shells could do no damage and waited till the British attacked. When the British guns stopped firing they went above ground and shot down the advancing troops. Far from the British breaking through, it was the worst day in the history of the British army. On the first day of the battle of the Somme, the British lost 19,000 dead and 39,000 wounded of the 100,000 soldiers who attacked. The battle went on until the end of November, with the British losing 418,000 casualties, the French 194,000 and the Germans 650,000. There was no breakthrough.

An eyewitness at the Somme

Hundreds of dead were strung out like wreckage washed up to a high water mark. Quite as many died on the enemy wire as on the ground, like fish caught in a net . . . It was clear that there were no gaps in the wire at the time of the attack. The Germans must have been reinforcing their wire for months. It was so dense that daylight could barely be seen through it. Who told the planners that artillery fire would pound such wire to pieces, making it possible to get through? Any Tommy could have told them that shell fire lifts wire up and drops it down, often in a worse tangle than before.

Quoted in *The First World War*, by Robin Lobban

The Russian Front

WITH THE GERMANS concentrating on the Western Front, the Russians took the chance to recover and attack in 1916. In March they attacked the German positions, but machine gun and artillery fire drove the Russians back, losing 100,000 men. The Russian General Brusilov had more success attacking the Austrians, however. The Russians won through on the Dneister river with the Austrians losing 600,000 casualties. Only German troops, rushed to the battlefield, stopped a complete Russian breakthrough. Russia lost over a million casualties, however, and though its population was vast, victory on such a scale was bought at too high a price.

Licensing laws

THE ACTIONS OF THE GOVERNMENT affected more and more people. In May 1916 the government introduced British Summer Time. This was designed to provide more daylight working hours for war production during the summer, though some farmers refused to follow it. Meanwhile the change in drinking laws was taking effect, and to reduce drunkenness the government watered down the beer and restricted spirits to 70 per cent proof. A government report stated that

The extent of the fall in public drunkenness may be judged broadly from the fact that in 1914 the total number of convictions in Greater London and the cities and boroughs in Great Britain with a population of over a hundred thousand, was approximately 156,000, and in 1916 was reduced to 77,000, the corresponding figures for women being 41,000 and 14,000 respectively. Increased efficiency and improved time-keeping have resulted.
Quoted Lobban *The First World War*

Irish Volunteers photographed during the Easter Uprising.

Conscription

BY THE START OF 1916, patriotic hysteria was mounting. Conservatives and their supporters, desperate for victory, looked for a scapegoat for the army's failure. The previous spring, shortage of shells had been the excuse, now it was a shortage of soldiers. Voluntary recruitment was in fact more than enough, and the army had more recruits than it could equip. Neverthe-less the Tories called for conscription – compulsory military service – and Lloyd George backed them. Asquith wavered, then gave in. In January 1916 the Military Service Act called up all unmarried men between the ages of 18 and 41. However this also brought in a system of exemption, which paradox-ically cut the number of recruits by half in the first six months of the scheme.

Ireland explodes

THE MILITARY SERVICE ACT did not apply to Ireland, a recognition that Southern Ireland was no longer really a part of the United Kingdom. This compromise did not satisfy the dis-contented minority of the Irish Volunteers, who were still armed. They planned an uprising for Easter Sunday, with German support. The German support did not turn up, and the Chief of Staff of the Volunteers cancelled the uprising. He was dis-obeyed by the Volunteers in Dublin, who captured the Post Office and issued a proclamation of independence. Four days of fighting followed. One hundred British and 450 Irish were killed before the rebels surrendered.

The uprising was unpopular in Ireland, and could have given the British a new start. However, the military commander, General Maxwell, executed the seven men who signed the proclamation of independence. All the Volunteer commanders were also shot, except the American Eamon de Valera. The shootings destroyed the authority of the peaceful Home Rule party under Redmond. The leaders of the Easter Uprising became martyrs, and from then on the Catholic Irish concluded they could only gain their aims by force.

Sport and the Arts

Painting in the East

ART AT THIS TIME was a truly European affair, and the experiments in the visual arts began to bear fruit even in Russia. The central figure in the Russian avant-garde was Vladimir Tatlin, who in 1913 had visited Picasso and been impressed by his Cubist reliefs. Back in Russia he experimented with Corner Counter Reliefs – believing that the visual arts should use 'real materials in real space'. In 1916 he organized an important exhibition of avant-garde art in a vacant Moscow shop. Two of the other exhibitors who were to become major figures in the Russian avant-garde were involved in the exhibition – Kasimir Malevich and Alexander Rodchenko.

Malevich was a leading Futurist, though in December 1915 he had developed this into a movement called 'Suprematism'. This was a pure, geometric abstraction, following a similar idea to that of Dutchman Piet Mondrian. Rodchenko was a close friend of Tatlin, however, and followed Tatlin's ideas, which were known as 'Constructivist'. Tatlin also attracted the talented Naum Gabo. At the Moscow exhibition, however, there was a fierce row between Tatlin and Malevich, and from then on there was distrust between the Constructivists and the Suprematists.

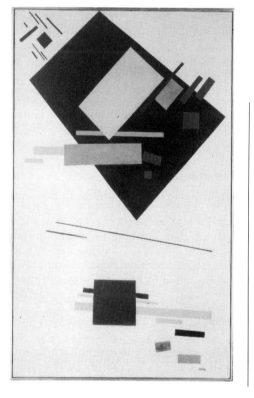

Suprematist Composition *by Kasimir Malevich.*

America marks time

1916 WAS THE LAST YEAR before the US entered the war, though few Americans could imagine this, as President Wilson had just won the Presidential election claiming he had 'kept America out of the war'. For America, High Art was still something which happened mainly in Europe. Both the two finest American poets, Ezra Pound and T.S. Eliot, were in Europe. In popular art, however, America led the world. D.W. Griffith's epic film *Intolerance* was released in September. Charlie Chaplin had another exceptional year, moving companies again. Essanay could not keep the biggest name in movies when Mutual offered Chaplin $670,000 for one year's work. Chaplin (only 26 at the time) accepted and made a stream of fine two-reel tramp films including *Carmen*, *The Floor Walker*, and *The Pawnshop*.

Artists and the war

ARTISTS IN THE MAJOR countries were affected by the war, and only those artists, like Picasso from neutral countries, or those in exile, could avoid it. Reactions differed. The French cubist Fernand Léger, mobilized on 2 August 1914 and in action until gassed and invalided out in September 1916, said later

The war was a major event for me. At the front there was a hyper poetic atmosphere which excited me greatly . . . The war brought me down to earth . . . I left Paris when I was painting almost entirely abstract work . . . suddenly I was at the level of the whole French people.
Quoted in Edward Lucie Smith, *Lives of the Great Twentieth-Century Artists*

Umberto Boccioni, composer of the Futurist manifesto of painting in 1910, had a less romantic view. He had believed in the futurist view that war was 'the only hygiene of the modern world', but found that

War, when one is waiting to fight, consists of just this: insects, boredom, obscure heroism . . . One thinks of life . . . past and of so many things which are now far away.
Lives of the Great Twentieth-Century Artists

Physics takes a leap

THE YEAR SAW ONE of the greatest steps forward in theoretical physics in history. Albert Einstein published his *Foundation of the General Theory of Relativity* in the Swiss journal *Annales der Physik*. Einstein argued that gravity was not a force, as Isaac Newton had said in the seventeenth century, but a curved field in the space-time continuum, created by the presence of mass. He suggested that this controversial notion could be proved or disproved by measuring the deflection of starlight as it travelled close to the sun. This would be difficult as starlight would only be visible in a lunar eclipse of the sun. Einstein predicted that the light would be deflected twice as much as Newton had suggested.

Albert Einstein, whose discoveries in physics revolutionized scientists' views of the universe.

The war in the air

AT THE START OF 1916, the French brought into action the Nieuport II fighter, the first Allied plane to rival the Fokker. It had a machine gun on the top wing, and when in April the British FE 2b became operational the Fokker was fully challenged. From then on no single fighter was supreme. The year also saw the first successful two-seater reconnaissance plane, the Sopwith 1½ Strutter, with a fixed forward firing gun and a moveable rear gun for the observer. Foreshadowing later developments in guided missiles, was the pilotless radio-guided 'Hewitt-Sperry bi-plane', built by Curtiss in America and demonstrated on 12 September 1916. The first European pilotless plane was the Siemens glider bomb which was tested in October. This type of weapon remained relatively undeveloped until the Second World War.

Radio makes waves

THE FIRST RADIO telephone message broadcast from the ground to an airplane occurred when a plane circling near Brooklands in England received the message from a ground station. This same year saw the germ of modern radio planted when David Sarnoff, contracts manager of the American Marconi Company, recommended setting up transmission stations for broadcasting speech, and manufacturing 'radio music boxes'. Although the idea was not taken up, after the war radio broadcasting took off as a new form of entertainment and communication.

A radio music box . . . the device must be arranged to receive on several wavelengths with the throw of a switch or press of a button. The radio music box can be supplied with amplifiers and a loudspeaker telephone, all of which can be neatly mounted in a box.
From David Sarnoff's original proposal

1917

Russian

Crisis

BY THE WINTER OF 1916-17, the people of Russia were close to despair. Despite huge sacrifices, the war was a disaster. A huge number of men had been called into the army, fifteen million men, but their efforts had been in vain against the better-equipped Germans. Five million Russians had been killed or wounded, and weapons were so short that at one point there was one rifle to every ten soldiers. Meanwhile back at home the shortage of men meant that farms could not produce enough food. Prices rose faster than wages, and fuel shortages meant that people in the cities froze as well as going hungry.

The Tsar and his wife were deeply hated. The Tsar had left the capital, Petrograd, to be with the army, leaving his wife in charge. The Tsarina relied on the advice of the notorious 'Holy Man', Gregory Rasputin, who seemed to be able to heal their sick son. Rasputin, dirty, drunken and a womanizer, shocked government ministers and at the end of 1916 he was murdered by a group of noblemen led by Prince Yusopov.

By the end of the winter, food began to run out and prices rose sky high. On 4 March 1917 workers at the Putilov factory went on strike for higher wages. Other factories came out in support, and on 10 March strikers clashed with troops. Sixty were shot dead. Riots spread across the capital and two regiments mutinied, refusing to go into the streets to shoot rioters. The government could not rely on its soldiers in Petrograd and the Tsar decided to return to the capital to take charge. Railway workers blocked the line and the Tsar realized he had lost control. The Romanovs abdicated and on 16 March Russia became a republic.

Bolsheviks and the Imperial Russian Army clash in Moscow during the October Revolution.

The provisional government

THE NEW GOVERNMENT was run by middle-class liberals who wanted to have an election as soon as possible, but in the months that this would take they continued to fight the war. Alexander Kerensky, a socialist whom the troops and workers respected, was made Minister of War. Meanwhile the Communist leader, Vladimir Lenin, was given a safe passage from exile in Switzerland to Russia by the Germans. On 16 April Lenin arrived in Petrograd by train at the Finland station. He was greeted by enthusiastic crowds and called for immediate revolution. Lenin realized that the army was near exhaustion, the people desperate for food, the peasants wanted land – so he announced that his Bolshevik Party would fight for Peace, Bread and Land.

At first, this did not seem to succeed. The army stayed loyal and on 18 June the Russians launched a major attack. It was the last. Within a month the better-equipped Germans had forced the Russians back, and soldiers began deserting in droves. Lenin said the army 'voted with its feet' for peace.

Revolution

The Communist Revolution

THE GENERALS BLAMED KERENSKY for the army's failure, and General Kornilov decided to march troops on Petrograd to form a military government. Striking workers, backed by Communist Red Guards, stopped the troops entering the city. Support for the Communists (known as Bolsheviks) soared, and they won elections to local councils (Soviets) in many big towns. The Bolsheviks used this increased power as a step toward ousting Kerensky and his government so that the Bolsheviks could form their own government. On 23 October the Bolsheviks decided to take over. This was supposed to be on behalf of the All-Russian Congress of Soviets, due to meet on 7 November. However the Bolsheviks feared this might not back them, so staged the insurrection on the night of 6 November. That night the Bolsheviks seized the railway stations in the capital, the banks, power stations, the telephone exchange, the St Peter and Paul fortress, and had the guns of the cruiser *Aurora* trained on the Winter Palace. On 7 November Kerensky left Petrograd. The Bolsheviks captured the Winter Palace and the rest of the city the same day.

It was already dark when we came out on the Liteiny, near the bridge where there had been a skirmish a few hours before between Tsarist and revolutionary troops. To the left the District Court was blazing. Guns had been set up at random near the Sergiyevsky. Ammunition boxes were standing behind them, in what looked to me a disorderly fashion. Something like a barricade could be seen there too. But it was crystal clear to every passer-by that neither guns nor barricades would protect anybody or anything from the slightest onslaught . . .

. . . but it was impossible to forget the other side of the picture; the arms at the disposal of the revolutionary people were, in their hands, certainly no protection against any organized force, but *Tsarism lacked that force.*
Nikolai Himmer, quoted in Anthony Wood, *The Russian Revolution*, Longman, 1986, p.78.

Resolution of the Bolshevik Central Committee 10 October 1917

The Central Committee recognizes that the international position of the Russian Revolution . . . as well as the military situation . . . and, finally, the obvious preparations for a second Kornilov affair . . . all this places the armed uprising on the order of the day.

Considering therefore that an armed rising is inevitable, and that the time for it is fully ripe, the Central Committee instructs all Party organizations to be guided accordingly, and to discuss and decide all practical questions (the Congress of Soviets of the Northern Region, the withdrawal of troops from Petrograd, the action of our people in Moscow and Minsk, etc.) from this point of view.
Quoted in Anthony Wood, *The Russian Revolution*, p. 83.

Lenin addressing a crowd in Moscow.

The Western Front

WHILE THE RUSSIAN ARMY collapsed on the Eastern Front, the French army suffered serious exhaustion in its battles against the Germans. The French again tried to break through by a big spring attack, this time in the Champagne region. Fifty-four divisions had been mobilized, with an astonishing bombardment of 11 million high explosive shells to begin the battle. Still the French failed, and this time French soldiers mutinied.

Camps were placarded with notices declaring the intention of the soldiers to refuse to go back to the trenches. A battalion ordered to the Front dispersed in a wood. Soldiers coming home on leave sang the 'Internationale' and demanded peace. Mutinies occurred in sixteen different army corps. A number of young infantrymen marched through the streets of a French town 'baa-ing' like sheep to indicate they were being driven like lambs to the slaughter'. (Lobban p.85)

Fortunately for the French the Germans did not hear of the mutinies, and the British under Haig kept them busy with a major attack at Ypres – the battle known as Passchendaele. This started in July and was one of the worst battles of the war. The bombardment by the heavy guns destroyed the drains, and when the rains came the ground turned to mud in which men drowned. There was no breakthrough and when the coming of winter forced the battle to stop, 360,000 British had fallen casualty and 245,000 Germans.

However, in the last battle of the year the British did make a breakthrough with a new weapon – the tank. Armour-plated, and with metal tracks instead of wheels, these petrol-driven machines could ignore machine gun bullets, which just bounced off them. At Cambrai in November 324 tanks and five divisions succeeded in punching a hole in the German lines. However, 179 tanks were lost, many breaking down, and the Germans rushed in reinforcements and plugged the gap. Nevertheless, Cambrai showed a way to beat the trenches and barbed wire.

Meanwhile at sea, the Germans switched back to using their U-boats to sink all merchant ships coming to Britain. They knew this would bring the Americans into the war, but calculated that the Americans would take a year to equip and train their army and ship it to Europe. In that time they hoped that Britain would lose so many ships and supplies that the British would be starved into surrender. The policy began on 31 January and America declared war in April. That spring the British did come close to defeat as the U-boats destroyed more and more shipping. At one point Britain had only six weeks supply of wheat left. However, rationing helped eke out the remaining food, while anti-submarine tactics were invented. Ships were told to sail in convoys, with warships protecting them, and the anti-submarine weapon the depth charge was used to blow up U-boats. Though six and a quarter million tons of Allied shipping was sunk in 1917, Britain survived – though only just.

Vessels of every kind, whatever their flag, their character, their cargo, their destination, their errand, have been ruthlessly sent to the bottom without warning and without thought of help or mercy for those on board, the vessels of friendly neutrals along with those of belligerents . . . The world must be made safe for democracy . . .
President Wilson's appeal to the US Congress to declare war, 2 April 1917.

Devastation at the Front: Ypres in October 1917.

U-Boat crisis

LLOYD GEORGE HAD ONLY been Prime Minister for two months when the U-boat campaign started. The navy had no solution to the crisis, Jellicoe saying 'there is absolutely no solution that we can see'. But in April one ship in four leaving Britain was sunk. Either a solution must be found, or Britain would be starved into surrender. On 26 April, Lloyd George persuaded the war cabinet to force the Admiralty to accept convoys – groups of merchant ships guarded by the navy. On 30 April he went to the Admiralty and forced the navy to accept the plan. The first convoy left from Gibraltar on 10 May.

Haig's trick

LLOYD GEORGE COULD DICTATE to the navy but not to the army. Haig wanted to launch a great attack in the summer, but the Prime Minister feared a repeat of the Somme. The politicians suspected the British army might mutiny like the French. To convince them that the men were in good spirits, Haig arranged a trick. He took the politicians to France and had a group of soldiers march past. At a signal, the soldiers cheered. This seemed to show they were in good heart. However, Haig had chosen men who were about to go home on leave – so they had every reason to cheer. Haig's trick worked and the politicians allowed him to launch the attack on 31 July. He had been warned that bombardment would destroy the drains and rains would turn the battlefield to mud. He ignored his experts and when the battle of Passchendaele proved a disaster the politicians came to distrust him even more.

Food shortages

MEANWHILE DISCONTENT WITH LIFE at home grew in 1917. Food and fuel ran short. Wages lagged behind rising prices until the government increased them to head off strike action. The government brought in National Savings to help pay for the war, and the British were urged to save spare money with the government to help pay for the war.

Labour supports peace proposals

PERHAPS THE MOST IMPORTANT development in British life in 1917 was the change in the Labour Party. After the Tsar was overthrown in March, the British Labour Party welcomed the provisional government at a convention in Leeds in June. The Convention endorsed the Russian peace proposals, and planned to send delegates to a peace conference in Stockholm to discuss a negotiated end to the war. The Government refused to take part in the negotiations and the chance to seek a peace without a fight to the finish was lost.

Sport and the Arts

Art and the Revolution

IN 1917, THE POLITICAL ferment in Russia spilled over into the lives of the experimental artists. While the Provisional government ruled the country, painters formed a trade union in Moscow and Petrograd. Rodchenko joined the most radical section, the Left Federation, which drew support mainly from the Futurists. He became secretary of the Moscow branch and after the Bolshevik revolution joined the Bolshevik Party. Marc Chagall and Vladimir Tatlin also sided with the Bolsheviks. Artists returning to Russia from abroad, like Naum Gabo and his brother Antoine, found themselves in the middle of artistic and political turmoil.

Artists in wartime

THE BEST-KNOWN GROUP of Russian artists in Europe, Diaghilev's Ballets Russes, stayed outside Russia, however, moving to Rome. Pablo Picasso joined them there, after the French artist Jean Cocteau had suggested Diaghilev invite the Spaniard. In Rome, Picasso worked on stage designs for the ballet *Parade*. Another major artist who left Paris in 1917 was Dutchman Piet Mondrian, who returned home and exhibited his pure abstract paintings in Holland. There he became involved in the De Stijl movement, publishing essays on abstract art in its magazine in October, and signing its manifesto in November. Despite the war, artistic experiment was continuing.

Wilfred Owen, who gave expression to the horror and futility of trench warfare.

War poets

SOME OF BRITAIN'S finest poets, Siegfried Sassoon, Robert Graves and above all Wilfred Owen were beginning to express their revulsion at the war. Sassoon, son of a banker, had known Rupert Brooke and like Brooke had joined up, considering it a patriotic duty, in 1914. Fighting with great courage, he had won the Military Cross at the Somme but had been sent home with a bullet wound in April 1917. As an invalid he came to believe the politicians were deliberately failing to end the war. He protested, throwing his medal in the Mersey. The military authorities, helped by Sassoon's friend Robert Graves, decided that Sassoon suffered from shell shock, and he was sent to a mental hospital. There he met another poet soldier, Wilfred Owen. Sassoon encouraged Owen's poetry, and under his influence Owen wrote the finest anti-war poetry of the Great War, including *Anthem for Dead Youth:*

What passing bells for these who die as
   cattle?
Only the monstrous anger of the guns.
Only the stuttering rifles' rapid rattle,
Can patter out their hasty orisons.
No mockeries now for them; no prayers nor
   bells,
Nor any voice of mourning save the choirs –
The shrill demented choirs of wailing shells;
And bugles calling for them from sad shires.

What candles may be held to speed them all?
Not in the hands of boys, but in their eyes
Shall shine the holy glimmers of good-byes,
The pallor of girls' brows shall be their pall;
Their flowers the tenderness of patient
   minds,
And each slow dusk a drawing down of
   blinds.

Enter the bomber

AEROPLANES DEVELOPED PIECEMEAL in the First World War, and military experts had spent little time thinking about their use. Most saw them as part of the established war machines, the armies and navies. Aircraft were supposed to act as observers, tackle enemy fighters, and drop bombs by hand to upset the enemy. In 1917 British experts came up with a more sinister view, which was put to the war cabinet by Jan Smuts in a report completed in October. The plan suggested that aircraft could win a war without the need for an army at all by using heavy bombing. Lloyd George was impressed. An independent air ministry was set up and Trenchard, head of the Royal Flying Corps, was made head of a new body, the Royal Air Force. Trenchard wanted 100 squadrons of heavy bombers, but got only nine. He claimed this was why he could not bomb Germany into defeat, and the theory that the bomber could win wars took on a life of its own.

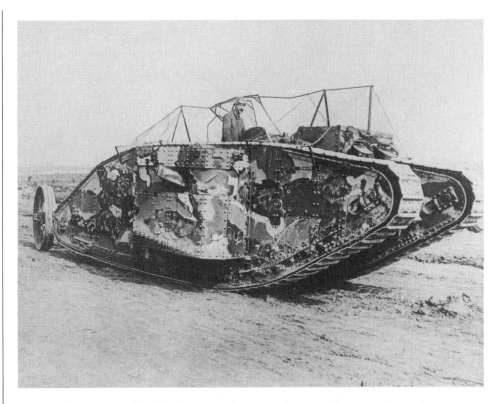

Machine-gun proof. Tanks became an important factor on the Western Front in 1917.

. . . and the tank

THE NAVY PROVED conservative in the face of the U-boat – but the army was little more intelligent tackling barbed wire and machine guns. The generals believed they could break through using gun bombardments, and then use the cavalry in open country. They kept hundreds of thousands of horses in France waiting for the breakthrough. It never came.

Meanwhile Churchill and his naval advisors had seen that an armoured vehicle might do the trick. In 1915 they tried putting an armoured car body on a tractor. When it worked, Churchill formed the Admiralty Landships Committee and its experiments were so successful that in February 1916 the British army ordered 100. The British lost the advantage of surprise by using them in small numbers on 15 September 1916 – only 49 were used – but they were so unsuccessful that the Germans thought them useless. The Germans changed their minds in November 1917, when the tank came of age at the Battle of Cambrai. An advance of six miles was achieved in twelve hours – previously without tanks it took months to advance so quickly.

Radio intelligence

RADIO ALSO CAME OF AGE as a weapon in 1917. British intelligence, intercepting U-boat signals, was able to radio information on U-boat locations. This was invaluable for convoys, which could avoid the danger. Unfortunately there were hundreds of ships which did not have radio, and though Allied shipping losses fell from 520,000 tons per month in 1917 to 281,000 in the first nine months of 1918, this still meant that two and a half million tons of shipping was sunk in 1918.

1918 All Quiet on the

Ludendorff's last gamble

THERE WERE FEW CELEBRATIONS at the start of the New Year. The leaders of the nations looked back on three and a half years of futile slaughter and could see no end in sight. Yet the more intelligent observers could see that 1918 might be the final year of the war. The Revolution had taken the Russians out of the war, and in March the Communists signed a peace treaty with the Germans at Brest Litovsk. Even before then, however, the Germans had begun shifting their troops from the Eastern Front to France. For the first time since August 1914, they could put their whole army on the Western Front. The German commander, Ludendorff, hoped that with these extra troops he could at long last beat the British and French.

US troops start to arrive

LUDENDORFF KNEW, however, that time was not on his side. The U-boats had failed to starve the British into surrender, and had forced the USA to declare war on Germany. Though the US army was slow to mobilize and get to France, as 1918 started a trickle of US troops were arriving. Ludendorff knew that this trickle would soon become a flood. He had only months to defeat the Western Allies before the new American troops tipped the balance and Germany was defeated.

Field Marshal Sir Douglas Haig

Council of war

ON 11 NOVEMBER 1917 Ludendorff had held a war council at Mons to draw up the battle plan for the coming spring. He decided to attack the British 5th and 3rd Armies on the front from Arras south to La Frère, where the troops were spread very thinly. The Germans decided not to have a long gunnery barrage but to rely on a short bombardment followed by waves of specially trained infantry – storm troopers – ordered to move quickly and avoid the machine guns.

The gamble fails

ON 21 MARCH 1918, 6000 German guns bombarded the British trenches for four and a half hours, then the storm troopers were sent in. Luck favoured the Germans, for heavy fog meant that the British could not see the Germans until it was too late. For two days the British fought, then began to retreat. It seemed that Ludendorff's gamble had succeeded. But the crisis led to the British, Americans and French agreeing at last on one supreme commander – General Foch, the Frenchman – and the Allies prepared to resist. As the British were forced steadily back, their commander, Haig, issued his famous 'backs to the wall' order on 11 April. His order to hold every position to the last man would have been little use, however, without the knowledge at the back of every Allied soldier's mind – 'the Yanks are coming'.

German army disintegrates

THE GERMANS HAD NO SUCH COMFORT. As they advanced, they discovered luxury in French towns they had not known for years – and their discipline broke down.

As the German army fell apart, the Allies retreated and waited. On 18 July Foch decided the time was ripe to counter-attack. Backed by 346 tanks, the French made the first breakthrough. It was only the start, and on 8 August British, Canadian and Australian troops broke through as six German divisions surrendered. The German army knew it was losing the war, and though it continued to fight as it retreated, its allies were surrendering. Bulgaria gave in on 30 September, Turkey a month later, Austria on 3 November, and Germany itself on 11 November. Exactly a year after the Mons conference, the Germans signed an armistice, and the guns fell silent on the Western Front.

8 August was the blackest day of the German army in the history of the war. This was the worst experience I had to go through. Our losses reached such proportions that the Supreme Command was faced with the necessity of having to disband a series of

Western Front

divisions
Ludendorff, second in command of the German army, Chief German war planner.

The surprise of the 8th was complete. The Germans had no idea that the Canadians were on my front, and believed them to be at Kemmel. The tanks were all up to time, and did splendidly, and some of our armoured cars got right through the German lines and surprised the headquarters of a German corps at breakfast. We have practically eaten up seven Prussian divisions. While everyone did splendidly, I think the spirit of the colonial infantry was probably the decisive factor. I am very proud to have

Crowds in London celebrate Armistice Day, 11 November.

commanded so magnificent an army in this historic battle.
General Rawlinson, commander of the British Fourth Army.

Wilson's Peace Plan

BY THE END OF 1917 President Wilson of the USA was under great pressure to spell out America's war aims – what the USA was fighting for. The Allies had been deeply embarrassed when the Communist government in Russia had published the secret treaties of Russia and her allies, which showed that the Allies' secret plans for the war were different, and much less honest, than those they had stated in public. The secret treaties suggested that the Allies were fighting to gain land at Germany's expense. British Prime Minister Lloyd George was forced to deny this on 5 January 1918, claiming that Britain was fighting to defend the rights of small nations, like Belgium. His statement was overshadowed when President Wilson spoke out.

On 8 January 1918 President Wilson set out his War Aims before a joint meeting of the US Congress. These were his famous Fourteen Points, which set out the terms for a peace settlement when the fighting was over. The first five points dealt with general principles for organizing international affairs. Points 6 and 7 – calling for the evacuation of Russian territory occupied by the Germans and the evacuation and neutrality of Belgium – were meant to prevent Germany gaining land from the war. Points 8 to 13 gave out ideas for redrawing the map of Europe after the war on a fairer basis to give small nations freedom and prevent another Bosnian crisis. The 14th point was for a League of Nations to avoid future conflicts. The Fourteen Points were greatly popular in the USA and among her allies.

Woodrow Wilson, the man who took the United States into the War.

Fourteen Points rejected

NEVERTHELESS, IF WILSON hoped they would lead to a negotiated peace, he was wrong. On 3 March the Communist government in Russia signed a separate peace with Germany, confirming what Ludendorff already knew, that the Germans could bring the whole of their army onto the Western Front and make a real bid for victory. The Germans accordingly rejected the Fourteen Points and only late in the year, when they were clearly losing the war, did they take an interest in them. By then it was too late. As Germany's allies collapsed, so did their governments. At the very end the Kings themselves lost their thrones. On 9 November the Kaiser abdicated and left Germany for neutral Holland. Two days later the last Hapsburg Emperor of Austria-Hungary, Charles, wrote his abdication on a piece of paper but was ignored. Austria-Hungary as a country had collapsed. That afternoon Lloyd George read the Armistice terms to Parliament with the fateful words, 'I hope we may say that thus, this fateful morning, came to an end all wars'.

It was a few minutes before the eleventh hour of the eleventh day of the eleventh month. I stood at the window of my room looking up Northumberland Avenue towards Trafalgar Square, waiting for Big Ben to tell that the war was over . . . suddenly the first stroke of the chime. I looked again at the broad street beneath me. It was deserted. From the portals of one of the large hotels . . . darted the slight figure of a girl clerk . . . Then from all sides men and women came scurrying into the street. Streams of people poured out of all the buildings. The bells of London began to clash. Northumberland Avenue was now crowded with people in hundreds, nay thousands, rushing hither and thither in a frantic manner, shouting and screaming with joy . . . Almost before the last stroke of the clock had died away, the strict, war straightened, regulated streets of London had become a triumphant pandemonium.
Winston Churchill, quoted Gibbons and Morican, *World War One*, Longman, 1979 p.p. 127-128.

Votes for women – at last

THE ISSUE OF VOTES FOR WOMEN was finally decided in 1918. The suffragettes had called off their militant campaign on the outbreak of the war, and had supported the war effort. Women had been drafted into the factories and other jobs normally done by men as the men had gone off to fight, and had proved they could do the jobs as well as the men could. There could be no doubt that women were equal to men, and a government committee had recommended they be allowed to vote. The Commons agreed and backed a bill giving the vote to all men over 21 and women over 28. Despite arguments in the Lords, the bill became law in June 1918.

Conscription extended to Ireland

IRELAND PROVED A DIFFERENT MATTER. Conscription had never been extended to Ireland, for the Easter Rising proved that so many Irishmen hated the British that forcing them into the British Army would only cause rebellion. Yet with the Ludendorff offensive in full swing, pressure mounted to force Irishmen to join the army. Lloyd George gave in, and extended conscription to Ireland. It was a disastrous mistake. The Irish Nationalist MPs walked out 'of the House of Commons, never to return, and joined Sinn Fein. The survivor of the Easter Rising, Eamon de Valera, became leader of the Irish Catholics. The Catholic Church in Ireland denounced the law, on 23 April there was a General Strike in Catholic Ireland, and the Sinn Fein leaders were arrested. Plans to conscript the Catholic Irish were hastily dropped, but it was too late. Ireland had served notice to quit on the English.

The Liberals split

THIS WAS NOT OBVIOUS TILL LATER, and meanwhile Lloyd George ruled supreme. In May he secured a personal triumph after a leading General, Sir Frederick Maurice, accused Lloyd George of lying about the number of troops in France. The Generals knew that Lloyd George hated the slaughter in France and kept reserves in England, away from Haig and his commanders. Nevertheless when Lloyd George had claimed there were more soldiers in France than in 1917, he was telling the truth. The Liberals under Asquith demanded a vote of no confidence, which took place on 9 May. The Tories and Lloyd George Liberals voted in favour of Lloyd George, and only 98 Liberals supported Asquith. Lloyd George won easily, and the Liberal Party was finally split completely in two.

Eamon de Valera.

The man who won the war

LLOYD GEORGE RODE ON THE CREST of a wave for the rest of the year. As the war turned against the Germans, his prestige rose and by the end of the year he was seen as 'the man who won the war'. He decided to use his popularity, and called a General Election for December 1918. It was an enormous triumph for Lloyd George. His supporters swept a great majority in seats – the Tories took 339 seats, Lloyd George Liberals 134 – against 26 Asquith Liberals and 59 Labour. Sinn Feiners captured all Irish seats outside Ulster save three, and refused to take part in the British parliament. Lloyd George had, however, made promises to 'make Germany pay' during the election campaign, to satisfy voters who wanted revenge for the war. He knew this was bound to cause trouble later, but his first priority was to win the election.

Revolutionary art

THE LEADING AVANT-GARDE painters in Russia became part of the artistic arrangements set up by the Bolsheviks after the revolution. Marc Chagall, who knew Anatoly Lunarchasky, the Minister for Culture, was appointed Commissar for Arts in September 1918. Vladimir Tatlin was appointed head of the Moscow section of Izo-Narkompos, the Department of Fine Arts at the commissariat for the People's Education. Rodchenko became first director of the Museum of Artistic Culture. In the ferment and excitement which followed the Bolshevik revolution, these artists were en-couraged to produce experimental art which could genuinely be regarded as revolutionary.

Surrealism

IN WESTERN EUROPE, artists also reacted to the earthquakes which were shaking Europe as the war reached its climax, but did so by evolving new ideas which rejected rational European aims and values. The experimental movements of the earlier years of the decade evolved into two new movements called Surrealism and Dada. Surrealism was the brainchild of Apollinaire, the French writer and poet. By 1917 Apollinaire and his friends had rejected the logical ideas of the Western World, arguing that if the brilliant results of the logical world of science was war and destruction, there was something badly wrong. They felt artists should abandon rational thought and try to get the unconscious to produce the art. In March 1917 Apollinaire had christened this idea 'Surrealism' in a letter to Paul Dermee. *Parade*, Diaghilev's ballet using Picasso, writer Jean Cocteau, and musician Eric Satie, was part of this movement, as was Apollinaire's play *Les Mamelles de Tiresias* in June 1917.

A ghost story

WILFRED OWEN WAS DISCHARGED from hospital and returned to the Western Front. As the war drew to a close, his unit was ordered to cross the Sambre canal. On the morning of 4 November, Owen led his platoon into battle. As he helped troops lay duckboards by the side of the water, he was hit by a German bullet and killed.

Seven days later, Wilfred's brother Harold was sailing on the cruiser *Astrea* off Africa. He had not heard of his brother's death, and when he returned to his cabin was amazed to see Wilfred sitting in his chair. The blood drained from his face, but he asked calmly, 'Wilfred, how did you get here?' There was no reply, but Wilfred's eyes did not leave his face. Harold did not feel fear – only great pleasure at seeing his brother. He spoke again: 'Wilfred dear, how can you be here, it's just not possible . . .', but Wilfred only smiled gently.

Then Harold turned his eyes away for a moment, and when he turned back his chair was empty. Suddenly he felt terribly tired and going to his bunk he lay down and fell into a deep dreamless sleep. When he woke up he knew with absolute certainty that Wilfred was dead.

Destructive Dada

DADA WAS A MORE DESTRUCTIVE movement, arguing that the existing social world had to be destroyed before a

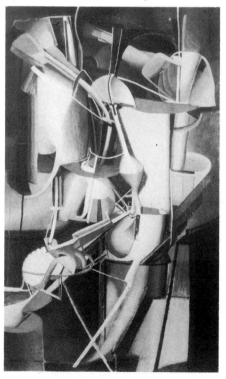

Louise and the Water *by Marcel Duchamp*.

new, healthier world could emerge. The Dada movement was formed in Zurich in 1917 and lead by Picabia, Marcel Duchamp and poet Tristan Tzara. In 1918 Tzara published a Dada manifesto, saying, 'Let every man cry out. A great destructive negative work needs to be accomplished. To sweep, to clean up'. This call to violence could have tragic results. One of the most influential figures in Dada, Jacques Vache, killed himself at the end of 1918 by taking an overdose of opium. Worse, he killed a friend at the same time by giving the same lethal dose of the drug to a friend who had asked to try some. Vache became a martyr to the followers of Dada.

Marcel Duchamp's Dadaism was not destructive. In 1913 he had produced the first of his 'ready-mades' – an everyday object displayed as art – in this case a bicycle wheel. In the same year he began work on a large abstract piece of work, *The Large Glass*, or *The Bride Stripped Bare by Her Bachelors, Even*. This work – neither sculpture nor painting – became a key step in modern art. Duchamp sold it to his patron, the American Walter Arensberg, in 1918.

An expanding industry

FEW AREAS OF SCIENCE and technology made as big steps forward during the war as aircraft. The tiny handful of planes on the Western Front in 1914 swelled to 3000 by the end of 1918. Altogether 55,000 aircraft were manufactured during the war years. The few hundreds employed by the industry in 1914 had swelled to 350,000 by 1918. The performance of the plane had improved out of all recognition. A typical two-seater fighter-reconnaissance plane in 1914 could fly at a maximum speed of 75 mph and could climb to 10,000 feet in 45 minutes. By the end of the war the best fighters on either side had a ceiling of 25,000 feet, a top speed, when flying low, of 155 mph and a speed of 140 mph at 10,000 feet. They could climb to this last height in about ten minutes.

Development of the bomber

THE FIGHTER PLANE had to be speedy and climb high and fast. Perhaps more important in the long run was the development of the bomber. This had to carry heavy loads of bombs over long distances, so flew slowly but steadily. It could cover great distances. In 1917 the British had introduced the twin-engined Handley Page 0/400 which could fly at 60-80 mph for eight hours with a bomb load of 1800 lbs, and the Germans had produced the Gotha which had a similar performance. Both sides produced even bigger machines. The Germans produced the five-engined Staaken R VI, and the British the Handley Page four-engine C/1500 bomber. This had a speed of 70-90 mph, a radius of action of 1300 miles, and a bomb load of 7500 lbs. Only the Armistice prevented this plane bombing Berlin.

The war had led to rapid development in aircraft technology. This is Baron von Richthofen's 'Flying Circus' squadron lined up in 1918.

Flu epidemic kills thousands

IF AIRCRAFT SHOWED that the human mind could work wonders, events during 1918 on the medical front showed that the limits of human ingenuity were still severe in the face of natural disasters. In 1918 there was an influenza outbreak so severe that by the time it had run its course in mid-1919 it had killed more people than died in the fighting of World War One. It may have started on 11 March in Kansas, USA, where an outbreak of flu spread among the 26,000 soldiers headed for France. The flu spread across the USA and Europe and into Africa and Asia. Some 27,000,000 died and an unknown number of people suffered from the illness – an estimated 20,000,000 in the USA alone. Doctors and scientists from Shanghai to California were at a loss to find a cure and councils issued almost desperate advice to people to stop borrowing books, stop shaving, or stop shaking hands. The disease reached a peak in November 1918, died down, then flared up again in the early months of 1919. Fortunately it died down permanently after that, for it took another 15 years before the National Institute for Medical Research in London identified the virus and enabled doctors to look for a cure. For the sufferers of 1918 and 1919, the breakthrough came too late.

Making the

Paris peace conference

THE ARMISTICE OF NOVEMBER 1918 had brought an end to the fighting – but the arrangements for Europe after the war still had to be made. To make these arrangements, delegates from the different countries came to Paris at the start of 1919 for a peace conference.

The Big Three dominate

NOT ALL COUNTRIES were invited to take part. Russia was excluded because its government was Communist and pledged to overthrow the capitalist countries of the West. Germany was excluded because it had lost the war and so was not allowed to negotiate. The defeated powers or their successors were in fact barred from the conference and simply forced to sign dictated treaties about which they had no say.

Even among the victorious Allies, most of the countries concerned played little part in the talks. Most of the key decisions were made by the three strongest countries – Britain, France and the USA – ignoring important countries such as Japan and Italy. This had serious effects later on, for these two countries came to feel they had been treated as badly as Germany, and lined up with their former foe in the run-up to the Second World War.

Clemenceau, Wilson and Lloyd George arrive in Versailles to negotiate the peace settlement.

Disagreement

THIS COULD HARDLY have been foreseen in 1919, but all politicians could see that the key issue at the Paris peace talks would be Germany. Germany remained the strongest power in Europe. Everyone knew how close she had come to winning the war – so how could Germany be stopped from making war again? On this vital question, the Big Three differed.

US President

WOODROW WILSON wanted a fair peace which would leave no country with a grievance that might lead to war. He believed that the cause of the war had been the way national groups, particularly in the Balkans, had been denied the right to form their own governments, and he was determined that all nations should govern themselves. Thus he was opposed to any attempt to break up Germany, the biggest national group outside Russia.

France calls for severe measures

FRANCE ACCEPTED THAT GERMANY could not be broken up, but wanted severe punishment for the Germans so that they would not want to go to war again, and indeed would be too weak to do so. Their leader, Clemenceau, regarded Wilson as weak and foolish. The leading British politicians, notably Lloyd George, thought the French desire to punish Germany dangerous. Germany would remain the strongest nation in Europe, so it was foolish to leave her resentful. Alas, in order to win the 1918 election, Lloyd George had given way to the British desire for revenge and had promised that 'the Germans must pay to the uttermost farthing, and we shall search their pockets for it'. Privately he knew that squeezing Germany was foolish but publicly he appeared to seek vengeance. The French thought he was on their side.

Peace

Lloyd George forced to compromise

WHEN LLOYD GEORGE went to Paris, then, he was handicapped in seeking a fair peace. In the opening talks he began to look for a way to seek compensation on the basis of what Germany could pay rather than taking every penny from her, and this annoyed the Tories: 370 Tory MPs sent him a telegram reminding him of his election promises, and Lloyd George had to return home to tell the House of Commons 'We want a stern peace, because the occasion demands it. But its severity must be designed, not to gratify vengeance, but to vindicate justice'.

This went some way to satisfying the British, but it cut no ice with the French, who accused Lloyd George of being soft on the Germans. Clemenceau wrote to Lloyd George arguing 'if the British are so anxious to appease Germany they should look . . . overseas . . . and make colonial, naval or commercial concessions'. Lloyd George was trapped. He knew his people would not accept him making any concessions to Germany, and he had to go along with some of the French demands to weaken Germany. In particular, both he and Wilson had to accept the transfer of Germans to the countries on the German border, though he knew this would cause trouble. He wrote:

I cannot conceive any greater cause of future war than that the German people . . . should be surrounded by a number of small states, many of them consisting of people who have never previously set up a stable government

Lloyd George takes his turn to sign the treaty, while the other leaders look on.

for themselves, but each of them containing large masses of Germans clamouring for reunion with their native land . . . [these proposals] must, in my judgement, lead sooner or later to a new war in Eastern Europe.

History was to show that Lloyd George was right, but in 1919 he could not stop the developments which he forecast would eventually lead to war.

Scene; the Hall of Mirrors, Palace of Versailles, 28 June 1919

The delegates arrive in little bunches and push up the central aisle slowly. Wilson and Lloyd George are among the last. They take their seats at the central table. Clemenceau glances right and left . . . 'Bring in the Germans' says Clemenceau . . . Through the doors at the end . . . come four officers of France, Great Britain, America and Italy. And then, isolated and pitiable, come the two German delegates, Dr Muller, Dr Bell. The silence is terrifying. Their feet upon a strip of parquet . . . echo hollow and duplicate . . . They are deathly pale. They do not appear as representative of brutal militarism. The one is pale and pink eye lidded; the second fiddle in a Brunswick orchestra. The other is moon faced and suffering; an ordinary private. It is almost painful . . .

There is general tension. They sign. There is general relaxation. Conversation hums again in an undertone . . .
Quoted in Gibbons and Morican, *World War One*, p. 133.

The peace treaties

AT THE PARIS PEACE CONFERENCE, treaties were signed between the victorious allies and the defeated powers – Germany, Austria and Hungary (the remaining parts of the Austro-Hungarian Empire), Bulgaria and Turkey. Officially 32 countries had allied together to defeat the Central Powers, but in practice only three mattered. Their leaders took the main decisions.

The Treaty of Versailles

THE MOST IMPORTANT Treaty signed after the First World War was that with Germany. It was signed in the Great Hall of the Palace of Versailles, and was called after the Palace. The Germans were not allowed to negotiate about the Treaty, which was dictated to them, and they never agreed with the Treaty, which they called the 'Diktat'.

Nevertheless, however unfair the Germans regarded the Treaty, they had lost the war and had no choice but to sign it, which their government did on 28 June 1919. By the Treaty, they lost land on their borders. Alsace-Lorraine, which Germany had taken after defeating the French in 1871, went back to France. Eupen and Malmedy went to Belgium, Schleswig to Denmark, Memel went to Lithuania, and most controversially of all, the provinces of Posen and West Prussia were given to Poland. Lloyd George was right to argue that the Germans would not accept permanently the loss of these provinces. Germany also lost all her colonies and was banned from uniting with German-speaking Austria.

Demobilized. Austrian troops returning home after the war.

Germany to pay compensation

THE FEARSOME MILITARY FORCES Germany once had were also banned. The army was to be reduced to 100,000 men. It was to have no tanks, heavy guns or aircraft. The navy was to have no U-boats, and it could have only six battleships of no more than 10,000 tons. The Rhineland was to be occupied for 15 years and both sides permanently demilitarized. But worst of all for the Germans, they were blamed for starting the war by Clause 231, and on this basis were forced to pay compensation. The compensation could not be worked out in 1919 and a special commission was set up to decide how much Germany had to pay out. The arguments about these payments went on for years, and Hitler exploited them to help the Nazis come to power in the 1930s. Repeal of the Treaty of Versailles was one of the most potent calls that the Nazis made. The Germans resented the whole of the Treaty and the way it was 'dictated' to them – they believed they should have been able to negotiate on the basis of Wilson's 14 points. Article 231 was the most bitterly resented, for the Germans pointed out that they did not start the war – the Austrians did by invading Serbia – so why should they have to pay the majority of the reparations?

A land fit for heroes

IN 1919, LLOYD GEORGE'S promise that the government would build 'a land fit for heroes to live in' looked as though it would be fulfilled. The troops were brought home and demobilized with surprising ease. The Ministry of Labour had at first tried releasing the key men most required for industry. These were usually the men who had been called up last, and the idea caused riots. Churchill scrapped the scheme and brought in a 'first in, first out' principle, and the trouble died away. By the summer, four out of five soldiers were discharged, and most found jobs quickly as the economy went through a post-war boom. Most people felt confident that pre-war living had come back, and the government told the army they need not expect another major war for at least ten years.

Housing shortage

THE MOST PRESSING PROBLEM facing the government was housing. The building of private houses had stopped before the end of 1914, and by 1919 610,000 new houses were needed. 'Homes for heroes' had been a popular cry in the election of 1918, and Lloyd George tried to fulfil the hopes raised. He had passed a Housing Act, which for the first time gave subsidies from the government to local councils for building houses. He also made Christopher Addison Minister of Health with instructions to increase building houses. Addison had worked with Lloyd George on munitions production in the war, and the Prime Minister hoped he would be equally successful in having council houses built.

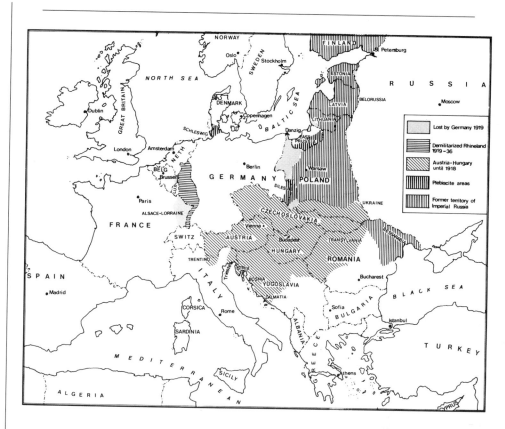

The shape of the treaty: Europe after Versailles.

The unions

MEANWHILE THERE WAS TROUBLE in the mines. In February the miners, transport workers and railwaymen revived their 'Triple Alliance' of the strongest unions. The miners suspended their planned strike waiting for the results of a government commission under a High Court Judge, Sankey. Sankey recommended nationalization, which Lloyd George refused in August, but the men were given a seven hour day by law. The railwaymen, meanwhile, went on strike in September over a plan to reduce their wages. Lloyd George stepped in to settle the strike on the railwaymen's terms. At this point, the unions were doing well.

Massacre at Amritsar

ABROAD ALL WAS NOT WELL with the British Empire. In 1917, when Indian troops were fighting for the British, India had been promised 'responsible government . . . as an integral part of the British Empire'. Yet after the war the British clung to control of the Indian Government. The Indian National Congress Party were now calling for Independence, under their leader, Mahatma Gandhi. Widespread discontent lead to disturbances. In April, at Amritsar, General Dyer ordered troops to open fire on an unarmed crowd. 379 Indians were killed. The Amritsar massacre completed the disillusion of the Indians with British rule of their country.

Sport and the Arts

Poetry

IN ANOTHER IMPORTANT year for poetry, T.S. Eliot and Ezra Pound were at the front of the avant-garde, while the Irish poet William Butler Yeats in middle age was enjoying second wind as a poet. Eliot this year was writing the poems which came out the following year in the collection named after the finest poem, *Gerontion*. Pound, who had followed his interest in Imagism with an interest in Chinese poetry, had now turned to classical Latin poetry. In 1919 Pound published *Homage to Sextus Propertius*, which uses the decay of the Roman Empire as a mirror for the collapse of the old Europe in World War One. Pound's borrowings from Latin were so obscure that Eliot later praised it but omitted it when editing Pound's *Selected Poems*. The more conventional, older Irish poet Yeats produced in 1919 a volume of poetry named after one of the poems, *The Wild Swans at Coole*. The poems dealt with the poet's growing into middle age, and the death of friends, some in the First World War. It included the poignant poem *A Song*:

I thought no more was needed
Youth to prolong,
Than dumb bell and foil
To keep the body young.
O who could have foretold
That the heart grows old?

The Bauhaus opens

A MAJOR EVENT IN THE VISUAL ARTS and architecture took place in April when Walter Gropius became director of a new art school in Weimar, the capital of the German province of Saxony. Called the Staatliches Bauhaus Weimar (Bauhaus for short), the school pioneered the style of architecture now known as the International Style because it has been adopted all over the world. Based on new building methods, notably the use of reinforced concrete and steel, the style allowed skyscrapers to be built and airy buildings with big windows. Curiously, there was no formal study of architecture or design at the Bauhaus. Gropius required his architecture and design students to undergo a practical training in materials and processes, based on handicrafts such as ceramics, weaving and stained glass design. The famous beginners' course produced by the Swiss painter and sculptor Johannes Itten made students explore design through simple materials such as wire, wood and paper. The students also benefited from having as teachers famous artists such as Paul Klee and Wassily Kandinsky, and later Laszlo Moholy-Nagy and Josef Albers. The Bauhaus became the most famous art and design school of the twentieth century.

Tragedy brought to the silver screen

FOR CINEMAGOERS, a major event of the year was the D.W. Griffith film *Broken Blossoms*. Griffith had made his name, with the two epics *Birth of a Nation* and *Intolerance*, dealing with epic stories and casts of thousands. In *Broken Blossoms* he turned to an intimate story with only three main characters – a brutal father, his daughter, and the Chinaman who loves her. A film version of a story set in London's poverty-stricken Limehouse area by Thomas Burke, it was a melodramatic but moving story which gave a powerful role to Griffith's favourite female star, Lillian Gish. The exquisite acting of Gish, the use of cross-cutting in the action sequences, the imaginative use of camera angles, notably the overhead shot of Gish trapped in a cupboard, made the film a milestone. While the story was not itself particularly memorable – the Chinaman loves the daughter, the daughter is killed by the brutal father, the Chinaman kills the father – the film marked an important step in the cinema's handling of emotional themes. The year also saw Griffith, with Charlie Chaplin and leading female actor Mary Pickford ('the Nation's Sweetheart') set up their own studio, United Artists. 'The Lunatics', said a cynic, 'have taken over the asylum'.

Broken Blossoms

This is a Limehouse which neither Mr Burke nor anybody else who knows his East End of London will be able to recognize . . . But *Broken Blossoms* is a genuine attempt to bring real tragedy onto the screen as opposed to machine-made drama, and Mr Griffith deserves the thanks of all who are convinced of the potentialities of the film.
Review in The *Times*

Across the Atlantic – by air!

FLYING EMERGED from the Great War into an era of spectacular feats which dramatized for all to see the great progress made in aviation. A note of high adventure was sounded by some of the exploits of the aviators, of which the most important was the attempt to fly the Atlantic. Given that the English Channel had only been flown in 1910, this seemed an impossible dream – but 1919 saw it accomplished.

In May, Harry Hawker and Mackenzie-Grieve had attempted a direct crossing in a single-engine Sopwith bi-plane, but they had to crash land and were picked up by a Danish steamer. The first completed crossing was made in stages between 16 and 27 May by the US Lieutenant-Commander A.C. Read and his crew in the Curtiss NC-4 Flying boat; it flew from Newfoundland to Lisbon with two landings in the Azores. The first non-stop crossing of the Atlantic was by the British flyers Alcock and Brown in a twin-engine Vickers Vimy bomber. They left St John's, Newfoundland, on 14 June, and crash-landed in a Galway bog the next day, after flying the 1890 miles in 15 hours and 57 minutes.

Alcock and Brown pictured after their non-stop Atlantic crossing.

The first scheduled air service

REGULAR AIR TRANSPORT spread slowly and erratically. The first civil airline for passengers started on 5 February 1919 when the German Deutsche Luftreederei opened a service between Berlin, Leipzig and Weimar. On 8 February, the French Farman Company opened a tentative Paris to London service with converted Goliath bombers. The world's first daily commercial scheduled service opened on 25 August with a flight from London (Hounslow) to Paris (Le Bourget).

The birth of space technology

A VERY DIFFERENT KIND of air transport took its first tentative steps in 1919 when, almost unnoticed, an American scientist, Dr R.H. Goddard, published a book called *A Method of Reaching Extreme Heights*. This book marked the birth of modern rocketry, as it dealt with the liquid fuel rocket, which after the Second World War was to put man into space.

Proof of relativity

BY FAR THE MOST IMPORTANT event in pure science, however, was the discovery that Einstein's Theory of Relativity had experimental proof. In 1916 Einstein had suggested his theory could be proved or disproved by measuring the deflection of rays of starlight as they passed the sun during a solar eclipse. In November 1919 the Royal Society of London announced that its scientific expedition to Principe Island in the Gulf of Guinea had photographed the solar eclipse of 29 May. After months of calculations, it had worked out that the observations verified the predictions made in Einstein's theory. The scientific world applauded Einstein's achievement.

Time Chart

World News	Sport and the Arts	Science and Technology
1910		
(January) British Genmeral Election, Liberals 275 MPs, Tories 273, Irish 83, Labour 40. Liberals form government with minority party support. (May) British King Edward VII dies. Kaiser attends the funeral. (December) Second British General Election. Liberals 272 MPs, Tories 272, Irish 84, Labour 42, Liberals continue in government with minority support.	Scots, Welsh and Irish Football Associations join FIFA. First British Rugby tour of South Africa since 1891. Jack Johnson beats Jim Jeffries to retain World Heavyweight boxing title. Debussy produces first two books of *Preludes*, Stravinsky publishes the *Firebird Suite*, and Elgar his *Violin Concerto*. E.M. Forster publishes his novel *Howard's End*.	(March 28) Claude Graham-White makes the first night flight in Europe. (May 31) Glenn Curtiss wins prize for first flight from Albany to New York City. (June 30) Curtiss makes the first dummy bombing run in a plane. Marie Curie produces a *Treatise on Radio Activity*.
1911		
The Agadir crisis; April French to Fez; June Germans send gunboat *The Panther* to Agadir; July 21 Lloyd George makes the Mansion House speech; 11 October Germany and France sign agreement. (10 October) British House of Commons passes Parliament Bill. (12 October) Army rebellion in Wuhan, China, marks revolution against the Imperial government.	Gordon Craig publishes *On the Art of the Theatre*. Thomas Mann publishes *Death in Venice*. Wassily Kandinsky and other painters form *Der Blaue Reiter* group. Walter Gropius designs the Fagus Factory at Alfeld an der Leine.	(January) Glenn Curtiss designs the first seaplane. (23 January) French Academie of Sciences rejects Madame Curie. (2 October) First air reconnaissance in history during Italo-Turkish war. (8 November) Madame Curie awarded Nobel Prize for Chemistry.
1912		
(10 April) *Titanic* sails. Sinks four days later. (9 May) Home Rule Bill passes British House of Commons. (June) Albania rebels against Turkish rule. Start of first Balkan war. (17 June) Young Turk government resigns after Albanian revolt.	Fifth Olympic Games. Kolehmainen of Finland wins three gold medals, Jim Thorpe wins the decathlon and pentathlon. Schoenberg writers *Pierrot Lunaire*. Premiere of G.B. Shaw's play *Androcles and the Lion*. Meliès produces early movie classic *A la Conquete du Pole*.	Monocoque – one piece – fuselage first used on an airplane. First Curtiss flying boat operational. (April) British Royal Flying Corps formed. (May) Wilbur Wright dies. (17 October) Marie Curie declared fit after near fatal illness.
1913		
(March) German government announces increases in German Army. (June) Emily Davison, suffragette, dies after incident at the Derby. (30 June) Start of Second Balkan War. (10 August) Bulgaria defeated, Treaty of Bucharest ends Second Balkan war. (28 November) British Tory leader Bonar Law calls on army to mutiny over Home Rule.	(29 March) Premiere of Stravinsky's *Rite of Spring*. D.H. Lawrence publishes the novel *Sons and Lovers*. G.B. Shaw has his greatest triumph with the play *Pygmalion*.	Neils Bohr devises the mathematics to explain Planck's quantum theory of the atom. (May) Sikorski exhibits the first four-engined plane – the Bolshoi. (19 August) First parachute jump. (20 August) Nesteror performs first loop-the-loop. Legagneux first man above 20,000 feet, setting height record of 20,079 feet.
1914		
(28 June) Archduke Franz Ferdinand assassinated at Sarajevo. (23 July) Austro-Hungarian ultimatum expires, attack on Serbia begins. (6 August) German army captures Brussels. (26-29 August) Battle of Tannenberg. Germans defeat Russians. (6-11 September) German advance into France stopped at Battle of the Marne.	(February) Charlie Chaplin makes first film, *Making a Living*. James Joyce publishes *Dubliners*. Ezra Pound edits the poetry collection *Des Imagistes*. (June) Wyndham Lewis publishes futurist magazine *Blast*. (November) Chaplin makes his first six-reel film, *Tillie's Punctured Romance*.	(28 June) Archduke Franz Ferdinand assassinated at Sarajevo. (23 July) Austro-Hungarian ultimatum expires, attack on Serbia begins. (6 August) German army captures Brussels. (26-29 August) Battle of Tannenberg. Germans defeat Russians. (6-11 September) German advance into France stopped at Battle of the Marne.

Time Chart

World News	Sport and the Arts	Science and Technology

1915

(March) army attacks in Champagne area, British army attacks at Neuve Chapelle. Failure of both attacks underlines problems for attackers.
(March) A joint Anglo-French naval force tries to open the Gallipoli straits. Defeated by Turkish mines.
(April) Western Allies including ANZAC troops make a military landing on the Gallipoli peninsula but are pinned down by Turkish army.
(15 May) German sub sinks the Lusitania. America threatens to declare war.

D.H. Lawrence publishes *The Rainbow*.
First Vorticist exhibition. Second edition of futurist magazine *Blast*.
(January) Chaplin moves to the *Essanay* film company for $1250 per week.
(March) D.W. Griffith premieres the film *Birth of a Nation*.
(11 April) Chaplin releases his film *The Tramp*.

(1 April) French ace Roland Garros invents the fighter by designing a gun which can fire through the propellor of a single seater airplane.
(1 August) First success for the Fokker fighter, the first effective German fighter plane.
(22 April-25 May) Second Battle of Ypres. Germans use poison gas – first time used in war.
(1 December) Junkers firm pioneers first all-metal monoplane.

1916

(February-November) German assault on Verdun. 315,000 French killed, 280,000 Germans.
(July-November) British attack on the Somme, 418,000 British killed, 650,000 Germans, 194,000 French.
(31 May) Battle of Jutland.
(Easter) Nationalist rising in Dublin.
(January) British government introduce conscription.

Tatlin exhibition Moscow. Tatlin becomes Constructivist, arguing with Malevich who advocates Futurism.
Chaplin leaves Essanay to join Mutual for a fee of $650,000 for one year's work. Produces *Carmen, The Floor Walker, The Pawnshop* at Mutual.

Einstein publishes his *General Theory of Relativity*.
First radio message made from ground to air at Brooklands.
First two-seater reconaissance plane.
(September) Pilotless Hewitt-Sperry bi-plane unveiled.
(October) Siemens invents the glider bomb.

1917

(Spring) French attack fails in Champagne region, army mutinies.
(July to November) Third Battle of Ypres. British attack and lose 360,000 dead. Germans lose 245,000 dead.
(31 January) Germans announce unlimited submarine warfare.
(2 April) USA declares war on Germany.
(23 October) Bolsheviks decide to launch a *coup d'etat*.
(6 November) Bolshevik takeover of government in Petrograd.

Leading Russian artists including Rodchenko, Chagall and Tatlin side with the Bolsheviks.
Picasso joins the Diaghilev ballet.
(October) Mondrian publishes his essay on abstract art in the Dutch magazine *De Stijl*.

(October) Smuts reports to Cabinet on role of air power in war. Argues that an air force could achieve victory by bombing. Royal Air Force set up in consequence of this report.

1918

(8 January) Woodrow Wilson announces US war aims – the '14 points'.
(3 March) Russians and Germans sign treaty of Brest-Litovsk.
(11 November) Armistice signed. All Quiet on the Western Front.

(September) Bolsheviks appoint Chagall Commissar for Art. Tatlin is appointed head of Moscow section of Department of Fine Art.
Tzara publishes the DaDa manifesto.
Duchamp produces *The Large Glass*.
Wilfred Owen is killed.

Advances in medical science mocked as influenza epidemic starts in March. There is no cure, and the epidemic kills millions.
Curie re-opens the Pasteur Institute, closed at the start of the war.

1919

(28 June) Treaty of Versailles signed. German sailors scuttle fleet in protest.
(April) British army massacres Sikhs at Amritsar.
Autumn: J.M. Keynes publishes *The Economic Consequences of the Peace*, attacking the reparations clauses of the Treaty of Versailles.

W.B. Yeats published poetry collection *The Wild Swans at Coole*.
(April) Gropius appointed director of the Bauhaus at Weimar.
D.W. Griffiths makes *Broken Blossoms* with Lilian Gish.
Griffiths, Chaplin, and actress Mary Pickford form United Artists Company.

(14-15 June) First non-stop flight across the Atlantic Newfoundland to Galway Bay by Alcock and Brown.
(1 August) First daily scheduled air service in the world, from London to Paris.
(November) British Royal Society announces results of Solar Eclipse in Guinea. Results confirm Einstein's theory of relativity.

Key figures of the decade

Charlie Chaplin (1889-1977)

ENGLISH-BORN FILM STAR. While touring the US with Fred Karno's British vaudeville company he was signed by Mack Sennett for the Keystone company (December 1913) to make one reel (ten minute) films. His second film for Keystone, *Kid Auto Races at Venice*, featured a tramp character who quickly became the most popular figure in the silent cinema. Chaplin injected pathos as well as humour into the Tramp and rapidly became the highest paid star in Hollywood.

George Clemenceau (1841-1929)

FRENCH POLITICIAN. After working as a doctor in the Vendee region he became the Republican mayor of Paris from 1871 to 1892, and was a deputy until 1892 and then a senator from 1902 to 1920. He was Premier 1906-09, then again became Premier 1917-20 at the invitation of President Poincare. In his second period as Premier he steered France though the last years of the War and represented France at the Versailles peace conference.

Marie Curie 1867-1934

POLISH PHYSICIST born in Sklodowska, moved to Paris in 1891 and in 1895 married Pierre Curie. They worked jointly on research which led to the discovery of the radioactive element radium in 1903. The Curies shared the Nobel Prize for physics with Bequerel. After her husband's tragic death in 1906 Madam Curie was appointed to her husband's professorship and was the first woman to teach at the Sorbonne. In 1910 she published her fundamental treatise on radium and in 1911 was awarded the Nobel Prize for Physics.

Glenn Curtiss (1878-1930)

AMERICAN AVIATION PIONEER. In 1904 he produced a motor which drove a dirigible, then turned to the aircraft pioneered by the Wright Brothers. In 1908 he won the Scientific American prize for the first US flight of one kilometer (0.6 miles). He turned his mind to sea planes and invented a series of sturdy and acrobatic machines. His Curtiss JN4 (Jenny) became the basic aircraft used for barnstorming aerobatics in the US after World War One and was used for the first Canadian mail flight over the Rockies.

Sergey Diaghilev (1872-1929)

RUSSIAN IMPRESARIO, founder *Ballets Russe*. Graduated in law from St Petersburg University in 1896. Moved to Paris in 1906, formed the *Ballets Russe* in 1909 to bring the best of the Russian ballet to the West. Enormously successful, especially in selecting artistic talent of the highest quality. Produced Mussorgsky's opera *Boris Gudonov* in Paris with Chaliapin in 1908. Employed dancer Nijinsky, poet Jean Cocteau, composers Stravinsky, Richard Strauss, Claude Debussy, Maurice Ravel and Sergei Prokoviev.

Albert Einstein (1879-1955)

GERMAN PHYSICIST. In 1905 published his doctorate and four research papers in the journal *Annalen Der Physik*, which challenged the foundations of conventional physics and set out the basis of a new physics of energy and matter. In 1916 he published his General Theory of Relativity, developing his theories in a form which could be tested by observing the deflection of light by large masses. This was done in 1919 during a solar eclipse and Einstein was proved right.

David Wark Griffith (1875-1948)

AMERICAN FILM DIRECTOR, with a background of acting and writing in the theatre. Sold screenplays for silent films to Edison and Biograph companies. From 1908 to 1913 he made 400 films for Biograph, mainly one reel (ten minutes). In 1913 he made *Judith of Bethula* in four reels. Developed techniques of close up, long shot, cross cutting, fade out and fade in which became standard for film makers. Invented the epic film in making *Birth of a Nation*, which opened on 8 February 1915 as *The Clansman* in Los Angeles. Followed up in 1916 with *Intolerance*, and though not always commercially successful, was a co-founder of the United Artists company with Chaplin, Mary Pickford and Douglas Fairbanks senior.

Jack Johnson (1878-1946)

AMERICAN BOXER, first black heavyweight champion of the world. Johnson won the title in 1908 by knocking out Tommy Burns. Lost to Jess Willard on a 26th round knockout in 1915. Encountered much racism, especially as he was married twice to white women. Former champion Jim Jeffries was brought out of retirement to face him as a 'great white hope' in 1912, but Johnson beat Jeffries with a knockout. Convicted under the Mann Act of immorality for transporting his (white) wife across a state line before their marriage, fled America and was a fugitive for seven years. May have thrown Willard fight hoping to get the conviction lifted. Eventually gave himself up in 1920 and served a year in prison.

Andrew Bonar Law (1859-1923)

SCOTTISH POLITICIAN. Born in Canada, moved to Glasgow and became an iron merchant. Leader of the Conservative Party 1911-23. Chancellor of the Exchequer 1916-19, Lord Privy Seal 1919-21. Conservative Prime Minister 1922-23. Took over leadership of the Conservative Party after the election defeats of 1910. Backed the protestant Ulster Unionists to the point of Civil War in the Ulster crisis. Demanded and got Conservative representation in the war cabinet in 1915. Backed Lloyd George to be Prime Minister in 1916, led opposition to him in 1922 and won election of 1922 for the Tory Party.

Vladimir Ilich Lenin (1870-1924)

RUSSIAN REVOLUTIONARY. Real name Ulyanov. Rebelled against Tsarist government and became a Marxist revolutionary. In prison 1895-1900, then exiled from Russia. Helped found revolutionary paper, *Iskra* (the spark) and form Marxist Social-Democrat party in 1900, then split it in 1903 to form a professional revolutionary party, the Bolsheviks. Banned from Russia by Tsarist government, then after fall of Tsar returned April 1917. Led the Bolshevik party to power in second Revolution (October 1917) then headed first Communist govern-

ment in history. Shot and seriously ill from 1922 to his death in January 1924.

David Lloyd-George (1863-1945)

WELSH POLITICIAN. Liberal MP 1890-1945, Chancellor of the Exchequer 1908-1915, Minister of Munitions 1915-16, Prime Minister 1916-22, leader of the Liberal Party 1926-31, Lloyd-George was the first Prime Minister who was not an aristocrat or from the upper middle class. Rose from poverty through ability, initially as a lawyer, then as a politician. Hated by the Tories because of his radical views, they backed him from 1916-22 as the only man to run the country in the war and immediately after, then ditched him. Lloyd-George split the Liberals by joining with the Tories in 1916. He represented Britain at the Versailles Peace Conference.

Pablo Picasso (1881-1973)

SPANISH ARTIST. In April 1904 moved to Paris and became leading innovator in what was the art capital of the world. From 1906 worked with Georges Braque to perfect the style known as Cubism. From 1917 to 24 he worked with Diaghilev in the *Ballets Russe*. After Cubism he moved into a surrealistic style. Militant opponent of fascism, whose painting about the bombing of the town of Guernica in the Spanish Civil war became legendary. 1944 joined the Communist Party. Became a leading member of peace movement.

Ezra Pound (1885-1972)

AMERICAN POET. From 1907, professor of Romance Languages in Indiana, threw up his job and in 1908 moved to London to live as bohemian. Befriended by novelist Ford Madox Ford, joined the imagist school of poetry and in 1914 edited the poetry collection *Des Imagistes*. Collaborated with James Joyce and helped publication of *Portrait of the Artist* and *Ulysses*. Helped T S Eliot start his poetic career. Went to Paris 1919, then lived in Italy 1924-44 and began working on *The Cantos*. Sympathised with the fascist regime and during war made pro-fascist broadcasts. Arrested by US troops as a traitor and was judged insane. 1946-58 kept in custody, working on *The Cantos*.

George Bernard Shaw (1856-1950)

IRISH PLAYWRIGHT and socialist. Failed as a novelist in the 1880s but discovered Fabian socialism and edited *Fabian Essays* in 1889. As a drama critic, advocated theatre of ideas on the lines of Ibsen. Wrote *Mrs Warrens' Profession* in 1893, denied a license until 1902 because it dealt with prostitution. Wrote prolifically, producing a comic masterpiece in *Pygmalion* in 1913, later won an Oscar for best screenplay when the play was filmed. In 1920 produced the tragic masterpiece *Heartbreak House* on life in England at the start of World War One. Awarded Nobel Prize for literature 1925, but refused to accept the award.

Igor Sikorski (1889-1972)

RUSSIAN AIRCRAFT DESIGNER. Graduated from the St Petersburg

Key figures of the decade

Naval Academy, resigned in 1906 to become an engineer. In 1909 began construction of a helicopter, abandoned scheme when aware that engineering skills were not able to cope. Turned to aircraft and built the S1 bi-plane in 1910. In 1913 built the first four engined plane in the world. In 1919 he moved to the USA and formed the Sikorski Aero Engineering Corporation. In 1939 he returned to his first love, helicopters, and built the VS 300, which flew on 14 September 1939, starting the history of the helicopter.

Igor Stravinsky (1882-1971)

RUSSIAN COMPOSER. Graduated in Law in St Petersburg 1905. Tutored by Rimsky-Korsakov from 1903-07. In 1909 invited by Diaghilev to join *Ballets Russe*. Successfully premiered *Firebird Suite* in 1910 at the Paris Opera. In 1911 enjoyed great success with the ballet *Petrushka*. Created a sensation on 29 May 1913 with the premiere of *The Rite of Spring*, choreographed by Nijinksy. Never returned to Russia. In 1940 became a US citizen and towards the end of his life became interested in writing serial music.

Jim Thorpe (1886-1953)

AMERICAN ATHLETE of part American Indian descent, voted in 1950 by US sports writers the greatest US athlete and greatest football player of the first half of the twentieth century. 1912 won the decathlon and pentathlon in the Olympic games, then lost medals because he had been a semi-professional baseball player in 1909-1910, violating his amateur status. From 1913 to 1919 he played baseball for a living then 1919-26 professional (US) football. First president of the American Professional Football Association.

Kaiser Wilhelm (1859-1941)

RULER OF GERMANY from 1890 to 1918. Child of Crown Prince Frederick (later Kaiser Frederick III of Germany) and Princess Victoria, eldest child of Queen Victoria of England. Becoming Kaiser after the death of his father, he allied himself with fervent German nationalists who wished to build German power and prestige. He was the moving force behind the growth of the German navy, a development which destroyed friendship between Britain and Germany. During World War One he lost power to the Generals and abdicated in November 1918 on Germany's defeat.

Thomas Woodrow Wilson (1856-1924)

US PRESIDENT. A Professor of History and Political Economy, in September 1910 he became Democrat governor of New Jersey. This position brought him national fame and in June 1912 he became the Democrat nomination for the Presidency, which he won that autumn. He won a second term in 1916, claiming that he had kept the US out of World War One, but pressure, including the sinking of the *Lusitania*, was building to join the war on the side of Britain and France. German submarine warfare in 1917 brought Wilson and the US Congress together and the US declared war. In January 1918 he devised his fourteen point peace plan, and tried to put it into operation at and after the Versailles conference. The Congress failed to accept his plan for a League of Nations, however, and he collapsed on 25 September 1919 while campaigning for support.

Acknowledgments

The Author and Publishers would like to thank the following for permission to reproduce illustrations: The Bridgeman Art Library for pages 25a, 25b and 58; Central Press Photos Ltd for page 33a; The Mary Evans Picture Library for pages 3b, 5, 7a, 7b, 9, 11, 27 and 42-3; The Hulton Picture Company for pages 4b, 10, 13, 14, 16, 17, 18, 19, 21, 22, 35, 37, 47, 48, 49, 52, 55, 56, 57, 59, 60, 62 and 65; The Imperial War Museum for the frontispiece and pages 33b, 39 and 53; The Mansell Collection for pages 3a, 23, 28, 30, 31, 34, 54 and 61; The National Library of Ireland for page 45. The maps were drawn by Robert Brien.

Books for further reading

World War 1

Cherry Gilchrist, *Finding Out About Life in Britain in World War 1*, Batsford, 1986

Robert Hoare, *World War One*, Macdonald, 1973

Stephen Hoare, *Finding Out About Fighting in World War 1*, Batsford, 1986

Richard Hough, *The Great War at Sea*, OUP, 1983

Peter Liddle, *World War One*, Longman, 1977

Craig Mair, *Britain at War 1914-19*, John Murray, 1982

Arthur Marwick, *Women at War 1914-18*, Croom Helm, 1977

Dorothy Morrison, *The Great War 1914-18*, Oliver & Boyd, 1981

C. Petrie, *The Drift to World War 1*, Eyre and Spottiswoode, 1968

Stewart Ross, *The Origins of the First World War*, Wayland, 1989

Richard Tames, *The First Day of the Somme*, Dryad Press, 1990

Richard Tames, *Living Through History: The Great War*, Batsford, 1984

Philip Warner, *Growing Up in the First World War*, Wayland, 1980

European and World History

David Arnold, *Britain, Europe and the Modern World 1871-1971*, Edward Arnold, 1973

Vera Brittain, *Chronicle of Youth*, Gollancz, 1981

Vera Brittain, *Testament of Youth*, Virago, 1978

Elizabeth Campling, *How and Why: The Russian Revolution*, Dryad Press, 1985

Elizabeth Campling, *Living Through History: The Russian Revolution*, Batsford, 1986

T.K. Derry and T.L. Jarman, *The European World 1870-1975*, Bell and Hyman, 1977

Michael Hodges, *Living Through History: Ireland, From Easter Uprising to Civil War*, Batsford, 1987

A. Raeburn, *The Militant Suffragettes*, Joseph, 1973

Emily Pankhurst, *My Own Story*, Paddington Press, 1979

L.E. Snellgrove, *The Modern World Since 1870*, Longman, 1968

Geoffrey Trease, *Living Through History: The Edwardian Era*, Batsford, 1986

Science, Technology and The Arts

E. Curie, *Marie Curie*, Da Capo, 1986

T.S. Eliot, *Selected Poems*, Faber, 1964

Robert Graves, *Goodbye to All That*, Penguin, 1969

John Gribbin, *In Search of Shroedinger's Cat*, Corgi, 1985

Christopher Martin, *The War Poets*, Wayland, 1983

Ezra Pound, *Selected Poems 1908-59*, Faber, 1975

E.M. Remarque, *All Quiet on the Western Front*, Picador, 1987

R.C. Sherriff, *Journey's End*, Penguin, 1983

John Silkin, *The Penguin Book of First World War Poetry*, Penguin, 1985

Denis Winter, *First of the Few, Fighter Pilots of the First World War*, Allen Lane, 1982

Index

Abyssinia 14
Addison, Christopher 63
Albania 26
Albers, Josef 64
Aldington, Richard 40
Amritsar 63
Amundsen, Captain 23
Apollinaire, Guillaume 40, 58
Armistice 54
Armory Show 24
Asquith, H.H. 12, 26, 33, 45, 57
Austria 8, 26, 54, 62
    Assassination of Archduke 30-31
    Dneister river battle 45
    War on Serbia declared 32
Aviation
    Aerobatics 29
    Atlantic crossing 65

Bombers 53, 59
Civil flights 65
Early flights 11
Long distance flights 17, 29
Military 23, 35, 41, 47, 59

Balfour, A.J. 15
Bauhaus 64
Beatty, Admiral 42
Behrens, Peter 16
Belgium 32, 56
Bennett, Arnold 10, 16
Bethmann Hollweg, Theobald von 8, 12
Blaue Reiter, Der 16
Bleriot, Louis 4, 5, 11
Boccioni, Umberto 10, 46
Bohr, Neils 29
Bonar Law, Andrew 20, 26

Bosnia 8, 30
Boxing 10
Brancusi, Constantin 24
Braque, Georges 10, 24
Brest Litovsk treaty 54
Brooke, Rupert 34, 40, 52
Brown, Arthur 24
Brusilov, General 45
Bulgaria 8, 20, 26, 54, 62
Bülow, Prince Bernhard von 8, 13

Cambrai, battle of 50, 53
Carson, Edward 20
Cezanne, Paul 4, 24
Chagall, Marc 52, 58
Chaplin, Charlie 34, 40, 46, 64
Charles, Emperor 56
China 15, 20

Churchill, Winston 26, 42, 63
  Armistice 56
  Gallipoli 38
  Landlords' tax 9
  Tank developments 53
Clemenceau, Georges 60, 61
Cocteau, Jean 52, 58
Conrad, Joseph 10
Conscription 45
Craig, Gordon 16
Cricket 10, 16
Crippen, Dr 11
Cubism 4
Curie, Marie 4, 11, l17, 23, 29, 35, 41
Curtiss, Glenn 11, 17, 47

Dada 58
Danysz, Jan 41
Davison, Emily 27
De Courbetin, Pierre 22
De Heresy, George Charles l29
De Stijl 52
De Valera, Eamon 45, 57
Debussy, Claude 10, 22
Defence of the Realm Act 39
Degas, Edgar 24
Derain, André 4
Diaghilev, Sergey 4, 22, 52, 58
Duchamp, Marcel 24, 58
Dufy, Raoul 24
Dyer, General 63

Edward VII 6
Einstein, Albert 4, 29, 47, 65
Elgar, Edward 10
Eliot, T.S. 46, 64
Expressionism 10

Fauvism 4, 10
Foch, General 54
Football 10, 34
Ford, Ford Madox 16, 34
Forster, E.M. 10
Franz Ferdinand, Archduke 30-31
Franz Joseph, Emperor 6
Futurism 10, 34, 40, 46, 52

Gabo, Naum 46, 52
Gallipoli 38
Gandhi, Mahatma 63
Gaudier-Brzeska, Henri 40
George V 6, 12
Gish, Lillian 40, 64
Goddard, R.H. 65
Gough, General 32
Graham-White, Claude 11
Graves, Robert 52
Greece 8, 20, 26
Grey, Edward 12, 20
Griffith, D.W. 40, 46, 64
Gropius, Walter 16, 64

Haig, Douglas 44, 50, 54
Haldane, Richard 20
Hipper, Admiral 42
Hitler, Adolf 62
Housing shortage 63
Hulme, T.E. 16

Imagists 5, 16, 34
India 63
Influenza epidemic 59
Ireland 20, 26, 32-33, 45, 57

Italy 14, 26
Itten, Johannes 64

Jeffries. Jim 10
Jellicoe, Admiral 42, 50
Johnson, Jack 5, 10
Joyce, James 34
Jutland, battle of 42

Kandinsky, Wassily 16, 64
Kerensky, Alexander 48, 49
Kitchener, Lord 33
Klee, Paul 16, 64
Kornilov, General 49
Kuhn, Walt 24

Landlords' tax 8, 9
Landsdowne, Lord 26
Lawrence, D.H. 22, 28, 40
Léger, Fernand 46
Lenin 48
Lewis, Wyndham 34, 40
Licensing Laws 45
Llewellyn, C.B. 16
Lloyd George, David 8, 15, 63
  Armistice 56
  Conscription 45, 57
  Election 1918 57
  Munitions Minister 39
  Naval convoys 50
  No confidence vote 57
  Prime Minister 50
  Versailles treaty 60, 61
  Warning to Germany 12
Lowell, Amy 34, 40
Ludendorff, Erich 54, 56
Lusitania 4, 36-37

Macke, August 16
McKenna, Reginald 27
Malevich, Kasimir 46
Marc, Franz 16
Marinetti, Filippo 10, 34
Marne, battle of 32
Matisse, Henri 4, 24
Mauretania 4
Maurice, Frederick 57
Maxwell, General 45
Melie, George 22
Moltke, Helmuth von 32
Mondrian, Piet 46, 52
Mons conference 54
Morocco 12, 13
Moseley, Harry 41
Murrow, E.A. 16

Nagy, Laszlo Moholy 64
National Savings 51
Neuve Chapelle, battle of 38
Nicholas II, Tsar 6, 48
Nijinsky, Vaslav 22, 28

Olympic Games 5, 22
Owen, Wilfred 52, 58

Paget, Arthur 32
Parliament Bill 9, 15
Passchendaele, battle of 50
Picabia, Francis 58
Picasso, Pablo 4, 10, 24, 46, 52, 58
Pickford, Mary 64
Planck, Max 29
Poison gas 41

Potiorek, General 30
Pound, Ezra 16, 34, 46, 64
Princip, Gavrilo 31
Proust, Marcel 28

Radio 11, 47, 53
Radio-activity 11, 29, 35
Rasputin, Gregory 48
Redmond, John 45
Renoir, Pierre Auguste 24
Rodchenko, Alexander 46, 52, 58
Rugby 10
Rumania 8, 26
Russia 8, 31, 32, 38, 51, 54, 56
  Revolution 48-49
Rutherford, Ernest 4, 29

Samuel, Herbert 27
Sarajevo 30-31
Sarnoff, David 47
Sassoon, Siegfried 52
Satie, Eric 58
Schlieffen Plan 8, 32
Schoenberg, Arnold 4, 22
Scott, Captain 23, 29
Seaplanes 17, 35
Seely, John 32-33
Serbia 8, 20, 26, 30, 31, 32
Severini, Gino 10
Shaw, George Bernard 4, 10, 22, 28
Somme, battle of the 44
Space rockets 65
Stravinsky, Igor 4, 10, 16, 22, 28
Suffragettes 15, 21, 26-27, 57
Suprematism 46
Surrealism 58
Sun Yat-sen 16, 20

Tanks 53
Tannenberg, battle of 32
Tatlin, Vladimir 46, 52, 58
Tennis 10
Thorpe, Jim 22
Tirpitz, Admiral 20
Titanic 4, 17, 18, 19, 23
Trades Unions 15, 21, 63
Tripoli 14, 20
Turkey 8, 14, 20, 26, 54, 62
Tzara, Tristan 58

U-boats 36, 50, 53
USA 36-37, 50, 54, 56, 60

Vache, Jacques 58
Verdun, battle of 44
Versailles, treaty of 61, 62
Villard, Paul 4
Vorticism 34, 40

Wells, H.G. 10, 16
Wilding, A.F. 10
Wilhelm II, Kaiser 6, 7, 8, 12, 56
Wilson, Henry 26, 56
Wilson, Woodrow 46, 50, 60, 61
Wright, Orville 4
Wright, Wilbur 4, 23

X-rays 35, 41

Yeats, William Butler 64
Yuan Shih-kai 20
Yusopov, Prince 48

Derek

Wine,
Cheese,
and now Bread...
Everything you could possibly want.
Love Neil

C000060174

THE BOOK OF
BREAD

JÉRÔME ASSIRE

Preface by
BERNARD CLAVEL

Flammarion

Paris - New York

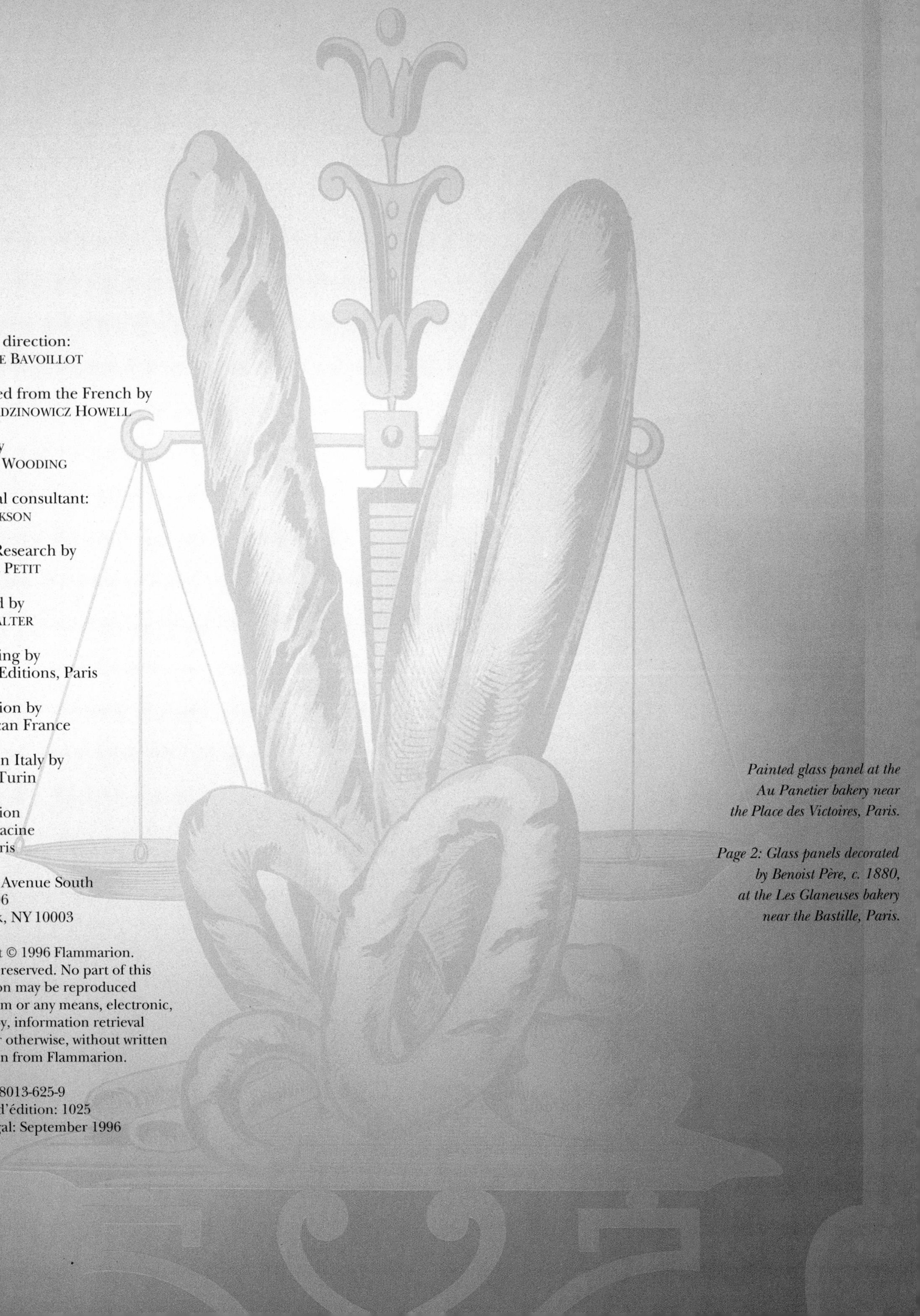

Editorial direction:
GHISLAINE BAVOILLOT

Translated from the French by
DAVID RADZINOWICZ HOWELL

Edited by
BERNARD WOODING

Technical consultant:
ROSA JACKSON

Picture Research by
BÉATRICE PETIT

Designed by
MARC WALTER

Typesetting by
OCTAVO Editions, Paris

Origination by
Colourscan France

Printed in Italy by
Canale, Turin

Flammarion
26, rue Racine
75006 Paris

200 Park Avenue South
Suite 1406
New York, NY 10003

Copyright © 1996 Flammarion.
All rights reserved. No part of this
publication may be reproduced
in any form or any means, electronic,
photocopy, information retrieval
system, or otherwise, without written
permission from Flammarion.

ISBN: 2-08013-625-9
Numéro d'édition: 1025
Dépôt légal: September 1996

*Painted glass panel at the
Au Panetier bakery near
the Place des Victoires, Paris.*

*Page 2: Glass panels decorated
by Benoist Père, c. 1880,
at the Les Glaneuses bakery
near the Bastille, Paris.*

Contents

7

THE TASTE OF BREAD
Preface by Bernard Clavel

*Bernard Clavel's father and grandfather
were both bakers, and as a young man,
he worked as a baker himself.
In his preface, the celebrated French
novelist evokes with nostalgia the bakeries
and breads of the past.*

12

THE STAFF OF LIFE

*Good bread is a feast for the senses, as
texture, aroma, and, of course, taste, all
contribute to the pleasure we take in eating
it. From the baguette to the bagel, bread
symbolizes nature, health, life itself.*

19

BREAD OF YESTERYEAR

*From the bread of ancient Egypt, leavened
with the water of the Nile, to the fateful
phrase, "let them eat cake," which
precipitated the French Revolution,
over four thousand years of human
history cannot be written without
an understanding of the pivotal
role bread has played.*

45

FROM SOWING
TO MILLING

*Whether it is wheat, rye, cornmeal,
or multigrain, bread is born of the sowing
of the fields and the milling of the grain.
Today, despite astounding technological
advances in genetics, cultivation, and
processing, the finest bread is still made
from old-fashioned stoneground flour.*

71

THE BAKER'S ART

*The kneading and rising of
the dough, the precise baking time and
temperature are the technical skills needed
to make bread. However, there
is always a touch of magic in the making
of truly great bread, and the kitchen of
a master baker is a place of mystery.*

93

BREADS OF FRANCE

*France offers an astounding selection
of breads as varied as the country's
legendary cheeses and wines. From the
fougasse of Provence to the pain brié
of Normandy, this chapter takes us on
a culinary voyage through the most
enchanting regions of France.*

113

BREADS OF THE WORLD

*German pumpernickel, Greek pita, British
scones, or American sourdough:
these and other national breads reflect
the history, culture, traditions, and indeed,
the identity of each people and reveal
the warmth and authenticity of their
character and lifestyle.*

147

BREAD FOR THE GOURMET

*Bread, like wine, is worthy of its connoisseurs,
experts, and enthusiasts. The selection of the
right bread to accompany different foods is
a highly refined art, whose fundamentals
are revealed in mouth-watering detail.*

161

CONNOISSEUR'S GUIDE

*A selection of the best addresses throughout
the world to find the finest breads, along
with a selection of practical information and
a glossary of technical terms.*

The Taste of Bread

Bernard Clavel

My father was born in 1873, and started working at the bakery when he was ten. He had known hand-kneading and the wood-burning oven, which had to be lighted with a candle when loading and unloading the bread. When he reached adulthood and had taken over his parent's bakery, he began his day at between ten in the evening and midnight and loaded his last batch around midday. He would then have something to eat and load his cart with bread, the aroma of which trailed in the air behind him. His mare, as well-trained as a circus horse, knew her round by heart, even though it was different for each day of the week. Once he had set the horse and cart in the right direction, the honest fellow would fall asleep on the seat. Whenever the cart would come to a halt, he would wake up, serve the customer, and climb back into the cart and go back to sleep. The rounds would end at about six or seven o'clock in the evening. He had a quick meal and then went to bed for just a few hours.

Not much of a life, I hear you say. Now I'm not so sure. Whenever my father spoke of that time—"when people knew how to live"—his voice trembled with nostalgia.

As he died shortly after the Liberation of Paris in 1945, this retired baker had also tasted that rare yet sticky concoction, which might even contain wood shavings, which we were made to eat during the German Occupation. And of course, he spent a good part of his old age griping about that "bread" which was scarcely bread at all. His recriminations had begun before the dark years of the war, however, just after he had sold his bakery and found himself unable to buy a loaf to his liking. In fact he thought that the whole world had lost its taste.

I always look closely at the way people cut their bread. They rarely do it as it should be done, by turning the loaf and sliding the blade across so as not to break the crust or crush the crumb.

My mother knew how to cut bread like that, just like my father. Their hands understood bread and, when they started a round or the small *jocot* loaf, having first made the sign of the Cross over it, they would cut off the first slice of crust, put it to one side, then, almost unconsciously, they would push the middle of the crumb with their thumb. This was their way of discovering whether the loaf was good or not, even before tasting it. If the crumb stuck to the fingers, if the hole took too long to close up, if the crumb was hard, then the dough had been kneaded for too long, or not long enough, enough yeast had not been used, or else the loaf had been cooked too quickly, or too slowly, or in a poorly heated oven.

This little pressure with the thumb was enough to tell them a thousand secrets and allowed them to judge the baker.

Their hands also knew what bread was worth: how much sweat it cost—and how much joy it could give.

I too took my turn at being a baker. Then I started writing. Every time the past calls to me, I wonder whether it is not more important to have written some books that a few thousand people read—and which will disappear one day—or to have kneaded dough all one's life. I know that my father would have replied without a moment's hesitation that it is more useful to make bread, as long as one makes it well and as honestly as possible; he put the quality of one's work above any profit gained. For it is in the quality of the work that the baker's real enjoyment resides. And if these basic joys are no longer enough for us, it is surely because we have lost all sense of what is meaningful in life, lost the sense that simple people have, like a tough grass that persists no matter how much upheaval the spring plowing brings.

The past can never be summoned up without some risk of pain. Nostalgia for time past can hardly be felt without some twinges, but it also offers us much joy, a joy so full of light that one might think it harbored an inner sun.

When I recall the bakery of my childhood, one of the things that strikes me the most is how much marvelous give-and-take there was. The shop was on a street which

Wood could be added to this list, as the forester who delivered the pieces of charcoal was paid throughout the year in loaves weighing 8 pounds, with which he would feed both his family and his woodcutters.

It cannot be denied that the arrival of electricity, of the kneading-machine, and of the automobile considerably shortened the work day and I shall not lament the time gained for rest and leisure activities. But I am by no means sure that the transformation of the bakery has really brought happiness. Surely if people today attempt to rediscover the taste of real bread by hurrying to buy it at those bakers who advertise "bread made with natural leaven baked in a wood-burning oven," it can only be because

led to the Montmorot saltworks. My mother would open up at five in the morning so that the salters could buy their bread on their way in to work. During his afternoon rounds, my father would serve a fair number of wine-growers, some of whom did not pay; the debt would be written into one of those little blue notebooks with sheets of pink blotting-paper alternating with lined pages. When the bread that had been delivered was worth a cask of wine, one was loaded onto the cart. And, when the bakery had run out of salt, we would stop at the saltworks to pick up a sack, which we would pay for in bread.

Who today has the courage to imagine that the exchange of these three treasures—bread, salt and wine—will ever occur again?

they are none too satisfied with the rubbery industrial *baguettes* they are customarily offered. But it is perhaps time to become more leery about "star" bakers and the kind of snobbism which surrounds old-style baking.

The most deplorable thing is the disappearance of the true artisan, who rejected industrial production but never took himself for a great artist. There is no more a Rembrandt of the roll than there is a Beethoven of the frying pan or a Mozart of the soccer ball. The real, the true bakers, those who believe in the greatness of their trade, know how to stay in their place; such fine artisans are too rare in this day and age not to receive their due.

About fifteen years ago, at Nevy-sur-Seille in the Revermont, in eastern France, Marie Daumard's bakery was still in business. It had been set up in an old mill and the kneader was powered by the flowing river. It was Stéphane, an old baker's assistant and former millhand, who did the work, and he would only make use of the best of what progress had to offer. To immerse myself once again in the atmosphere of the old trade, I went to spend a few nights in his company. He lent me a long white apron and let me put my hand to the dough again.

Of course, the kneading was done mechanically, but we did the dividing, weighing, and shaping manually. One night, up in the barn, I unearthed a brand new divider lying dormant under a covering of empty old bags. I was surprised that it was not being used. "It's the boss," Stéphane explained. "She wanted to help me keep up the

if he had been describing the creation of life itself. In my adolescent stupidity—forever dreaming of other things—I sometimes even laughed at his words, the true meaning of which was, at the time, beyond me. My laughter probably pained this old man who loved me. He was talking about what had given his life meaning—and I gave it little heed.

But his words have not been lost forever, as now they come back to me in all their grandeur. And when I speak of grandeur it is because I know the great worth of the respect and love a person shows for a real trade. My father fulfilled a role on this earth. He was proud of it and he was right to be proud, for not all men have such an importance.

pace. One day, without a word to me, she had it brought here. It was meant to be a surprise—it sure was! It's really a kind of press, you see; it means you don't have to weigh, of course, and it saves time, but it squashes the dough and that kills the bread!"

The old baker's boy did not want his bread "killed," as he realized that killing the bread also meant killing off his trade. And he loved the work too much to stand by and watch it die. After spending a few nights working with him in that antiquated bakery, where time flowed like the waters of the river, I could appreciate exactly what he might fear from the death of his trade.

In his company, I found myself once more in the presence of the words and gestures of my father. In my youth, I had heard him talk of his trade with the same passion as

Such recollections of his trade were not limited to what he had lived through personally; the roots of memory reached back beyond his birth into the rich subsoil of labor that his parents had known before him. I can hear him still, tirelessly recounting the same stories. He drew the most profound pleasure from earlier years, which he could only have learned about through tales told him by his parents, whom I had never had the chance to know.

My grandfather was a chimney sweep from Savoie, who came to Lons-le-Saunier with all his belongings tied in a scarf slung over his shoulder. One day he swept the oven chimney at the bakery and fell in love with one of the bakers' daughters. As he did not know how to write, he had to ask one of his traveling companions, who was about to return to Savoie to tell his family that he was going to marry a girl from the Jura, and that he was abandoning soot and taking up flour. He then learned how to knead and his new trade never left him the time to go back to his village.

This story used to get on my nerves a little, but today it moves me deeply.

It was on a winter's morning, kissing my father on his deathbed, that I began to fathom just how much I had fallen short in my love for him. The passion he felt for his work had often seemed so excessive.

One never forgives oneself for such mistakes—for nothing can salve a past which flows in our veins like molten lava.

Gazing on my father's hands folded forever on his chest, I cried as I thought of all the toil they had endured, kneading, stoking the oven, pulling out the embers, directing the duct, loading and unloading the batches. I really wept to think of such suffering. Today too, the same feeling seizes me; but I also remember all the joys, the real happiness.

I can see him now, as he touches the dough feelingly in the kneading basin, cuts a piece to weigh, shapes a round loaf or some big crown. In retrospect, his gestures—a dance of toil—for me embodied immense richness.

One day, when I used to live in Quebec, tired of only eating sandwich loaves sold in transparent wrapping, I decided to make some bread. That night, having bought some yeast on the sly the day before, I got up without making a sound and started kneading. We were then living in an old farm out on the vast plain which stretches between the Saint Lawrence and the Outaouais. A nor'easter howled across the frozen snow, the blizzard swirled against the windows. And in the snug kitchen, I was kneading dough.

Around seven o'clock, my wife was awoken by the smell of warm bread (and of warm *brioches*, for I had baked some of those too) as it rose up to the floor above, just as the scent of the bakery used to drag the baker's wife from her slumbers. My Canadian wife had not at that time read Henri Béraud's masterpiece, *La Gerbe d'or*; it was the first time she had been woken by such a smell.

That warm bread in the heart of winter was quite a feast! For her it was a discovery, but for me it was just as if a vast expanse of my past was once more brought to life. I was like those children who, on Christmas morning, gaze at all the presents Santa Claus had put in their stockings during the night, but do not dare to approach them too closely.

It does not take much to overwhelm a man: salt, some yeast, flour and water. But above all, love, a great deal of love.

The universe of bread is made up of a nostalgia for one's childhood, the hard work of farmers, millers, and bakers, and the distinctive pleasure given by something "authentic" and flavorful.
Page 6: Le Petit Parisien, photograph taken by Willy Ronis in 1952.
Page 8 and 9: the "life cycle" of bread in the 1930s, from the fields to the old bakery.

Right: "pain Ravoux," a bread made in the old-fashioned way, is served in the inn at Auvers-sur-Oise where Van Gogh died. Facing page: Michel Cousin, a great Parisian baker, with his "giant" pain de campagne. At L'Autre Boulangerie he sells, in addition to traditional bread, the kinds of innovative loaves (such as rye bread with orange peel) that are becoming increasingly popular.

The Staff of Life

Without a love of the simple things, would life be worth living? The things we see and use every day are mysterious because they are, if one stops to think about it, the most valuable of all. This is the case, for example, with daylight, which the ancient Egyptians had good reason to worship every morning. Among the things we eat, it is so with good bread and water. "Barley bread and water give exquisite pleasure," wrote the ancient philosopher, Epicurus, an expert on matters relating to pleasure. His opinion was echoed by Seneca: "Bread and water—these are the things nature requires. For such things no man is too poor, and whosoever can limit his desire to them alone can rival Jupiter for happiness."

Learning to appreciate these elements of life is not easy; such pleasures are often obscured by the daily grind. Water and bread especially have suffered the sad effects of habit—indifference, over-familiarity, even neglect. Water has long since lost its rightful place on the table and it will not be very long before children, drowned in milk and soda, will stop drinking it altogether. I hope the ghost of Epicurus will forgive me, but I shed no tears for plain water. The best is transparent, odorless, tasteless and not particularly good for the digestion. On the other hand, bread, unfortunately less abundant than water ("Oh! If only springs could run with bread!" exclaimed Crates the Cynic in the fourth century B.C.), was essential to the human diet until the 1950s. Fernand Braudel cites statistics showing that, as late as 1800, the average family in Berlin spent forty-four percent of their total income on bread. Consumption has diminished considerably, however (in northern Europe by almost three-quarters this century

alone), and even in France one often encounters unfortunate souls who have simply no idea what real bread is like.

French bread—especially the *baguette*—has gradually permeated the consciousness of the Western world. Associated with good eating and a carefree lifestyle, it is also strangely suited to the modern pleasures of "country in the town" living. Countless movies and advertising posters have made this picnic-perfect shape into a cliché, but a friendly cliché, of France itself. For the French themselves of course, bread is not limited to the *baguette* alone; there are a plethora of loaf-shapes, made with many varied techniques, some regional, some now to be found all over the country. At every turn, the traveler through France meets with fine specimens such as the *pain de campagne*, which should be made with natural leavening, as well as such variants of the ubiquitous *baguette* as the *bâtard* and the *ficelle*.

French bread is generally what is known as "oven-bottom" baked, that is, it is baked on the sole of a brick oven, unlike the Anglo-Saxon "tin" or "pan" bread baked in metal containers. Of the "oven-bottom" varieties, the *baguette*-family in particular is made in a very different way from almost any other bread in the world. The adopted "Vienna" technique (which will be outlined in the chapter "The Baker's Art") is ideal for obtaining an airy crumb from the less absorbent soft flour used in France. The technique of incorporating liquid leaven makes for lighter bread, and the "Vienna" ovens, with their steam injectors, though they are not used by the best bakers, have popularized a soft and giving inner texture, resulting in the much-loved "holey" grain structure typical of a loaf the French do

There is a law of baking which allows for no exception: a good loaf must also look good. Bakers are artists who work as hard to satisfy the eye as to delight the taste buds. Previous page: baguette, pain de campagne, and bread-cutter at a good Parisian bakery.

Below: this tartine with chocolate shavings is a subtle combination of flour and cocoa. French grandmothers used to prepare this treat, which is coming back into fashion.
Facing page: petits pains which their creator Jean Jeudon charmingly calls flûtines. They are sold only on Saturdays and Sundays at his bakery in the Ménilmontant district of Paris. Like all good loaves, they seem to have been baked to be shared. Once pulled open, a creamy crumb appears with a pleasant aroma of hazelnut.

not regard as a mere vehicle for butter and jam: "May God grant me bread with holes and cheese without," goes a particularly gastronomic French saying. The special steam jets often built into the oven perhaps also account for the fact that home-baking is even rarer in France than in Britain and the United States. These jets alone (or else a high initial heat) make for an impressive, glossy crackle on the outside. In the early days before steam, this crust, prepared simply in a very hot oven with a primitive form of bakers' yeast, was so hard that, to adapt it to eighteenth-century English palates, the loaf had to be "chipped" or grated. As for the off-white color of the heart of a *baguette* (which seems more like cream than the milk of a typical tin loaf), it derives from the fact that, unlike in Anglo-Saxon mills, neither artificial flour-bleaching, nor the use of additives which make the average British or American loaf such an anemic affair, are permitted.

The English were importing the makings of a "light bread known as French bread" as early as 1288, when it was baked from wastel (the same flour used to make up the "cheat bread" we will encounter in "Bread of Yesteryear"). The last fact that should be borne in mind when tasting French bread, especially a *baguette* compared to a sourish British "country" loaf, is that vinegar is not employed as an additive just as, historically, ale barm was not generally used in fermenting the dough. It is a combination of these differences which makes French bread unique (and not only the *baguette*, as the regulations also apply to other kinds of bread).

Unlike most other peoples, the French still eat bread at every meal and with every course except dessert: they dunk it in their soup, use it for trying sauces, and to give body to salads or to mellow strong cheese. Bread thus fulfils a utilitarian role devoid of the pleasure dear to Epicurus. To experience that sudden feeling of well-being that can come with a single mouthful of bread, we have to sharpen our dulled senses considerably. Of course, it has to be good bread, not a factory-made product, injected with chemicals and wrapped in plastic, nor one of those dishonorable mock "baker's loaves," lacking all consistency, each

What can one do to avoid taking bread for granted, to avoid becoming indifferent to its beauty and flavor? For a start, one should eat only good bread. It should be tasted it as one would taste a fine wine. Finally, one should share it: "We have learned to see in bread an instrument of community between men . . . the flavor of bread shared has no equal" (Antoine de Saint-Exupéry, Flight to Arras).

one whiter and more insipid than the last. It simply has to be real bread. It could be *pain de campagne* made with natural leaven, for example, or else an authentic *baguette* that a good baker will have taken five hours to make.

Take a goodly sized, attractive-looking loaf and put it on the table. Look at it closely, like the poet Francis Ponge in his ode on the contemplation of ordinary things, *Le Parti pris des choses*: "The surface of bread is a marvelous thing primarily because of the almost panoramic impression it makes, as if one held in one's hand the mountains of the Alps, the Taurus or the Andes." Later in his prose poem, soberly entitled "Bread," Ponge, referring to the crust of a *baguette*, evokes its "valleys, ridges, undulations, crevasses." Closely observed, bread is a volcanic landscape of the earth's infancy, as if it could serve as a daily reminder of the chaos from which we arose. Bread crust—the texture of which is variously smooth, rough and sharp-edged—illustrates one simple truth: among all the things that humanity has invented, nothing is closer to nature than bread. For example, are there any colors more natural than those of the crust? Look at the splendor and harmony of this grainy texture, marbled with gold, amber-yellow, and deep brown.

Now listen to it. Without doubt, bread's most wonderful song is to be heard as it emerges from the baker's oven, crackling like dry kindling. But now just tap the base of the loaf—just as bakers do to assure themselves it has been cooked all the way through—and listen to it resonate like a big bass drum. Then press it between your fingers and listen to it crackle. Bread sings and breathes. Alive, it seems to speak to you, inviting you to open it up. Break into the *baguette* and listen to the crust snapping, or else plunge the blade of a sharp knife into a *pain de campagne* and make the crust quiver like shaken velvet.

It is then that the crumb comes into view, like a soft and delicate lacework underneath the firmness of the stone-like crust. As smooth as ivory, it has a pearl-like iridescence. A good *baguette* should have an aroma of one thing and one thing only: fresh bread. It is the smell which used to make me slow down when I passed a bakery on the way to school. The telltale scent of fresh flour, that of the ripe wheat grain, is the same you get in a mill; it has just a hint of milk, of almonds, hazelnuts, and fresh-cut hay. Leavened *pain de campagne*, American sourdough bread, or English farmhouse loaf, on the other hand, provide a richer source of aromas. Naturally the dominant one is that of the leaven itself, slightly sour, acidic, like green fruit, more redolent of the bakehouse than the mill. The crumb exhudes scents of damp earth, of wet leaves and moss, with sometimes an ephemeral fragrance of cherry, sandalwood, and faded rose.

Supreme, of course, is the moment of tasting. Bite into your *baguette* and feel immediately the sublime contrast between crunchiness and softness, the crust which cracks between the teeth and the crumb which melts on the tongue. No other food, not even the most sophisticated, can offer such a balanced contrast in consistency. The same harmony of contrasts extends to the flavor. The four basic tastes mix with more mutual respect than in anything else we eat: there is saltiness, because salt is added to the dough, sweetness, because of the starch, bitterness, due to the slightly caramelized crust, and then there is the sourness of the yeast. After chewing for a moment, there arise more fragrances of wheat and hazelnut. The initial, slightly toasty taste can remind one of a field of ripe wheat in summer. In his novel *Tante Martine*, Henri Bosco encapsulated these sensations in a solar image: "Their wheat makes bread, a real bread with real flour. There can be no better. It's like eating the sun."

Now take a *pain de campagne*. Here the landscape evoked is altogether starker, more bracing. The crumb is already denser, more highly structured and amply nourishing. Its first onslaught of tartness—though not a harsh one—means that sour has the edge over the three other primary tastes. Soon follow more rustic and woodland flavors, a country world of wild plants without which the loaf would scarcely deserve the term *de campagne*, mixing with savors of walnut, truffle, and mushroom. After a moment's chewing, the vista changes from summer to autumn as a second acidulous wave breaks like unripe fruit—blueberry, perhaps, or apple, plum, or grape.

These, then, are the typical, but by no means the only, tastes of French bread. This book is intended to make bread more delicious still, by treating its history and its symbolism, describing its origins, and evoking how lovingly it is made by a good baker. In its shape, the vocabulary used to refer to it, and by the ways in which it is made and eaten, bread belongs to a sensual world where a certain rawness or jovial bawdiness is not excluded. Is it by chance for example that the French call a variant of the *baguette* a *bâtard* ("bastard"), while round loaves are called *miches* (slang for "buttocks" or "breasts")? So this book is intended to make you appreciate bread as fully as possible, to understand what it is, what it has meant in history and what it can symbolize today: nature, health, life itself.

Bail Joseph

Bread of Yesteryear

From earliest times, bread has been a symbol of conviviality. The bakery, where everyone went regularly, was the perfect place to meet and exchange gossip. The baker played a major role in social life. The traditions of the bakery and bread shop go back four thousand years; and some have remained unchanged and are the pride of the profession to this day. Top: detail from an anonymous eighteenth-century Venetian painting, The Art of Baking. *Facing page:* Interior of a Bakery, *Joseph Bail (1862–1921). Above: detail from a table of trade guilds, painted wood (fourteenth century).*

Few actors on the stage of history can have played a more significant role than bread. Crucial to human nutrition, bread has been instrumental in molding civilizations for centuries. Essential to life, it has influenced the domestic and foreign affairs of nations, precipitated wars and revolutions, and driven technological advances. A symbol of both material and spiritual life, it has nurtured religions, fostered countless traditions, forged legends, and enriched every language with proverbs and metaphors. From the nomads and the peasants of antiquity to today's fast-food customers, over four thousand years of world history cannot be written or understood without taking some account of the pivotal role bread has played.

A Fortuitous Birth

People have been consuming cereal products for at least ten thousand years. Early agriculture tended to favor barley, oats, wheat, and rye. For several thousand years, all sorts of grain (including millet) were eaten raw, boiled, or roasted. Ground, turned into dough and cooked over an open fire, they were made into a sort of thick, flat cake. And then, probably by accident, grain was eventually transformed into bread.

Bread, as against the earlier flat cake, is made from fermented dough, that is to say the dough is changed by micro-organisms after being left for a certain time in contact with air and water. A process of natural fermentation gives off carbon dioxide, which makes the dough swell so that when cooked it becomes relatively bulky, springy, and light, far tastier than any flat bread.

Who was the first to let dough stand and ferment before cooking? A number of clues suggest that leavened bread was probably first made in ancient Egypt. In the first place, the earliest known pictures of bread are to be found painted on walls of Old Empire tombs dating from around 3000 B.C. As offerings to the gods, as currency, or as provisions to be carried by the deceased on his last journey, Egyptian bread appears in a number of different guises. Just how significant bread was for the Egyptians is evident from the fact that a thousand years later funerary art (and even toys) continued to portray people working in the

Wheat, barley, spelt, and millet are mentioned many times in the Scriptures. In the New Testament, bread, identified with the body of Christ, is the symbol of spiritual food, of the presence of God on earth.

Hence, in Christendom until the twentieth century, it was a central metaphor for the sacred in daily life. Facing page: The Eucharist, Giovanni Battista Ramacciotti (1628–1671).

fields and master bakers with their loaves and ovens. In the earliest bakeries, barley or wheat grains were crushed or pounded either with a muller (a stone "rolling pin") or else in a flatter stone "slab-mill." The resulting meal was then crudely sifted. The dough was subsequently kneaded in large earthenware jars before being cooked in the fire in simple preheated molds or more sophisticated "beehive" or stepped ovens. There were three basic kinds of loaf: wide and oval, flat and round, or conical. Some were flavored with honey and others enriched with butter, eggs, or milk. All contained an essential ingredient which might in itself explain why raised bread was born in Egypt: the water of the Nile in which the dough was kneaded. Rich in the silt which makes the soil fertile, the waters are also full of *Saccharomyces cerevisiae*, the very yeast strain used in the bakers' yeast of today. It is enough to leave the dough standing for a few hours for fermentation to start of its own accord, resulting, after baking, in a real loaf of bread.

Sacred Bread

The oldest text referring to leavened bread is the Book of Genesis, in which bread, fermented or not, appears often. The first mention of leaven occurs when Jehovah, having decided to destroy Sodom, sends two angels to Abraham's nephew Lot to forewarn and rescue him. Lot welcomes them into his house: "And he made them a feast, and did bake unleavened bread, and they did eat" (Gen. 19:3). Such quotations, as well as other references in the Old Testament, have induced historians to conclude that Hebrew bakers discovered leavened bread independently and that they reserved unleavened bread for all their rituals. It is, however, more probably the case that the originally nomadic Hebrew tribes learned of the leavened variety through contact with the Egyptians. The Scriptures, distinguishing frequently between leavened and unleavened bread, reveal another salient fact: unlike the Egyptians, the Hebrews considered the former type to be unclean—as it was the result of a kind of putrefaction—and unworthy to be used as an offering or at religious festivals. Modern Jews

In the form of a golden loaf, the "bread of life" appears in a more or less attested episode from the life of St. Paul of Thebes in the third century A.D. He was reputedly the first anchorite, predating even St. Anthony the Great. In his hermitage in Egypt, St. Paul received from the beak of a raven a half-loaf provided by God. When St. Anthony visited St. Paul, God sent them a whole loaf. Below: St. Paul and St. Anthony, *Alonso Sánchez Coello (c. 1541–1588).*

still use only unleavened bread (now called *matzos*) to celebrate Passover, in remembrance of the Exodus: "Unleavened bread shall be eaten seven days; and there shall no leavened bread be seen with thee, neither shall there be leaven seen with thee in all thy quarters" (Exod. 7:7).

One thousand five hundred years after the Exodus, the points of contact between bread and religion would increase considerably in scope with the advent of Christianity. This new dimension was heralded by Jesus's birth in a place called Bethlehem—in Aramaic, "the house of bread." At that time, Judea was a Roman province where, as in Samaria and Galilee, starvation was commonplace. The vocabulary employed by Christ in his teaching, often couched in the terms of a rustic parable—complete with sheep, plowing, sowing, reaping, wheat, and above all, bread—was intended to be easily assimilated by hungry ears. However, Jesus offered spiritual food only, not the daily bread often lacking in Palestine's markets; this misunderstanding between Christ and the people grew steadily. The problem is set out in the Gospel of St. Matthew, in the episode where Jesus is led after his baptism to the desert in order to undergo the ordeal of hunger and temptation: "And when he had fasted forty days and forty nights, he was afterward an hungered. And when the tempter came to him, he said, If thou be the Son of God, command that these stones be made bread. But he answered and said, It is written, Man shall not live by bread alone, but by every word that proceedeth out of the mouth of God" (Matt. 4:2–4). Later, Jesus did nonetheless perform the miracle of the Feeding of the Five Thousand, when he gave bread to the crowd who were following him after the death of St. John the Baptist. This is the crux of the misunderstanding as narrated by St. John. The astonished people called Christ the Messiah, and prepared to acclaim him king, but Jesus elected instead to retire alone to the mountains. Then, after the miraculous walking on the water, he traveled to Capernaum, where he was joined by the people. Once in the synagogue, Christ then alluded to his remarks on the "bread of life": "Verily, verily I say unto to you, Ye seek me, not because ye saw the miracles, but because ye did eat of the loaves, and were filled. Labor not for the meat which perisheth, but for that meat which endureth unto everlasting life . . . I am that bread of life . . . this is the bread which cometh down from heaven, that a man may eat thereof, and not die . . . if any man eat of this bread, he shall live forever" (John 6:26–27; 6:50–51). Christ made this identification with bread even clearer at the Last Supper, when, surrounded by his disciples, he instituted the Eucharist: "And he took bread, and gave thanks, and brake it, and gave unto them, saying, This is my body which is given for you: this do in remembrance of me" (Luke 22:19).

Christ, by identifying himself with bread, invested this simplest and most ordinary of foods with a hallowed aura. The holiness of bread is revealed in a number of traditions which have only recently fallen into disuse: the old aversion to throwing bread away, or to feeding it to animals; the sign of the Cross made over bread before cutting it (occasionally in the belief that this will keep it from going stale); the feeling of guilt when one accidentally drops bread on the floor (a sin forestalled by picking the bread up and kissing it); and the fact that one is respectfully careful not to put a loaf upside down on a table. This notion is also encountered in countless popular legends, such as the one recounted by the Brothers Grimm of the woman who, having gone insane after fashioning a pair of shoes made of bread for her since dead child, only recovers her reason when the infant is eventually exhumed and the sacrilegious shoes are removed.

Greek and Roman Bread

Cereals and bread were of considerable importance in the nutrition of the ancient Greeks. Homer himself had already described men as "flour eaters." The daily bread of the Greeks—known as *maza*—was closer in fact to an unfermented flat cake made from barley, griddled on red-hot stones. For the average Greek, wheat bread, or *artos* (whose dough might sometimes contain olive oil) was reserved solely for festivals. Bread was most probably unleavened in the fifth century B.C., hence Herodotus's surprise when visiting Egypt: "We all worry about food fermenting; but the Egyptians deliberately make dough so that it does fer-

ment." In towns, bread making slowly but surely left the domain of the private house and became concentrated in bakehouses, where the more onerous tasks such as kneading were alloted to slaves. The slaves were often malnourished and it was not unknown for a kind of wide ring to be fitted around their necks to prevent them being able to put their hand to their mouth and so eat any of the dough. Greek bakers also improved the oven, which was soon to replace the archaic preheated molds and earthenware cones placed on stones. There was equal progress in bread gastronomy: by the second century B.C., just before the Roman era, seventy-two different loaves and cakes were sold in Athenian bakeries. It is believed that among the earliest of these types must have been loaves of raised bread, flavored with herbs and olives, delicacies which were to transform the baker's art.

The Romans first had to catch up somewhat with the Greeks, though they subsequently developed bread-making techniques still further. In fact, just at the time when the best Athenian bakeries were overflowing with delicious loaves, the Romans, if one is to believe Cato Censorius (234–149 B.C.) in his *De agri cultura*, regarded the accidental fermentation of their dough as a disaster. In the later second century B.C., however, they realized that fermentation was an advance and it was the Romans who introduced leavened bread into Britain in the wake of their invasion of 55 B.C. Back in Rome itself, the earliest bakers soon organized themselves into a strictly regimented guild which had great influence over matters political and religious. Thanks to Greek bakers, whose reputation in the Mediterranean world was already one to be reckoned with, this *ars pistorica*—the art of "pounding," that is, baking—soon took off, and in its wake came some remarkable technical advances. Though a few texts survive (Pliny the Elder and Virgil are both illuminating), our information about this *ars* comes mostly from numerous archaeological finds. The "Street of Bakers" in Pompeii, preserved by the lava from Vesuvius, and the frieze decorating the tomb of a major Roman baker, Marcus Vergilius Eurysaces, outside the Porta Maggiore enable us to reconstruct the work of a baker in detail. To start with, the grain was ground

between two large conical millstones originally operated by slaves or prisoners, and later by mules or horses; then the flour was sifted by hand using bolters. As for kneading the dough, techniques underwent spectacular improvements in Rome, at least as regards the more prosperous bakers. Kneading was now performed in a cylindrical vat by a rod on a horse-driven mechanism. This distant relative of the mechanical kneader had no descendants for two thousand years. The loaves were rounded, then baked in brick ovens resembling a present-day wood-burning oven (one such oven was unearthed among the ruins of Pompeii).

The most common type of Roman loaf was round, like the one found in Pompeii. It is clear from the texts which do survive that even at this early stage white bread was preferred, brown loaves being termed *panis secundarius*. Whatever the flour, however, Roman bakers were possessed of fertile imaginations, and concocted loaves to order in a myriad of shapes. At banquets, loaves in the form of lyres or birds were much appreciated, while for weddings interlocking rings were made. Certain Romans were keen on naughty or even obscenely modeled loaves, which enhanced the good humor of the guests and stimulated the appetite. Also discovered in the ruins of Pompeii were eighty-one star-shaped loaves.

However, despite these advances the history of bread in Rome can be summarized in a single word: penury. From the second century A.D., thousands of starving and impoverished peasants deserted the countryside and flooded into Rome. To prevent social unrest was the first concern of successive consuls, and later emperors, which Juvenal encapsulated in one of his satires by a notorious phrase: "Bread and Circuses!" Flour, made from imported Egyptian wheat, was thus distributed free to the poorest by state-employed bakers. By 59 B.C., under Julius Caesar, Rome counted two hundred thousand recipients of free flour. Three centuries later, during the reign of Aurelian, there were three hundred thousand, each receiving a ration of two loaves per day. This support for the destitute became so routine that the Emperor eventually decreed that the *tessera*, the token showed as a pass to receive the free loaves, would become hereditary.

Buried beneath ash from Vesuvius on the 24 August A.D. 79, the city of Pompeii provides exceptional evidence of the Romans' passion for bread. The town set aside an entire street for the bakers. Mills and ovens have been excavated, as well as numerous loaves, which, though burned to a cinder, have retained their attractive shape.

Facing page: The Baker, fresco from Pompeii. The only flour the Romans liked was wheat. It is this cereal that the poet La Fontaine described as a "rich gift from blonde Ceres," a goddess venerated in particular by the Roman plebeians. Below: Ceres, Baldassare Peruzzi (1481–1536).

The Age of Feudalism

During the Middle Ages, extremely arduous conditions in the countryside did not entirely prevent progress in the development of new techniques in the long and laborious chain of tasks which extends from the field to the finished loaf. During this period the collar harness, which permitted the animal to draft much heavier loads without strangulation, the wheeled plowshare and the flail all came into use. More importantly, the windmill appeared. The windmill's origins are shrouded in mystery, but the first Euro-pean example might have been built in ninth-century England (an illustration survives in Norfolk dating from 1349), and in France three hundred years later.

In rural Europe, the feudal system had become established. Its various privileges included rights of banality over both mill and bakehouse, which were both the property of the suzerain. To bake their bread, the peasants were obliged to use these and these alone, and had to pay a duty to do so. The laborer first had to carry his load of grain to the mill by unsafe and, in winter, impassable roads. Then, once at the mill, he often had to wait hours for some rough millings, sometimes mixed with sand by a much-hated miller. Then he had to go back to the farm, where he kneaded his dough. Then he went to the communal bake-house, generally situated right next door to the mill, where the baker would eventually hand over an often half-baked loaf and charge him a further toll.

This peasants' bread, a huge loaf of at least 10 pounds, was never made from wheat alone. Even in good years this food, which represented at least 50 percent of a peasant's diet, often comprised the scarcely sifted meal milled from maslin, a crop of wheat and rye sown and reaped together. Such plentiful years, however, were few and far between. Between the ninth and the fourteenth centuries, the European countryside was plagued by many periods of scarcity and famine, and there was often even a dearth of barley and oats. At times like these famine bread was eaten: loaves baked from a smattering of meal, with straw, clay, or ground tree-bark, or cakes made from acorn or horse chestnut meal or else from crushed roots and herbs, all more or less roasted in embers. In southern England, as late as 1439, the poor were in such straits that they made flour from pummeled fern roots.

As one can well imagine, things were very different at the tables of the lords and kings and the rich, who all lived through a less arduous Middle Ages, and later through the splendors of the Renaissance. Du Cange, one of the greatest French scholars of the seventeenth century, has left us a list of the types of bread eaten by the wealthy during the medieval period: the court loaf, the lord's loaf, the Papal loaf, the knight's loaf, the squireling's loaf . . . right down

In France, the talemeliers, *medieval bakers, provided townspeople with a wide range of leavened loaves, from the rough and ready* pain ballé *(containing bran) to the very sophisticated* pain de Gonesse *(after the town of the same name), carefully prepared and baked from pure wheat flour.*

Above: The Bakery, *miniature from a fifteenth-century Franciscan missal. At that time, even the best wheat bread made for lords and the wealthy was never pure white. Facing page:* Man with a Wine-glass *(Portuguese School, fifteenth century).*

From 1665, with the appearance of brewer's yeast, the superior breads acquired more variety, and became lighter and tastier. Below: Still Life with Cheese, *Floris van Dijck (1575–1651).*
Facing page: Still Life with Figs, *Luis Eugenio Meléndez (1716–1780).*

Both paintings show bread as it was baked until the beginning of the twentieth century, without pumping steam into the oven. The crust was thicker and less shiny than today's, although this loaf, thanks to the painter's talent, gleams in the light.

to the humble loaf eaten in the scullery. We are not sure exactly how these breads differed, but they were all of pure wheat flour. We do know, however, what the main use for bread was among the nobility until the seventeenth century: a sort of plate made of bread around 2 inches thick, upon which was placed the meat. The *tranchoir*, or trencher, absorbed the meat juices and was eaten at the end of the meal, or else thrown to the servants.

It was for these privileged few and also for townsfolk that the bakers busied themselves before their ovens. In France medieval bakers were known as *talemeliers*, a word whose origins are obscure and which was only supplanted by *boulanger* (from *boule*, the round of dough) in the fifteenth century. In the major towns it was only in the twelfth century that King Philip Augustus granted bakers the right to possess their own ovens. In Paris their trade was then regulated by royal authority and placed under the control of the prevost (or appointed mayor), assisted by a Grand Panetier (known in England as the Royal Panter) in charge of bakery. Meanwhile in England, in 1155, the bakers formed a guild. The Assize of Bread was established in 1266 to enforce comprehensive and somewhat draconian baking regulations. In both countries from the fourteenth century onwards, a journeyman desiring to join the guild was required to serve an apprenticeship with several master bakers and afterwards present his "masterpiece." Judged by twelve adjudicators designated by the Grand Panetier, this decorated piece, depicting an historical event or a miracle, for example, was designed to show the aptitude of the applicant to join the ranks of the masters. Similar regulations governed the "pastmasters" of the Worshipful Company of Bakers in London until the early nineteenth century.

Even prior to the thirteenth century, the best bakers in Paris and the surrounding region could offer a considerable range of more than thirty breads which varied as much in their ingredients as their shape. Among these were the basic *pain de brode* (a brown loaf made from rye and unmilled wheat grist); the superior white flour *pain de Chailly* made from wheat; and the *pain coquille* (shell loaf), which had a puffy crust. The *pain de Gonesse*, from the town of the same name in the Val d'Oise to the north of Paris,

was the most famous and already much praised by Henri IV. It was made from pure, well-kneaded leavened flour and continued to be one of the most prized until the French Revolution. There was also the *pain ballé*, a rougher loaf containing bran (the so-called *balle* of the grain); a *pain de deux couleurs*, a two-color loaf prepared with a layer of rye laid over one of wheat; and *pain rousset*, a russet-colored loaf made from the unsifted meal of wheat and rye. Of course, such a profusion of varieties depended above all on the quality and the quantity of the harvest, something which for many centuries remained a matter of chance.

Fermenting the French Revolution

On the eve of the French Revolution, a combination of archaic agriculture and an inadequate transportation system made for serious problems of food supply. Moreover, regions rich in wheat tended to stockpile grain in case of poor harvests, thereby depriving the poorer areas and precipitating higher prices. In an effort to expand and modernize cereal farming in 1787, the government further worsened the situation by trying to raise the price of grain through deregulation of both transport and export. The price rises had an immediate effect, further exacerbated by the very poor harvest of 1788, and they increased in an accelerating spiral until the fateful month of July 1789. Inflation in turn had dire repercussions on the price of flour and bread, playing no small role in the circumstances of the Revolution.

In eighteenth-century France, the gravest problem was not the lack of bread but its price. In fact, never before had the town bakeries—above all those in Paris—offered so many varied and high-quality loaves, but only the wealthy could afford to buy them. Several publications of the period attest to the great strides made in the baker's art, for example *Le parfait boulanger* (The perfect baker) by the agronomist Antoine Augustin Parmentier, published in 1778. Parmentier is best known in France for having introduced potato-farming. It is less commonly known that he intended the potato to be milled so as to replace flour during shortages. In 1780 Parmentier obtained the authoriza-

tion to open a "baking academy" in Paris designed to study the "new combinations of farinaceous substances from which it might be possible to bake bread in times of famine." The scientist then carried out a number of trials on various kinds of "bread," combining potato, oats, buckwheat, and corn. Ten years later, the revolutionary mob massed outside Parmentier's academy yelling: "Why doesn't he eat his potatoes himself? We want bread!" However, the agriculturist survived to witness the triumph of his cherished tubers during the First Empire.

Le parfait boulanger described the process of making bread in practice at this period: hand-kneading the dough, fermenting with natural leavening, shaping the loaf, and baking in brick, wood-burning ovens. The book also refers to something new: adding salt to the dough, unusual until that time due to its high price. It was realized that salt improved the texture of the dough, allowing it to rise higher. Parmentier also referred to brewer's yeast, which a Parisian baker had first added to leaven in 1665 in the production of a loaf called *pain mollet*. This soft luxury bread, produced from fine-sifted flour, had known great success at the court of Louis XIV. A century later, it could still be found in the bakeries of Paris and had pride of place among the thirty or so loaves listed in Diderot and d'Alembert's monumental *Encyclopédie*. Some of these pure wheat breads, such as the *petit pain* or the *pain chapelet* (rosary bread), both enriched with butter and milk, seem to be of

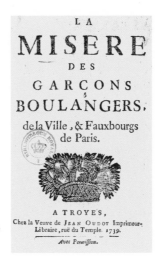

LA
MISERE
DES
GARÇONS
BOULANGERS,
de la Ville, & Fauxbourgs
de Paris.

A TROYES,
Chez la Veuve de JEAN OUDOT Imprimeur-
Libraire, rue du Temple. 1739.
Avec Permission.

Bread traders and baker's boys bore witness to the dire conditions of the Parisian poor under the ancien régime. *Facing page:* The Bread Vendor and the Water-Carrier, *Jean Michelin (1623–1695). Left: an oft-republished anonymous verse pamphlet complaining of the working conditions of the baker's boys.*

an astonishing extravagance given the social conditions of the time. Several others incorporated brewer's yeast like the *pain mollet*: for example, the *pain à la Reine* (Queen's bread) or the *pain de festin* (festival bread). Less unusual were the *pain bis* (with bran) and the less costly oatmeal, barley, and rye breads. One might also still come across the old *pain de Gonesse*, and one could always buy the huge 12-pound *pain de Brane*.

All these loaves, however, lay well beyond the means of the poor. It had been calculated in France that, to ensure that the workers remained adequately nourished, the price

of bread should not exceed two *sous* per pound. In July 1789 bread cost four *sous* in Paris, and twice that in provincial towns. To an angry populace stirred up by rumors it was obvious who was responsible for the inflation. It was believed that those instrumental in starving the people had conspired in a "famine plot." First in line came the *seigneurs* themselves who earned a tax from cereals and so stockpiled them to sell later on at a higher price. Next came the millers and bakers who were accused, occasionally not without foundation, of fraudulent speculation on the price of grain. Bringing up the rear of course was the government, in the shape of Finance Minister Necker, suspected of particular complicity. From spring 1789 on, hunger riots broke out in practically all the main towns and in Paris on 14 July a furious crowd stormed the prison of the Bastille in the misplaced belief that the plotters had stored wheat there.

During August, which also saw the abolition of all feudal privileges, a catastrophic drought hit the country and there was not enough water to drive the mill wheels. The small quantity of wheat harvested in July could therefore not be ground and bread prices soared. Who could save the people from starvation? On 5 October, a ragged army of women, men, and children, armed with staves and scythes, marched from Paris to Versailles and forced the king, queen, and Dauphin (nicknamed "the baker, the baker's wife, and the shop boy") to return to the capital. A fortnight later, however, the people of Paris still had no bread. Pillage occurred in a number of city areas, and one incensed mob dragged a baker suspected of hiding flour from his bakery near the cathedral of Notre-Dame to the place de Grève in front of the Hôtel de Ville, where public executions took place, and hanged him.

Structural shortcomings in French agriculture were soon compounded by the war against Austria, which depleted the farmland of peasantry. Disastrous harvests and spiraling inflation prolonged the dearth of food for many years. Meanwhile, the guillotine was brought into action against speculators. Any man found guilty of slowing down a passing corn cart risked the death penalty. In 1792, the government of the Convention forbade all sale of white bread. Millers and bakers had their bolters and sifts

In the eighteenth century, bakeries in towns were piled high with loaves made from finely-sifted wheat. The wheat harvests were nonetheless always uncertain, flour was expensive and the poor could not afford good bread. In France, the high price of bread was one of the underlying factors of the Revolution. Above: interior of a bakery, around 1770. Facing page: The Girl returning from Market, Jean Siméon Chardin (1699–1779).

confiscated, while the only loaf permitted to be sold was the *pain-égalité*, an "equality bread" of the coarsest kind with which rich and poor alike had to make do.

It was once more in the name of equality that wheat was to supplant all other cereals after the revolution. Whereas white-flour wheat bread had formerly been reserved for the rich, it was at last to become a bread for everyone. However, for the starving thousands of those years, the famine, which hit England by 1794–1795, did not abate until 1796.

The Birth of Modern Baking

Brewer's yeast had been produced on a small scale and used in baking since 1665. Bakers using it discovered, however, that their bread would frequently fail to rise. Around 1780, some Dutch distillers concerned themselves with this problem and came up with a more reliable yeast which was sold in the form of a paste. This process was further improved by the German yeast-maker Tebbenhof in 1825. He perfected a dehydrated yeast and sold it as a compressed cake (this is the way brewer's yeast is marketed today). Even that was not ideal and, in 1867, a Viennese distiller—spurred on by the

ample reward offered by Dutch bakers to whomsoever might develop the perfect yeast—discovered a new means of production from grain must. He got his reward and yeast produced by this novel method was quickly taken up by bakers and employed throughout Europe until 1914.

Naturally, progress in yeast-making made for parallel advances in baking. It was, apparently, a Polish baker who, at the beginning of the nineteenth century, was the first to take a decisive step on the road to modern baking by discovering a way of doing without leaven. This method, a version of the sponge dough technique, became known in French as *poolisch*. It consisted in replacing the leaven by a liquid mixture of flour, yeast, and water, which was allowed to ferment. The bread thus obtained was obviously less sour than that fermented with a natural dough leaven, and it preserved unaltered all the taste of the flour. This method soon took over in Austria, where it was used in the rising of a high-quality wheat dough, occasionally enriched with malt extract. In 1840, a chamberlain at the Austrian court, Baron Zang, having heard several visiting members of the French royal family in Vienna singing the praises of this type of bread, undertook to introduce it to France. He recruited several bakers and opened a shop in Paris on the

Facing page: the Encyclopédie by Diderot and d'Alembert (from which this plate is taken) informs us that there were 250 bakeries within the walls of Paris around 1750. Some 1,500 bakers or stallholders from Paris and the outskirts, however, also sold their produce at the fifteen twice-weekly bread markets in the capital (including place Maubert in Saint-Germain, rue Saint-Antoine near the place des Vosges, and place du Palais-Royal). Work in bakeries hardly changed from antiquity to the end of the nineteenth century, the hardest job being the manual kneading of large quantities of dough. Above: a bakery in Italy, anonymous (Italian School, eighteenth century). Left: a German bread- and milk-seller's sign adorned with a pretzel.

Around 1850, new fermentation methods and progress in milling made it possible to produce softer, finer bread. Bakers also began to sell cakes and their shops became temples to the taste buds. Above: a German bakery around 1850 (lithograph after a drawing by T. Streich). Left: The Appetizing Baker's Wife (nineteenth-century lithograph).

rue Richelieu. This bread, fermented using the *poolisch* sponge-dough method and christened *pain viennois* (known in English as "French Vienna bread"), was to enjoy immense success, especially in the larger towns, before being supplanted in the 1920s by other fancy breads.

There were simultaneous improvements in kneading techniques. In the last few years of the eighteenth century, the first mechanical kneading-machines made their appearance, designed to save the baker's boys from the most arduous part of their job. These kneaders took the form of a wooden kneading trough turned with the aid of a crank. The results were far from conclusive, however, and, throughout the following century, other, more advanced hydraulic or horse-driven machines were devised. They were complicated and unwieldy, and were hardly feasible for use in small family bakeries in towns. It was not before the end of the nineteenth century, and the development of electric and gas-powered engines, that mechanical kneaders really came into their own. Nonetheless, progress was slowed by a distrust of this new "mechanical bread" on the part of both the consumer and the baker, for whom hand-kneading, with all its symbolic and sensual ramifications, made his job what it was. As for the baker's boys who did most of the kneading, they were hostile to this apparatus, which threatened to put them out of work. The outbreak of the First World War resulted in their mobilization, however, and developments accelerated. By the middle of the 1920s, hand-kneading had totally disappeared from bakeries.

Neither did baking ovens escape the effects of progress. Heat resistant brick ovens, allowing baking at higher temperatures, became more widespread around 1840. Ten years later, some ovens were being lighted by gas lamps or jets. Wood-burning ovens were subjected to considerable advances around 1900 with the introduction of a hearth beneath the baking chamber. A mouth connected the two parts, directing the flames and combustion gases upward to the brick chamber. Hitherto the wood had burned out on the oven floor, where the bread was laid once the oven was heated to the right temperature and the embers removed. From 1920, however, bakers began to fit their ovens with gas or fuel-oil burners, while the same period saw the appearance of the earliest continuously heated ovens (fueled by coal, gas, or oil). In these, hot-air or steam tubes maintained the baking chamber at a constant temperature, making it better suited to smaller loaves, such as the *baguette*. Finally, the earliest electric ovens appeared, becoming widespread with the lowering of electricity costs.

There were also technical and scientific advances in other stages of the bread-making process. Modern milling was born with the introduction of the steam mill at the end of the eighteenth century in North America. In fact, two mills of this type had been developed by James Watt on the banks of the Thames in the 1780s, but they had been burned down by local millers who saw them as a threat to their livelihoods. The idea was taken up and considerably improved in the 1830s by a technical wizard from Philadelphia named Oliver Evans. Following the earlier steam revolution, mills were also

This steam-powered kneader in a bakery in the rue Saint-Maur, Paris, in 1862, was just one of many kneading-machines experimented with during the nineteenth century. Mechanical kneaders only became widespread after the First World War.

to experience a "roller revolution." Legend has it that an engineer from Zurich, a certain Müller (German for miller, as it happens), had the idea of replacing millstones by metal rollers after a visit to his dentist. The dentist had told him how chewing cereals wore down the teeth and, to prevent this, he was going to strengthen them with metal.

Improved by another Swiss engineer, Jacob Sulzberger, this idea soon resulted in the creation of roller mills, first in Switzerland and then in Hungary. Patent—high-grade—Hungarian flour, which could be made into sublime cakes and Viennese pastries, was soon to become famous throughout the world. Roller mills then spread to the United States.

Finally came improvements of the wheat itself. Gregor Mendel, the botanist monk who founded the science of genetics, was to completely transform humanity's relationship with nature. His experiments into plant hybridization, which had begun in 1860, were applied to wheat during

A round loaf is the very image of good cheer and plenty. All over Europe, until the twentieth century, the large round quartern loaf (4 pounds) was the daily bread in the countryside. The French wheat loaf, prettily dusted with flour (above: Dinner at the Hospice de Beaune, by Joseph Bail); the dense German rye cob, baked in the village oven, with a few pretzels to delight the children (facing page:

Coming Home from the Baking Oven, by Hermann Sandermann, 1880). Below: a votive loaf made of gold, created by the goldsmith Cahier for the coronation of Charles X of France.

the first years of the twentieth century. For example, a new hybrid of wheat was grown in Sweden, where the cereal had never before been cultivated. Research into wheat hybrids that can withstand insects and inhospitable climates, as well as provide higher yields and superior baking qualities, has continued unabated.

The Quest for White Bread

Bread—or rather the lack of it—has played a preponderant role in twentieth-century history, particularly in the two world wars and during the major economic crises of the 1930s. In Europe, the First World War mobilized the rural workforce on all fronts and it was only thanks to massive grain imports from America that people were able to con-

tinue eating bread at all. Coming into the war on the side of the allies in 1917, the United States deprived Germany and Austria of wheat, thus precipitating the moral, political, and economic collapse of the two countries.

In the euphoria of the 1920s the French were to see the triumph of a delicious form of bread which was to ensure a worldwide reputation for French baking. This type of bread was the product of a new, so-called "direct" method of fermentation, which consisted in incorporating the yeast straight into the dough just before kneading. Less sour than leaven bread, easier to prepare than a dough with *poolisch*, what was initially termed *pain de fantaisie* (fancy bread) was first made by city bakers. It rapidly seduced consumers with its thin, crunchy crust, its light and spongy cream-colored crumb and its pleasant, wheaty taste. Bakers made it into long loaves of various sizes, which gradually became known by the names still in use today: *baguette* (stick), the shorter *bâtard* and thinner *ficelle* (string).

The terrible economic crisis of the 1930s again found bread high on the agenda, but for rather more somber reasons. In the larger cities of France, as in the rest of Europe and America, tens of thousands of unemployed people demonstrated in the streets, chanting a slogan which encapsulated their plight: "Work and bread!" There was no bread at all for the poorest and there was soon to be very little for anyone.

From 1935 onwards, Nazi Germany brooded over her revenge and the entire country retrenched itself into one vast encampment. Even before the war, one and a half million acres of good arable land were set aside and turned into military bases and parade grounds. A few months after the outbreak of war, millions of tons of wheat, stockpiled in Poland, Holland, Belgium and France, were seized and transported to Germany. The spectre of hunger then haunted occupied Europe. In France bread was already rationed by summer 1940: every Frenchman had the right to slightly more than 1 pound of bread per day. By October of the same year daily "bread tickets" had appeared, now worth only around 12 ounces. It was not long before the daily ration fell to around 9 ounces, and this just as the general shortage was giving bread added importance as a staple

Two forgotten sights: an itinerant bread vendor (above: photograph by Eugène Atget, Paris, c. 1900); kneading dough for homemade loaves (facing page: a farm in the Vosges region, 1934).

food. The grayish loaf provided, made from whole wheat mixed with substitute flour (milled from crops such as beans, rice, corn, barley and potatoes), was like chewing cardboard pap stuck with bran. In unoccupied but increasingly destitute England meanwhile, the "national loaf" was officially allowed to contain potato-flour from 1943.

To this day, most French people who lived through the Occupation cannot bring themselves to eat whole-wheat bread because one of their recurrent dreams during those dark days was of a return to white bread.

It was this dream which was to be realized by French bakers once peace was restored and wheat was in good supply. The end of the 1950s was marked by a whiter than white bread. A new "intensified" kneading technique in which bean flour was used as an additive, resulted in a snow-white loaf, thanks to excessive oxidation of the dough. This was a response to demand from consumers, who were convinced that whiteness was synonymous with quality, but it also suited the bakers as this new method reduced their workload. This method had a drawback, however: the crumb not only turned white, but also uneven in texture and tasteless into the bargain, while the almost translucent crust crumbled like a thin biscuit so that the loaf only kept for a few hours. Initially hoodwinked by appearances, consumers slowly saw the light, and ended up rejecting such

poor-quality bread. In the 1930s, when bread was good, a Frenchman consumed more than 1 pound a day; by 1970 the quantity had fallen to 7 ounces and to around 5½ ounces in 1980. The rising living standards of the period, which meant that bread lost its supremacy as a foodstuff, cannot alone explain this change.

The post-war years also saw the emergence of industrial bread. The increasing use of yeast and the development of kneading-machines in the 1920s had already promoted the growth of a new type of baking, no longer conceived of as a small-scale business but as an industry. As one might expect, this transformation initially took place in America, where the first "bread king," William W. Bard, had founded the Continental Baking Corporation, which, in entirely automated factories, each year turned six million metric tons of flour into bread. Reaching Europe just after the Second World War, the bread-making industry was aided by the advent of the supermarket. By the middle of the 1970s, factory-produced

bread was everywhere, glutted with preservatives, sliced and ready-packed. The introduction of the deep-freeze into bread production, transforming many bakeries into "baking terminals," where factory-prepared frozen dough was simply put in the oven, made the picture grimmer still.

Army bakeries were the first to mass-produce bread as they followed the troops on campaign. Facing page, above: French army bakers with "mobile ovens" during manoeuvres in 1892. It was only from the 1920s

Facing page, below: a bakery on Ellis Island in New York Harbor, 1923. Below: an industrial bakery in Germany.

Echoing similar tendencies in England and the United States, a reaction began in France in the 1970s. This was initiated by a few isolated artisans, and spurred on by the commercial dynasty founded by of one of their number, Lionel Poilâne, himself the son of a Parisian baker. His celebrated country loaf (*known as Pain Poilâne*), made in the traditional way but distributed by a network of hundreds of outlets throughout France, has revived, in the wake of a general

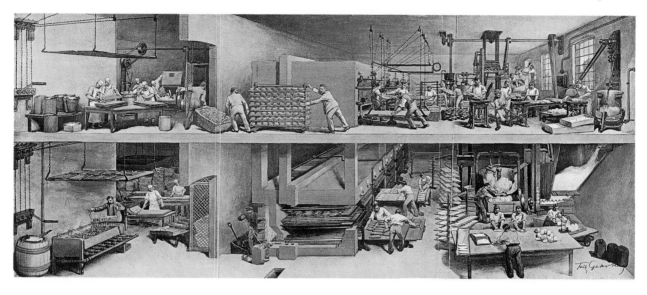

on that, under the impetus of influential entrepreneurs, large-scale industry took over bread making.

Below: a delivery truck from the bakery of the London department store Harrods, from the early years of the century.

enthusiasm for authentic and natural products, the age-old taste for good French bread. Numerous bakers, encouraged by a surge in demand, have rediscovered the advantages of wood-burning ovens, of natural leaven and of a dough kneaded less but fermented for longer. French bread, which has suffered such denigration for so long, has, for the last fifteen years, gradually been restored to its former glory.

A similar reaction has been going on in a number of other industrialized nations such as the United States, where a new-found enthusiasm for good bread has been much in evidence in the last ten years. But traditional bakers all over the world are faced with severe competition from industry and from supermarkets. Only those who are fired by a desire to produce really good bread can be sure of surviving. The renaissance is already in full swing and the image of the baker's trade is regaining its prestige. If this trend continues, the twenty-first century will at long last be the century of good bread for everyone.

From Sowing to Milling

"If pleasure-seeking town-dwellers only knew just how much work it takes to make their bread they would be horrified," wrote Voltaire in his Dictionnaire philosophique. *Arduous work and uncertain yields were for a long time the lot of every peasant. But the end of a good harvest was the opportunity for much rejoicing, enlivened by* the warmth and long days of summer. Facing page: Summer, *Jakob Philipp Hackert (1737–1807). Above:* Landscape with Wheat Threshers, *Niccolò dell'Abate (c. 1560). Right: an old peel belonging to an Italian artisan (nicknamed "Il Macinato," meaning "the milled"), adorned with a grain hopper and millstone.*

W hat Victor Hugo described as the "august gesture of the sower" disappeared long ago. For centuries it symbolized the agricultural way of life, that of men and women taming nature with courage and affection. Harvest festivals, with their religious rites and popular celebrations, drunkenness and dancing, are now but a distant memory. Only a few windmills and water wheels still turn today, the last remnants of a bygone age. Nowadays, the bread we eat—or more accurately the cereals which are its raw materials—are a product of scientific know-how exercised in a laboratory. The grain is then sown and harvested by complicated contraptions, before being milled for the most part in highly automated and computerized modern factories. Technology has forever replaced ancestral customs and expertise. From sowing through to milling, genetics, mechanics, electronics, physics, and chemistry have, in a single century, supplanted all the rudimentary tools which embodied the dignity of farm work. This dignity, however, was not without its share of suffering, hardship, and famine. For thousands of years, the quality and even the very presence of the bread on our tables was dependent on the caprices of the weather. The peasantry, as well as the poor in towns, were ever at the mercy of a severe winter, a dry spring, or an invasion of pests. At present, we are living in age of almost complete mastery over nature, even if people are still working to improve technology. Engineers, agriculturists, and millers not only make sure we get our daily bread, but also, together with the bakers, ensure that it is of high quality. They are in effect guardians of our eating pleasure.

Cereals: Our Daily Bread

Because its flour could be worked easily into a tasty, airy, white loaf, wheat has ousted all other cereals. Until the nineteenth century, however, it was also common to eat bread made from barley, corn, or rye (still the predominant cereal in Scandinavia). According to circumstances and the prevailing local traditions, these loaves might also contain oats, millet, or buckwheat, cereals more often reserved for animal feed. In fact, only wheat and rye flour can be made into worthwhile bread; the other grains lack the necessary baking qualities if left unblended.

The Search for a Perfect Wheat

Wheat is a plant from the grass family, the Gramineae, of the genus *Triticum*. As everyone knows, its hollow stalk—the straw or haulm in botany—terminates in a fine golden ear comprising the grains which are milled to produce flour. Two species, comprising some several thousand varieties, are grown today: common or "bread" wheat (*Triticum aestivum*), used in baking, and durum, used mainly for making pasta (*T. durum*).

Gathered since time immemorial, already cultivated in Asia Minor nine or ten thousand years ago, wheat, from its wild species to those of today, has undergone a number of radical changes through the kind of empirical selection that was already being alluded to by Virgil. At the end of the nineteenth century there appeared the very first hybrids, resulting from crossing local races better adapted to the prevailing soil and climate with others of higher yield. From the 1950s sophisticated genetic manipulations, in tandem with test tube cultures in the laboratory, further advanced research into ideal varieties. Consequently the oldest cultivated species—*T. emmer* of the ancients, *T. einkorn*, Abyssinian *T. spelt*—and all the other wheats which were turned into the earliest types of bread, have all vanished and are only distantly related to present-day varieties. Only spelt, commonplace right up until the First World War, still survives in parts of Europe

The symbolism of the harvest has often led to idealization. It was a major theme of Western art up until the twentieth century. Above: The Harvest, *by the Franco-Russian painter* Zinaida Serebriakova *(1884–1967). Facing page:* The Arrival of the Reapers in the Pontins Marshlands *(detail), Léopold Robert (1830).*

thanks to its nutritional qualities, which exceed even those of common wheat. It can be found mixed with other cereals in certain special breads concocted by bakers with a taste for things rustic. But such wheats suffer from the considerable handicap of not being machine-threshable.

Several dozen new strains of laboratory-grown common wheat appear each year. In France, around two hundred, developed for baking, are officially listed, the majority dating from the last twenty years. The more common cultivars have such poetic names as Soissons, Sidéral, Thésée (Theseus), or Scipion. The oldest French variety is one of the best: Florence-Aurore, developed in 1963. All over the world, research into new varieties has to respond to numerous different objectives, such as higher resistance (to disease, parasites, cold, drought, etc.), improved yield (since the beginning of century this has increased on average from around 13 to 55 U.S. bushels per acre) and, above all, good baking qualities, that is, a capacity to produce a flour and a dough which satisfies the bakers. These baking qualities are today laboratory-measured on a "trial milling" in accordance with a wide range of parameters: the solidity (or rather "tenacity") of the dough; its elasticity (or workability); its rising properties; and its gluten and protein content. Hence our wheat, and in consequence our bread, is nowadays fostered by scientists in white coats—biologists, agronomists, biochemists and geneticists—using complex procedures.

Facing page: summer in the Gers, Gascogne, when on the hillsides flows what Victor Hugo called, in Odes et Ballades, *"the golden flood of the yellow harvest." The golden color of ripe wheat is also that of a good loaf.*

Working in the fields. What began in a test tube must end up sooner or later in the fields. Wheat grows phenomenally well in temperate climates. Around –10°C (18°F), it begins to suffer and freezes at about –16°C (4°F). It favors snow, which offers it protection in winter, but extreme heat can scald and wither the kernel, preventing ripening. It does not need much water, but requires rich, clay or silty soils. Whoever has seen the earth of Brie or Beauce in France newly tilled knows the kind of deep and buttery soil in which wheat thrives. Such conditions are to be found in a number of countries, including China, the United States, the countries of the former USSR, India, and France; these five main producers alone provide two thirds of the world's yearly wheat yield of more than a billion metric tons.

"That morning, Jean, holding open with his left hand the pocket of the blue canvas seed-bag tied over his stomach, took a handful of seed every three strides with his right and, in single, fluent gesture, cast it. As his body swung smoothly, his big shoes kicked divets out of the fat earth . . . Alone, onward he marched, as if growing taller." This dance of the sower, here captured so vividly by Émile Zola in his novel *La Terre* (Earth), has been performed across our landscapes since antiquity. What remains of the way people used to work in the fields? Just a few traces (and not for many more years) on some forgotten plots sheltered from the effects of modernization. In parts of the Turkish or Spanish countryside, some farmers still use the ancient *tribulum*, a plank stuck with flints or metal rollers dragged over the scythed wheat to detach the grain from the ears. Like the scythes and sickles used for harvesting, the flails for threshing the grain, and the winnows or fanners to separate the grain from the chaff, these *tribula* are today displayed in museums or else stand in antique shops. The hard and sometimes fruitless toil represented by these tools is only a memory.

The present-day farmer is essentially a driver of various kinds of machines. Except at harvest time, he is always to be seen at work seated on his tractor. His first task is to prepare the soil before sowing in winter or spring, depending on the variety. The field is first weeded, then turned over by plowing, broken up with a harrow, and

At Brouckerque, in French Flanders, harvest festivals are celebrated in the traditional way; everyone wears old-time costume, the sheaves are tied as of old, and the antiquated thresher is once more pressed into service.

The grain, however, has changed: the oldest varieties presently in use were born in laboratories during the 1960s. Each year new ones appear, ever more resistant, of higher yield, and of improved baking quality. But the farmer who weighs the seed in his hand and rubs it between his palms, making it glisten in the sun, expresses, through gestures as old as time, an ever-lasting love of the soil.

enriched with fertilizer. In France, sowing of the winter wheat begins in October, using a seeder which drops the seeds into the furrows. Between November and January, the farmer lovingly nurtures its first leaves, fragile shoots at the mercy of weeds and insects, and sprays them with weed-killer and pesticides. Of course, such chemical treatment of wheat is proscribed by so-called "organic" farming, and is replaced by other methods such as hoeing, vegetal insecticides, and organic fertilizer. From February to April, several secondary shoots—tillers—appear at the base of the wheat stalk. Before being harvested, the wheat will "rise," that is grow, and then, around the end of May, it will "ear," each ear containing about fifty grains. In the spring months fertilizer will again be applied to the fields.

In temperate Europe, wheat is ripe by July. The standing stalk bends under the weight of the full, silky ears and the golden fields shimmer in waves under the summer sun. This beautiful sight, an eternal symbol of the abundance of nature, is seen in January in Argentina and Australia, February in India and Brazil, May in China and Texas, mid-July in the American Midwest and southern England, August in Sweden and northern England, and October in Russia. The farmers check the ripeness of the wheat by its color, and often by chewing a few grains, which should be dry and crunchy. To be surer still, measurements are taken in a laboratory of the wheat's relative humidity, which should not exceed 15 percent. Reaping begins to the sound of combines. These extremely sophisticated machines head the wheat, thresh it to separate the grain from the straw and shoot the grain into a box-wagon, while another machine is towed behind to pick up the straw and bind it into bales. All this is done with a speed and efficiency that would have astonished the peasants of the past.

A treasure trove in a grain of wheat. Except for water, salt and the optional yeast, everything which goes to make bread is contained in the *Triticum* seed, the wheat grain. This minute fruit measures around 1/4 inch long and is of varying color—from a pale gold to ochre or reddish-brown—depending on the variety. If one wants

52

to know exactly what bread is made of, one has to prise open this tiny fruit: but how? Its creased casing is so tough that the seed has to be crushed to reveal its secrets. In fact, the husk is comprised of a series of very strong cellulose envelopes, known collectively as bran, which cannot be absorbed by the human body. It comprises between 13 and 16 percent of the total weight of the grain. Highly prized for its digestive properties, it is only to be found in whole-wheat bread or added to "bran" loaves. The admirable protection afforded by it, however, has a purpose. The capsule harbors a real treasure trove: a creamy-white, floury kernel, comprised of tiny grains of starch contained in a kind of natural protein cement, the gluten. It is the latter that gives the dough elasticity and imparts taste and lightness to the bread.

Crammed with energy and low in fat, the kernel supplies our bodies with easily absorbed monosaccharides. Crushed to produce flour, it represents around 85 percent of the weight of the grain. There remains the germ,

a plant-embryo, which, when it is sown again, will produce another grain. Wheat germ (only about 2 percent of the weight of the grain) is so extraordinarily beneficial to human health that it is even sold separately. It contains a concentrated cocktail of vitamins (B and E), seasoned with mineral salts, protein, and the healthiest fatty acids. The flour which goes to make whole wheat and some other high-quality breads includes this germ, giving the bread a delicious flavor of hazelnut.

Rye: the cold climate cereal. Apart from wheat, rye is the only cereal that is readily made into good bread. Its quality, however, as attested by the words of this peasant from northern France around 1830, was not always to be envied: "We used to eat bread as black as pitch, and gritty, as if it contained a good handful of sand from the river. It was made of unsifted, milled rye; the whole husk was mixed with the meal, as this was supposed to be more nourishing." For a long time, rye, which cost half as much as wheat flour, was the base of a number of "black breads" among the peasantry. Bread was also often made from masnil, the rye/wheat blend sown and harvested in the same field.

Prospering at high altitudes and low temperatures (even as a shoot it can endure –20°C) and in dry climates, rye, *Secale cereale*, thrives where wheat could not possibly do so. Rye is an ascetic; it prefers acid, thin soil, and, during sowing in September or October, it should be dry too. "Sow wheat in dirt [soil], and rye in dust," an old proverb goes. So rye is cultivated throughout northern Europe, from northern France to Scandinavia, passing through Germany (the major Western European producer, with more than six million metric tons per year), and in Poland, Russia, and in some regions of North America and Asia. World production does not exceed fifty million metric tons, however, and declines annually.

Rye is harvested in July and August. Essentially the same size, though narrower than a grain of wheat, the rye grain, which can be anything from light brown to bronze in color, cannot furnish all the gluten required to make a soft, light, but firm loaf. The all-rye loaves consumed in Scandinavia and Germany, though delicious, are extremely dense. In France, where preference is for a more airy crumb, "rye" bread also incorporates up to 35 percent wheat flour, though all the slightly sour, mineral flavor of the rye can still be appreciated.

A bouquet of cereals. Nowadays, no other cereal is transformed, unblended, into bread. From earliest antiquity to the dawn of the twentieth century, cereals still more

Facing page: the stars of mills and bakeries—wheat (left) and rye (right)—united in a field in Beauce, before being brought together again at the mill to produce traditional maslin flour. In his Journal du voleur, *Jean Genet spoke of "a field of ripe rye, the blondness of which was that of the hair of Polish youths." Right: wheat, rye, barley, and oats.*

deficient in gluten than rye, such as barley, millet, corn, oats, and buckwheat, were used in the preparation of heavy, rustic loaves intended for the poor. With the arrival of wheat for all, these coarse loaves were at length discarded. The cereals themselves, however, mostly blended and incorporated into wheat flour, still go to make up a number of specialty breads.

Corn, Christopher Columbus noted in his journal for 5 November 1492, "tastes good and all the inhabitants of this country live on it." This traditional food of the indigenous peoples of pre-Columbian America was imported into Europe and cultivated from the sixteenth century, before reaching Asia and Africa. Requiring high temperatures and much sunshine, corn in Europe spread mainly to the Iberian peninsula, Italy, Crete, Turkey, and southern France (where it was known as *blé turc*, "Turkish

54

wheat"). Genetically-controlled improvements gradually enabled it to be introduced into cooler climates, such as northern France, where it is today an important crop. Its many qualities, and above all its high starch content, have made it, in a natural or prepared state, into a favorite food of endless variety: simply cooked or boiled (Italian polenta, the *mamaliga* of Rumania) in fritters (*cruchades* in southwest France), as cornflakes and popcorn, in flat cakes or corn bread, in pancakes (Mexican *tortillas*, eaten as bread, but made with unfermented corn flour), not forgetting bourbon and hominy grits, as well as certain types of beer. Corn does unfortunately suffer from a serious drawback, however; its low gluten content makes it difficult to turn into proper loaves. Sometimes during times of hardship there was no choice but to eat it, as was particularly the case in France during the last war. A tradition of cornmeal bread has grown up nonetheless in a number of countries (Portugal and the southern United

States, for example), where the yellow crumb, if the meal is blended with wheat flour by an expert baker, can delight even the most discriminating of palates.

"As rough as barley bread," a French saying used to go, referring to a bread which, according to the Bible, fed the Five Thousand. Barley, the hardiest of all cereals which can be cultivated in almost any climate (it is found in the Arabian peninsula as well as 13,000 feet high in the foothills of the Himalayas), is today employed far more in brewing and for animal feed than in baking. Added in small quantities to wheat or rye flour, it can impart a distinctive, slightly bitter, and somewhat wild flavor.

Millet, perhaps the earliest cereal consumed by man in tropical regions, is particularly rich in magnesium and gives bread a slightly acid note. Oats, a cereal set aside for horse feed since earliest times, would have disappeared as a food without the Anglo-Saxon love of porridge—oat flakes boiled in milk or water. This would have been a pity, since the "swish" of fields of ripe oats when the wind blows is one of the most attractive and musical sounds in the vegetable kingdom, like paper rustling. It is cultivated for the most part in northern Europe, where, above all as porridge, it was the staple diet until the end of the Middle Ages. Extremely rich in energy and a stimulant, oats are ideal for combating the cold and bread baked from them can serve as a winter warmer.

Buckwheat (or "Saracen corn") has also practically vanished. One has to comb the countryside of central Europe, or countries such as Canada, China, and Japan to catch a glimpse of the marvelous sight of buckwheat fields in flower, studded with tiny white and pink blossoms. The grain, on the other hand, is blackish, hence its French common name, *blé noir* (black wheat). Once the husk is removed, however, the flour can be milled very white and can be used to make succulent pancakes, drop scones, or gruel. Buckwheat, thanks to its high phosphorus content, can transform bread into a food that increases brain power.

A number of bakeries today offer a wide range of multigrain breads. "Five-grain" is a Swiss specialty composed of wheat and rye, together with three other cereals such as spelt, barley, oats, buckwheat, or millet. Some bakers, however, go further to create even more refined mixtures. The Swiss bread known as *sako* comprises wheat and rye flour, oatmeal, soya meal, linseed, and sesame, pumpkin, and sunflower seeds. Jean Jeudon, a baker on the rue de Ménilmontant in Paris, offers a wheat-flour loaf which also contains rye, oats, rice, barley, sunflower seeds, and cottonseed, sprinkled with sesame seeds—in all, eight different ingredients.

The mills of old. "The people got into the habit of sending their wheat to the big mills and the poor windmills were starved of work . . . The age of windmills was over, like that of bells on the Rhône, regional *parlements* and flowery frock coats." In "Le secret de maître Cornille," one of the most famous stories from his collection *Lettres de mon moulin*, Alphonse Daudet evoked in 1866 the sorry state of local millers in competition with modern milling methods. "Deranged by his plight," the poor miller

Facing page: on the little island of Karpathos in Greece, whose terracing forestalls all mechanization, the women still harvest wheat with a sickle.

Above and below: in France wheat is ripe in June. The character of the wheat— depending on variety, climate, and soil—influences the color and flavor of the bread it goes to make.

Cornille could not bear to see himself fallen so low and let the empty grindstones run on, loading sacks of white dust on his donkey to keep the pretense alive. A century later and Cornille the miller, less pathetic it is true, is still with us. To my knowledge, no French baker is still making his bread entirely from flour produced by a mill powered solely by wind or water. There exists, however, a water mill where bread from its flour is made and sold, the Bassilour mill, at Bidart, in the French Basque country. There are also a few bakers in the Maine-et-Loire who use the glorious flour from the Moulin du Rat in Challain-la-Potherie, but this mill runs on electricity when the wind

"Beware," replied Sancho, "what we can see over there are not giants but windmills, and what looks like arms to you are the sails, which, turned by the wind, themselves push round the millstone." (Cervantes, Don Quixote).

Windmills have always fired the imagination of artists. Above: section through a windmill. Facing page: Windmills in Normandy, *Richard Parkes Bonington (1802–1828).*

drops. The few dozen paddles and vanes that are still turning are only kept alive by people who love the mills of old. They are often owned by local councils or else by associations, and their fine old machinery clanks into action a few Sundays every summer for wide-eyed visitors, who leave clutching little packets of freshly milled flour. The majority of old mills survive only as treasures of the national heritage and have been transformed into museums. It is for this reason all the more gratifying to come across a real working mill, situated at a bend in a country lane, which the enthusiasm of a single miller keeps turning. I have met with a few in the Beauce region (the "breadbasket of France" to the southwest of Paris), that "ocean of wheat" as the poet Charles Péguy described it.

It is worth visiting Beauce in summer, just before the harvest, to admire the beauty of the sunsets on the immense, gold-bedecked plain. You are also sure to see a few windmills standing out on the horizon. The reason for their presence here is obvious enough: on this endless plain there may be only a few slow-moving rivers, but nothing stands in the way of the wind. Beauce, a land of wind, a land of wheat, was also once one of windmills; there were five hundred of them at the beginning of this century. Since then, many have been abandoned and left to fall into ruin. Some continued to mill grain for animal feed, while others ground enough wheat for the miller's personal needs. Only about ten still turn today, and most of those do so only very occasionally for demonstration purposes. The Chesnay mill, standing in the middle of fields some distance outside the village of Moutiers, between Chartres and Orléans, has been luckier. Here, Edgar Barbier, the son of a professional miller and a miller himself for the love of it (he earns his livelihood as a builder), works his mill whenever he can, whenever there is enough wind. He produces a whole-wheat flour, which he supplies to the local farms for their animals, and, more occasionally, a less coarse flour which he gives to his friends or his wife, who makes pancakes with it. Not surprisingly, such an enterprise is not economically viable and does not even cover the running costs of the mill itself. But Edgar Barbier looks after the mill

Right: the sails of the mill at Saint-Pierre, Fontvieille, in the south of France, have not turned since 1915. Today it is the Musée Alphonse Daudet.
In Lettres de mon moulin, *Daudet tenderly and humorously evoked the dignity and demise of the ordinary artisan millers.*
Below: section through a water mill (c. 1780). France at one

time had hundreds of working water mills and windmills; only a few dozen still grind grain today.
Facing page: a miller at work in Casalta, Corsica. From the hopper, the grain falls into the millstones.

carefully, repairing and restoring it; the sails and the millstones must turn, whatever the cost, because a mill which does not turn soon dies.

The magnificent windmill at Chesnay was built in 1788, on the site of an older mill, some of the timbers from which were reused (one piece carries the date 1770). It is a perfect example of a post ("German") mill, which is different from the tower ("Dutch") mill. The former is comprised of a wooden framework mounted on a well-braced wooden post, which is socketed into a horizontal beam located on the second floor of the mill. The sails can thus be turned around a vertical axis to face the wind. The second type, developed later, is a stone- or brick-built tower, housing the stones and gearing, which has a movable top, or "cap," to which the sails are fixed. The top can be swiveled on a track or curb. The earliest illustration of a tower mill dates from around 1420. Both types were turned by means of a long tailpole, which reached right down to the ground outside the mill. The automatic fantail, invented in England in 1745 by Edmund Lee, made life easier for the miller. It has a set of five to eight smaller vanes which are mounted on a tailpole of a post mill at right angles to the sails. The vanes are connected by gearing to wheels running along a track around the mill, so that when the wind strikes the vanes and makes them move the wheels turn as well, rotating the mill until the sails are facing the wind again.

There were further refinements over the centuries, such as the spring sails invented by, Andrew Meikle in 1772. He replaced the sails with hinged shutters which could be controlled by a connecting bar. The spring could thus be adjusted to the power required. In 1789, in England, Stephen Hooper replaced the shutters with roller blinds and invented a remote control making it possible to adjust the blinds simultaneously while the mill was in operation. In 1854, in the United States, Daniel Halladay created the annular-sailed wind pump, which, although inefficient, was popular for its cheapness and reliability. It consists of a number of small vanes set radially in a wheel. The pump is totally automatic, thanks to the tail vane and the off-center position of the wheel; as the wind increases

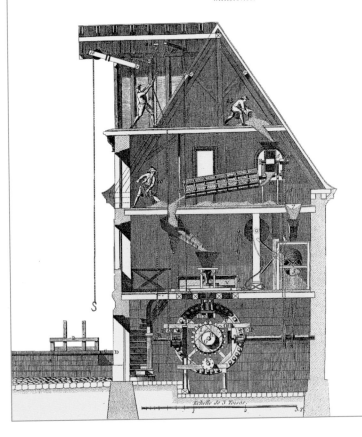

Traditional millstone grinding produces a creamier flour, and a richer and more flavorful bread than that milled between modern steel rollers. Above: an old mill in Périgord.
Facing page: the windmill at Chesnay, in the Beauce region.
Right: a 50-kilo (over 100 pounds) flour sack. Following double page: these "flour strong men" in The Flour Porters *(Louis Carrier-Belleuse, 1885) used to lift sacks of 24 bushels (around 350 pounds). The 50-kilo sack only made its appearance in 1922.*

in strength the mill rotates on the vertical axis, thereby reducing the effective area and, as a result, speed.

Edgar Barbier rotates his mill by turning a crank. There is a breeze and the sails are turning quietly. The mill is entered by climbing a small, wooden stairway. At the top one breathes in the fresh flour, which here, rather strangely, brings to mind the aroma of apples. A fine white dust hovers in a ray of sunlight; it has a poetic name in French, the *envolage*, or "beeswing" as it is sometimes known in English. The dust accounts for a difference of about 2 percent between the weight of the grain on arrival and that of the whole-wheat flour. Through this milky, gossamer cloud—which is also found in the bakery and which Lionel Poilâne calls "flour air"—we can make out the two grindstones, the mechanism of the mill, some hemp ropes lying on the floor, and, hanging on the wall of wooden planks, metal dressing hammers which are used to furrow the millstones when they needed sharpening.

And the mill sings, its stones keening as they turn. The song is accompanied by the regular beat of a short length of wood on the first floor, which, as it moves, allows the grist to pour out of the hopper and onto the millstones. This is an ancient song, unchanged through the centuries, as here all works as it did before the industrial era, by no power other than that of the wind.

What strikes one above all in a windmill is the extreme simplicity of the wooden mechanism, which forms an unbroken chain from the sails to the stones. Here, in Beauce, the sails are not the same as those on Greek, Dutch, or Spanish windmills; they are wooden shutters designed to simplify the task of the miller, who can veer them without leaving the mill by using a striking lever called the *araignée* (spider). One can only see these vanes in the regions of Beauce, Charente, in the Loire Valley, and in the Vendée, and nowhere else in the world. The vanes turn the huge oak wind shaft, which lies set across the entire upper floor. Onto this is mounted a great spur gear almost 7 feet in diameter that rotates a pinion, known as the *rouet* (referred to as a "wallower" in English), which, by turning the vertical iron spindle (sometimes known as the "quant"), spins the upper millstone (the "runner"). The lower stone (the "bedder" or "bed stone") does not turn at all. The rotating iron spindle also sets in motion the slat of wood in the hopper which lets the grist funnel into the hole (the "eye") in the middle of the runner. This is how the grain, crushed between the set of stones, turns into flour, which is then channeled to the floor below and into a tun or a sack. The whole wheat is packed up as it is. To obtain a finer flour, Edgar Barbier simply bolts it by hand in a silk sieve to sift out the bran.

"Meunier tu dors, ton moulin va trop vite" (Miller, you're asleep, your mill's turning too fast), says the old French song. A seventeenth-century English proverb echoes the sentiment: "In vain does the mill clack, if the

Louis CARRIER-BeLLeuse

miller his hearing lack." Vigilance is indeed the essential quality of the miller. He continually has to regulate the speed of the runner; if it races, it might heat up the stone and jeopardize the quality of the flour. Above all, he must make quite sure that the stone never turns when the hopper is empty as the resulting heat could set the entire mill ablaze. Hence, a little device was installed which would ring a bell to wake up the sleeping miller whenever the stones lacked grist. At Moutiers, however, the windmill goes to sleep before the miller. At sunset, Edgar Barbier immobilizes the sails and everything stops—the song of the stones and the "beeswing" of flour in the air. There is not even any light, because the mill at Chesnay is without electricity.

The Secrets of Great Flour

When, at the beginning of the century, the mill at Chesnay was turning every day there was wind, it would grind about 165 metric tons of flour a year. The large industrial

Facing page: some of the cereals used in baking. From left to right and top to bottom: sunflower seeds; brown linseed; whole-grain buckwheat; yellow linseed; durum; rye; organic wheat; sesame seed; bread wheat; millet; spelt. Only wheat, spelt, and rye can be made into loaves unblended. Other cereals may be composed into multigrain flours. Below: the triumph of American industrial milling.

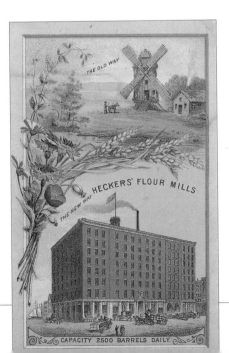

mills of today produce ordinarily 220 tons a day. One of the world's best flours, however, is the result of a happy medium, a mill of human scale (a workforce of thirteen), where 16 to 17 tons per day are bagged. A mile or so from Meaux, to the northeast of Paris, in the little village of Précy-sur-Marne, the Decollogne-Lococq mill grinds rye and wheat for the kings of French baking: Jean Jeudon, Basile Kamir, Max Poilâne, Jean-Luc Poujauran, and for several famous chefs who make their own bread, such as Joël Rebuchon, Alain Sanderens (Lucas-Carton, Paris), and Alain Ducasse (at the Hôtel de Paris in Monaco). That such sublime loaves are all made from a raw material that comes from the same mill tells us clearly enough that there can be no good bread without first-rate flour, however skillful the baker may be.

One day, to get to the bottom of the mystery of this extraordinary flour, I knocked on the door of the mill. It is utterly different from a little windmill and still more so from the vast factories which produce commonplace flour. Since 1926, the Lecocq firm of millers (in association with the Decollogne millers since 1974) have been based in a fine old farm. One can still recognize the farmhouse in the middle (it has been turned into offices), and the range of barns and the stables which today house the laboratories and the machinery. Guy Derécourt welcomed me and showed me around the property. He is the great-grandson of a miller and runs the company with the assistance of the Lecocqs, father and son: Pierre, the father, is the company's technical director; Pascal, the son, has designed and supervises the automation of the plant (the mill also functions at night, without personnel, an alarm ringing in the event of a mishap).

Guy Derécourt took me first to the "laboratory." It was a small room on the first floor reached by climbing a wide and magnificent wooden staircase. Here we encountered the first secret of fine flour: selecting the grains. To ensure that the quality of the finished product is consistently good, all millers blend different wheat varieties. No flour is the result of milling one single variety, and here the selection of the various wheats is stringent to the extreme. The company deals only with the best producers, for the most part

Right: the raising of the "runner," the top stone, weighing more than 2 tons, to dress, that is sharpen, the worn stone. The stone-dressers used to have their own guild, all the more respected as the task, performed in a thick cloud of stone dust, was bad for the health. The best millstone came from a quarry at Ferté-sous-Jouarre in Seine-et-Marne, which has unfortunately closed down. The millstones hewn from this stone were exported the world over.

Facing page: an operation which requires much experience and a high degree of exactitude—checking the various grades of milling (here, master miller Xavier Maurice at the Giraud mills, in the Vaucluse).
Preceding double page: different kinds of flour. 1. organic wheat; 2. and 3. wheat; 4. corn; 5. whole wheat; 6. malted wheat; 7. oats; 8., 13. and 15. multigrain 9. buckwheat; 10. rye; 11. durum semolina; 12. light rye mix; 14. barley; 16. spelt.

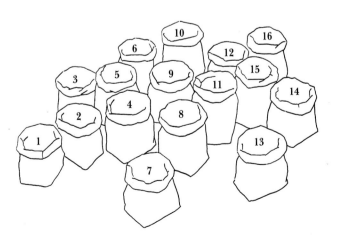

practitioners of organic farming who do not use chemical fertilizer or pesticides. Such farmers are no longer to be found in the Beauce itself (where the water table is already very polluted), but in the Loire Valley, in the Côte-d'Or in Burgundy, and in the Vaucluse to the east of Avignon. The mill receives small lots of grist from each of them which are analyzed in the laboratory with an infrared apparatus so as to assess their quality with respect to certain parameters, such as humidity level and protein content. Using these analyses, the miller then decides with which mixture of grain he is going to produce his flour. Once the mixture is prepared, he checks the quality of the final output by carefully analyzing a trial milling.

The selected grain ordered from the farmers then arrives at the mill, where it is stored in immense silos. These silos hold the second secret of good flour. Here, the grain is stored without pesticides, which might impair quality. To avoid any degradation, ventilation is continuous. The grist is cleaned meticulously in a series of machines: it is first brushed, then passed through a magnetic field to extract all metal particles, and finally washed thoroughly in fresh water. It is then left to settle in the silo for forty-eight hours. When it has restabilized to the ideal moisture level (around 15 percent) it is ready to be milled.

The third, and final, important secret of Decollogne-Lecocq flour lies in the traditional millstone grinding. Today's ordinary flours are obtained from roller milling, a process invented in the nineteenth century: the grain is crushed between large, steel-ribbed rollers rotating in opposite directions. The system has many advantages but one drawback. Unlike grindstones, rollers do not wear, removing the kernel from the husk quite impeccably. But they also separate and expel the germ. For the majority of millers, this ensures better storage as the germ oil often makes the flour spoil more quickly. For others, however, like the Lecocqs, it is a disadvantage, as the germ represents the jewel of the wheat grain. Millstones crush the germ as well; the shelf life of the flour is reduced, but every drop of flavor and nutrition is extracted.

Guy Derécourt then took me to see the millhouse. As in a windmill the air is full of flour dust, but the sound is no longer a soft sing-song but rather the din of electrical turbines and scraping stones. Eight pairs of stones of varying size turn at a speed of about two revolutions a second. Since the death of the last French millstone-maker, who worked not far from Précy, at Ferté-sous-Jouarre, replacing them has posed a problem. A millstone lasts on average forty years. At Précy the oldest are about fifteen, and Guy Derécourt occasionally unearths workable examples in old mills. Pascal Lecocq dresses them every six weeks by hand with a hammer. It is a long and exhausting process; the running stone (which weighs around two tons) has to be raised and moved, and then furrowed with a dressing hammer for several hours in a thick cloud of stone dust.

To be turned into finer flour, the grain passes through eight pairs of millstones, each placed closer together than the last. After each grinding, the grist is drawn by pneumatic duct into a plan-sifter installed on the floor above. Invented in Hungary in 1887, this machine is a screen serving to sift the millings and is found in all modern mills. Hanging from the ceiling and revolving in a horizontal plane, it comprises any number of differently gauged screens placed one on top of the other (in Précy there are ninety-six). The more or less finely milled stock from the sifting then finds its way back to a pair of closer-set stones, again through a pneumatic duct. At the end of the treatment, the fraction milled by the eighth set of stones can go through the finest screen, made of pure silk. If whole-wheat flour is required, containing the germ and bran, the whole grain is milled in this way. For white or grayish brown flour, the larger bran particles extracted by the coarser screens are jettisoned.

The same process is followed in roller mills; the steel cylinders are set progressively closer together and the grooves are progressively thinner (the last pair are entirely smooth). Decollogne-Lecocq possesses six such pairs, each equipped with their own plan-sifter. Occupying another part of the installation, they furnish non-organic flour, which represents at most 20 percent of the mill's total output; their specialty remains organic flour. Guy Derécourt proudly show me this marvelous flour, inviting me to take some in my hand and smell it. The

milling has preserved the germ and crushed its oils into the flour, hence its creamy color and its fattiness. Indeed, it is of such a delicious unctuosity that I can, by pressing it into my palm, make it into a tight little ball. The germ also accounts for the subtle aroma of hazelnut emanating from it, an aroma we also find in the bread of the finest bakers.

The Decollogne-Lecocq mills produce only wheat and rye flour. Other, larger firms also provide buckwheat, barley, millet, oat, or ready-to-use blended flours. All these flours—after being left to stand before bagging so they are not, as bakers say, "hot off the mill"—are delivered to the bakery in sacks of around 220 pounds. There they will be transformed into bread. The flour, no matter how sublime it may be, cannot alone ensure the excellence of the bread. That requires an unfailing instinct, an expertise and a love of a job well done; in other words, the flour needs a good baker.

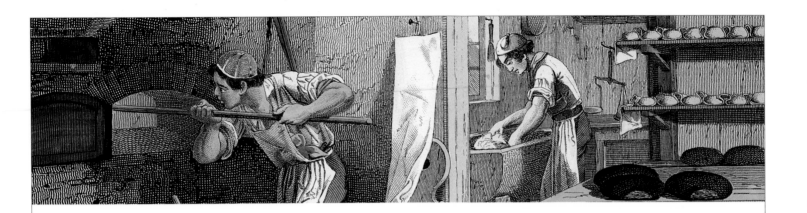

The Baker's Art

Even since the advent of machinery, the atmosphere inside a bakery has not changed since the beginning of history: the heat from the oven, the aromas of flour, yeast, and dough, the baker's hard-working fervor . . . not forgetting that little night music evoked by Arthur Rimbaud: "And when, as midnight sounds, / Shaped,

crackling and yellow, / The bread is taken out, / When, beneath smoke-clad beams, / Scented crusts sing, / And the crickets . . ." (Les Éffarés). Facing page: The Bakery, Helena Sofia Schjerfbeck (1862–1946).

Top: Colored engraving (c. 1870) showing bakers at work. Above right: a sign from a bakery in Lyon.

The French have a saying "Bon comme le bon pain" (literally, good like good bread), and it is particularly true of good bakers. I recommend that the bread-lover verify the truth of this statement one day by asking to be allowed to visit the place where the bread is actually baked. You will probably be taken down a staircase which leads to the holy of holies, a mysterious but still homey place where your bread is born. With each step towards the heat, the smell of the oldest scent known to man, that of hot bread, becomes more intense. The warmth, however, does not come only from the ovens, but also from the welcome you will receive: a good family baker is proud of his work and is always more than ready to show it. Once in the warmth of the bakery, among the mingling aromas of hot bread, flour and leaven, you will be astonished by the baker's skill even before you taste his bread.

Right: a French bakery ledger dating from 1934, inscribed with the name of the customer, where his purchases on credit payable at the end of the month were noted. The accounts were usually kept by the baker's wife. Why is it that the same flour from the same mill does not always give the same dough or the same bread from one day to the next? And why, with the same leaven, does the second batch rise slower than the first? The baker, constantly confronted by mysteries of this kind, has to be meticulous: he softly fingers the flour,

strokes the leaven, presses the dough between his fingers the better to get to know the living substance he is to shape. Below and facing page: these photographs were taken in 1933 and 1934.

Perfect Dough

To create a good, smooth dough by kneading a mixture of flour, leaven (or yeast), salt and water, is the baker's first task. This used to be very arduous work indeed and nowadays no baker does it by hand. To work 200 pounds or more of dough daily was akin to an athletic feat, and so bakers welcomed kneading-machines, as they also produced better results—something which is not true of other machines invented since.

Old kneaders whose hands still work the dough survive to this day in some of the very few villages in France where a communal bakery still operates. At Montvernier in the Maurienne valley, a tiny village perched 3,000 feet up in the French Alps, the inhabitants still make their own bread every three weeks, baking it in a wood-burning oven built into the foundations of the village hall. The tradition has survived solely thanks to a love of good bread, of dense loaves full of flavor, and those crispy flat breads called *cressenes* that French children love so much. Naturally, each individual family kneads the dough by hand and the batch delivered has to be large enough to last three weeks. Georges Balcaen, an alert seventy-year-old who drinks his own wine and eats his own fruit and vegetables, has been making his own bread too for at least half a century. His old wooden kneading trough is kept in a shed next to the chalet. Outside, in his shirt sleeves, he transforms 35 pounds of white flour, around 2 gallons of water, more than 2 pounds of leaven (sourdough from the previous batch stored under a layer of coarse sea salt in an earthenware vessel), and three and a half handfuls of curing salt into dough.

The effort required for these quantities is considerable, although they are insignificant compared to those worked every day by bakers in the past. Leaning over the trough, keeping up the same rhythm for more than half an hour, his gestures precise and energetic, Georges Balcaen's breathing is audible as he works. Having made a hollow in the center of the flour and poured in the water and the salt, all the ingredients are mixed for a long time during the first kneading. The dough is then divided into

pieces, which are thrown hard against the far side of the trough (just like "knocking back" in a bakery). Each one is then taken and pulled upwards several times and folded back on itself to give it some air (the "stretching" and "folding" stages), until a unified, smooth dough is formed which is neither too firm nor too soft, sticking neither to the sides of the kneading trough nor to the hands. After ten minutes of such exertion, Georges Balcaen's face has turned purplish and he is wiping the

drops of sweat on his forehead with his shirt sleeves. In bygone days, the "dough-boys"—assistants whose principal task it was to knead the dough—would let their sweat drop into the dough; the nitrogenous matter helped activate the leaven and would impart an inimitable taste to the bread.

Today, the best bakers obtain even their finest dough through the use of kneading-machines. Where formerly it took a man's hands, now electrically-powered metal arms

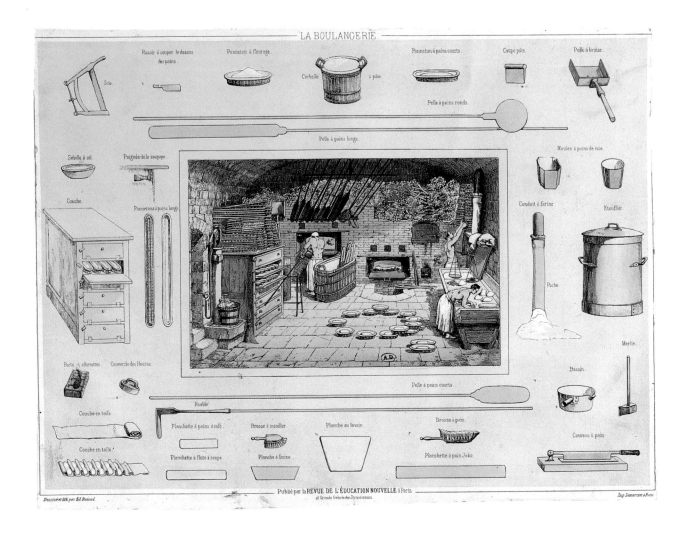

Kneading, weighing, shaping, rising, and baking: whether in a small-scale bakery or in a factory, the five steps leading from flour to bread are the same. There exist numerous middle ways between the artisan who does everything by hand (save the kneading) and the factory where only machines are seen at work. But all great bakers say the same thing: the fewer machines there are in a bakery, the better the bread.

knead the four basic ingredients together in a large basin. There exists a wide range of machines, each transmitting a different type of motion to the arms, and every baker defends his own model. Only Bernard Ganachaud—a baking genius, the inventor of the delicious *baguette* called the *flûte Gana*—has not bought his machine ready-made; helped by a wrought-iron craftsman, he spent two years developing a special kneader with slanting rods.

There are not only many types of kneading-machine but also many methods of kneading. The first mechanical dough mixer was invented in ancient Greece and consisted of a large stone basin in which wooden paddles, powered by a horse or donkey walking in circles, kneaded the dough mixture. More recently, in the 1960s, a method of high-speed and sustained kneading became common which greatly oxygenated the dough. This method artificially increases the "stiffness" of the dough, that is its capacity to retain the carbon dioxide resulting from fermentation, and hence makes for a more substantial loaf. By destroying the pigments in the flour, this method also produces the extremely white crumb that is preferred by the majority of consumers. However, such rapid kneading also reduces, or even eliminates entirely, the initial "proofing" stage intended to enhance the strength of the dough but also to give taste to the bread. The result of this practice is all too obvious today: a bulky, but insipid and lighter-than-air loaf, with a crumb of immaculate whiteness but no consistency, and with a crust so thin that within two hours the loaf is stale. If there is one golden rule with which all bakers would agree, it is the need for a slow and not excessive period of kneading—around fifteen minutes. The bread is less white and of reduced volume, certainly, but the crumb is denser and tastier while the thicker crust lengthens shelf-life. When it is ready, the dough has a silky sheen and is thrown around the mixing bowl in one piece, stretching elastically without breaking.

If the kneading-machine has considerably improved the baker's task, it has not removed the need for careful control. The dosing of the ingredients (above all the amount of water, which can vary greatly depending on the quantity of flour), the temperature of the dough (maintained by the temperature of the water to around 25°C,

no matter how hot it is in the bakery), and its stiffness (which can be regulated throughout kneading by adding either water or flour)—all these present a vast array of problems to be resolved, of decisions to be made. And everything has to be done speedily; there can be no slacking in a bakery, and the very finest bakers are those who solve all the riddles without thinking twice, relying on

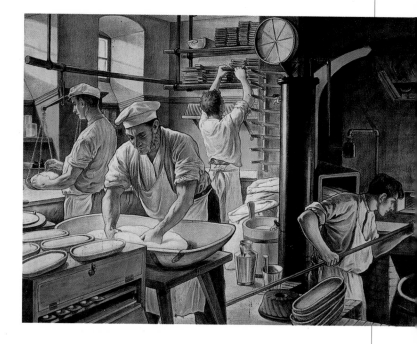

experience or instinct. This is why, for example, there is no thermometer either in Lionel Poilâne's Paris bakery or at his larger bakery in Bièvres (just southwest of the capital) which turns out ten thousand loaves a day. This is the man who has revived the French taste for good bread, and he trusts solely to his baking instincts and his sensibility,

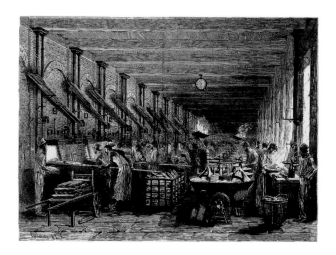

Except for a few details, a bakery run by a good baker still resembles the nineteenth-century ones seen here (facing page and above). The factories, on the other hand, have changed: molders and traveling tray ovens have replaced the baker. Left: one of the first industrial bakeries, in Germany (c. 1870).

his "feel." It is simply by feeling the warmth of the bakery and by plunging their hands into the flour that Lionel Poilâne's bakers regulate the temperature of the water: they use no thermometer, just their fingers. And bakers trained at Poilâne's school never get it wrong.

Rising Time

"The act of starting and nurturing fermentation is the most exalted task the baker performs, the one which gives nobility to his art. It is an act which creates life." Lionel Poilâne's words underline the crucial importance of fermentation. All breads are created by baking fermented dough, making the art of baking special in that it is living organisms that transform its raw material. First and foremost then, a baker has to learn how to control life itself.

There are two basic reasons for letting the dough rise: to increase the loaf's volume and to give it flavor and aroma. Fermentation occurs naturally through the encounter between the dough's sugars and microscopic fungi, which are either already present in the flour or else cultured and supplied industrially as baker's yeast, in the form of a pressed cake or powder. To survive and multiply, these microorganisms feed on the sugars and turn them into alcohol and carbon dioxide. These are the two substances which make the dough rise, giving bulk to the loaf, aerating the crumb and giving leavened bread its particular taste. Fermentation begins during kneading and stops with baking.

Yeast or leavening? There are a number of ways of giving life to dough. Fermentation with baker's yeast, which appeared in the 1920s, is the most common today. It is particularly suited to French breads such as the *baguette*, the thinner *ficelle*, and rolls such as *petits pains*, as it guarantees that the crust is at once crunchy but thin. The yeast is derived from the industrial culturing of a microscopic fungus of the species *Saccharomyces cerevisiae*. It is marketed as a compressed cake, which is crumbled or diluted with water before being kneaded into the flour.

Comprised of microscopic fungi which catalyze the fermentation of the dough, yeast (below) conserves the taste of the wheat flour, makes for a lighter crumb, and is ideal for loaves such as the French baguette, *providing it is not overused . . .*

Above: old advertising poster. Springer yeast is still produced today at Maisons-Alfort, in the Paris region.

Ready-to-use, reliable, and quick-acting, it has the added advantage of preserving all the delicate aroma of the flour, as long as the yeast is used in moderation, the dough is not over-kneaded, and a bulk fermentation time of four to five hours before baking is adhered to. Unfortunately, all too many bakers, to reduce rasing time, use high doses in tandem with high-intensity mixers. The resulting bread has an overwhelming yeast flavor. On the other hand, some bakers improve the quality of yeast fermentation by incorporating a small quantity of starter from the previous batch fermented for at least three hours. This addition enhances the flavor of the bread and improves shelf-life.

The most traditional method, which the very best bakers are beginning to employ once again, is fermentation using entirely natural leavening. There are people who will only eat bread made with natural leavening, and prefer the slightly sour taste, fruity aroma, and rustic look of such loaves. They are by no means easy to make, however, and demand thorough fermentation; they are therefore synonymous with high quality. As it produces a thick crust, natural leavening is ideal for *pain de campagne.* If the baker can be considered the "father" of his bread, it is above all in carefully preparing this leaven, an elixir of life which fructifies the dough. It begins with the preparation of a starter from a piece of dough particularly high in ferments, obtained either from added fruit or from flour. Basil Kamir, one of the top Parisian bakers, makes the sponge dough afresh every five to six weeks. In winter, 7 ounces of dough is worked up with a touch of stoneground whole-wheat flour and the juice of an orange (other bakers prefer grapes or apple). This is left to ferment for twelve hours, then $1^3/_4$ pints of water and slightly more than 2 pounds of stoneground flour are worked in. This is left to ferment for a further seventy-two hours at room temperature to give a $4^1/_2$ pound dough piece. In summer, the warmth which naturally encourages fermentation means that the orange juice can be dispensed with; some stoneground-flour dough will simply be left to ferment for around seventy-two hours. The sponge dough is "revived" at five-hour intervals by adding flour and water, which will increase the weight of the dough from 2 to 15

and then to around 175 pounds. This will be enough to serve as a starter for two or three daily batches, weighing more than 660 pounds in all. Because natural leavening is extremely fragile and the slightest change can effect its "growth," especially in winter, a minute quantity of yeast is added prior to kneading which will have the added advantage of giving volume to the loaf. For a month, it will be enough to make starter from a $1^1/_2$ pound piece taken from the previous day's batch, "revived" twice to attain the required 175 pounds.

Poolisch: **the sponge-dough method.** Another method of fermentation, used primarily in France, is a variant of the liquid sponge and dough process, known in French as *poolisch*, as it was apparently developed in Poland around 1840. Max Poilâne, Lionel's elder brother and an excellent baker himself, calls *poolisch* sponge "pâte à crêpe" (pancake batter). It is true that its most obvious characteristic is its liquid appearance. The sponge is composed of equal quantities of flour and water and an amount of yeast which varies depending on the temperature in the bakery (from 0.02 to 0.2 ounces per pint). This liquid curd is allowed to ferment at room temperature until it has tripled in volume. Depending on the season, between two and twelve hours are required to attain this level of fermentation, called the tolerance. It is then poured into a mixing bowl and more flour, water, salt, and yeast are added before kneading.

Whoever has tasted a loaf made using the *poolisch* sponge method knows all the benefits it brings to the bread, especially to the *baguette.* The crumb has very little acidity, and the complex aroma of the flour is retained. Provided the flour is of good quality, the perfectly crunchy crust is neither too thin nor too thick and the bread has a taste vaguely redolent of hazelnut.

Not just resting. The fermentation of the dough begins once the yeast, leaven, or sponge mix is worked into it during kneading. At the end of mixing, the baker leaves his dough standing for first proofing (preliminary rising). Ostensibly, the dough is simply "resting," but in reality it is subjected to intense chemical and physical reactions which transform it completely. The ferments break down the sugars, transforming them into carbon dioxide and alcohol, the latter producing organic acids which fix onto the flour's gluten and contract it, making the dough more resilient, firmer, and bulkier. At the same time these acids play a role in the gradual evolution of the bread's aroma. The baker's art consists in making this period last for the maximum length of time, without, however, going too far and producing dough liable to tear at the shaping stage. Here one can understand how the fermenting method, the type of kneading, and the length of first proofing are inextricably linked to bread quality. The faster the necessary dough strength is obtained—by high levels of yeast and by intensified kneading—the shorter first proofing can be, and the

bread will accordingly lack taste and consistency. Anything which lengthens first proofing—by using leaven and above all by a short but slow kneading process—improves the quality of the bread. Though it is unknown among all too many of today's bakers, in a bakery where pride is taken in the work proofing of this kind lasts one or two hours (depending on the ambient temperature).

The more it is left to nature, however, the less the process of fermentation can be controlled. Mysterious and untoward things can often happen, making the baker's task more engrossing, certainly, but also more complicated. The masters of the craft confront the unpredictable with a sense of exaltation. This applies to twenty-seven-year-old Thierry Tabu, a fine baker working at the Moulin de la Vierge on rue Daguerre in Paris, who exercises his art in public—a mere glass partition separating the shop from the bakery. I went to see him one fine September morning, a difficult one for him as his mix had not "risen" well during first proofing. "It's like chewing gum," he complained, poking at the soft, sticky dough. He had used exactly the same flour as the day before and observed the same kneading and fermentation time, while neither the temperature nor the humidity of the air had changed. What mystery lay behind the dough's not rising normally? Thierry Tabu inspected his flour, of the organic, stoneground variety. It was of course from the same miller as always, but, if you felt it and smelled it, it became obvious that it was too young, that it was "hot off the mill" as some millers say. It was September, so the very first sacks of flour from the new harvest were making an unannounced early appearance in the bakeries. The next day, Thierry Tabu had solved the problem by mixing the new flour with another, less "green" one from a different mill. He was glad to have figured it out, but gladder still to have encountered the problem at all: "I'd change my job if I wasn't constantly confronted by all sorts of unforeseen circumstances."

The first proofing is an opportunity for the baker to have his first direct contact with the dough itself. To assess its strength he prods at it with his fingertips, uses his palm to make it shudder against the sides of the mixing bowl and stretches it carefully. Dough can be temperamental

"This ingredient is magic, for an amount of it is enough to transform all the dough and give rise to an extraordinary result: bread*," wrote J.M.G. Le Clézio on leavening in his novel,* L'Innconu sur la terre *(The Unknown on earth).*

Above: the three ingredients required for the finest bread are written on the window of the Moulin de la Vierge bakery, in Paris: natural leaven, wood-fired oven, and stoneground flour. Facing page: natural leavening at Lionel Poilâne's bakery.

and should be treated with respect. When Max Poilâne is pleased with its consistency, its softness and its shimmering in the light, he smiles and murmurs: "It's like silk . . ."

Magic Hands

The dough, now smooth and silky, but firm enough to be worked, can be "divided" by hand into dough rounds which will each be made into a single loaf. Hand-dividing, which has generally been replaced by mechanical dividers, is gradually disappearing and nowadays there remain very few bakeries where this fascinating spectacle can be seen. Though in theory there is nothing so very extraordinary about the process, the dexterity it requires has to be seen to be believed. Armed with a plastic spatula, a "dough slice" or "divider," the baker takes up a piece of the dough about the size of a loaf, weighs it on the scales, removes or adds a little if it is too heavy or too light and places it on a floured board, where it will rest for a short time to recover from the "felling" or cutting. The speed and accuracy of the whole operation is astonishing. Speed is of the essence because often more than a hundred dough rounds need to be produced quickly and they must not be fermented for too long lest they tear during shaping. But speed alone is not enough: one also needs to be accurate, as adjusting the weight of a dough piece wastes time. Whenever a correction has to be made, precision is again imperative: one should add, if possible, one extra dollop and one only (adding several impairs the quality of the shaping). Hence, expert bakers can be recognized by the way they scale up the dough; not only will they work swiftly but also the rounds they gather up with the slice will weigh exactly the required amount seven or eight times out of ten. It is as if the scales are not really there for weighing the dough but simply for the conscientious craftsman to confirm the accuracy and magic of his or her handiwork. In Max Poilâne's bakery, for example, eighty-five dough pieces are divided, weighed, and placed on the board in just twenty minutes. The calculation is easy: that makes fourteen seconds per piece!

The weighing of the divided dough rounds, like their shaping on a floured board, requires a dexterity that some bakers consider a gift from God. Traditional hand weighing is now only practiced by the very finest bakers. Facing page: this photograph was taken by François Kollar in 1933. Above: at Lionel Poilâne's bakeries weighing is done by hand. The pile of wicker breadbaskets lined with linen, in which the divided dough is fermented, is also a sure sign of a good bakery.

Taming the dough. Once the last round is placed on the board, the first, which has been "resting" for twenty minutes, it is shaped into a loaf. Here, too, all the processes are nowadays normally done by machine. Good bakers will tell you, however, that there are two reasons why nothing can replace real hand-shaping. The first is to do with quality: manual "handing-up" (shaping) and "knocking-back" (massaging) are less rough than machine work, which tends to compress the dough. It thus gives the loaf a less even crumb complete with larger holes, making it pleasanter to chew and more flavorful. The second reason is an ethical one; since the disappearance of hand-kneading, the baker has no other opportunity to roll up his or her sleeves and get to grips with the raw material, to feel its density and its texture, and, by picking up and fashioning a shapeless piece of dough, to actually *make* a loaf. For the finest artisans, losing this intimate contact with the sensual, living dough would amount to losing something of their baker's soul.

Watching a baker hand-shaping enables one to appreciate the dexterity, the knack, the skill, and the great concentration required. The baker must have an instinctive awareness of the dough itself and be able to react immediately to any stiffness or thinness. He or she must sense and adapt to the dough's moods, thereby taming it and turning it into bread. The whole performance takes less than thirty seconds and is repeated a hundred times. That is why the final hand-shaping, where the baker's gestures are necessarily individual, cannot be taught. All the bakers I talked to agreed; with the best will in the world some will never acquire this innate ability. "It is difficult to show someone how to have good hands; either one has, or one hasn't," Bernard Ganachaud confided. This baker, who has been an enthusiastic proponent of

hand-shaping for years, does not lose sleep trying to work out why it is that his daughter Isabelle (like her sister Valerie, also a baker) should be far more skilled at shaping than he is himself. "There's just no accounting for such things."

For the classic loaves all the magic of shaping lies in one or two operations, depending on whether the baker is making round or long loaves. For the former, the work is confined basically to *boulage*, "rounding" or "rolling" the dough on a lightly floured board. The piece is first pressed down hard with the palms to expel the carbon dioxide and make the dough more compact. The edges are then folded back into the middle to make a round ball, which is then turned over and rolled softly against the board with the palms. Long "oven-bottom" loafs—such as the *baguette*—are first fashioned into a kind of small log. The dough piece is then flattened out into an oblong before being folded back on itself three times. Then the long cylinder shape is pushed out by moving the palms back and forth from the center towards the ends, pressing down very gently. Observing a baker at this task, it is immediately obvious whether he or she has the knack or not. In Lionel Poilâne's bakery at Bièvres I watched two bakers working side by side: the nervous hands of one were fashioning a ball of dough; from the expert and gentle hands of the other was born a prettily rounded body, pliant, its skin perfectly even and smooth, the whole quivering with life.

Baker's Weather

Good bakers occasionally leave the bakery to look at the sky, sniff the air, and get a feeling for the wind. The weather plays a considerable role in bread making, especially during the last stage of fermentation, *apprêt*, or final proofing. During this standing phase prior to baking, the starch in the flour breaks down into sugar, which then itself turns into alcohol and gases. The rounds experience at this time a sharp rise in carbon dioxide content and acquire their final volume. Here again the baker must be vigilant: too short a time and the loaf will not rise sufficiently; too long, and the dough piece might collapse during the initial stages of baking. The length of final proofing is at least an hour, but varies appreciably depending on the ambient temperature and humidity.

In traditional bakeries, for this final stage of fermentation the shaped dough pieces for long loaves (*baguettes* and *pains parisiens*) are laid side-by-side on floured bolts of jute or linen called *couches*. They are housed in a kind of high-sided trolley with a number of shelves, called a *parisien*, which protects the loaves from drafts and should keep the humidity level constant. The round loaves are put in charming little round wickerwork baskets, called *bannetons*, lined with floured, unbleached linen (in Britain, special "dough bowls" are used). These baskets are placed on wooden shelves and covered with a tarpaulin. While fermenting, the dough releases a sourish, acidic smell which is one of the bakery's most distinctive perfumes.

At his bakery in Bièvres, Lionel Poilâne proudly showed me his *bannetons*; the linen cloth is covered with a thick layer of old flour which has turned into something as subtle as an artist's palette, awash with pink, blue, and green mold. "It is life which gives bread its taste: one should let it do so." The majority of other bakers elect to wash their baskets and cloths thoroughly.

There is no more unpredictable time in bread making than the final proofing. A change in atmospheric pressure, a downpour, a lightning storm, or a door left ajar can all have a deleterious effect on the

"The magic resides in the long chain formed by these actions which, like some ritual, come down to us across the generations. On the board, the shaped bread . . . slowly taking form, awaits baking. Perhaps nothing created by man is more truthful, more complete. Working dough by hand is like the demiurge fashioning the human body while the leaven is like the ferment of life." (J.M.G. Le Clézio, L'Inconnu sur la terre). Facing page and above: shaping and fermenting the dough. Below: the baker Basile Kamir with some of his sublime pains de campagne.

Ten thousand of Lionel Poilâne's famous miches de campagne—whose fine floured crust is decorated with four cuts reminiscent of Chinese calligraphy—are made daily. In his extraordinary circular factory in Bièvres,

near Paris, Lionel Poilâne and his bakers, all trained at his school, follow the finest traditions of bread making on a large scale. For Poilâne the hand is a fantastic tool, ideal for gauging the flexibility, the texture, and the temperature of dough.

Facing page, top to bottom: "dividing" the dough after kneading; manual weighing of the dough rounds; fermenting in wicker dough baskets. This page, top to bottom: the baker hard at work at his brick wood-burning oven, where batches are put into and taken out of the oven with a flat shovel called a "peel"; "slashing" with a razor just before baking; the fine, golden loaf just ready to be taken out of the oven. Loaves placed low down in the oven will be slightly more cooked than the others, and have a taste which some bread lovers appreciate.

This pain Poilâne, *which has been behind a resurgence in French taste for fine, authentic bread, accompanies cheese and* charcuterie *to perfection. It can keep for a good week.*

Right: another baking genius, Bernard Ganachaud. The son of a baker from Nantes, he has two daughters who are also bakers. This "bread fanatic" has perfected a marvelous blend of flours—the exact recipe is a secret—which is used in the preparation of a delicious baguette *christened the* flûte Gana. *Bernard Ganachaud also believes in hand working and favors the* poolisch *method of fermenting, which imparts a pleasant, hazelnut flavor to the bread.*

fermenting dough even if it is not in the open. When the dough is fermenting too slowly, the baker can only wait. When it does so too rapidly, then he or she is reduced to using a few archaic tricks of the trade, such as uncovering them and placing them in a draft (*croûtage*, a method employed by Thierry Tabu); the "crusting" or drying of the outside of the dough halts its fermentation. If the baker does not mind waiting or speeding up the process, the customer, on the other hand, wants to find his bread cooked on time, and this is particularly true of a loaf like the *baguette* which is eaten freshly baked. Hence the enthusiasm of many bakers, even some of the best, for a more modern procedure which enables the baker to control the final proofing: the *pousse contrôlée.*

For *baguettes*, the dough pieces are placed on shelves in a "retarder proofer," which is a free-standing, hermetically sealed cabinet in which the temperature and humidity can be precisely controlled. The essential goal of these "retarding" machines is to slow down fermentation by chilling the dough. For example, *baguettes* are fermented for twelve hours at 6–12°C (42–50°F). This cabinet has revolutionized the bread-making industry. Not only does it enable the baker to satisfy the requirements of the customer by supplying bread on time, but it also obviates the need for night working, which many bakers viewed as the major drawback of their chosen occupation. There is now no need to rise at two or three in the morning to be able to serve fresh *baguettes* when the bakery opens, as the bread can have been shaped the day before and put in the retarder cabinet at night.

Nothing would induce some bakers, however, to abandon night work. For them it is as if bread can only be born during the dark and mysterious night hours. In front of the hot wood-burning ovens of Jean Jeudon—who, on Bernard Ganachaud's retirement, took up his bakery, and who possesses half a dozen retarder proofers—I met Laurent Boucherès, aged seventeen, the son of a fine baker and himself a good apprentice. "My father can only work at night," he told me, loading the loaves with a peel. "He bought a few cabinets but that hasn't stopped him getting up every morning at one o'clock. I take after him a bit. I'm supposed to start work at six, but I always arrive at five to get started before dawn. Because I like the nighttime . . ." The soul of baking, of the men who used to make a little light in the middle of the night, is getting rarer, but it has not quite vanished.

The Ordeal of the Oven

Bernard Ganachaud is an ardent partisan not only of hand-molding but also of each baker's personal *coup de lame*, or cutting technique (also known as "slashing"). Slashing denotes the cut the baker makes into the dough after final proof and immediately before loading into the oven. The cuts are made with a razor and enable the steam and carbon dioxide in the dough to escape during baking, allowing the loaf to achieve good all-round volume and to bake through well. *Baguettes* have from five to seven cuts, while 14-ounce *pain parisien* have four or five. In both cases, the slashes are parallel and at a slight angle to the axis of the bread. Round breads (such as the *miches*—round loaves resembling flattened coburgs—made by the two Poilânes) are docked with four slashes arranged in a square. These cuts require a degree of experience because the razor penetrates to a different depth depending on the stiffness of the dough. Because connoisseurs can recognize an individual's slash immediately and a master baker can always tell which of his men or apprentices made a particular batch, the cut is considered by some to be a sort of signature, a trademark that should not be imitated. Bernard Ganachaud is attempting to prevent his method of slashing the *baguette* (one long slash down the middle) being used by others.

The dough is at last ready for its final ordeal: the oven. Traditional solid stone or red-brick ovens, with their often elaborate decorative ironwork, large dark openings, and hearths glowing with embers, are impressive in their beauty. These ovens are preheated and the hearth put out before the bread is loaded; the heat stored in the bricks decreases as the bread is baked, making for a thick crust which guarantees good shelf-life and suits farmhouse loaves perfectly. Continuously heated modern ovens (of the electric, oil-fired, hot-air, and steam-tube varieties) all give a thin, crackly crust, making them better for *baguettes*. But only the old ovens, scarcely different from the stone ovens of the Romans, give the baker a sense of battling with the elements—with fire, earth, and water—to bake his bread. Hence, these ovens

relate more to the philosophy of bread making than to its folklore, and all the bakers who use them love them.

Wood-burning ovens. Up until the beginning of the nineteenth century, all the ovens built of fire-proof stone were heated by burning wood on the sole, that is to say on the very spot where the bread was actually placed. This two-thousand-year-old ritual is still alive in a few places: at Montvernier in Savoie, one of the very few villages in France where a working village oven is still lit periodically, or else in Jean-Pierre Veyrat's bakery, also in Savoie, the only one I know of which still uses such an oven. A large wood-fire is lit on the sole of the oven and is kept going until the bricks at the crown are white-hot. The embers and ashes are removed with the peel, the

Loading bread into a wood-burning oven with a peel is a complex skill which requires experience, concentration and dexterity.

In The Baker from Valorgue, *directed by Henri Verneuil in 1952, the French actor Fernandel captured perfectly the facial expressions and gestures of a baker loading his oven.*

sole cleaned with an *éouvillon*, or scuffle (an oven mop or a long handle fitted with a wet rag soaked in the nearby water tub) and only then are the loaves loaded with the peel. If a little ash remains on the sole, or if the logs burnt are fragrant, the loaves take up the slight woody taste. Bernard Ganachaud remembers that his father, a baker in Nantes, heated his oven with bundles of furze from the Vendée delivered by ox cart. In a novel by Marcel Pagnol, a baker promises that, if the villagers bring his wife Aurélie back, he will "mix a little rosemary with the embers in the oven."

Nowadays, the influence of wood-burning on the taste of bread has become a highly controversial subject. Since the beginning of the century, wood-burning ovens have functioned differently from their predecessors. The wood burns off in a hearth situated beneath the sole and the flames are funneled through to the baking chamber by a swan-neck burner. As the wood is no longer placed directly on the sole, it is difficult to understand how it could flavor the bread. The advantage of today's wood-fired ovens in fact resides entirely in the fire-proof materials which accumulate heat and allow for baking at gradually decreasing temperatures (from 230 to 180°C, or 450 to 350°F), ideal for the larger loaf. If proof were needed, one should taste a *pain de campagne* cooked in an old brick-built, wood-burning oven re-equipped for use with gas-firing: they are just as good. But wood remains a noble material and the heat it gives out still burns brightly in the hearts of some bakers. "One can tell the

heat of a wood-fired oven with one's eyes closed," Max Poilâne told me once. "One doesn't feel the heat from an open fire or from a radiator in the same way . . . Mysterious it may be, but wood cooks bread to the very heart in a more gentle way then any other fuel."

I met the king of the wood-burning oven in the Moulin de la Vierge bakery on the rue Daguerre. Young Thierry Tabu (who like his colleague does the afternoon shift) is admirable if only because he works with a single oven, built in 1930, in which he has to bake more than one type of bread at a time. This acrobatic exercise, which in earlier times was a daily occurrence, is extremely rare nowadays. It requires good organizational skills and unstinting vigilance.

The first task is to heat up the oven. I should really have said "reheat it," as a brick oven cools so slowly that it is still lukewarm after a fortnight without relighting. Thierry Tabu sets a flame to some little chunks of compressed sawdust (other bakers prefer beech, ash, or acacia wood). Once the fire is kindled, the oven heats to around 250°C (480°F) in about an hour, though the heating time depends as much on the ambient temperature as on atmospheric pressure, and can vary from twenty minutes to two hours. However long the oven takes, the bread must be loaded at the exact moment final proofing is complete, neither before nor after. This means that one has to be acutely aware of the prevailing weather conditions before firing the oven. As the oven he uses, like

Like old millstones, real wood-burning ovens are gaining a second lease on life thanks to a new breed of bakers proud of their trade and their traditions. They are very heavy, cumbersome, costly, not very commodious, and somewhat unpredictable . . . but they bake the best bread, especially pain de campagne. *Nothing would induce a baker who owns one to exchange it for a modern oven. Facing page and above: a baker at work in Lionel Poilâne's bakery, which has been equipped with twenty-four specially built wood-burning ovens.*

those of old, is not equipped with a thermometer, Thierry Tabu has a few tricks up his sleeve to gauge its temperature. The first is the color of the bricks at the crown, which should be white-hot. Then comes the paper test: he places a bit of yeast packaging on the peel and thrusts it into the oven for a few seconds to see how quickly it turns brown. To be absolutely sure, he might even throw a pinch of *fleurage* (powdered olive stones used primarily during loading) to see what happens: if they spark, the oven is too hot.

Once the oven has reached the correct temperature, he removes the embers from the hearth with a metal shovel, then wipes the sole with the damp scuffle. Then the oven is left for forty-five minutes while the stored heat spreads throughout the refractories, reducing the temperature by around 30°C (85°F). The oven is now ready. It only needs some steam to slow down the dehydration of the bread and give a sheen to the crust. It will enter the oven by way of a reservoir or hydrator placed against the oven.

The fragrance of newly baked bread and its crackle as it is drawn from the oven spreads a sense of joy throughout the bakery. Unloading the oven is like assisting at a birth. Facing page: batches of freshly baked miches *at Lionel Poilâne's. In 1920, Marcel Proust told a journalist: "If paper was no more to be had, I think I'd like to become a baker. It is an honorable thing to give men their daily bread."*

The time has come to load the first batch, consisting of around one hundred and fifty *baguettes*, which must be seized at a high temperature. These are followed by one hundred and eighty other long loaves, *pain parisiens*, then eighty crusty *boules*, and finally thirty-two coburg-like *miches*. The last batch is loaded a full hour after the first so that the *baguettes*, baked in a mere twenty to twenty-five minutes, will leave the oven before the *miches* are even loaded. For an hour, Thierry Tabu performs the rapid and precise movements of a choreography which has not changed for centuries, that of the *brigadier*, the oven master. Depending on what part of the oven the bread is placed, he selects one of five wooden peels of different sizes, laying it horizontally between the sill of the oven, the "stock," and a stilt (the "peelhead"), sprinkling it with a *fleurage* of finely ground olive stones to prevent the dough from sticking. To make it good and slippery, the peel is also dusted with *fleurage* or finely ground bran. Flour cannot be used for this purpose as it would tend instead to make the dough stick to the peel and prevent the base of the loaf from cooking thoroughly. Thierry Tabu places the dough on the peel, flours it, and then slashes it several times with a razor. He then takes up the peel and neatly offloads the dough onto the oven sole. The whole process lasts about ten seconds. And he also has to stop occasionally to take out the baked loaves or else to adjust the hatches which supply the in-draught.

The smell of fresh bread fills the bakery; the crackling sound of burning-hot *baguettes* can be heard as they are

laid in their wicker dough baskets. By inspecting their golden-brown crust, Thierry Tabu has judged that they are cooked. For the larger loaves, which must be baked right through, he will look rather at how well the sides of the crusts are doing: they should be brown and firm. He will then tap the base of a loaf to see if it sounds hollow. All the freshly baked loaves are then brushed to remove the *fleurage*. The crust, where golden and wood-brown hues intermingle, looks like a magnificent relief map with raised plateaus, deep valleys, craters, and gorges. This is because the *coups de lame* bit well into the dough. Even before it is eaten, good bread is already a work of art.

Thierry Tabu took three months to get to know and really understand his oven. He says that he could never forsake it for a modern contraption, for example one with a wide "setter" tray for loading the loaves. Trained in an entirely mechanized bakery, he discovered the old traditions at the Moulin de la Vierge and with them experienced a new-found pleasure in his work. The young apprentice, Laurent Boucherès, senses it too. At seventeen, he has other ideas, other dreams, and is still wondering whether to devote his life to baking. But he confessed to me that, going into a bakery when he is on vacation, he feels a sudden urge to get up at three in the morning, go to the bakery, and thrust his hands into the dough. His father, also a baker, told him once that the trade, the best in the world, was also like a drug: "Once you've tried it, you can't do without it." Laurent is beginning to believe it. If all apprentices were like him, the art of baking would not be in danger of disappearing.

Breads of France

A recent invention, the
baguette, *at once soft and
crunchy, is the embodiment of
French bread throughout the
world. But two-thirds of the
loaves eaten in France are not*
baguettes: *bakers offer their
customers a whole gamut of
shapes, tastes, and amusing
names, such as the* chapeau
(hat), the cordon *(cord), the*
pain polka *(like chequerboard
loaf), and the* pain plié
("folded loaf" or "turnover").

*Top: a selection of French
breads.*
Facing page: The Bread
Vendor, *autochrome by Paul
Castelnau (Reims, February
1917). Above: Fernandel in*
Le Boulanger de Valorgue.

It is for good reason that the perennial and universal cliché which associates the French and the
baguette has become so ingrained, for no nation is
more passionate about bread. There are, of course, peoples who consume more bread, but France remains special in the richness and imaginativeness of its traditions.
It is, for example, customary that every course of a
meal, from the appetizer to the cheese, be eaten with
bread. The skill of French bakers forms an ancient tradition; these artisans, who can possess as much expertise and inventiveness as great chefs, offer breads of
extraordinary variety and high quality. Even two centuries ago, thirty different types were described in
Diderot's *Encyclopédie*, including the *bis* (a brown loaf
with bran), the *cornu* (with its "horns"), the *pain mollet*,
and the split loaf, the *fendu*. This variety was admiringly
captured by Marcel Pagnol in *La femme du boulanger*

94

(1939): "Those large round loaves, all neatly arranged, looked like a fortification. Then above these, the fancy breads: there were long ones, double ones, ones with heads . . . ; there were *fougasses*, looking like a kind of golden grate, and little round *pompettes* for breakfast, with an onion and an anchovy; and on the counter, biscuit breads, as brown as gypsies . . ." Today's bread lovers can still experience a similar feeling of wonder on entering any good French bakery. Commonplace loaves, such as the *baguette* and the *pain de campagne*, regional breads, or else specialty breads, such as those prepared with a number of different grains or flavors, make up a fascinating tapestry, mixing the most varied shapes with a sublimely modulated artist's palette, from creamy white to dark brown. Just like that composed by a selection of wines or cheeses, such a picture invites the food lover to partake of all the authentic tastes that France has to offer.

Everyday Loaves

Until the nineteenth century, the everyday bread of the immense majority of French people was baked in the farmhouse or at the village bakery. This "homemade" bread took the form of large, dense, round loaves weighing at least 6 pounds, called *pain ménage* (the equivalent of the English "household bread"). There are a few exceptions, but in general this custom has today died out. In those days, a French person would eat at least a pound of bread a day. Today, France has thirty-five thousand bakeries and people consume, on average, less than 6 ounces a day. For the most part this is white wheat-flour bread, with a giving, well-aerated crust, the kind that has established the reputation of French bakers throughout the world.

A third of all loaves eaten today are in the form of the *baguette*, the king of French breads. Ten million of these loaves measuring around 27 inches long and normally weighing 9 ounces (250 grams), are sold daily in bakeries and supermarkets. It is a familiar sight in a city street or a village in France: a golden *baguette* protruding from a shopping bag or else being carried by a schoolboy of much the same size, nibbling at the crust on his way home from school. The *baguette*, however, only originated in Paris at the beginning of the 1930s, in conjunction with the ideal method for making it, which entailed adding baker's yeast to the dough just prior to kneading, without the need for culturing ferments. In tandem with the advent of mechanical kneaders and dough shapers, this method—and the *baguette* itself—soon gained a foothold in the whole country. Before the name *baguette* became popular, these loaves were called *pain de fantasie* (fancy bread). This is the term employed by Marcel Pagnol in the text cited above ("the long ones"). They differed from both the old *pain français* with leaven, and the Vienna breads, born of a particular type of fermentation, the *poolisch* sponge-dough method.

For lovers of "real bread" that is to say enthusiasts for the traditional half-quartern French loaf, the notion of the *baguette* was regarded—and still is—as a superfluous Parisian fad. Jean Giono (whose *Jean le Bleu* inspired Pagnol's *La femme du boulanger*) went so far as to call it an "infamous dough glue which disagrees with the stomach." More recently, the uncompromising food

Baking bread in the communal oven is one of the finest French traditions, unfortunately vanishing nowadays. Facing page: a communal bread oven in the east of France, in 1934. Above: a bakery on the rue des Blancs-Manteaux, in Paris (photograph by Eugène Atget, c. 1900). From 1850 to about 1930, bread made with leaven was termed pain français *to distinguish it from the newly arrived* pain viennois, *which was made using the* poolisch *sponge-dough method. Left: Raimu in Marcel Pagnol's* La femme de boulanger *(1938): "I'll make you a bread so good that it won't just be an accompaniment to something else but will be a delicious food in itself."*

Long loaves are typical of French baking. The baguette *has been exported the world over, but there is also the* pain parisien *or* gros pain, *the close-crumbed* bâtard, *the smaller* flûte, *and the thin* ficelle.
Below: a baker's boy in 1938. Facing page: The Bread Vendor *by Albert Dubois-Pillet (1846–1890). Both the vendor and baker's boy would deliver what are called in France simply* pains, *long, wheat-flour loaves*

weighing 14 ounces. But, as Jean-Luc Poujauran's bakery in Paris proves (following double page), the range of French bread is vast. Apollinaire alluded to this variety in L'Hérésiarque et Cie.: *"There were long, thin* flûtes, *then* pains polkas *like round crowns—chevroned with gold because of the crust and with silver because of the flour sprinkled on top; little Vienna cobs, like pale oranges, household loaves called round or split, depending on their appearance."*

writer La Reynière bluntly described it as "a tid-bit for bimbos," while Lionel Poilâne wrote that the *baguette* was "a banal fancy, very Parisian, in the deprecatory sense of the word." How unfair! A real *baguette*, which happily has nothing to do with the product as normally sold, is in fact truly delicious. An authentic *baguette* is the product of conscientious work on the part of a real craftsman, as well as good-quality flour, little yeast, no additives such as bean flour or ascorbic acid, slow kneading, and a four- to five-hour fermentation. This results in the crustiest and yet softest loaf imaginable, one which must be eaten as fresh as possible. From its dense but well-aerated and creamy-white crumb emanates the unadulterated scent of pure wheat flour, while its unassertive taste and its melt-in-the-mouth consistency can accompany even the most delicate dishes.

Unfortunately, since the 1960s the good *baguettes* of old have been replaced by loaves thrown together all too rapidly, afflicted with a crust as thin as cigarette paper and an insipid, cottonwool crumb. Today, however, the French are rediscovering the real *baguette*, which is being sold by more and more bakers, especially in the major towns. So as they can be distinguished from the other, slightly cheaper sort, they are sometimes floured and sport strange labels, such as *baguette à l'ancienne* or *baguette de tradition*.

Belonging to the same family as the *baguette*, as they are made in the same way, are the *pain*, the *bâtard*, the *flûte*, and the *ficelle*. These are readily found in any bakery and are differentiated from the *baguette* solely by their weight and size. What is often simply called a *pain* (bought above all in the country) weighs 14 ounces (400 grams), the *bâtard* (a "bastard" or "cross" between the *baguette* and the *pain*) weighs the same as the *baguette* but is slightly stouter, the *flûte* is a little 7 ounce (200 gram) *baguette*, while the thinner *ficelle* traditionally weighs half a *baguette*. The *petits pains* (like rolls) also belong to the same family. They weigh nearly 2 ounces and share with *croissants*, *brioches*, and milk breads (*pains de lait*) the honors of the table at breakfast or teatime. These two meals can also be

accompanied by sliced and toasted *pain de mie*, a familiar tin loaf whose crumb is enriched with milk powder, fat, and a little sugar before being baked.

Another loaf regularly eaten in France is the *pain de campagne*, a sourdough country bread. Contrary to its name, this loaf was actually invented in Paris, and has always been a favorite of customers in cities. In fact, the term does not designate a specific type of bread; its ingredients, weight, and appearance vary according to the baker. It is usually either long or round and weighs slightly over a pound. Certain characteristics are always present, however: a thicker, often floured crust, a closer and darker crumb than that of the *baguette*, and a somewhat sourer taste. Bakers often add a touch of rye to the white wheat flour used, while others, to enhance the taste, mix in some fermented dough from the day before in conjunction with yeast before kneading. Others again opt for a real leaven, which imparts a marvelously fruity taste to their *pain de campagne*. Whatever the technique, a correctly baked *pain de campagne*, as well as being a feast for the taste buds, should also give one the impression of being absolutely authentic and natural, without which it would hardly deserve its name.

The same sensation should come from eating a *pain de seigle*, rye bread, the indispensable complement to a favorite French dish: oysters. Both its shape and weight may vary, but French rye bread, unlike the German or Scandinavian varieties, has a light crumb due to a greater proportion of wheat flour. To justify its appellation, however, it must contain at least two-thirds rye flour (otherwise it should be termed *pain au seigle*, bread with rye). Finally, bakers provide, for those who are eager to benefit from the nutritional value of whole wheat, the *pain complet* (a long or round whole-wheat loaf weighing slightly over 1 pound), which includes the kernel, the germ, and the husk. These whole-wheat breads can be succulent—as long as the flour is of good quality—and they are also very healthy, provided that they are made with organic flour ground from wheat grown, stored, and milled without the addition of noxious synthetic chemicals, which accumulate in the bran.

The best French bakeries combine authenticity and refinement. In sometimes opulent interiors, humble baguettes *lie next to more sophisticated concoctions, such as the* pain de gruau, *a fine-grained wheat bread, and other fancy breads. Above: the Louis XVI counters of marble set with bronze in the Boulangerie Azrak, Paris, dating from around 1910. Below: a delicious rye bread with figs, prepared by a baker from Saulieu, and proposed by Bernard Loiseau at his restaurant, La Côte d'Or.*

Bread and Fantasy

The French, who have fastidious palates, are not satisfied with these various kinds of everyday bread, delicious as they are. Constantly on the lookout for new tastes, French bakers have spent much time and effort devising new, subtler recipes, thereby making bread into a dish in itself. They have also been busy concocting loaves in new shapes, prepared in a thousand mouth-watering different ways and worthy of being served at elegant dinners.

The most traditional of these fancy breads is the *baguette viennoise*, which appeared in France at the end of the 1940s. It should not be confused with Vienna bread—the *pain viennois*—already known in Paris in 1840 when Austrian bakers introduced the new *poolisch* method of yeast-based, sponge-dough fermentation. Until around 1920 any yeast-fermented loaf was called *viennois*. The *baguette viennoise* and rolls of today differ from normal loaves by their shiny but soft crusts, which are molded "sausage-style," that is to say decorated by deep horizontal cuts every fifth of an inch or so. Devotees particularly value their delicate, tender, slightly sugary crumb, enriched with milk and butter. Others prefer the *pain de gruau*, often *baguette*-shaped, also with a delicate crumb, but no sugar. Traditionally, it is made with a high-quality patent flour made from *gruaux*, the purest parts of the milled kernel. Under its

thin, light crust is to be found a marvelous, butter-like crumb tasting faintly of hazelnut.

In addition to these luxurious versions of wheat bread, the best French bakers also provide a fantastic range of round loaves flavored with the most varied ingredients. The exact recipe and, in particular, the proportions of the ingredients chosen are up to the individual baker. One of the most common, the *pain au noix*—with walnuts—originally a specialty from Alsace, is excellent with salads, cheese, and especially red wine. French bakers offer every conceivable shape of wheat or rye flour loaf. A casual exploration of the wares produced by the most inventive might yield: *pain aux olives*; *pain aux figues* and *pain au thym* (both equally suitable for accompanying game); *pain aux oignons*; *pain à l'ail* (excellent with red meats and incorporating just a few cloves, but not to be confused with "garlic bread"); *pain au fenouil* (flavored with fennel, for fish dishes); various *pains au fromage* (made with cheese ranging from delicate cream cheese or strong Roquefort or Parmesan); *pain au lard* (with bacon pieces); the somewhat heavy *pain à la pomme de terre* (the potatoes improve shelf-life); *pain au cumin* (with certain cheeses); and the delicious *benoîton*, a charming little rye round stuffed with currants. As the best bakers are never short of imagination, such a list is naturally far from exhaustive.

Top: baguettes viennoises, *made in a characteristic "sausage" style. Right: advertising poster for a patent flour dating from 1900.*

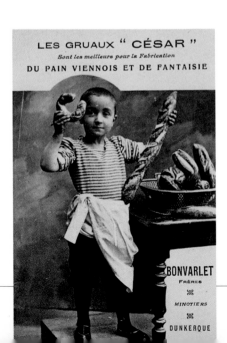

LES GRUAUX " CÉSAR "
Sont les meilleurs pour la Fabrication
DU PAIN VIENNOIS ET DE FANTAISIE

BONVARLET
FRÈRES
MINOTIERS
DUNKERQUE

The same variety is to be met with in the realm of another type of baking which is increasingly in vogue in France: *pain aux céréales,* or "multigrain" loaf. The classic example is the rye bread, which in France always contains a proportion of wheat flour. But there are breads which contain, three, four, five, even up to twelve different grains, specially invented for those looking for a bit of variety in their diet. Professional gourmets are slightly dubious about the culinary interest of these strange cocktails, mixing—and mixing up—tastes of flour from wheat, rye, barley, millet, oats, corn, sorghum, spelt, soya, buckwheat, linseed, and cottonseed. Most bakers make these breads from ready-blended flours supplied by the flour mill.

For consumers concerned about their health or their waistlines, bakers have also become chemists, transforming bread into a pharmaceutical product. There exists a whole range of breads designed to serve as dietary supplements or to obviate medical complications arising from eating normal bread. People who should not take salt can find bread made without it, while bran loaves (which are not whole-wheat loaves but white-flour loaves with added bran—up to 20 percent of the total weight) are good for the digestion. Gluten bread, low in carbohydrates and caloric, is recommended for diabetics. White bread with added wheat

Facing page: the épi *(wheat ear), especially when it is made into a* couronne *(crown), is one of the finest French loaves. Like the* baguette, *it is at once fresh-tasting, light, and crusty. Above: a baker's van specially designed by André Citroën for bread deliveries.*

Below: two French bakeries, around 1900. Unlike other types of stores, in France the appearance of the boulangerie *has remained largely unchanged this century; bread is above all synonymous with tradition.*

germ is highly caloric and perfect for athletes and convalescents. For those suffering from dietary deficiencies, there is soya bread, a good source of protein, and bread made with seaweed, full of mineral salts, that the professor of bakery, Raymond Calvel, humorously recommends to those who enjoy scuba diving.

Bakers can just be bakers too, however, and one specialty of French bakers is the decorative loaf, designed to adorn the dining table like a work of art. One of the most common is the *couronne,* found all over France and shaped like a large ring; it is perfect for carrying on the handlebars of a bicycle, a fact not entirely unconnected with its commercial success. Another is the magnificent *épi* (wheat ear), the dough of which is cut with scissors into the stylized shape of a wheat ear so the loaf breaks conveniently into a dozen or so little rolls of equal size. The same allusion to bread's raw materials is made in the British "wheat-sheaf" festival loaf. Some bakers are like true sculptors and design loaves depicting various objects, such as fish, cornucopias, violins, and baskets. Others follow local traditions in their choice of subjects, a fact which alone can make traveling through the regions of France a gastronomic experience.

Regional Breads

The richness of French gastronomy has its roots in the country's regional differences. Each part of France—on occasion under the influence of the neighboring foreign country—has developed its own cuisine in keeping with the particularities of the local soil and climate. As a staple food, bread still bears witness to regional particularities. While the *baguette* and the *bâtard* have permeated national life, others remain confined mainly to their birthplace. France has around a hundred of these regional breads. This century has seen the disappearance of many, thanks to mechanization (most of them can only be baked by hand) and the growing uniformity of eating habits. There remain, however, a few good bakers who are alive to this predicament. They are craftsmen, who, by safeguarding recipes and upholding old skills, have saved several dozen traditional types of bread from oblivion. As France gradually returns to its traditional baking values, these regional loaves are beginning to make their presence felt once again.

As we have seen, Marcel Pagnol, the novelist of the traditional Midi, evoked one of the most famous of these regional recipes in *La femme du boulanger*: the *fougasse*. Although it hailed originally from Italy, it is now a famed specialty of Languedoc and Provence. There is more than one sort of *fougasse* (a tasty variant of the recipe is known as ash-cake in Britain) and they vary immensely in shape and flavor. They are always large, flat, openworked loaves, generally depicting branches or a cogwheel. The *fougasse* has a soft crust and a sourish taste, and is made from leaven-fermented wheat dough which has been "quick"-baked at a high temperature. It can be stuffed with olives, bacon pieces, anchovies, or walnuts, and flavored with rosemary, aniseed, or olive oil. Another "sculpted" loaf, also from Provence, is the *main de Nice*, in the shape of a thumbless hand. Here the wheat flour is kneaded with plenty of olive oil, which makes the crumb delicate in texture and taste. The town of Aix-en-Provence, to the west, also has its own loaf, the *pain d'Aix*. Baked with well-fermented leaven, it has a

The breads of Provence, celebrated in the writings of Giono and Pagnol, mingle the scents and mouth-watering tastes of the sea and of the stony scrubland of the garrigue. Fresh wheat flour is married to olives, garlic, rosemary, thyme, aniseed, and anchovy to delight the taste buds.
Facing page: fougasses (a type of ash cake) and anchovy bread in Provence.

Above: in the Camargue on the Rhône delta, a fougasse, a couronne, and decorative loaves stand on an old dough trough. Above is a local bread cabinet, which, like the breadbasket, was used to keep the loaves fresh. Both dough troughs and breadbaskets are much sought after to decorate country houses.
Below: a bread vendor in Nice in the 1950s.

pronounced, slightly sour taste. The most curious thing about it is its shape, obtained by folding the dampened dough over a number of times. The *pain de Beaucaire* is from a small town on the Rhône north of Avignon, famous for its massive medieval fortress. This loaf, which has a strong taste of leaven, is shaped into a double dome with a delightfully matte golden crust somewhat reminiscent of stone. Being a favorite among grape-harvesters, it used to be common throughout the south of France. It can still be bought in some bakeries today. In Languedoc, in addition to the *fougasse*, the *département* of Hérault harbors the *pain de Lodève*, a white or brown loaf made with leaven and named after the historical town. It can be of almost any form because it is not shaped, the dough being fermented in a large *banneton* before being cut into more or less equal parts. There is also the *charleston*, a big loaf slashed diagonally, leaven-fermented

Below: Lionel Poilâne in his bakery. Facing page: some loaves from Alsace, illustrating its enduring tradition of gastronomic excellence: pretzels, made from interlaced lengths of dough—with or without salt— are often served with an apéritif; the slightly floured masnil round, delicious with Alsace wine, ham and walnuts; a long masnil loaf with walnuts, recommended with Munster cheese;

sübrot, made up of four equal-sized little rolls, a must at breakfast with cherry or quince jam; moricettes, *with their wide "slash," perfect for light sandwiches; braided poppy seed* berches; *and a Jewish festival bread. These breads were made by Daniel Helmstetter, a baker at Colmar, whose initials can be seen on the masnil round.*

with a brown crumb. From further south, in Perpignan, comes the *pain coiffé*, of the same type as the *charleston*, but made up into a crushed, coburg-like shape.

The Alps to the north are still home to communal village ovens where families come to bake household loaves. The little village of Villar d'Arène, some 5,000 feet up in the Hautes-Alpes, has kept alive a unique tradition: on the third weekend in November each year, the communal wood-burning oven is set to cook *pain bouli* (or *bouilli*). This large, round loaf, weighing around 10 pounds, is baked from rye flour kneaded with scalding water and then boiled for around an hour. Five batches, amounting to more than one hundred loaves, are baked and the bread can be kept for up to a year. The *couronne de Bugey*, another Alpine specialty, is somewhat less esoteric and can even be found in the odd bakery. This wheaten loaf, made with leaven, is shaped like a ring, as are the other French loaves of this type, but the hole in the middle is molded with the clenched fist. Since the loaf is baked for an especially long time, the magnificent, uneven crust is almost black. Finally, Alpine bakers offer the *pain fendu;* long and floured, this is a split loaf decorated with a deep lengthways channel made during final molding with a wooden roller 1½ inches in diameter. Such split loaves, of varying weights, are much appreciated throughout the country.

To the west of the Rhône, the Ardèche and the Auvergne are regions famous for their simple but delicious rustic cuisine, which is always accompanied by substantial and nourishing bread. In the Ardèche they eat the traditional *maniode*, a rye-wheat loaf made with leaven with a highly floured crust. The Auvergne also has its rye bread, in the form of *baguettes*, *pains*, or else rounds topped by a sort of flat hat, rather like a coburg. These loaves, tricky to shape, are called *tabatières* (snuffboxes). In this region, the *pain de méteil* (maslin bread), of a flour milled from rye and wheat grown in the same field, is a large, circular loaf. Another specialty of the region is the *tordu*, also to be found in the Charentes in the west, in the Gers to the southwest, and in the Limousin to the west of the Massif Central. This wheat bread is twisted

during shaping and, once drawn from the oven, looks rather like a wet rag that has just been wrung out.

Passing through Burgundy, with its pretty *cordon*, a fancy bread weighing 2 pounds and decorated on top with a wavy strip of dough, and Franche-Comté, home to the magnificent *fer à cheval* (horseshoe), we reach Alsace, a region of gastronomic delights, which include fine breads. The *sübrot* ("one *sou* bread") is a favorite, customarily eaten at breakfast. This light, attractively shaped loaf, weighing about 7 ounces, is formed from two pairs of rolls joined together at the sides which can easily be split into four when eaten. Normally made with leaven, it can be of white or grayish brown flour, with a lightly floured golden crust. Less common is the three-sided *pain à la bière* (beer bread), an excellent accompaniment to sauerkraut or Munster cheese. The aroma of this dense crumbed loaf is as subtle as its taste, and its dough is a combination of wheat and rye

flours prepared with creamed potatoes and brushed prior to baking with a mixture of rye flour and beer.

Alsace is also known for many other types of bread, which can frequently also be found in Germany and elsewhere in central Europe. The pure wheat *pretzel*, in the shape of a ring inscribed with a figure-eight, is prepared from poached dough coated with egg white which is studded with sea-salt and golden baked. This recipe makes for a real loaf, with a firm but not dry crumb and a crunchy crust. Alsace also offers pure rye or slightly wheatened *pumpernickel*, with a compact crumb which keeps its freshness, succulent walnut breads, and fruit breads (with apples, pears, plums, etc.), as well as milk-enriched, braided loaves, often sugared and flavored with aniseed or poppy seed.

The local breads of the region to the north of Paris are generally less elaborate, but there are gourmet loaves to be had here too. One of the most common is the round *pain boulot*. Often sold ready-sliced at the *boulangerie*, its pure white crumb with very small air holes makes it delicious for sandwiches (it is even called *pain à tartines*, sandwich bread). It is also baked as a long loaf weighing slightly more than 1 pound, while the oblong version is tin-baked and called *pain platine*. Another famous bread from the north is the *faluche*, a small loaf made with leaven and weighing around 7 ounces. It is baked at a very high temperature, its top crust splitting during "oven spring." The resulting hole can thus be filled with butter, jam and so on, providing a traditional workman's snack. The most intriguing thing about the loaf, however, is its consistency: dropped into a jute bag directly after baking, the steam renders it dreamily soft.

Heading along the Channel coast to Normandy, we encounter a land of numerous excellent breads. Some disappeared long ago, like the seawater loaves made at Cherbourg, which must have been delicious indeed. The *pain épi*, on the other hand, which originally came from Rouen, has become well known all over the country. The *gâche*, however, is a specialty confined to the Cotentin peninsula around Cherbourg. Seized in a hot oven, it is a round, flat wheat-flour loaf weighing in excess of 2 pounds, recognizable by its square-docked, golden crust.

207 — INDUSTRIE SARDINIERE EN BRETAGNE — La Vie à bord des Sardiniers — ND

The most idiosyncratic and probably finest Norman bread is still the *pain brié*, introduced to the region in the fourteenth century by Spanish monks shipwrecked from a galleon on rocks in Calvados. The *pain brié* owes its renown to its long shelf-life, particularly appreciated by seafarers. The secret lay in the manner in which the dough was worked. The technique of *briage* consists in removing from the dough as much of the air as possible to ensure the bread does not spoil. This was achieved by the use of a sort of long wooden lever or punner, the *brie* (nothing to do with the cheese), which was dropped onto the dough in the kneading trough. This punner was later replaced by a mechanical rammer, before being superseded completely by a technique of turning the whole dough basin by hand for twenty minutes after compacting the dough at the bottom (it should not, of course, get caught around the kneader paddles). This *pain brié* can be molded into pieces weighing 1 or 2 pounds, into a *bâtard* or a round, both decorated with deep cuts. The tough crust protects it from the air, while the incredibly dense crumb exudes a strong aroma of wheat flour and leavening. It needs to be thinly sliced and eaten in canapé-sized mouthfuls.

A little to the south, Brittany, whose salt from the Guérande salinas is used by bakers all over the country, has its own mariners' fare: the *pain bateau*, which has almost completely disappeared today. It used to be called *biscuit* (simply "twice cooked"), or even *biscuit de mer*. The double-cooking procedure was the reason for its exceptionally long life, which seamen valued so much. It was

Mariners' bread is designed for long sea journeys, whether it be the pain bateau *or* biscuit— *(literally, "cooked twice") of the Bretons (top), or the Norman* pain brié, *with its dense crumb (facing page). Both keep at least a month and do not deteriorate in damp conditions. The former has virtually disappeared, but the latter can still sometimes be found in various parts of France. It is a delicious accompaniment to seafood as well as cheese. Below: wedding celebrations in Brittany at the end of the last century.*

fouée is an excellent example. Bakers from Tours often make these little loaves (weighing anything from 3 to 7 ounces) for themselves, from leftover dough. The secret behind their exquisite taste lies in the fact that they always incorporate a piece of old sourdough into the mixture, which makes for its tartness. The dough is flattened by hand, before being quick-baked in a very hot wood-burning oven. The crust should be crunchy and the crumb butter-soft; this bread is preferably eaten warm, opened, and filled with butter, pork cracklings, or rillettes.

Another type of bread eaten by bakers, and which is so tasty that customers sometimes ask if they can have some, is the *soufflâme*, which comes from the Charentes. It owes its name to its peculiar baking method. It is nothing more than a little round of flattened dough, often pierced by two deep cuts into a figure-eight. It is laid directly on the oven sole in the middle of a ring of flaming embers and left to slowly burn out. The original idea was simply to check the oven temperature before loading a batch. Some bakers still bake *soufflâmes*

fashioned into large loaves weighing between 9 and 11 pounds, with a thick, almost black crust. Brittany is still home to a number of other traditional breads, in general of pure wheat, though very varied in shape. They include the *pain plié*, an original, folded preparation complete with a turn-down on the base of the loaf, the *pain rennais* (from the town of Rennes), like a large flat cake, the top crust divided into squares, and the *chapeau* (hat), an attractive loaf built from two smaller rounds one on top of the other. In the Loire-Atlantique region, the *tourton* is noted for its extraordinary taste adored by children at both breakfast and tea: it is a round loaf weighing about a pound, made from wheat flour and leaven, enriched with eggs and a fair amount of sugar, the crust being squared (like the English chequerboard loaf). Some prefer this delicious bread toasted, when the butter and homemade jam make the marriage between the sourness of the leavening and the sugar still more harmonious. The Loire is also home to the *pain polka*, an attractive, large, oval but flat loaf, baked with leavening, well floured, with a closely textured crumb and a crust hatched by deep razor cuts.

The historic area around Tours is known, in particular, for its *matelote d'anguille*, eels stewed in fine Bourgueil wine. The region has fine bread too, however, and the

for fun, just because they like the taste, with its over-tones of ash and smoke. The *pain collier* (necklace), admired above all for its shape, comes from the Char-ente-Maritime in Poitou. It resembles a large oval crown of gold lying resplendent on the table.

The most majestic *couronnes*, however, are from Bor-deaux—sun-like discs composed of eight or nine equal-sized rounds of wheat-flour dough, attached to form a ring like a chain of rosary beads. In the center, a charm-ing thin collaret of dough covers half the rounds, creat-ing an intriguing color contrast, and the baker artistically flours the finished ring. At mealtime, breaking this loaf, after having admired its form, becomes a kind of game.

Still farther to the south, the Landes region, facing the Bay of Biscay, possesses a very singular bread which has almost totally vanished from bakeries. It is the *méture*, a cornmeal loaf, fermented with leaven, with a compact yellow crumb. Continuing towards Spain, the French Basque country and neighboring Béarn have a more resilient survivor in the *tignolet*, a wheaten loaf made with leaven, weighing 1 or even 2 pounds, which is turned over during final shaping so that it resembles a big shell. Between the Pyrenees and the Mediterranean lie the Gers region (home of the *tordus* mentioned earlier) and the Haute-Garonne, where a few bakers perform the tour de force which is the baking of one of France's finest loaves, the *porte-manteau* (coat hanger): first pulled out in a roll 18 inches long, the ends of the dough are rolled back towards the middle, leaving a gap of about 8 inches between them. When one comes to eat this golden loaf, one discovers that the crumb at the ends is much denser than that at the prettily plump center.

These surviving regional breads are not just examples of French popular culture but also stand as evidence of an enduring history. In this they join the more cele-brated monuments of French bread making (such as the *baguette*) and the original creations of the great master bakers. They are part of a culinary heritage and the French are determined to protect them. Good bakers, who re-create these treasures in the bakery, are the cura-tors of this heritage, and as such deserve our gratitude.

Facing page, above: méture, *a cornmeal loaf from the French Basque country and the Landes. It is a rarity nowadays, but is still to be found at the Moulin de Bassilour, in Bidart. It can be eaten spread with goose rillettes, dunked in milk, or lightly toasted with eggs. Facing page, below: the attractive* couronne *from Bordeaux, to be found only in the Gironde. Above:* pains polkas *in a Paris market.*

Breads of the World

Bread is a vehicle for the history, culture, and identity of every nation. Each has put into its bread something of the authenticity and warmth of its particular approach to life.

Facing page: a Catalan baker near Barcelona.
Top: grissini *(bread sticks) and* carasàu *bread from Sardinia (also called "music paper" because it is so thin).*
Above: an Italian farmhouse loaf, made by restaurant owner Paolo Petrini, Paris.

Whereas the seafaring English say "he's sailed the seven seas," for someone who has led a peripatetic existence, the agricultural French speak of "eating more than one kind of loaf." Every region of the world has its own individual breads whose qualities reflect a climate, particular farming and cooking techniques, and differing cultural and religious traditions. Bread can be said to lie close to the very heart of a people, revealing the incredible assortment of lifestyles on our planet. Except for a few polar regions, anyone whose passion and curiosity about bread leads them to travel in search of varieties they have never eaten will rarely be disappointed. No other foodstuff is as characteristic as bread. To search for its different types is at the same time to explore the world itself in all its diversity. From eastern Europe to the western United States this chapter takes us on a journey in search of bread.

Northern Europe: Rye and Sponge Dough

The frosts of northern Europe mean that rye—which thrives in cooler weather—is the predominant cereal and it is this crop which is made into a wide range of tasty breads. But it is among the soft-wheat fields of Great Britain that our journey commences, a land saved from such climatic extremes by the Gulf Stream.

At once light and soft, the sandwich tin loaf is one of British gastronomy's finest achievements. The best is of course freshly baked, but there are some decent-quality, ready-sliced, industrial versions which are now packed without preservatives. One of the most famous is the brown Hovis, also available fresh in certain bakeries, which has been part and parcel of the British breakfast since 1886.
Facing page, top: the impressive bakery counter at Harrods Food Hall soon after its opening in 1903.
Facing page, below: some Scottish and Irish specialties. A split soda bread, raised with bicarbonate of soda, and three baps with sunflower, sesame seed, and mixed grains—ideal breads for hamburgers.

From breakfast to dinner: British bread. In Britain, as in other countries, people like to make their own bread. It was the only kind of manual work at which Virginia Woolf excelled, if the testimony of her cook Louie Mayer is to be believed. Woolf taught her how to make beautiful loaves as soon as she had hired her. It is at breakfast that one can enjoy Britain's greatest baking specialty: the sandwich tin. The milk bread variety is served with sweet foods (especially jam), whereas the standard is also used for savory spreads and cheeses. Simply buttered, but better toasted and spread with marmalade, this breakfast loaf, through its taste and the melting softness of its crumb, can reach the summits of refinement. Later in the day, its fine crusts are sliced off and it becomes an afternoon bread, used to make the classic cucumber, tomato, hard-boiled egg, or watercress sandwiches which are served at high tea. A real baker's sandwich tin, which is unfortunately becoming increasingly rare nowadays, is made with a special process called sponge dough, which gives it an original taste as well as improving the shelf life of the loaf. Sponge dough is a ferment based on baker's yeast, flour, and water added before kneading, and is occasionally used in France for the *brioche*. The dough also contains a limited quantity of sugar and milk powder, additions also incorporated in the mix of numerous butter-soft smaller loaves made using the same method. Among these number the sponge-dough rolls, and, especially in Scotland, floured baps, together with the sweeter scones and buns.

Britain is not only a country of soft breads, however, but also one of more substantial loaves. In that Ali Baba's cave which is the Food Hall in Harrods of London one can get a fair idea of the variety of British bread. There one can of course find Italian bread and French loaves like the *baguette*, but above all there are native wheat or rye breads made with leaven, both brown and whole wheat, as well as breads made from a plethora of different cereals. These variants on European bread are joined by some typically British or Irish specialties. The Irish, in particular, have developed over the ages a succession of delicious bread types, such as their traditional soda bread. The name comes from the use of bicarbonate of soda to make the

dough rise in much the same way as yeast. The recipe employs whole-wheat flour (sometimes mixed with white flour), as well as buttermilk or yoghurt, to produce loaves of various shapes and sizes, but all having the same delicious, slightly sour flavor. Soda bread, which used to be cooked in a skillet hanging over the fire, is found in many guises, flavored with bacon pieces, raisins, or caraway seed. Black treacle bread, another Irish specialty, also contains bicarbonate, as well as a pinch of ginger. This slightly sweet bread can be eaten hot, covered with butter and cheese. Britain itself has its own gingerbread, containing a few other spices, the most in evidence being cinnamon. It is left standing for two days before being cut and eaten, and has an unforgettable balance of tastes and aromas.

Of course, no visit to Britain would be complete without going into a pub. The British not only go there to drink beer, but also, frequently, to eat. Perhaps the most popular pub snack is the ploughman's lunch: a slice of

bread, often brown, with farmhouse cheddar and pickled onions—an excellent accompaniment to a pint of ale.

German rye. Crossing the Channel from England to Germany, we move from the soft texture of wheat to the wholesome density of rye. The situation should not be oversimplified, however, as there exist two hundred types of bread in Germany and rye is not the only grain used. However, the country is still Europe's number one rye producer, so it is hardly surprising to discover that the German word *Brot* needs no other adjective when referring to wheat or rye bread while all other cereals must be referred to by their own special names. The simple term "rye bread" hardly does justice to the profusion of loaves one finds in German bakeries made from this hardy crop. Nevertheless, they do have certain qualities in common: their darkish color—from light brown to pitch black—their density (rye is low in gluten), and their outstanding shelf life. But their shapes and sizes, and the recipes that go to make them, confer on each a distinct personality. To taste the real flavor of rye, with its sapid reminders of undergrowth in the fall, reminiscent of moss or slightly bitter mushrooms, one should chew on a piece of authentic, unmixed, 100 percent rye *Roggenbrot*. This is a black, oblong loaf, with a crust which is often studded with whole grains. Like many rye breads, it is normally baked in an oven with steam jets. Pure rye *Landbrot*, more of an everyday loaf, comes in all manner of shapes and sizes. It has the same flavors as *Roggenbrot* but, being necessarily baked faster and at a higher temperature, its often floured crust is thinner and more brittle. A number of loaves marry rye and wheat flour in various proportions. *Schwarzenwalder bauerbrot* (Black Forest peasant bread) is a large loaf weighing around 7 pounds, made from half rye and half wheat flour, fermented with yeast. The *Mischbrot*, which contains only 30 percent rye flour, has a smooth, golden crust and resembles a British or American "light" rye loaf. As for *Pumpernickel*, the German bread best known abroad, it is also widely eaten both in the Netherlands and Scandinavia and has been exported all over the world. There are a number of basic types of this bread, which is often sold

In his French Campaign, *on 24 September 1792, four days after the battle of Valmy, where he was accompanying the Prussian armies, Goethe wrote: "White bread! Black Bread! This the war cry, the shibboleth which separates the French from the Germans."*

Germany is indeed a rye paradise, a country where black bread reaches new heights. Facing page: seventeen rye breads, from the dense Roggenbrot *(wholemeal) to the* Mischbrot *(30 percent rye). Left: a poster for the Berlin Great Baking Exhibition at Leipzig in 1914. On the "Maypole" hang tempting pretzels (Salzbrezeln). Below: homemade sesame seed rolls, a German tradition on holidays.*

ready-packed: pure rye or mainly rye, with varying proportions of wheat flour. Its success is not unconnected with its slightly sweet taste and its impressive shelf life, both a result of its lengthy bake and the addition of a touch of vegetable oil during kneading. *Pumpernickel*, which retains its softness for a long time, has a magnificently brown crumb obtained by adding a little molasses, or even a touch of coffee. As with many other German breads, it is sometimes flavored with caraway seed.

The Germans have such a passion for bread that there is even a special evening meal built around it. This *Abendbrot* (evening bread), eaten cold, traditionally comprises cooked meats such as salami, with, on occasion, cheeses and salad, served on substantial slices of good bread.

In Denmark, poppy seeds are traditionally used to decorate loaves.

Below: a mixed rye and wheat tin loaf with poppy seed and a pure wheat bread.

Scandinavian open sandwiches. The story of Hansel and Gretel, recounted in the fairy tales of the Brothers Grimm, tells of two lost children who, imprisoned in a house made of gingerbread by an evil old witch, escape by pushing her into the burning oven. In remembrance of this story at Christmas, Swedish children build gingerbread houses decorated with candied fruits. In Scandinavia, bread made from wheat-flour is eaten primarily at Christmas. A loaf made from wheat flour is often called a "French bread," but most bread is made from rye. Loaves come in various shapes and mixes, connoisseurs favoring black loaves with a tightly textured crumb. The bread keeps well due to the fact that it is mixed with fat (as in the case of Danish *pumpernickel* and *rugbrød*) and is often baked with buckwheat and sesame seed. Sliced thinly, rye loaves form the basis of sublime open sandwiches (in Danish *smørrebrød*, "butter bread") which are laced with meat, marinated fish, smoked salmon, or cheese. Served in a similar way or as an accompaniment to a meal is the famous Scandinavian *flatbrod*, a crunchy and slightly salty kind of unleavened bread baked from unfermented wheat-flour or rye dough.

Switzerland: a taste for mixes. Switzerland is a melting pot of very different cultures, peoples, languages, and cereal crops. So, though it too has its rye breads, its reputation is based above all on its loaves concocted from various flavorful grain mixes. A loaf from the Valais, for example, blends oats and rye, while the *Apfelnussbrot* has wheat, rye, barley, spelt, and millet, combined with walnuts and apples. In fact, each regional canton proposes its own particular, even peculiar bread, with its own shape, baking recipe, and flavor. The most splendid are to be found beautifully arranged in the windows of certain bakeries in the Valais, near the French border in the south of the country. Here one finds, for example, large golden rounds of rye decorated with floral patterns or with the arms of the local town. However, the most common bread, which is found all over the federation, is Zürich bread, which, when sliced, reveals its light whole-grain wheat crumb.

Belgian *pistolets*. Before leaving northern Europe entirely we should stop briefly in Belgium to sample its baking specialty: the *pistolet* (pistol). Every Sunday morning, when the French are eating their *croissants*, the Belgians have their *pistolets*. It is quite simply one of the best tea-breads in existence. It is round with a depression in the middle (made with a stick dipped in oil just before baking) and is filled to bursting with a smooth crumb under a thin, glossy, golden crust. Also on Sundays, an afternoon snack in Belgium is taken with a few slices of nourishing *cramique*, a whole-wheat loaf, prepared with butter and milk, stuffed with raisins and sugar chips.

Above: if Belgian pistolets *are small, butter-soft milk bread treats, traditional Swiss close-textured bread, on the other hand, is a warming tonic for both body and soul.*

Right: the round sako *(a cracked multigrain with eight cereals) and the long* Bängeli *from Basel, which often accompanies a fondue, are Swiss specialties.*

Traces of bread made with some kind of leavening dating from the fourth century B.C. have been found in Switzerland, a country which has a number of nourishing and often exquisite traditional recipes. Wheat is not a common cereal and is normally mixed with rye and barley.

Above: a multigrain Apfelnussbrot *with walnut and apple, a wheat and spelt flour* Sauserbrot *with chestnut and grape must, and a rye* Zwetochgenbrot *with plum and walnut. Left: a wheat and rye* Urigsbrot (*puckish bread*) *whose name is derived from its extravagant shape.*

Above: one of the most original and nourishing of all Swiss breads is the Körnlipicker. It is made mainly of whole grains of wheat, barley, and rye, scarcely held together by a modicum of crumb. It is best eaten after a day on the mountains.

Creators of singularly beautiful breads, the Swiss are good hands at shaping: the extremely attractive Bauerruch (left) is a close-crumbed round loaf with a magnificent crust whose shape is reminiscent of a seashell.

*As their cuisine shows,
the Portuguese have great
respect for bread. It is to be
found in soups, sauces, and
stews. They also make smooth-
tasting faties (a type of
French toast).*

*The traditional bread
is the broa de milho,
a corn bread containing
wheat whose crumb can
be a vivid yellow. Above:
at the market in Ribiera,
Oporto, on the banks of the*

*Douro. It accompanies
caldo verde (cabbage soup),
as well as beans cooked with
ham and chorizo doused
with a fine vihno verde.
It is best, of course, when*

*cooked in the old wood-burning
ovens which seize the bread
and give it a divine aroma.
Above and right: ovens
lit for a local feast in
Sintra (Estremadura).*

Southern Europe

The poorer people are the more bread they eat. This perennial nutritional law is particularly true of Europe, where less bread is consumed in the north and more in the south. But southerners do not eat bread just to feed themselves: they too have developed countless mouth-watering recipes which have made bread one of the enduring elements of Mediterranean gastronomy.

The yellow bread of Portugal. In the north of Portugal, the favorite loaf is the delicious *broa de milho*, a corn bread. In former times, this peasant's bread was only baked on farms, but today it is to be found in numerous bakeries all over the country. From the outside, it looks just like a round farmhouse loaf with a splendid, rather irregular, lightly floured crust. It has to be cut open (with a good sharp knife as it is dense and heavy) to reveal its yellow, sometimes bright yellow, crumb. This crumb, which is tight and chewy, has a characteristic taste which fills the palate. As there exist many different varieties of corn, the color of the crumb ranges from pale yellow to a more surprising gray. The proportion of cornmeal used, always blended with wheat flour, without which the loaf would not rise, also has an influence on the color of the *broa*. The taste remains distinctive however, as does the aroma, especially toasted, when, spread with a touch of butter, the bread is truly delicious. The Portuguese eat cornmeal bread with

sardines, salted cod (*bacalháo secco*), and as a traditional accompaniment to the *caldo verde*, a cabbage soup flavored with some slices of chorizo sausage and a few drops of olive oil.

The white bread of Spain. In some Castilian villages, women potters still specialize in making little domestic bread ovens, earthenware domes with an opening at the base. Spain's rapid modernization has tended to accelerate the disappearance of the old homemade loaves, while *panaderias* (bakeries) offering a wide range of products have sprung up all over the country. Bread baked from all sorts of cereals and blends can be found in Spain, but the majority (made into every conceivable shape) are baked from yeast-fermented wheat flour. The crumb, beneath a smooth, rarely

In the Algarve in southern Portugal, near Castro Marim, women carry bread into a house for a feast. On festive occasions in this region, bread accompanies mutton stew, roast pork, or arroz de langueirão, *a rice and shellfish dish.*

123

floured crust, is often of an immaculate whiteness, soft and fine yet close-grained, occasionally betraying the presence of a drop of milk in the dough. This rich and flavorful bread is used in the preparation of Andalusian *gazpacho*, the delicious cold soup made from tomatoes, garlic, vinegar, and finely pounded bread crumbs, into which cubes of fresh or toasted bread are dropped prior to serving. Rustic *migas*, a nationwide favorite, are made from slightly stale bread, which is dampened, grated, and wrapped overnight in a cloth, then fried the next day in olive oil and garlic. Though this can be enjoyed at any time of the day, it is particularly welcome at breakfast time. A Catalan delicacy, the ever-popular *pa amb tomàquets* unites the four elements of Mediterranean cooking: a slice of toasted bread, covered with a layer of tomato purée (or simply rubbed down with half a tomato), then spread with garlic and olive oil. Nothing could be simpler, but the combination is superb.

Attractive shapes and the use of snow-white wheat make these Spanish rolls particularly appetizing. The originality of Spanish bread, however, lies in the use of the country's delicious olive oil. It is poured over bread with tomatoes in Catalonia (facing page), but is also used to give a delicious taste to the wheat flour. This flavor of oil in bread remained vivid in the memory of the Andalusian writer, Agustín Gómez-Arcos: "Recess smelled of olive oil. The child pulled out of his pocket a round roll, warm and soft, baked by his mother that very morning, undid the paper wrapped around it, and very gently squeezed the golden crust with an expert hand so that the olive oil, sugar, or salt that Maria had poured into a hole in the dough ran through it. Then he ate it. A gourmet pleasure, this refined taste of olive oil with each mouthful. Olive oil and wheat together: the Word of food" (The Bread Child).

The thousand breads of Italy. The Italians say that they have a thousand different kinds of loaves. They may be right, as there are countless varieties, though these are really "shapes" of bread as the majority are made from wheat flour. On the one hand, there are loaves found all over the peninsula, and, along with the regional specialties, no bakery (*panetteria*) is big enough to contain all of them. The "national breads" include: the *pagnotta*, a large, round farmhouse loaf baked with leaven using varying proportions of whole-wheat flour depending on the latitude; the *ciabatta*, a large oval which has a wonderful consistency, ideal for toasted Italian sandwiches (*panini*); the irresistible *biova* from the north, primarily in Piedmont, which is made with lard added to the dough, has a cylindrical shape with pointed horns, and a thick crust and light-as-air crumb; the *michetta* (called the *rosetta* in Rome, where it is shaped into a flower), a round roll as rich in crust as in crumb, an excellent vehicle for succulent sandwiches. Also from Turin come the bread sticks for which Napoleon had such a penchant, known as *grissini*, which have been exported the world over in their industrially produced version, and which are nibbled in restaurants throughout Italy. They are long, thin, hand-rolled batons, baked from wheat flour with a touch of olive oil, often eaten with an *apéritif*, as they are dry and very crunchy. The supreme bread in that department, however, is the finely delicate crumb loaf from which the little sandwiches known as *tramezzini* are made. These are enjoyable lunchtime eating in a city café.

Then come all the regional loaves. Romans can be divided into partisans of the *rosetta*, already mentioned, and fans of the *ciriola*, a longer, golden-crusted loaf with more crumb. *Francesine*—a kind of fatter *grissini* with a fresher crumb—are enthusiastically eaten in Milan and in the rest of Lombardy. As for Tuscans, they swear by an unsalted bread which leaves unaffected the subtle flavor of the wheat: the *pane sciapo*. An extraordinary and very tasty loaf is eaten in Apulia, a large round made from the durum wheat normally used for pasta, which requires special preparation: the *pane de Trani*. A much-loved dish which is always cheerfully received is *pan cotto*—pieces of stale bread simply boiled for a few minutes in a garlic, broccoli, and potato soup, seasoned with a drop or two of olive oil. Equally delicious, and just as simple, is the *bruschetta* from Umbria and Tuscany, a slice of bread or a loaf cut through the middle, covered in olive oil and garlic and eaten as it is, or else with finely chopped fresh tomatoes and basil. Here we are already entering a different domain, that of dishes based on bread, or at least on a dough mixture, an area in which the Italians are masters. *Focaccia*, in which the dough is kneaded with olive oil and even, on occasion, with boiled potatoes, is a soft, toasted bread base, sprinkled with sea salt and spread with anything from herbs (normally rosemary), onions, and cheese, to Italian smoked ham. The *tortino* is based on a large loaf with a dense crumb, stuffed with, for example, spinach or olives. Nor should we forget the internationally renowned pizza. There are many other incredible breads, from Calabria, Sardinia—the astonishing *carasàu* or *carta de musica* (music paper), as thin as unleavened bread—and from Sicily. These would also merit investigation, but the world of bread is a big place.

Below: at the legendary Harry's Bar in Venice, which used to be frequented by Toscanini, Truman Capote, Charlie Chaplin, and Hemingway, Arrigo Cipriani offers customers little puff breads, leavened with brewers' yeast, which are delicately rolled during shaping.

Italy is a bread paradise. Every imaginable shape of loaf can be found, while dough mixture is used in recipes such as pizza and focaccia. *The inventiveness of Italian bakers finds expression particularly in shaping, but also in the creation of crusty breads, often enriched with fats (such as olive oil). Previous page: a few of Italy's marvelous loaves, just out of the oven in Galli's bakery, the oldest in Florence. They include: the* mezza luna *(half-moon); the two* rosette, *graceful, flower-shaped Roman specialties; and the soft-crusted, oblong* ciabatta, *perfect for making Italian sandwiches (*panini*).*

In Greece, the "communion wafer" of the Orthodox Church is, in fact, a real bread with leaven. Below: on the island of Karpathos it is baked in the village oven exclusively by women, for, according to the men, "only they are clean and wise." Right: in a chapel on the island, high above the sea, a papa *incenses and blesses the Eucharist bread.*

Facing page: a village woman carrying her prettily shaped loaves to the oven.

The sacred bread of the Greeks. Whoever would become more closely acquainted with the Greek soul should enter a village church to join in an Orthodox mass, breathe in the heavy perfumes of the incense, glimpse the glimmering gold of the icons through the shadows, listen to the mysterious chant, and then go up to the altar rail to receive the host. Here, unlike at Catholic mass or Anglican communion, the host is a real leavened bread, a large, round loaf of fine white flour which the priest slices and shares out among the faithful. It is special in that it bears—imprinted on the dough with a wooden stamp before baking—stylized patterns evoking the Passion: instruments of the scourging or of the crucifixion—lance and sponge—or the tomb. It is prepared by the village baker and brought to the church by the congregation. That the host should be a round loaf of white bread and not a specially made wafer highlights the significant role of bread in Greek life. As for everyday bread—Greeks are the leading bread consumers in Europe—it is eaten for the most part in the form of a large farmhouse loaf, long or round, whose golden crust is occasionally covered with sesame seed. But the Greeks also have the famous *pita* bread, flat, round, or oval and extremely soft, without any crumb to speak of at all. It can be folded or split open to receive practically any filling, producing a copious sandwich. With the pita, we are already at the gate to the Orient . . .

saving resource of the destitute.
*Above: distributing bread to
Kurdish refugees.
Below and facing page:
in a bakery in Tbilisi,
capital of Georgia.*

*From central Europe to western
Asia, bread is ever-present,
whether it be for everyday
consumption, feast days or
as a gesture of hospitality.
Sometimes it is the last, life-*

Eastern Europe

From the Danube to the Urals, bread is still very much
a staple food. Everyday breads and breads for festivities
or rituals constitute a cultural and culinary anthology of
great richness which has sometimes remain unchanged
throughout the centuries. Each country has its own customs, but a few traditions have become more widespread, forging a shared identity around a number of
basic breads: black bread, braided bread, and loaves
reserved for farming or religious festivals.

Black bread. The often cold climate of eastern Europe
has meant that it has been the more hardy cereals that
have established themselves, providing a valuable reserve
of energy. One such is buckwheat, cultivated on a large
scale in Poland and Russia, where it is used in the making of *blinis*, and, when the bran is not removed totally,
black bread. But its low gluten content dictates the
addition of a quantity of wheat flour, without which the
loaf would resemble rather a stone-hard flat cake. In
Poland, the blend (80 percent buckwheat meal for 20
percent wheat flour) results in a black, round, flattish
loaf with a rather strong taste of lard (it is added to the
dough) and an oily crumb. It is often spread with butter or else eaten with a warming soup. However, it is
rye that remains the base of most black breads, and
Pumpernickel-type breads are found all over eastern
Europe. Rye bread has always been eaten in rural areas
of Russia. This is the same bread that was fed to prisoners and was sculpted by them into little figurines (Lenin,
for example, made his inkwell out of a piece of stale
rye). In Belarus, some peasants still make their bread
on the farm, oven-baking it on a bed of oak, maple, or
cabbage leaves placed on the peel just before loading.
The flavor of the leaves mingles deliciously with that of
the crust, giving the whole loaf—traditionally baked
without salt—a unique flavor. In the Ukraine, the peasants accompany their meals with *chernyi khilb*, a large
loaf of black rye.

Above: delicious Jewish rolls
from central Europe have
become an American favorite.
Soft little loaves, often prepared
with cumin, poppy seeds, or

onions, they can be cut open
and made into delicious, melt-
in-your-mouth "sandwiches."
From Alsace to Russia, all of
central Europe has a tradition
of braided bread.
Left: a poppy seed
challah, the bread of
the Jewish Sabbath.

Braided breads. Braided breads, made mainly from wheat flour, are another characteristic loaf of eastern Europe. Here, the art of the baker comes to the fore in the shaping of at least two strands of dough into a braid or "twist." Often enriched with milk to make the crumb soft and tender, braided loaves are especially prominent on tables on the Sabbath and holidays. They are very common in Russia and in those regions of central Europe where they were adopted centuries ago by the resident Jewish population. Every Jewish bakery in the world offers them in all shapes and sizes for religious festivals. There is, for example, the *hallah* or *challah*, a braided bread sometimes stuffed with raisins or lightly sweetened with honey and prepared especially for the Sabbath dinner. Once placed on the traditional embroidered tablecloth, it is then blessed by the head of the family, who breaks it and hands a piece to each guest, symbolizing the divine gift of bread. To make

these spectacular loaves still more attractive and flavorful, bakers garnish them with poppy seeds, or, more rarely, with cumin.

Festival breads. Both religious and pagan festival breads are still popular in eastern Europe, where traditions remain deep-rooted. We have just mentioned the Jewish Sabbath breads, while Christian children are still to be seen eating traditional Christmas breads of fine white wheat flour that are hung on the fir tree. In rural areas of Poland and Bulgaria special loaves are made to celebrate the New Year. They are decorated with pictures of wheat fields, farm animals, and plows, and symbolize the rebirth of nature and the enduring fertility of the earth. During harvest festivals loaves are molded into wheat sheaves, stocks of rye, or bunches of grapes and shared out at thanksgiving feasts in the Czech Republic, Slovakia, and Bulgaria. In Bulgaria, Russia, Belarus and the Ukraine,

Slav weddings are celebrated around a fancy bread, sometimes molded into a heart shape. The newlyweds bow before the loaf, kiss each other, then break it and hand it out to their guests. In Poland, the loaf eaten at the wedding reception is often delicately adorned with doves and flowers. In all these lands, bread is used as a celebration of—or as a plea for—peace, plenty and happiness. In all of these countries, a symbolic offering of "bread and salt" is presented to special guests—a large loaf on which is placed a saucer filled with salt.

Above: bread vendors in Jerusalem. Bread is sacred for all the three great monotheistic religions of the Holy City.

Moroccans for the most part prepare their bread at home, then take it to the baker to be cooked. This wheat bread made with leaven, often enriched with a little peanut oil, accompanies tajine *dishes. Above: a bread vendor in Marrakech.*

Right: a woman in Morocco cooking her bread in an archaic but very effective nomad's bread oven. Whatever its ingredients, a loaf cooked on a bed of kindling always seems tastier than any loaf baked in an electric oven. Facing page: A mella, *a Tunisian loaf which is covered in sand before being cooked on embers.*

The Middle East

From Egypt to Afghanistan, the bread of the Middle East takes us on more than just a voyage through space: it is also a voyage through time, back to the very earliest bread ever baked. The archaic cooking techniques used and the particular uses to which bread is put give us an insight into ancient baking customs and the savors enjoyed by the farmers, shepherds, and nomads of antiquity.

Bread ovens: nomads and peasants. In an excellent book on bread by Bernard Dupaigne, published in 1979 (regrettably out of print, even in French), the author describes a journey he made on foot with some merchants traveling to Faizabad in Afghanistan. "Hunger came. They stopped. One of them took out of his pocket a few handfuls of dough and began to knead them in a wooden bowl with a little of the water they'd brought. Another went off to collect a few of the many camel pats . . . The fire (made with the dung) once lit, the embers had to be plentiful. One, with the staff he used for walking, pushed the glowing embers aside and placed the dough, which had been worked into a disk scarcely 2 inches thick, on the bed of hot ash. The embers were then raked back over the dough piece, making an oven in which the bread could bake. About a quarter of an hour later, the embers were once again cleared away with the stick, to reveal a cooked flat bread."

From the Middle East to India, the dominant tradition is that of a soft-crusted flat bread, which can either be stuffed to create a sandwich, or else be used as a tool to pick up food. In houses and village bakeries, bread is cooked in earthenware ovens. As it is rare, and therefore valuable, wood is rarely used. In Egypt, for example, cottonwood, corn cobs, or dried cow pats are employed to stock the oven.
Above: a bakery in Afghanistan.
Left: a Tunisian kesret, *a loaf cooked in a* tajine.

If it is rare to come across bread cooked over camel dung today, it is quite common, on the other hand, to discover in villages little clay ovens where the bread bakes vertically, stacked against its sides. These ovens are open at the top and have a hole pierced in their base for air intake. A fire of kindling is set at the bottom of the oven and, once the walls are red-hot, flattened cakes of dough are leaned against the walls while the glowing embers are left inside. Such ancient ovens, identical to those painted on tomb walls in ancient Egypt, where bread was invented, are still in use in certain villages in Egypt even today, as well as in the countryside in Lebanon, Syria, Turkey, and Yemen. Less antiquated ovens exist of course throughout such countries, particularly in the cities, but the bread—with the exceptions of various imitations, more or less successful, of French loaves—has not changed significantly.

The tradition of flat bread. In Egypt, guests are seated on straw mats on the ground around a low table. There are no plates or cutlery: a large plate of rice cooked in oil, often garnished with vegetables and, more occasionally, with some pieces of lamb or chicken, is accompanied by a mountain of round flat breads. The meat is eaten with the fingers and the rice with pieces of bread, which are bent inwards slightly to scoop it up. Not a single mouthful is taken without bread; this is general practice for the poorest people everywhere. This way of eating bread is common to all Middle Eastern countries. The round flat loaf—the most common of all breads—is called by different names depending on the country: in Egypt, *aesh*; *khoubz* (simply "bread" in Arabic) in the Arabian peninsula, Syria, Lebanon, and Yemen; and *pide* in Turkey. This bread is in fact none other than the *pita* already met with in Greece—a soft-textured wheat bread, often without any crumb to speak of. Another flat bread is also to be found in these countries, as well as in Armenia and Iran: the *lavash*. Round or oval, extremely thin, but often impressively large (up to 2 feet in diameter), it is an unleavened—or very slightly leavened—bread, as crunchy as a cracker.

Of course, there are other breads which are also enjoyed in the Orient. Walking idly through the streets of Istanbul or Cairo, one encounters itinerant vendors of *simits*, dry and crusty little ring-shaped loaves, sprinkled with

poppy seeds, often eaten as a snack between meals. In Turkish towns, a special favorite is the *francala* (pronounced "frandjala"), a long loaf weighing around 1 pound, with either a white, airy crumb with "eyes" (like French bread—hence its name), or else based on whole-wheat flour. Iranian tables are, for their part, often decorated with the very attractive *barbari* bread, whose dough has added olive oil. These loaves are also round or oval and relatively flat, and, like some French *fougasses*, pierced by five long slashes.

Above: a bakery in the Fener district on the Golden Horn, in Istanbul. In Turkey, luxury breads called francala *(as their name suggests they are an imitation of French bread)*

are baked from finely bolted wheat flour.
Left: during a hunt in Tanzania bread is baked every day at camp.

Asia

Bread enthusiasts would be wrong to think that there is no bread to be found in Asia, though it is true that little is eaten in relation to the amount of rice consumed. In fact, there is more than enough bread in India to satisfy anybody, while China has its surprises, and even Japan and Vietnam are far from being *terrae incognitae*.

Naans and chapatis. Indian cuisine is undeniably one of the richest in the world, and its refinement is very much in evidence in its breads. They are very varied but have the common characteristic of being oval or round, and flat. There are, however, two distinct families, divided into those with leaven and those without. The marvelous *naans* are the best known of the leavened sort, and are found in the north of India, especially in the Punjab, as well as in Pakistan and Bangladesh. The *naan* is traditionally cooked in a *tandoor*, a clay oven dug into the earth, in which Indians also cook chicken, lamb, and fish. Its secret lies in the yoghurt added to a highly fermented, very fine wheat flour, which is responsible for its smooth, soft crust and its slightly sour taste. Bakers, restaurant owners, and mothers at home all add various flavors to their *naans*; some are sprinkled with poppy or sesame seed, others contain onion, or cheese, eggs or milk, while others are spread with *ghee*, a boiled, clarified butter. They are always served warm.

If the *naan* is a bread in the true sense of the word, the *chapati*, served with meals throughout India, is rather a kind of thick pancake, as it is made from unfermented dough, griddled on a large metal hob. They too are served warm, spread with *ghee*. In general, *chapati* are baked from finely crushed wheat flour, but varieties also exist from corn flour, making for a crustier griddle cake. There also exists a richer, flakier, and moister version of the wheaten *chapati*, the *paratha*, whose dough contains some milk or *ghee*, and a deep-fried adaptation with the same dough, the *puri*, which should be eaten almost straight from the pan.

From steamed delights to the *baguette*. Chinese cuisine is also, of course, among the finest in the world. In Peking and throughout the north of the country people eat a bread which seems, on the face of it, somewhat disconcerting: its dough, made from wheat flour, yeast, and a little sugar, is fermented scarcely more than an hour before being rolled into little sausages. These are then put in a wicker basket and steamed for twenty minutes over a saucepan of boiling water. These *man to* are eaten warm as an accompaniment. Such warm, soft, rubbery, and slightly sugary rolls will, of course, prove to be something of a

Facing page: cooking chapatis *on a griddle called a* tava, *in India. Like* naan, *which is leavened bread, a* chapati *is both sustenance in itself and an implement for picking up other foods.*

There are still traces of French colonization in Southeast Asia, such as a predilection for good, crusty bread. Above: a market at Dalat, in Vietnam.

surprise to palates used to other sorts of bread. The Chinese adore them, however, and have exported this tasty recipe to Vietnam, Laos, and Cambodia. Normally, however, when bread is eaten in any of these three countries, it is an unoriginal, crusty loaf baked in a European–style oven with a white and airy crumb—no doubt a legacy of French colonialism. On a journey through Vietnam, an excellent French baker, Dominique Saibron, detected a soupçon of rice meal in these white loaves. French bread, especially the *baguette*, is also found in Japan's larger cities, where, for the last few years, French bakers have been making inroads. China too, as she experiences the delights of the all-American "bun," is gradually discovering real French bread: an industrialist from Nevers, southeast of Paris, has already exported around thirty bread-making units, including dough-freezing plant and cooking terminals. The first French loaf introduced, however, was a *baguette* 2½ feet in length, but it was soon necessary to replace these with shorter loaves as the Chinese were in the habit of carrying them home strapped to the back of their bicycles and they were always being snapped off in the traffic.

South America

Crossing the Pacific we arrive in Latin America. Here there is certainly a great variety of breads, but surprisingly little originality, and the ordinary bread resembles that of the French, the Spanish, or the Germans. One country stands out from the rest, however, by its interesting use of cornmeal: Mexico.

The *tortilla*. The national Mexican "bread," thousands of years old, is not a true bread at all. What the Maya called *uah*, and the Spanish christened *tortilla* because it looked like their own omelet, is in fact a griddle cake made from unfermented cornmeal. Rural Mexicans, however, consume it in exactly the same way as the French do their *baguettes*: daily, with all their meals and with every imaginable dish. In these farming communities, where corn was first cultivated and where the conquistadors discovered it before bringing it to Europe, the preparation of *tortillas*, a task performed solely by women, has not changed at all. The corn kernels are first boiled in a cooking pot for several hours, then pounded on a stone (the *metate*) to obtain a dough (called the *masa*). The cook then flattens the pieces of dough between her hands into little griddle cakes that she cooks on an earthenware slab supported above a wood fire. In cities the dough mixture is sold ready-made, and town dwellers with the time like to cook them at home, as *tortillas* are best served and eaten warm. They are eaten instead of bread to accompany traditional Mexican dishes. They are used like spoons to pick up other foods, or else both *tortilla* and sauce are eaten together, forming a delicious mixture. They also form the base for succulent sandwiches, the famous *tacos*.

Left: a traditional Spanish leavened bread in a Bolivian market. Facing page: the Mexican national dish, - the tortilla, *which is in fact an unleavened cornmeal flat bread, still prepared as it was by the Maya.*

North America

Henry Miller once lamented that he could travel fifty thousand miles in America without once tasting good bread. It is a pity that the writer did not live until he was one hundred. Miller died in 1980, thereby missing the extraordinary revival in American bread making, which started in the 1980s and continues today. This renewal might introduce more Americans to good bread—at present Americans consume on average half as much per capita than the French. In the years of "cocooning" and of a return to basic values, numerous bakeries have sprung up, offering a new generation of gourmets, tired of the industrialized, plastic-wrapped loaf, an extraordinary variety of delicious breads. These include not only French and Italian examples but also old American recipes that used to be eaten on the ranches of the pioneers.

The bread of the pioneers. The earliest American farmers, faced with tracts of untilled land and an unpredictable climate, preferred the security of corn, a resistant crop already cultivated by Native Americans, to the uncertainty of wheat yields. The United States is to this day the biggest producer of corn, responsible for half the world's yield. Not surprisingly there is a variety of corn breads available in the country. The oldest, which is also the simplest, is directly inspired by an old Native

In North America, bread making remains a deeply rooted tradition. Left: a husband gazes admiringly at a loaf of homemade bread. Facing page: baking bread in the Canadian West in the 1920s.

American recipe: the corn pone is a small moist loaf made from cornmeal with a little lard and buttermilk. However, numerous other recipes exist which marry cornmeal and wheat flour. An example is the classic corn bread which is found all over the United States, baked from equal proportions of the two crops. To make the bread moist, butter, milk, and eggs are added to the mixture. Corn imparts its particular flavor to the excellent pioneer bread, composed of white and whole-wheat flour, rye flour, and sunflower seeds. Such breads can also be fermented with leaven and mixed with a little maple syrup or honey. Another classic mix from the American farm is wheat flour and potato bread, which also incorporates milk, the dough being kneaded into the water in which the potatoes were boiled. Toasted in slices, it is eaten mainly in winter.

Some regions in the United States offer other succulent and age-old specialties based on bread. The well-known hoagie is a favorite of Philadelphians. It is a sandwich of white-bread roll, sausage meat, onions, tomatoes, and lettuce, with a modicum of pepper, and olive oil. In the southern states, nothing is more typical than spoon bread: this is another corn bread, doused in so much corn syrup and butter that one has to eat it with a spoon. For those who are not partial to corn syrup, there is a version of spoon bread with honey and milk. There are of course people who cannot stomach sweet-tasting breads at all. For them as well, the south has a tailor-made specialty: corn bread with bacon bits. New Orleans has a penchant for breakfast with *pain perdu*, an old Creole recipe for French toast using stale bread. The bread is first soaked in a mixture of eggs (hence its occasional name "eggy bread"), cream, honey, orange-flower water, rum, and orange zest. The pieces are then fried until golden brown in butter, before being served sprinkled with sugar and grated nutmeg. California, above all San Francisco, is the American capital of sourdough bread, a fine wheat flour loaf made with leaven, which is becoming fashionable once more thanks to a number of excellent bakers.

The Americans call it the "bread rush." In the last ten years, many Americans have discovered good bread and now debate the respective merits of the baguette, ciabatta, bagel, or pumpernickel. All over the country numerous excellent bakeries are opening their doors.

Below: an armful of delights, carried by Sophie, the daughter of Wendy and Michael London, excellent bakers in Greenwich, near New York (the Rock Hill Bakehouse). Below right: the shop sign of a famous bakery in Berkeley, Acme Bread, specialized in French bread with natural leavening. Facing page: two bakeries in New York in 1937 (left: photograph by Berenice Abbott) and today.

Bread and immigration. The United States and Canada are immigrant countries and therefore a kind of living museum of bread. Germans and Scandinavians brought their rye, the Irish their soda bread, the Italians, *grissini* and *focaccia*. Italian bread is among the most appreciated in the United States, and every large city has its own specialized Italian bakeries. The Jewish communities of central Europe, for their part, brought their braided breads and the bagel. The tastiest bagels on the planet are to be found in certain American cities and above all in New York, the city with the world's largest Jewish community. The distinguishing characteristic of these little rolls is their "donut" shape. But how can such a delicious "roll with the hole" be so crunchy and glossy on the outside and so soft and moist on the inside? First, butter, egg white, and milk are added to the mixture; then a special cooking method is used in which the bagel rings are plunged for thirty seconds into boiling water or put under steam for a full minute before they are placed in the oven. Bagels are often eaten sliced into two to form two flat rings which are simply buttered or eaten as a sandwich with cream cheese and smoked salmon. They are occasionally sprinkled with poppy seeds or sesame seeds. Caraway-rye bagels, cinnamon- or raisin-flavored bagels are just some of the other varieties enjoyed all over the city. The specialized Chesapeake Bagel Bakery sells seven

ACME BREAD COMPANY · BERKELEY

hundred thousand bagels through its thirty-five outlets in the Washington, D.C. area alone. Unfortunately, a bizarre but all too common accident has made its appearance in hospital emergency departments: "bagel injury." It results from the knife being pushed into the roll and meeting some initial resistance from the crust before going right through the soft crumb more quickly than anticipated and wounding the hand holding the bagel.

In spite of the relative paucity of French immigrants, French bread making has met with extraordinary popularity throughout the United States. The best bakeries, many of whose owners have trained in France, offer succulent loaves made with natural leavening, *baguettes*, *fougasses*, *bâtards*, *ficelles*, and walnut and raisin bread. As for Lionel Poilâne's famous loaves, Americans, for the sum of forty dollars each, can receive them freshly baked and flown over from France by airplane.

Bread and fast food. It would be impossible to conclude an overview of American bread, however brief, without mentioning the loaf that is eaten the most often, one that has conquered the whole planet: the fast-food hamburger roll. The champion in this domain, McDonald's (fifteen thousand restaurants around the world), has a recipe which has hardly changed in thirty-five years. These very soft and slightly sweet-tasting buns are made from milk-enriched wheat flour containing an additive, lecithin, a fatty substance extracted from soya which improves both freshness and taste. These buns are produced industrially and delivered for the most part deep-frozen to the outlets. Some are sprinkled with sesame seeds and they are always lightly toasted before being filled with the burger. Such is the most recent incarnation of the continuing and universal success of bread.

This is the final stage of our trip around the world of bread. We could cross back over the Atlantic and start the process all over again, so numerous are the breads that remain to be discovered. From industrial bread prepared in a factory to the flat bread cooked on a camel pat, the history of bread has lasted thousands of years and stretched thousands of miles. Its presence on tables all over the world should be appreciated for what it really is: an everyday miracle.

Bread for
the Gourmet

Bread gastronomy is a tricky matter which a number of chefs and master bakers have pondered. Above: at his restaurant La Côte d'Or, in Saulieu, in the Morvan, Bernard Loiseau provides his diners with little rolls called pains gris de Morvan. These are wheat and rye blends, made with leaven, and delicately flavored with a hint of toasted wheat millings and honey. By combining the four basic

tastes (sweet, sour, bitter, and, salt), the rolls go with practically every dish. Facing page: the simplicity of a white farmhouse loaf is a good match for the strong Mediterranean flavors of tapenade *(olive paste) and fresh goat's milk cheese. Below: wheat loaves baked in Sologne birch containers. The wood gives the crust a slightly scented aroma.*

Real bread lovers do not eat bread just to appease their hunger, nor do they eat it through force of habit or because it is convenient. They eat it consciously for what it is: a flavorful food in itself, a true delicacy. They might spread a little smooth butter onto a fresh *baguette,* but if they do it is not simply to wolf it down, rather they savor the unforgettable marriage of wheat flour and butter. And if they put two pieces of cooked sausage between two slices of a farmhouse bread made with natural leaven, it is not because such a sandwich is a simple thing to throw together, but because the sourdough taste of the leaven is an excellent foil to the taste of pork. Bread, which, like wine, is born of natural but carefully controlled fermentation, is also worthy of its own body of connoisseurs, experts, and enthusiasts. Though such expert knowledge leads to still greater eating pleasure, to attain it requires intelligent and regular exercise of the taste buds. But first of all it is necessary to familiarize oneself with the fundamental principles that form the basis of bread gastronomy.

Selecting Bread

How is one to separate the wheat from the chaff among all the loaves—*pain de campagne*, *baguette*, sandwich, oven-bottom—that bakeries provide? And even before that, how should one select a decent baker, where one can go and buy one's bread every day? This is a more delicate question than might at first appear, because everyone has their own ideas about bread quality and might find a loaf someone else thinks sublime, inedible. For my part, I have built up my criteria through my dealings with great bakers, people who are to be recognized not only by their bread but also by their passion for their chosen trade. Such people are surely the best judges and they all generally agree on a number of essentials.

With the eye alone, I can already spot certain clues which make me think that a particular loaf is worth avoiding: a thin, shiny crust, the base still bearing the imprint of the industrial oven plate; an over-regular shape; a uniform color; an overall form reminiscent of an inflated balloon. Inversely, there are signs which make my mouth water: a fine, solid crust, none too shiny, somewhat mountainous looking and irregular with a good color contrast, a sturdy mass which gives the impression of density when I hold it in my hand. These clues are clearly evident when one compares a pathetic ordinary "mock" *baguette* with an authentic exemple of the same species (nicknamed in French bakeries *à l'ancienne* or *1900*). The latter, weighing the same as the former, is always slightly smaller, and tastes better. At this stage—that is, whenever I have to choose bread from its appearance alone—I am never lulled into a false sense of security by a floured crust: some unscrupulous bakers do not shrink from sprinkling flour on their loaves to give them the "country" look which city-dwellers fall for. There is no guarantee that such a loaf is equally rustic on the inside.

Breaking the bread gives me far more information. When a loaf has not been prepared according to the rules of good baking, it is poorly dressed in a thin, fragile crust which does not crumble when I cut it with a knife but comes off in big "scales"—a sure sign that all is not well.

Small bread rolls are ideal for entertaining friends. Above: these very soft white rolls from the Auvergne, made with fine, patent flour, are shaped to have a sort of cap.

For special occasions, the name of each guest can be painted on top using a brush and coffee essence and the roll can be placed on the napkin as a place marker.

When I bring a knife to a good crust, only a few irregularly shaped crumbs drop off—these I pick up and nibble. The structure, consistency, and color of the crumb are the best clues to ascertaining the quality before actually tasting it. The crumb of French loaves such as the *baguette* should not be white as snow, but rather creamy-white. This is not, of course, for merely aesthetic reasons but because an off-white color proves that the dough was not excessively oxygenated during kneading. Excessive oxygenation is a common practice because consumers tend to prefer white bread, but unfortunately the process deprives the loaf of all taste. This delicate, creamy tone should be even throughout the loaf; a mottled crumb with darker, tighter-textured areas implies that the dough has been insufficiently fermented. As for *baguettes* and *bâtards* made with leaven, their crumb should possess a slight grayish tint. *Pains de campagne*, on the other hand, cannot be judged by their crumb in the same fashion as bakers prepare them in so many different ways, some being baked with a flour similar to that used for *baguettes*, others being made from brown whole-wheat or rye-enriched types.

Apart from color, crumb structure provides other unmistakable indications of quality. A good crumb has a supple, springy, airy texture, with, particularly for French breads, "holes" of different sizes. Around these air holes, the crumb itself should have good body and density. A tight, highly regular hole structure, forming a see-through, cotton-wool crumb lacking in firmness is the telltale sign that the baker has opted to hoodwink his customers by increasing the volume of the loaf, thereby spoiling the taste and aroma into the bargain. The customer is robbed of the smell of fresh bread: the scents of ripe wheat seed, with sometimes a whiff of hazelnut or fruit, or else, with leavening, fall undergrowth and wet earth, or any other of the one hundred and fifty aromas detected in fresh bread by the "noses" on the laboratory staff of the French Institut National de Recherche Agronomique. These many perfumes (grass shoots, rose, mushroom, and potatoes, for example) are replaced by feckless bakers with the stench of pure yeast or soggy cardboard.

Inseparable from aroma, the flavor of bread and its "chewiness" form the inevitable culmination of any gastronomic examination. Taste depends on a wide range of factors and can vary a great deal from bread to bread. In *Le Goût du pain*, a rather technical volume written for professionals, the professor of baking Raymond Calvel lists five main factors: the ingredients of the dough, the type of kneading, the method of fermentation, the handing up of the dough, and the oven baking itself. Each stage is approached very differently by individual bakers for each particular loaf and so it is obvious that "the taste" of good bread does not in fact exist, any more than it does for great wine. For example, the *baguettes* made in summer and winter by the same baker using the same methods can taste different because the fermentation of the dough varies according to the season. How can one be sure then that a particular loaf is a good one? For my part, it is when I have evidence that I am eating a natural product, one in which all the raw materials that go to make it can be individually tasted. Like a good cheese which is identifiable by the aroma of the cow's or goat's milk which it contains, I recognize a good loaf of bread by the smell of wheat—or rye—grain, of freshly milled flour. I like the aroma of hot bread just out of the oven, when it has the taste of freshly toasted cereal grain. I am glad when I also get a whiff of sea air, as with the flavor of Guérande rock salt, that used by the best French bakers. Whether the loaf is a *baguette*, a fancy loaf flavored with figs or garlic, or a large, round loaf made with leaven, if these basic tastes each remain discernible, the baker has earned his laurels. To achieve this, he must, for example, avoid incorporating too much yeast into a *baguette* dough and take care that the leavening he uses does not make his *pain de campagne* too sour.

The *mâche* (chew) of a loaf is just as important. Never again will I buy loaves which give one the disagreeable sensation of chewing on fresh air, or worse still, on a piece of absorbent cotton wool which dries out tongue and palate. Bread should be soft and creamy, but dense as well. The grainy crust and the soft crumb should merge as they are chewed, while the taste fills the mouth right up to the moment it is swallowed.

Bread as an Accompaniment

Once you have unearthed a decent baker, you can start discovering the infinitely varied world of bread, with its everyday delights and its more refined delicacies. Artisan bakers can supply a vast array of different loaves and you would therefore be wrong to stick to just a few. To begin with, you would soon become bored of such a routine and, what is more, you would never experience one of the great delights of bread: the many ways it can be served as an accompaniment to other dishes. In the best restaurants, such marriages are arranged in the subtlest way, to ensure that they are as harmonious as possible. At L'Espadon, the Ritz's Parisian restaurant, for example, Guy Legay officiates in the kitchen and Bernard Burban at the oven. The two men, who have both received the French prize of "Meilleur Ouvrier de France" (best craftsman), work in tandem to delight their customers. Six rolls are placed on each table, whatever the dish served:

Joël Robuchon in his restaurant proposes mini-baguettes and farmhouse rolls made with leaven all served—like so many dollhouse toys—in a banneton (the same basket that is used for handing up the dough).
Facing page: a colorful selection of rolls offered by the baker

Bernard Burban at the Ritz in Paris. They incorporate, variously, red wine and shallots, cumin, pure rye, and rye with walnuts. There are also whole-wheat brioches and mini-baguettes. The rolls can be eaten on their own or with selected dishes.

a "mini-*baguette*," a roll with bacon pieces, a wheat-flour base with cumin, and a light rye with walnuts, together with a wheat-flour roll and a heavy rye mix, both made with leaven. Such tid-bits can of course be nibbled at while waiting for the entrée to arrive, but the real idea behind this assortment is to create the perfect match between the dish served and one or other of the rolls. The Ritz is not the only restaurant in France where this practice is followed and it is an idea that might be copied in the home for a dinner party, as any dish can be greatly improved by a bread which goes with it. It is cheap and easy, and also makes quite a splash, to serve four different breads (either sliced or, in the case of rolls, served whole): a good *baguette*, a farmhouse loaf, and two other breads chosen to harmonize with the dishes served. Bread should always be put in baskets or placed on side plates so that guests can help themselves whenever they wish without having to ask. Whole loaves should be sliced just before people take their place at table. A sharp knife which is not serrated should be used, as serrated knives tend to tear the crumb and break it into little balls.

But which bread should be eaten with which dish? A number of good bakers, such as Jacques Mahou in Tours, Pierre Gauducheau in Nantes, Claude Mesnier in Besançon, and Jean-Jacques Poujauran in Paris, simplify this task by advising their customers on what the best combinations are. There is, however, one general rule: *baguettes* and other white yeast loaves, with their unassertive taste, should accompany delicately flavored foods, while farmhouse *pains de campagne* made with leaven, with their stronger flavor, go best with sturdy, somewhat rustic dishes. Thus *baguettes* and *ficelles* are ideally suited to salads and raw or green vegetables, as well as grills, roasts, creamed or poached filleted fish, and the less strong cheeses like camembert, brie, emmental, comté, and fresh goat's milk cheeses. Leavened breads (as well as masnil and mixed ryes) are at their best with *charcuterie*, game, dishes made with strong traditional French sauces (*coq au vin, boeuf bourguignon, cassoulet,* pickled pork with lentils, etc.) and strong cheeses, such as Roquefort, Époisses, Munster, and all goat's milk cheeses.

Special breads bring countless nuances to these basic principles. Rye bread goes well with all seafood dishes, such as oysters, with *charcuterie* and, in particular, with all smoked foods, such as ham and salmon. Walnut bread is somewhat difficult to marry to other dishes, but is suited to game, snails, mixed salads, and full-bodied wines. When it is very slightly stale, I like to heat it up in the oven and eat it with a little cake of warm Chavignol goat's milk cheese. Dense *pain brié* seems to have been created specifically to be eaten with all cheeses and with fish in sauce, whereas olive bread is a wonderful accompaniment to mild goat's milk cheeses. Some bakers propose loaves which tone down the taste of strong cheeses. We have already mentioned *pain brié* and cumin bread (whose peppery taste joins forces best with Munster and Livarot cheeses), but there are also hazelnut, chestnut, and wine-flavored loaves. At the Ritz, Bernard Burban has concocted a red wine and shallot loaf, while Claude Mesnier, at his bakery in Besançon, bakes one flavored with an Arbois wine. A light raisin rye, which can be eaten as it is or spread with butter, also goes well with goat's milk cheese. Certain specific dishes naturally seem to require particular types of bread: blood sausage with apple bread, for example, or duck with orange-flavored rolls, classic salads and rolls with bacon pieces, exotic salads with soya or seaweed breads. Other still more inventive combinations can also be surprisingly good: fig loaves with marinated game (deer or wild boar), fennel rolls with fish, and poppy-seed bread with fowl.

The only dishes which do not go with any type of bread are those themselves based on cereals: pasta, couscous, and polenta, for example. A Judaeo-Spanish proverb from Morocco puts it in a nutshell: "Bread with bread is a meal fit for fools" (*pan con pan, comida de tontos*).

The tricky subject of the marriage between two such divine substances as bread and wine seems to depend largely on personal preference. A few years ago, Alain Senderens, the chef at the prestigious Lucas-Carton restaurant, brought together an eminent group of wine experts, wine waiters, and a baker, Lionel Poilâne. Their mission was to discover the best combinations of wine and bread by means of a tasting. These two delicacies are of course rarely consumed in isolation, without an accompanying dish, but it was felt that the exercise would be worthwhile as a means of engineering more refined culinary harmonies. Bread and wine are nevertheless eaten together outside meals by winegrowers. I discovered this fact at an extraordinary tasting of Burgundies at Auxey-Duresses. To highlight all the savors of his nectars, the wise and warm-hearted winegrower Jean-Pierre Prunier proposed that I drink the whites with a Comté cheese bread and the reds accompanied by a walnut loaf: the flavors thus created were sublime indeed. Alain Senderens's gourmet conclave analyzed the thirty-six possible marriages between six different wines and breads. Judgments were almost unanimous with respect to the *baguette* eaten with a Muscadet, a Riesling (which it made "more amiable") and a Bourgueil (made "more fruity"). A farmhouse bread with leaven went with Sauternes perfectly but not at all with Muscadet or Riesling. The latter, on the other hand, married wonderfully with a rye bread (whose dry, well-nigh "withered" edge was pleasantly improved by the process). Rye, however, also accompanied to perfection light red wines such as Beaujolais and Bourgueil. The walnut bread found its soul mate in the shape of a white Burgundy, the Saint-Véran, but was somewhat overbearing when allied with Sauternes, Beaujolais and Bourgueil. Raisin bread, somewhat paradoxically, went with neither reds nor whites.

Finding the best combinations of bread with other food, apparently a mysterious art, is in fact governed by the mingling of the senses. The mineral savor of rye goes well with all salty seafoods, and hence rye breads suit oysters and black, whole-grain rye accompanies smoked fish. Fig bread and apricot bread gracefully join forces with Sauternes, the better to envelop the oily softness of foie gras. Walnut and raisin breads have pastoral undertones which harmonize perfectly with goat's milk cheese, giving it a wholesome, rustic flavor.

The Art of the Sandwich

Lord Sandwich, who lived during the eighteenth century, was a fortunate man indeed. He gave his name both to two archipelagos and to a small but world-famous culinary concept, devised for him by an inspired cook. An inveterate gambler, the Lord of the Admiralty would rather have

The sandwich is an art form with its own schools of thought. Some opt for a sandwich loaf, others for a farmhouse loaf, some like it hot, others want butter . . . Imaginative gourmets can come up with inventions that would make those accustomed to the commonplace ham sandwich turn pale. An example was provided by Joris-Karl Huysmans in his novel Là-bas, *published in 1891: ". . . would you pass me the* pain d'épices . . . ; *cut it into wafer-thin slices and then take an equally thin slice of normal bread, butter both, put them together and eat. Now just tell me, doesn't this sandwich have the exquisite taste of fresh hazelnuts?"*

Above: preparing sandwiches for the crowd at Wembley Stadium, London, at the beginning of the century.

Facing page: Monsieur Bouscarel and his sandwiches in his bistrot, La Tartine, near the Place de la Bastille in Paris.

died of hunger than left the green baize at mealtimes. So the cook dreamed up a simple cold snack which was nourishing and, above all, could be eaten with one hand: Lord Sandwich was saved from starvation. Almost any bread in the world can be used to make a sandwich, which has many different names. Many of the most delicious, including the classic sandwich as eaten in Britain and the Italian *tramezzini* (sometimes toasted), are made from the sandwich loaf. All kinds of bread can be used to make delicious sandwiches, however. The French *baguette*, for example, is the basis of the famous *jambon-beurre* (split down the middle with butter and ham), while there is also the hot dog, the American bun in the form of hamburgers, the French roll (*petit pain*), and the very Provençal *pan-bagnat*, an original sandwich of anchovies, tuna, olive oil, and vegetables. The Middle Eastern *pita* bread is usually stuffed with spitted meats, while in Scandinavia black rye rolls are often filled with smoked fish. It has become fashionable to lampoon the sandwich as an indigestible nefarious snack that is misguidedly eaten at lunchtime instead of an honest meal. We will address the question of bread and nutrition below, but for now we will just ask whether sandwiches have their place in a balanced diet. At the risk of shocking gourmets, I have to say that for bread lovers nothing is as tasty as a sandwich. The sandwich, it goes without saying, has to be a good one: here are a few rules which should be observed to guarantee that this is the case.

The most important is to only use the best bread and avoid sandwich loaves with the texture of cotton wool. There is nothing worse, when it comes to sandwiches, than to have to chew endlessly on a piece of bread that resembles dry cardboard. One should also select the bread which goes best with the chosen fillings—the best combinations follow the same general principles outlined above. The marriage is only successful, though, if the proportions between filling and bread are correct so as the tastes of both come through. As there is generally more bread than filling, this normally means that the bread must be cut thinly and should in general be a sandwich loaf which has a light crumb and an undemonstrative taste. These loaves, made from wheat or rye, can be used to make the ideal sandwich for buffets at cocktail parties or receptions. They can be served arranged on a tray or, better still, concealed in a large loaf from which the crumb has been removed. At receptions, a sandwich loaf can form the basis of canapés, those tiny delicate sandwiches with colorful and tasty fillings, such as ham, salmon, asparagus heads, caviar, and Roquefort butter. The thin stick *ficelle* loaf is ideal for sandwiches, but the *baguette*, though it can also be filled, is more suited, because of its size, to the *tartine*, the French open sandwich.

Bernard Burban, the baker at the Ritz, is one of the very few in his profession to openly declare his passion for the sandwich. I wish that everyone could taste the

admirable bread made from stone-ground flour which is used to make the warm sandwiches of chicken breast, cold roast beef, and smoked salmon served at the Ritz bar. If that is not a gastronomic experience, may I be forever starved of bread!

The Delights of Toasted Bread

Another delicious way of eating bread, above all at breakfast time, is in grilled slices: toast. Bread used to be toasted over glowing embers on metal toasting forks equipped with long handles. The toast was thereby impregnated with a smoky taste which pleasantly excited the taste buds. Today, the best way of making toast is to use a good electric toaster which can accept different thicknesses, toasting both sides simultaneously. (The asbestos or perforated metal plates often used in continental Europe are to be avoided as they impart a disagreeable taste to the toast.) Though any wheat-flour

Bread was long toasted over a direct flame or on embers using a trivet or fork with a long handle, allowing the bread to be placed right next to the heat source. Today's toasters are all electric and do not give the same smoky flavor to the bread.
Right: a drawing by Jessie Wilcox Smith (1903).

Facing page: pain perdu or French toast—the most delicious way of making something out of stale bread.

WOMEN HAVE COOKED AND DREAMED IN THIS EMBER-GLOW SINCE THE WORLD BEGAN

bread can be toasted to taste, my own preference is for a fresh *baguette*, which comes out of the toaster as soft as it went in, with a still lighter crumb and a crunchy crust. It is the ideal accompaniment to *foie gras* (which can be eaten with toasted *pain de campagne*, providing it is not too sour, or with saffron bread or *méture*, Basque corn bread). Bread can be kept soft after toasting by placing it immediately in a hermetically sealed container for a minute or two—holding the steam in prevents the toast from drying out. One should not, however, toast rye bread at all as this can damage it beyond recognition; corn bread, on the other hand, is better toasted than fresh.

Toast is often eaten with butter and jam. At a British or American breakfast it can accompany not only marmalade but also fried eggs, bacon, sausages, and potatoes. In Britain is also eaten with a semi-hard cheese, such as Cheddar or Double Gloucester. In Italy and Spain toasted bread laced with olive oil, garlic, and tomato forms the basis of many tasty snacks such as the Italian *bruschetta* and Catalonia's *pa amb tomàquets*. In France, Lionel Poilâne has called the slices of toasted bread which are spread with all kinds of savory preparations (based on vegetables, cheese, or herbs) *croustons*. My own recommendation would be an open sandwich with a generous helping of eggplant caviar or guacamole.

Long Live Fresh Bread!

How best to conserve bread depends on its type. French *baguettes*, *ficelles*, and *bâtards* were designed to be eaten fresh, which is why good bakers prepare at least two oven loads daily. They should, however, not be eaten straight out of the oven as the damp, doughy crumb makes them difficult to digest. That said, if a poorly baked *baguette* bought in the morning is only fit for the garbage by the afternoon (its paper-thin crust making the crumb quickly dry out), an authentic one should always be good enough to turn into a last little snack at midnight. The next day, even when a little stale, it will regain its freshness for a few minutes if moistened and heated up in the oven. Larger

detached during freezing, although this amounts to a minor disadvantage if the loaf is a good one. Thawing is best achieved in one of two ways: either directly in the oven, for five minutes at around 200°C (400°F), or else at room temperature, being careful to shelter the bread from drafts. Freezing bread, as long as these rules are observed, is a godsend: it enables those bread lovers who live too far from a good bakery to be able to go every day to eat daily perfectly fresh bread made by the very best bakers.

It should not be forgotten that toasting can often make slightly stale bread delicious and that even when bread is totally stale it still may form the basis of countless dishes using bread crumbs, or as bread soup, bread pudding, summer pudding, or French toast.

Cooking with Bread

Some absolutely delicious dishes can simply not be eaten without bread, such as the Savoie *fondue*, for example, (with a close-crumbed farmhouse loaf), or Andalusian *gazpacho* (with white bread cubes). For other dishes, bread forms an essential ingredient in their preparation. This is once again the case with *gazpacho*, made from bread, tomatoes, garlic, and vinegar processed together in a mixer. An onion soup without a few slices of *baguette* covered with melted cheese scarcely deserves the name. In the Middle East, *koftas* are little meatballs made of minced mutton with a good helping of bread crumbs, that is stale bread baked golden in the oven then crumbed. Added during preparation, stale bread has the gift of making a multitude of soups marvelously creamy. Steeped in milk, stale bread is also used to make the fruit cakes of which the English are so fond. Other dishes also have bread as their principal ingredient. *Panade*, for example, is a soup which was long popular in France. It is nothing other than a broth of stale bread made smoother with the addition of milk or dairy cream. Stale bread is the basic ingredient of *pain perdu*, known as Poor Knights of Windsor in England and French toast in the United States. Slices of stale bread are dipped in a mixture of milk and beaten eggs, fried golden with

farmhouse loaves—especially the thick crusted ones baked in brick-built ovens—can keep their delicious taste for at least ten days. They should not be left in an atmosphere which is either too dry or too damp but should be stored in a receptacle which allows the bread to breathe: in a paper bag (plastic, which makes bread go soft, should be avoided at all costs), a dishtowel or placed in a metal—or better still wooden—bread bin. Lionel Poilâne has designed a very useful wooden box, equipped with built-in slicer and crumb tray, which he sells in his bakeries.

The recent practice of home freezing has made it possible to conserve bread for longer periods. It is possible to freeze *baguettes*, small loaves, and even larger ones, provided they are sliced first. But to ensure that it keeps all its freshness the bread must be sealed hermetically in a plastic wrapping before being placed in the freezer as the cold in fact dehydrates and dries out bread. If it has been well protected, however, a *baguette* quickly regains its original freshness after four or five days freezing, and sandwich and Viennese loaves keep for a week. Beyond this time, bread can still be fresh but pieces of the crust may become butter and finally sprinkled with maple syrup, sugar, cinnamon, or vanilla.

Before concluding these lines on bread in cooking, I cannot refrain from alluding to one of my favorite dishes, the French ham and cheese toasted sandwich called the *croque-monsieur*, which is absolutely divine when prepared as it should be. It requires some simple ingredients which are often lacking in cafés in France: good bread, good ham, and good cheese. Sandwich bread can be used, but I personally prefer an oven-bottom *pain de campagne*. The slice of Paris ham should be thick and juicy and the cheese used should be Comté (from the Franche–Comté region) rather than Gruyère. Cut two long and rather thin slices of bread from a loaf; cover one with the Comté grated into wafer-thin strips and lay the slice of ham on the cheese and sprinkle it with more grated cheese. Then place the second slice of bread on top. The sandwich should be pressed together and kept tight by a length of kitchen string. It should then be put in a hot oven for five to ten minutes (a frying pan is not recommended for browning and cooking the *croque-monsieur* as the butter required makes the sandwich too fatty). The sandwich should be taken out of the oven as soon as the bread is golden brown and the cheese has melted. Simply cut the string and enjoy.

Right: as early as 1931, Parisian bakers were concerned to provide their customers with a healthy product.
Facing page: Mark Furstenberg, a baker in Washington, D.C. and one of America's staunchest defenders of good, natural bread.

Page 160: Swiss Traubenbrot.
Page 161: Ceres in the Stohrer bakery, in Les Halles, Paris.

Bread, Health and Fitness

Bread has not always enjoyed a good reputation among those who are concerned with their health or are trying to watch their weight. They consider that it contributes a few extra pounds in weight to the body and nothing much else. In fact the opposite is the case: nutritionists are unanimous in ascribing bread with extraordinary virtues. It is in fact a complete food in itself, perfectly balanced and digestible. An ordinary *baguette*, for example, contains 35 percent water, 54 percent carbohydrate, 7 percent protein and 1 percent lipids, as well as a little salt, phosphorus, calcium, and vitamins B1, B2, and niacin. A whole-meal loaf contains approximately 40 percent water, 9 percent protein, 42 percent carbohydrate, iron, calcium, zinc, magnesium and potassium and vitamins B1, B2, and niacin. It also makes for 8.5 percent dietary fiber.

Can bread make you fat? The answer is no, as long as the bread is not swathed in bacon fat or covered by a thick layer of butter! The main dietary qualities of bread derive from its low fat content (only 1 percent of lipids in normal bread) and in the *type* of carbohydrate it comprises. In a balanced diet, which must contain carbohydrate, protein, and fats, the first make up 50 percent of the caloric value. For the purposes of discussions about diet, there are two main groups of carbohydrates, however. The first consist of monosaccharides such as sugar, honey, jams, and fruits. These stimulate rapid insulin production and make one feel like eating again soon after. The second group consists of polysaccharides, such as starch-rich foodstuffs like bread, pasta, rice, and potatoes. These reduce the desire for sugars and therefore do not encourage over-eating. Hence, if one wants to reduce weight, one should avoid rapidly absorbed sugars and concentrate on the "slow" ones. Contrary to popular opinion, bread does not make one gain weight, and can even help the overweight in a diet. As carbohydrates are unavoidable, a number of slimming diets allow for the eating of bread—as it provides "good" carbohydrates—or else allow for its gradual reintroduction after initially

forbidding it. What is more, bread contains a variable amount of dietary cereal fiber which reduces the likelihood of constipation.

Very healthy and easy to digest, bread also releases its energy content gradually throughout the day. Because of this, rolls or bread with fillings or spreads should form part of every breakfast. Thanks to its high, slow-release carbohydrate content, bread works rather like a high energy battery which only slowly runs down. The body assimilates its sugars slowly, thereby avoiding that all-too-common empty feeling around eleven o'clock resulting from a drop in blood sugar levels.

Bread from organic and stone-ground flour. Because bran (the envelope around the grain) contains the residue from herbicides, fungicides, and pesticides used in modern agriculture, it is far better to eat only loaves containing it—brown and above all whole-wheat loaves— which have been made from organically grown flour free from such chemicals. The chemical residues are of course minute and for the most part entirely harmless. Nonetheless, it would be as well for all those who eat whole-wheat bread to keep to the organic variety, which is found readily in most good bakers and in health shops. In general, excessive consumption of whole-wheat bread is not to be encouraged; if the dietary fiber they contain is undeniably beneficial to all those who suffer from constipation, it has the disadvantage of reducing the body's intake of iron, calcium, and magnesium present either in the bread itself or in other foodstuffs. In high dosages, bran can also adversely effect the intestines.

All flour milled to make "stone-ground" bread should also ideally come from organic farming, as millstones (unlike rollers) never succeed in eliminating all the bran. Once again, however, this is most important in the case of brown flour, as white breads contain very little bran at all. Such stone-milled loaves are certainly the best, for their health-giving qualities as well as for their aroma and flavor. The wheat germ, which stone-milling does not remove from the grain, is a rich, life-giving concentrate of proteins, mineral salts, vitamins, and fatty acids. There is a drawback for those who have to watch their weight, however, as the wheat germ is so fatty that the stones turn it into oil during milling.

Excellent for one's health, full of flavor when it is made by artisans who love their work, a wonderful accompaniment to countless dishes, bread remains today the boon to humanity it has always been. Its role in our nutrition has evolved, however, and this shift has meant that bread itself has undergone change. It was the basic foodstuff among the peasantry for centuries, when it was for the most part somewhat rough and made from dubious and scarcely bolted flour. Since then, it has become a non-essential, above all in the developed world, where it has been much refined and diversified; bread must attract solely by virtue of its gastronomic and dietary qualities. Since it is these very qualities that have been neglected by bakers over the past thirty years, bread consumption has continued to decline. Even in bread-loving France, for example, it has dropped from 8½ ounces to 5¼ during this period. Bread was no longer the staple it had been and, as it was unappetizing, what incentive was there for people to continue eating it? Bakers would do well to reflect on this. Bad bread will end up by disappearing. Bread will only survive in its most mouth-watering and flavorful manifestations, forms which are already the pride and joy of certain master bakers, as well as the delight of many a connoisseur.

Connoisseur's Guide

Good Bakeries 162, Appellations 176, French Chefs and their Bread Suppliers 177,
Flours 178, Mill-Supplied Bread Mixes 179,
Making Your Own Bread 180, Museums 182, Bread Accessories 184, Glossary 185,
Becoming a Baker 187, Bibliography 188, Index 190

G O O D   B A K E R I E S

Where can one go to find good bread, made according to the age-old precepts of the baker's art? Where can one find novelty and fancy breads, loaves for special occasions or holidays? The following directory lists some of the best bakers and bakeries in Europe and the United States. In France, there are thirty-five thousand bakeries, several hundred of which are good enough to be included in our list. Because of lack of space, we have decided to list only those that we know personally or to which we have been referred by other bread enthusiasts worthy of our trust. We have given preference to bakers who use stone-ground flour and bake their bread in real wood-fueled ovens. This is not for reasons of nostalgia, but simply because such baking practices, which make shortcuts impossible, are evidence of a love of the trade which has, in the past, been sorely lacking. Many of the bakeries outside France have been selected according to similar criteria: we have either visited them personally or they have been warmly recommended to us by connoisseur friends. Inevitably there are omissions: a guide of this kind cannot be comprehensive. The simple solution, particularly in large towns where consumers have more choice, is to look for a bakery where people are waiting to get in: that is almost certainly where the best bread is to be found!

UNITED STATES

Since the beginning of the 1980s, Americans have been rediscovering good bread. Some bakeries have become famous for the quality of their bread, whether it be of American or foreign origin.

ACME BREAD (photo p. 144)
1601 San Pablo Avenue, Berkeley, CA 94702.
Tel. 510-524-1021.
Steve Sullivan, formerly head chef at Chez Panisse, the famous restaurant in Berkeley (he remains its bread supplier), became a full-time baker in 1983. It was during his honeymoon in France that he perfected his specialty: bread made with natural leaven (which he fermented with a starter made from grape juice). Indeed, his shop is a monumental and delicious collection of breads made with leaven. There is the walnut coburg round with a thick, prettily molded, crunchy crust, in addition to *bâtards*, *baguettes*, and a whole-grain loaf. Steve Sullivan also uses two other traditional methods: leavening with a touch of yeast (for, the ryes and Italian breads), and yeast alone (for among other things, *baguettes*, *bâtards*, a rosemary-flavored *fougasse* with olive oil, and a whole-wheat loaf with sesame and poppy seeds). All except the *baguettes* are hand-shaped, and some are made from stone-ground organic flours.

AMY'S BREAD
629 Ninth Avenue and Sixth Street, New York, NY 10036.
Tel. 212-977-3856.
The inventive Amy Scherber has created a range of aromatic breads flavored with rosemary, fennel, and toasted nutmeats.

BAKER'S PLACE
1386 Cambridge Road, McLean, VA 22101.
Tel. 703-790-1700.
This chain of bakeries (seven to date in Maryland and Virginia) offers thirty-five different kinds of fresh bread, from the popular buckwheat and walnut loaves to garlic and Parmesan loaves and seven-grain multigrains. They also make the striking Italian *pugliese* loaf, which is shaped like a wheel.

BAKER STREET ARTISAN BREADS
8009 Germantown Avenue, Philadelphia, PA 19118.
Tel: 215-248-2500.
This bakery makes more than two dozen varieties of hand-crafted breads, baked in a stone-hearth oven imported from France.

BALLARD BAKING CO.
5909 Twenty-fourth Avenue, NW, Seattle, WA 98107.
Tel. 206-781-0091.
A specialist in earthy types of bread, which have a rustic appearance and a defined crust—ideal for people who are concerned about health as well as flavor.

BLUEPOINT BAKERY
1307 East Sixth Avenue, Denver, CO 80218.
Tel. 303-839-1820.
From potato-onion scones to sun-dried tomato leaves, the numerous irresistible specialties of this recently opened bakery have quickly made it impossible to pass by.

BOULANGERIE
2200 North Forty-fifth Street, Seattle, WA 98103.
Tel. 206-634-2211.
This bakery specializes in traditional French bread.

BREAD ALONE
RT 28, Boiceville, NY 12412.
Tel. 914-657-3328.

A love of basic, natural ingredients helped to create this bakery, known for its variety of breads baked with organic flour. One of the favorites here is the rich, buttery, cinnamon-scented *brioche.*

BUCKHEAD BREAD CO.
3070 Piedmont Road, Atlanta, GA 30305.
Tel. 404-237-8396.
Chosen as one of the best bread shops in America by *Bon Appetit Magazine*, Buckhead serves skillfully shaped, resiliently textured, crisp-crusted bread.

CHEZ PANISSE
1517 Snattuck Avenue, Berkeley, CA 94709.
Tel. 510-548-5525.
Alice Waters, the owner of this restaurant known for its high standards, was frustrated that she could not get good bread, so she asked chef Steve Sullivan, a passionate baker, to make its *baguettes.* Sullivan went on to found the Acme Bread Company (see above), and continues to supply the restaurant with bread.

D'AMATO'S ITALIAN AND FRENCH BAKERY
1124 West Grand Avenue, Chicago, IL 60622.
Tel. 312-733-5456.
For genuine Italian pizza, tomato breads, and *focaccia*, this European-style shop in Chicago is highly recommended.

DEAN & DELUCA
121 Prince Street, SoHo, New York, NY 10012.
Tel. 212-254-7774.
Also: 560 Broadway, New York, NY 10012, tel. 212-481-1691; Rockefeller Plaza #1, New York, NY 1002, tel. 212-664-1365; 46 Newtown Lane, East Hampton, NY 11937, tel. 516-324-5790.
This reputable store sells a vast array of carefully selected delicacies. The displays are so neat and attractive that it feels more like being in a museum than a delicatessen. The breads are supplied by six different bakers and include Swiss peasant bread and an Italian country loaf.

D & G BAKERY
45 Spring Street, New York, NY 10012.
Tel. 212-226-6688.
Unequaled even among the fabulous bakeries of New York, this establishment specializes in delicious *prosciutto*, cheese, and olive oil breads. Baked in a brick oven, the fresh breads all sell out quickly.

E.A.T.
1264 Madison Avenue, New York City, NY 10028.
Tel. 212-772-0022.

The owner of this restaurant, Eli Zabar, was one of the first to treat bread as an important part of a restaurant meal. Customers can expect a wide variety of breads with their meals, including whole-grain rolls, crusty sourdough *baguettes*, *focaccia*, or breadsticks.

ECCE PANIS
1120 Third Avenue, New York, NY 10021.
Tel. 212-535-2099.
This New York bakery is famous for its breads flavored with herbs, raisins, and olives, and also for its delicious Italian *focaccia*.

ELI'S BREAD
431 East Ninety-first Street, New York City, NY 10128.
Tel. 212-987-0885.
Eli Zabar, regarded as one of the best bakers in the country, recently opened this wholesale bakery to continue the tradition of quality baking. Crusty *ficelles*, onion sourdough *baguettes*, raisin pecan loaves, garlic sourdough loaves, and enormous farmers' bread, all hand-shaped, catch the eye and tease the taste buds.

FRENCH MEADOW BAKERY
2610 Lyndale Avenue South, Minneapolis, MN 55408.
Tel. 612-870-4740.
Now there are no obstacles to obtaining fresh bread anywhere, anytime: this mail-order bakery transcends the distance barrier. The organic sourdough bread baked here can be shipped anywhere in the country.

GRACE BAKING
3655 College Avenue, Oakland, CA 94618.
Tel. 310-428-2662.
The pre-dinner rush brings in a steady stream of customers who have a variety of forty kinds of bread from which to choose.

GRAND CENTRAL BAKERY CO.
214 First Avenue South, Seattle WA 98012.
Tel. 206-622-3644.
Also: 138–107th NE, Bellevue, WA 98004, tel. 206-454-9661; 2230 SE Hawthorn Boulevard, Portland, Oregon 97214, tel. 503-232-0575.
This bakery is widely known in the United States for its range of rustic European breads. The dough is well fermented before being hand-shaped, then baked in a brick-built oven imported from Italy. It provides: Italian (or Italian-style) breads, such as *ciabatta* or the *solemio* (a wheat and rye round with leaven enriched with olive oil); two kinds of *baguette* (yeast and natural leaven versions); a walnut bread flavored with thyme, olive oil and pepper; a rye bread; and a corn bread fermented with *biga* (an Italian version of sponge-and-dough). They are sold in strong paper bags (ideal for keeping them fresh), on which is written a de-

tailed résumé of their ingredients and useful hints as to how they should best be enjoyed.

GREENWOOD BAKERY
7227 Greenwood Avenue, N. Seattle, WA 98103.
Tel. 206-783-7181.
This bakery specializes in earthy, wholesome bread.

HAWTHORNE VALLEY
R.D. 2, Box 225A Ghent, NY 12075.
Tel. 518-672-7500.
A bio-dynamic, self-sufficient farm selling breads, baked goods, homemade cheeses and granolas at the Farmer's Market in Union Square, New York City.

HONEST BREAD
169 Mariner Drive, Southampton, NY 11968.
Tel. 516-283-6161.
The demand for quality has led to the rapid expansion of this recently opened bakery.

IL FORNAIO
101 Greenwich Street, San Francisco, CA 94111.
Tel. 415-391-4622.
With sixteen retail bakeries, ten restaurants, and six production bakeries in California, Il Fornaio is breaking records with its delicious breads, sublime *biscotti*, and pastries. Its rustic Italian breads are baked and preserved using methods imported directly from Milan.

JACQUES
Oka Street, Kilauea, Kauai, HI 96754.
Tel. 808-828-1393.
This bakery brings a bit of France to Hawaii, with its delicious and popular loaves, cinnamon rolls, and *croissants*.

LA BREAD BAKERY
624 South La Brea Avenue, Los Angeles, CA 90036.
Tel. 213-939-6813.
This small bakery sells sumptuous, European-style breads, including a rosemary and olive oil loaf, a potato and dill loaf, and a Greek olive loaf. The bakery supplies its own restaurant as well as other nearby establishments.

LA MADELEINE FRENCH BAKERY AND CAFE
307 Mockingbird Lane, Dallas, TX 75205.
Tel. 214-696-0800.
With its chain of bakeries and adjoining cafés throughout Texas and New Orleans, La Madeleine is well known in the South. Founded and run by a French chef, it serves wonderful breads, as well as breakfast, lunch, and dinner with a genuine French touch.

MACRINA BAKERY CAFE
2408 First Avenue, Seattle, WA 98121.
Tel. 206-448-4032.

This establishment serves as a neighborhood meeting place, as well as a source of crispy, mild, sourdough bread which was judged one of the best in the West.

MARVELOUS MARKET (photo p. 159)
5016 Connecticut Avenue, NW Washington, D.C. 20008.
Tel. 202-686-6779.
Mark Furstenberg opened his bakery in 1990 intending to produce good bread in the best French tradition. He has often been to France to meet the country's best bakers, and has become friends with many of them. He is today a virtuoso of baking with leaven, using the *poolisch* method, or *levain-levure* (sponge process). All his various types of bread are marvelous, ranging from French-inspired loaves, such as *baguettes*, coburg rounds, *ficelles*, *flûtes*, *fougasses*, and *pains de campagne*, to Italian breads, like the "Bostoni" (a sort of *grissini* with olives, onions, and Parmesan), and Jewish recipes (the *challah*). Mark Furstenberg is the inventor of "Palladin bread" (created for Jean-Louis, the famous French chef of the restaurant in Washington, D.C. which bears his name). It is a light and tasty bread, based on wheat flour and rye, enriched with olive oil and milk.

MONDRIAN
250 East Fifty-fourth Street, New York, NY 10022.
Tel. 212-750-3829.
Amy Scherber makes different breads every day at this restaurant, almost eclipsing the celebrated cuisine.

NEIGHBORHOOD BAKING COMPANY
3310 NW Yeon, Portland, OR 97210.
Tel. 503-221-1829.
This bakery produces one of the top sourdough breads in the country: a natural *pain de campagne* with an extraordinarily chewy texture.

ORWASHER'S BAKERY
308 East Seventy-eighth Street, New York City, NY 10021.
Tel. 212-288-6569.
Another old-time bakery which conjures up the taste and smell of mother's home baking.

OUR DAILY BREAD
33 Hudson Avenue, Chatam, NY 12037.
Tel. 518-392-9852.
Homemade and handmade breads sold at the Farmer's Market in Union Square, New York City.

PANINI BAKERY
406 Washington Street, Boston, MA 02143.
Tel. 617-666-2770.
A top choice of food critics, this bakery illustrates why bread consumption has been increasing recently.

POLICASTRO BREAD CO.
138 Park Avenue, Hoboken, NJ 07030.
Tel. 201-963-4281.
While maintaining the traditional quality of its bread, this forty-six-year-old bakery has recently added six new types of bread to its menu. A mix of old-time flavor with unusual novelties is the secret of this bakery's success.

ROCK HILL BAKEHOUSE
21 Saratoga Road, Gansevoort, NY 12831.
Tel. 518-743-1627.
Celebrated as one of the twelve best bakeries by *New York Magazine*, touting their sourdough bread as the "chewiest, crustiest, and most flavorful available in Manhattan." George Balanchine accepted no other *croissants* than those that came from this Saratoga Springs bakery.

ROCK HILL BAKERY (photo p. 144)
Spraguetown Rd, Greenwich, NY 12834.
Tel. 518-692-2934.
Michael and Wendy London are two of the best-known American bakers. Their bakery, located right next to a fine farm they own in Greenwich, supplies organic-flour breads baked with natural leaven. Their *baguettes*, *pains de campagne*, and ryes are all great successes. Not long ago, the Londons installed a real, direct-heat, wood-fired oven, built in 1995 by a baking-oven builder who was born and learned his trade in Germany.

SEMIFREDDI'S
372 Colusa Avenue, Kensington, CA 94707.
Tel. 510-596-9935.
The hand-crafted rustic bread sold here is so rich in flavor that it does not need butter or toppings. The three-seeded *baguette*, coated with fennel, poppy, and sesame seeds, has been a main attraction here since the bakery was opened in 1984.

TASSAJARA BREAD BAKERY
1000 Cole Street, San Francisco, CA 94117.
Tel. 415-664-8947.
Whole-grain loaves are a specialty in this bakery, which was started by Zen Center students in San Francisco.

THE BALDWIN HILL BAKERY
Baldwin Hill Road, Phillipston, MA 01331.
Tel. 508-249-4961.
This bakery offers six different varieties of organic sourdough bread.

THE BREAD SHOP
3139 Broadway, near 123rd Street, New York, NY 10027.
Tel. 800-873-9119.
This bakery, which has an adjoining café, serves healthy and delicious five-grain and herb-flavored loaves, as well as airy buttermilk biscuits, monkey bread, and herb onion rolls covered with melted cheese . . . enough to make one's mouth water.

THE CORNER BAKERY
516 N. Clark Street, Chicago, IL 60610.
Tel. 312-644-8100.
This company, which started up five years ago, now has a number of stores and supplies

---

FRENCH BAKERY CHAINS

CARREFOUR. A hundred or so supermarkets belonging to this French chain have their own bakery on the premises.

LE FOURNIL DE PIERRE. This firm was created by Pierre Desnos in 1980. Today, the twenty-six stores trading under the sign "Fournil de Pierre" are not, as their French name would imply, places where bread is actually baked, but rather what are termed *boulangeries froides*, where bread prepared at an industrial bakery in Saint-Denis is delivered several times a day. Forty types of bread are supplied, including a pleasant *flûte* on a leaven, and a *pain de campagne* called the "Fournil de Pierre," which is sold by weight and contains a touch of rye.

PAUL. Founded in 1889, this company now owns around a hundred bakeries throughout France, some operating out of supermarkets. The bread is always prepared and baked on the premises. Bread lovers will discover some hidden marvels here: a fine loaf made on a leaven; an excellent *pain à l'ancienne* baked with well-fermented dough; and an equally succulent *pain de campagne* from stone-ground flour with natural leavening. The whole-wheat loaf, sandwich loaves, ryes (80 percent), and the multigrain with six different ingredients are all on the same level. Paul compares favorably with the best of the independent bakers.

LE PAIN QUOTIDIEN. This Belgian chain has around twenty bakeries. They provide some very good breads made on a leaven, baked in a brick-built oven with a stone sole. They range from large loaves (weighing 5 pounds) to fine wheat-flour rolls, ryes, and walnut loaves. The *baguettes* and *flûtes parisiennes* are also above reproach. Each branch of the Pain Quotidien also serves breakfast and snacks throughout the day, notably sandwiches made with a bread on a leaven and beef tartare (with basil and Parmesan), or Tuscan sandwiches (bread, cream cheese, and sun-dried tomatoes).

---

150 restaurants, delivering twice a day. Ric Scicchitano, who says he learned baking in the school of hard knocks, oversees the baking of the thirty-five different breads. The range includes various herb breads, a potato and dill loaf, rye bread with onion, and a highly popular chocolate cherry formula.

TOM CAT BAKERY
42-45 Vernon Boulevard, Long Island City, NY 11101.
Tel. 718-786-4224.
Noel Comess, who used to be a cook before becoming a baker, offers a wide range of breads in a number of different shapes and sizes. His whole-wheat and wheat-flour with leaven are available in rounds or French longs. They are much admired by connoisseurs, as are the *poolisch*-method *baguette*, the rye with yeast, and the seven-grain multigrain. Most of these loaves are shaped by hand and all are well fermented. They are to be found at markets and in fine food stores.

UPTOWN BAKERY
3313 Connecticut Avenue, Washington, D.C. 20008.
Tel. 202-362-6262
This bakery features hard-crusted, European-style breads baked on the premises in stone-hearth French ovens with a traditional slow rising method.

VESUVIO BAKERY
160 Prince Street, SoHo, New York, NY 10012.
Tel. 212-925-8248.
Delicious bread is baked in the ovens of this closet-sized shop, which was opened in 1920. *Biscotti*, Italian pretzels, and round white sesame-seed loaves are displayed in the window, luring customers into this haven of fresh, satisfying bread.

ZABAR'S
2245 Broadway, New York, NY 10024.
Tel. 212-787-2000.
The bread department of this legendary New York delicatessen offers eighty kinds of bread.

GREAT BRITAIN

THE BAGATELLE CONCEPT
44 Harrington Rd, London SW7.
Tel. 0171-581 1551.
A real French bakery in the heart of London, offering forty-five types of bread each day. The flours and the bread-making techniques are all French. One can even find *pain brié*, produced according to an old Honfleur family recipe, and the "Saint-Tropez," a loaf which brings to mind Provence and which contains olive oil, tomatoes, black olives, and basil. But there are also some succulent recipes from other regions of the world,

notably the "San Francisco," made from an excellent stone-ground flour fermented with rye leaven, and the "Jerusalem bread," containing semolina, olive oil, and sesame seed. All these loaves are hand-shaped and baked in an oven with a refractory brick sole. Baker Jacky Lesselier also supplies both restaurants at the Connaught Hotel, where one can have, to accompany the cheese board, a "petit pain Louisiane," made with pecans.

BAKER & SPICE
46 Walton Street, London SW3.
Tel. 0171-589 4735.
Food lovers are flocking to this bakery, inspired by Poilâne in Paris, and presided over by master baker Philippe Dadé. The bread is baked in two listed brick ovens.

BRICK LANE BEIGEL BAKE
159 Brick Lane, London E1.
Tel. 0171-729 0616.
This tremendously popular bagel store, opened sixteen years ago, sells a variety of fresh and inexpensive filled bagels, including classic favorites such as smoked salmon and cream cheese. They also sell white, rye, and wholemeal loaves baked in-house.

CARLUCCIO'S
28a Neal Street, Covent Garden,
London WC2.
Tel. 0171-240 1487.
This is a long-established delicatessen selling various Italian breads, such as *foccacia*, *campagna*, and *ciabacca*. They also have a range of flavored breads, made with walnuts, garlic, apricots, or sun-dried tomatoes. All the loaves are baked in-house.

CLARKE'S
122 Kensington Church Street, London W8.
Tel. 0171-229 2190.
Clarke's is at once a fine London restaurant and an impressive bakery. Clarke's provides a wide range of all sorts of breads: French ones like the *baguette*, *ficelle*, and *miche de campagne*, Mediterranean specialties such as *fougasses* (with herbs), and loaves with Parmesan, olive oil, tomatoes, or black or green olives. There are also more Anglo-Saxon offerings, such as horseshoe-shaped apricot breads, corn bread, a wholemeal bread with honey, and rye bread with poppy seeds and cumin. These breads can also be purchased in the excellent cheese shop, The Neal's Yard Dairy, in Covent Garden.

HARRODS (photos pp. 43, 115)
Knightsbridge, London SW1.
Tel. 0171-730 1234.
Every day, thirty thousand people shop at this London temple of consumerism and more than a few concentrate their efforts on the marvelous Food Hall. The décor, which dates from the turn of the century, was restored a dozen or so years ago. The fabulous bread counter offers one hundred and thirty different kinds of bread—French, Italian, American, Scandinavian, German, traditional Jewish, and, of course, British. It has all the breakfast rolls and soft tea-breads imaginable (scones, baps, buns, etc.), sandwich loaves, a number of sourdough breads, breads baked with leaven, and loaves made with stone-ground flour. There is also the Irish contingent of soda breads, with their pleasant, almost sourish taste. Harrods also supplies the exquisite "Rétrodor" *baguette*.

HARVEY NICHOLS
109-125 Knightsbridge, London SW1.
Tel. 0171-235 5000.
This well-known department store sells a wide variety of freshly baked breads.

KONDITOR AND COOK
22 Cornwall Road, London SE1.
Tel. 0171-261 0456.
Opened in 1993, this store sells specialty breads and cakes. There can be anything up to fifteen types of bread on any one day. The range includes loaves with hazelnuts and raisins, cheese and onion, and green and black olives, in addition to granary and sunflower cobs. Although the store does not bake its own bread, quality is excellent and they can arrange for special loaves to be baked to order.

LE PONT DE LA TOUR
The Food Store, Butlers Wharf Building, 36d Shad Thames, Butlers Wharf, London SE1.
Tel. 0171-403 4030.
This delicatessen, opened by Terence Conran, is situated on the banks of the Thames, a stone's throw from Tower Bridge. It sells excellent bread baked the same morning. The range includes *baguettes*, *pains de campagne*, *ciabattas*, corn bread, and rye loaves, as well as a dozen flavored breads (cumin, lemon, tomato, Parmesan, onion and bacon, date and walnut). All the bread is baked in the bakery that Terence Conran, very much a bread lover himself, has had built for his restaurant, Mezzo (see below).

MEZZO
100 Wardour Street, London W1.
Tel. 0171-314 4065.
This bakery and patisserie was opened in September 1995 and is attached to Terence Conran's newest restaurant. There is a varied range which changes constantly. More unusual loaves include such ingredients as rosemary, walnuts, and lemon. The bakery also makes *pains de campagne*, olive bread, and soda bread.

MISTER CHRISTIAN
11 Elgin Crescent, London W11.
Tel. 0171-229 0501.
This delicatessen sells no less than forty types of bread, some of which, such as the *foccacia*, are made in-house. The range includes loaves made with Gruyère, herbs, sun-dried tomatoes, lemon, orange, and spinach.

NEALS YARD BAKERY
6 Neals Yard, Covent Garden, London WC2.
Tel. 0171-836 5199.
This bakery uses organic flour to make a variety of loaves. Ingredients include whole wheat, poppy, sesame seeds, linseed, cheese, herbs, and a mix of olives and garlic.

SELFRIDGES
Oxford Street, London W1.
Tel. 0171-629 1234.
The bread department in Selfridges' impressive food hall sells over sixty different loaves, all fresh. The selection is international in scope: in addition to *baguettes* and French pastries, which are all baked in-house, you can buy German, Swedish, or Ukrainian loaves, as well as Greek *pita* bread.

THE FRESH FOOD CO.
326 Portobello Road, London W10.
Tel. 0181-969 0351.
This mail-order company sells organic and specialty foods. Its featured product is a pack of Innes breads and cheeses, including a traditional brown sourdough loaf, a wholewheat loaf with walnuts and sultanas, and an Italian-style sourdough loaf with sun-dried tomatoes and pesto.

THE GRAIN SHOP
269a Portobello Road, London W11.
Tel. 0171-229 5571.
This long-established bakery sells a variety of delights, all baked in-house. Of particular note are the rice bread, corn bread, sunflower seed loaves, and sourdough rolls.

FRANCE–PARIS

BOULANGERIE JULIEN
75, rue Saint-Honoré, 75001 Paris.
Tel. 42 36 24 83.
Closed Sundays.
In 1995, Jean-Noël Julien won the Grand Prix de la Baguette, organized by the City of Paris, so lovers of this exquisite Parisian bread will be more than satisfied here. The victorious *baguette* in question was a "Rétrodor," made from an excellent flour developed by the Viron mill in Chartres. It has an attractive-looking crust and a superb, well-aerated crumb, which has all the aromas of fine wheat flour. The last *baguettes* are unloaded

from the oven at 7:30 p.m., which means that if you buy one for dinner it is sure to be fresh.

AU PANETIER (photo p. 4)
10, place des Petits-Pères, 75002 Paris.
Tel. 42 60 90 23.
Closed Saturdays and Sundays.
This is one of the oldest bakeries in Paris. Its magnificent tiled interior and the wood-fired oven date from 1896. The bread made by Bernard Lebon also deserves to be listed as a national monument. He makes two white-flour specialties: a marvelous "Saint-Fiacre," little kneaded but well fermented (made using the excellent "Rétrodor" flour); and the "pavé des Petits-Pères," made from a blend of the same flour with a stone-ground variety. The taste of these two loaves is truly exquisite. The bakery also sells a fine organic-flour loaf, a number of different kinds of *pains de campagne*, and a specialty from Normandy, *pain brié*.

AU LEVAIN DU MARAIS
32, rue de Turenne, 75003 Paris.
Tel. 42 78 07 31.
Closed Sundays.
In October 1994, the baker Thierry Rabineau left the Moulin de la Vierge bakery (see p. 164) and took over this pretty wood-paneled shop in the fashionable Marais. It has a tiled ceiling delightfully decorated with a blue sky and pastel flowers. The bakery, which had until then been struggling, with declining sales, was given a new lease of life by Thierry Rabineau and his wife Dominique. They decided to break with the methods used by the previous owner and to make, quite simply, for the same price, good bread made with fine flour. Tasty *baguettes*—with a dense "holey" crumb—*flûtes de campagne*, and whole-wheat bread are all made from the superb organic flour milled by the Decollogne-Lecocq mills and well fermented with a starter. In addition they make a rye bread and an impeccable multigrain loaf (with six different cereals), as well as anchovy and bacon *fougasses*. Now the bakery is, of course, a roaring, and salutary, success!

LERCH
4, rue du Cardinal-Lemoine, 75005 Paris.
Tel. 43 26 15 80.
Closed Mondays and Tuesdays.
André Lerch is better known as a first-rate pastry cook than as a baker. His bread is delicious, however, particularly the specialties from Alsace, notably the poppy seed *pain au pavot* (a magnificent braided variety is available to order) and the *pain gris* with various grains (the rye much in evidence), both of which are supplied to restaurants such as Dodin-Bouffant and Le Beaujolais. The more common loaves baked here are every bit as good, and the small, hand-shaped, wheaten

loaves are to be found gracing the tables of the Tour d'Argent. All the bread is hand-shaped and baked in a good oven which has refractory bricks on the sole.

BEAUVALLET-JULIEN
6, rue de Poissy, 75005 Paris.
Tel. 43 26 94 24.
Closed Wednesdays.
This little bakery resembles its owner: unpretentious and friendly. Mohammed Ousbih, a Moroccan who came to Paris at the age of twelve and was apprenticed to a baker two years later, is a somewhat enigmatic character. How does he manage to make some of the best bread in Paris employing methods which are no different from those of many another good but unexceptional bakers? When this question is put to him, he smiles and simply says: "I work gently." His *baguettes* are long and thin, hand-shaped, crunchy, and full of the flavor of wheat flour (as are his *bâtards* and larger *pains longs*). His *pains de campagne* (long, round, or in the form of magnificent *couronnes*) contain a touch of rye flour and have a subtle taste—the best kind of bread that can be baked without leaven.

STEFF LE BOULANGER
123, rue Mouffetard, 75005 Paris.
Tel. 47 07 35 96.
Closed Sunday afternoons and Mondays.
Stéphane Delaunay's bakery, situated at the bottom end of the rue Mouffetard, is unusual. To begin with, this former fish dealer's store has no door and as you walk in it is like entering a mill. Behind a long, glass-fronted counter, Stéphane Delaunay is hard at work tending his ovens, while, behind the cash register, another baker is kneading and molding. "Steff" was a pupil of Bernard Ganachaud and set up shop here in 1992. In addition to the delicious "Gana" range (*flûte, petite flûte*, and large *pavé*), he also makes succulent and tender *pains de campagne* with leaven, with a good crust and soft crumb, baked from a stone-ground flour enriched with wheat germ. Also on offer is a specialty from the Gers region in the south, updated slightly by Ganachaud, called the *tougnole*. This bread, which has a light, smooth crust, is made from rye (55 percent) and wheat flour and comes in two forms: with walnuts or with raisins. Both are wonderful lightly toasted. The multigrain bread is also excellent.

CHARCUTERIE ALSACIENNE
10, rue de Buci, 75006 Paris.
Tel. 43 54 93 49.
Open every day.
There are several of these pleasant shops in Paris. They supply traditional dishes from Alsace and such breads as pretzels and *morciettes* (here made into wonderful sandwiches).

JEAN-CLAUDE GAULUPEAU
12, rue Mabillon, 75006 Paris.
Tel. 43 54 16 93.
Closed Mondays.
Jean-Claude Gaulupeau is not only a fine chocolate-maker and pastry cook, he is also a superb baker. Situated opposite the Marché Saint-Germain, his bakery also serves as a tea shop where you can taste the various kinds of bread on offer, all of which are made from organic flour and are fermented for a long time. The loaves all look magnificent (many are shaped by hand) and are as flavorsome as his pastries and chocolate concoctions.

POILANE (photos pp. 79, 81, 84-85, 88-90, 106)
8, rue Cherche-Midi, 75006 Paris.
Tel. 45 48 42 59.
Closed Sundays.
Also: 49, boulevard de Grenelle, 75015 Paris.
Tel. 45 79 11 49.
Closed Mondays.
This is the tiny bakery where two of today's greatest French bakers were brought up in the trade by their father, the baking genius Pierre Poilâne. We will encounter the elder of the two, Max, later on; here the master is Lionel, the most famous baker in the world. His unquenchable passion for bread lies at the root of its extraordinary new lease of life in recent times. Six hundred outlets supply his well-known and ever-fresh *miche de campagne*, which weighs $4^{1}/_{2}$ pounds. It is made from prime selected brown flour, fermented with leaven, hand-molded and baked in a wood-fired stove, which gives the bread its brown, floury crust and dense crumb structure. His walnut bread, rye-flour loaves and little rye rolls with raisins are delicious: it is a pity that he is such an enemy of the *baguette*. His bakeries supply wooden bread bins of his own devising, as well as his publications, in particular his excellent *Guide de l'amateur du pain*.

POUJAURAN (photos pp. 98–99, 102)
20, rue Jean-Nicot, 75007 Paris.
Tel. 47 05 80 88.
Closed Sundays and Mondays.
This bakery may be narrow, but the pink storefront can be seen from afar. Jean-Luc Poujauran is the son of a baker from the Landes in the west of France. He opened his bakery in 1977 and has established himself as one of the finest bakers and pastry cooks in the capital. On entering the store (probably after having waited on line), you realize why he has such fine reputation: the loaves—piled high on a magnificent wrought-iron and brass counter—look beautiful, and if they look good they must taste good. Jean-Luc Poujauran only uses flour from the Decollogne-Lecocq mills—for the most part, the stone-ground organic variety. The baker remains reticent about the methods he uses to turn the flour into such perfect

end products. Does he prefer to keep it a secret or is it all too intuitive and complex to be described? The *baguettes*, for instance, are baked with leaven, with yeast, or with a starter from the previous day's batch. The precise alchemy depends on the season. Whatever the choice, the bread remains excellent. The exquisite-tasting *pains de campagne* made with leaven are light-crumbed beneath their thick crust; the *couronne-épi* is exceedingly appetizing and crunchy. The Piedmontese walnut bread goes well with cheese and there are extraordinary black olive, olive oil, and thyme rolls. Also on offer is a strong-tasting *fougasse* (with anchovies from Collioure) and a divine rye bread with raisins, best eaten with butter. There is not enough room to describe all the other breads, but they are all of the same high calibre.

AU PAIN BIEN CUIT

111, boulevard Haussmann, 75008 Paris.
Tel. 42 65 06 25.
Closed Sundays.

The words "sculptor in bread" are painted on the window of this bakery, which has been the delight of many a passing child since it opened in 1965: bread rabbits, cats, horses, bicycles, and Eiffel Towers are a few of the specialties made by the friendly owner, René-Gérard Saint-Ouen. Their dense, white dough, enriched with fats, allows the sculptures to survive baking intact. The bakery is also a restaurant where unpretentious breakfasts and lunches are served, accompanied by another specialty: wholesome white bread. *Baguettes*, 1-pound *pains*, *demi-couronnes* (half "crown" shapes), and rounds are all made from the excellent "Rétrodor" flour from the Viron mill. A *baguette* baked by René-Gérard Saint-Ouen won the 1994 Grand Prix de la Baguette, organized by the City of Paris. The crumb is light and creamy, and extremely tasty. The robust crust is as crunchy as could be.

DANIEL DUPUY

13, rue Cadet, 75009 Paris.
Tel. 48 24 54 26.
Closed Tuesdays.

As soon as one enters this charming little bakery, one is struck by the admirable appearance of the *pains de campagne*. They have a marvelously brown and "mountainous" crust, with a coppery shine—the unmistakable sign of hand-shaping. They come in the form of long loaves and rounds, weighing from $\frac{1}{2}$ pound to 2 kilos ($4\frac{1}{2}$ pounds). Those who have bitten into their crunchy crusts will hardly be surprised to learn that Daniel Dupuy is regarded as one of the best bakers in Paris. His two *baguettes* are exceptionally fine: one, named "Rochetour," made with natural leaven, was invented by the mas-

ter (its preparation remains a closely guarded secret); the other, recognizable from the square docking on the crust like that of a polka, is made from organic flour. The latter won second prize in the Grand Prix de la Baguette in 1994.

L'AUTRE BOULANGE (photo p. 11)

4, rue de Montreuil, 75011 Paris.
Tel. 43 72 86 04.
Closed Saturday afternoons and Sundays.

Michel Cousin is one of the three or four bakers in Paris whose names are passed from one gourmet to another—some people are prepared to cross the city just to buy his bread. Customers are never disappointed, for Michel Cousin excels at everything: traditional breads (stone-ground *pain de campagne* with natural leaven, the classic *baguette* "1900," rye breads and whole-wheat loaves), or specialty bakes (rye with orange peel, large *pavé* with raisins, the *pain des moines*, or "Monks' bread," with organic spelt flour, and the *fougasses* with their various flavors). Each has a natural, yet subtle taste.

BREAD AT PARISIAN MARKETS

Some bakers sell at one or other of the many markets in Paris. One such baker is André Lupo, who abandoned his store on rue Monsieur-le-Prince. His bread, which he makes in his bakery in Clichy, can be found at the markets at Port-Royal, Bastille, Convention, Monge, Lecourbe, Point-du-Jour (avenue de Versailles), Lefebvre, Popincourt, and Porte-Molitor. *Baguette* lovers will adore his *baguette campagne à l'ancienne*, the dough for which is fermented fully seven hours, and be agreeably surprised by his *baguette* with leaven. Other delights include: a large farmhouse round with leaven made from stone-ground wheat; a stone-ground whole-wheat loaf; and a splendid flat polka. The walnut bread (rye with crystallized orange peel) and the *acajou* (rye bread with walnut, almonds and raisins) are all succulent. The most recent of André Lupo's inventions is the "forestier," a wheat-flour and rye blend base, with sesame and sunflower seeds, cornseed and linseed. These breads are also available at La Mie du Pain (photo p. 111), who can be found at the Cours-de-Vincennes, Auguste-Blanqui, and Edgar-Quinet markets. At the organic ("bio") market on boulevard Raspail, there are stalls representing stores which specialize in organic bread and flour, such as Le Pain de Midée, Borsa, and Boisnard.

ROGER FREUSLON (photo p. 101)

83, avenue du Docteur-Arnold-Netter,
75012 Paris.
Tel. 43 07 67 48.

Roger Freulson is a real baker in the classic tradition, who starts work at 2 a.m. every morning. His *pains de campagne* made with leaven (the starter was begun twenty years ago using some honey and olive oil) are delicious. Also sold are linen and cotton bread bags for keeping loaves fresh.

MOISAN

114, rue de Patay, 75013 Paris.
Tel. 45 83 80 13.
Closed Tuesdays.

Few bakeries in Paris smell so intensely of leaven. The bread is baked just behind the counter and Michel Moisan's leaven is one of the most delectably fruity I know of. In 1993, it was decided to divide the bakery into two sections, one side for organic-flour breads, the other for classic varieties. One thousand five hundred customers buy their bread here each day. On the classic bread side, one can find a perfect "Banette" (see p. 179), a really good *baguette* (third in the Grand Prix de la Baguette for 1995) and a very tasty *flûte à l'ancienne*, whose rye/wheat flour blend is fermented for twelve hours. The wares produced by the "organic" side of the store are particularly fine: the stone-ground flour comes from the Coutelet mills at Meung-sur-Loire. Natural leaven, salt from the Guérande salt marshes, lengthy fermentation: all these elements make for magnificent *pains de campagne*; a nice soft whole-wheat loaf; a fine rye; and an astonishing 100 percent whole-wheat *pain intégral*, baked, and sold, in a wooden container.

MAX POILANE

87, rue Brancion, 75015 Paris.
Tel. 48 28 45 90.
Open every day.
29, rue de l'Ouest, 75014, Paris.
Closed Sundays.
42, place du Marché-Saint-Honoré,
75001 Paris.
Closed Saturdays and Sundays.

Max Poilâne is a very great baker. An unpretentious and generous man, when he talks about bread he is a true poet. His bread is baked in his image, and it would be difficult to find a better in all Paris. There are no *baguettes*, however. The master himself works in the little bakery on the rue Brancion. His admirable farmhouse round with natural leaven is made from stone-ground brown flour with salt from the Guérande salt marshes. After lengthy fermentation, it is baked in one of his two wood-burning ovens. The end result is a masterpiece. The rye is delicious, while the rye with raisins and the wheat-flour loaf with walnuts are both perfectly balanced. There is only one white-flour bread: the so-called *pain au prélevain* (weighing 10 to 11 ounces, and fermented on yeast but shaped in a most eye-catching fashion), whose light, airy crumb has a fine, floury savor. Perfection.

MOULIN DE LA VIERGE (photos p. 13, 78)
166, avenue de Suffren, 75015 Paris.
Tel. 47 83 45 55.
Closed Sundays.
Also: 82, rue Daguerre, 75014 Paris;
105, rue Vercingétorix, 75014 Paris.
Basile Kamir, regarded as one of the two or three supreme bakers in the French capital (photo p. 83) entered the trade in an unusual fashion. In the 1970s, he decided to try and get the former bakery on rue Vercingétorix, where he worked in the record business, listed as a historic building. To do so, however, he had to turn it back into a bakery . . . and become a baker. He refurbished the two old wood-fired ovens, which were languishing in the basement, and took up baking, using a method which he had loved as a child in the Aveyron: natural leaven. Today, the three Moulin de la Vierge stores offer sumptuous *pains de campagne* (from flour milled by Decollogne-Lecocq), *flûtes*, and *baguettes*, all baked in wood-fired ovens (except for the *baguettes* on avenue de Suffren, where the oven used is electric), a sublime rye loaf, an anchovy and olive *fougasse*, an unforgettable six-cereal multigrain, and a *quignonnette* (a white-flour loaf, between the *baguette* and the *bâtard*, kneaded in a special way), which should be eaten fresh. For an account of how master bakers like Basile Kamir work, see chapter four, "The Baker's Art."

LENOTRE
44, rue d'Auteuil, 75016 Paris.
Tel. 45 24 52 52.
Open every day.
Also in Paris: 44, rue du Bac, 7th *arrondissement*; 15, boulevard de Courcelles, 8th; 3–5, rue du Havre, 9th; Lafayette Gourmet, 40, boulevard Haussmann, 9th; 61, rue Lecourbe, 15th; 193, avenue de Versailles, 16th; 49, avenue Victor-Hugo, 16th; 121, avenue de Wagram, 17th.
The reputation of this chocolate-maker and pastry cook is well established, but few people are aware that his stores supply excellent bread (which, like the other products, is made in Plaisir, just outside Paris). All the loaves are carefully prepared: the *baguette paysanne*, the country round—both made with leaven—and the *boule Lenôtre* (another round), made from stone-ground flour, and spectacular large long loaves weighing almost 2 pounds. The multigrain breads are exquisitely shaped into horseshoes, thin *ficelles*, and rolls.

MANZAGOL
33 bis, rue Doudeauville, 75018 Paris.
Tel. 46 06 13 11.
Open until 9 p.m. Closed Sunday afternoons and Thursdays.
One of the best farmhouse *pains de campagne* you could wish to find is baked here. The Manzagols are a dynasty of bakers from the Auvergne who pass on the secrets of their baking from generation to generation. Today, Manzagol supplies two hundred restaurants (among which, the Royal Monceau and L'Ambassade d'Auvergne) with bread from its large bakery. The bread is baked in a large, bare room smelling of leavening. Long wooden peels and an old kneader full of wicker dough baskets provide the only decoration. The loaves are piled up on a long wooden table. Only two main types are baked: a rye (the short one weighs almost a pound, and the long and round versions more than 4 pounds) and a *pain de campagne* made with stone-ground flour. How the rye tastes so toasted and fruity, and the *pain de campagne* so crisp, yet without the slightest sourness, is a well-guarded secret for which we are sincerely grateful.

AU PAIN D'ANTAN
2, rue Eugène-Sue, 75018 Paris.
Tel. 42 64 71 78.
Closed Sundays.
The baker Jean Sousa has kept the accent of his native region, the Aveyron, and also a taste for its wholesome traditional breads. There are no *baguettes* or flavored breads to be found in his store, but extraordinary, hand-shaped farmhouse loaves made with leaven, well fermented in wicker dough baskets and baked in a brick peel-oven. All his various breads (ryes, whole-wheats, granaries and multigrains), not just the huge 7-pound *grand pain*, keep for at least a week.

LA FLUTE GANA
226, rue des Pyrénées, 75020 Paris.
Tel. 43 58 42 62.
Closed Sundays and Mondays.
Bernard Ganachaud's two daughters are, as far as I am aware, the only two qualified women bakers in France. They uphold the traditions of their illustrious father and bake a perfect version of the famous *flûte*. The organic loaves, *pains de campagne* (both with natural leaven, like the *flûte*), and the range of specialties (whole-wheat, multigrains, rye with raisins, *tordu de Gers*, etc.) attract customers from far and wide. Not every loaf is available at all times, however: each day is reserved for just one of the specialty loaves.

RAOUL FOYART
143, boulevard Davout, 75020 Paris.
Tel. 43 61 20 38.
Closed Saturdays.

Raoul Foyart, whose name is not as well known as it should be, has worked in baking for around fifty years. He is, as far as I know, the only baker making *baguettes* from stone-ground flour (from Decollogne-Lecocq) baked according to the special liquid sponge and dough process called *poolisch*. Costing the same as an "ordinary" version, this is the ideal *baguette*, with a flavor which is rich and subtle, delicate and complex. M. Foyart uses stone-ground flour and salt from the Guérande salt marshes. With a starter begun in 1974, he makes two exceptional ranges of *pains de campagne*, ranging from the *ficelle*, to the round: a standard range containing some rye, and an organic wheat range. The whole-grain rye loaf and the organic bran loaf are every bit as good as these marvels.

GANACHAUD (photos pp. 14, 15, 86)
150, rue de Ménilmontant, 75020 Paris.
Tel. 46 36 13 82.
Closed Sunday afternoons, and Monday and Tuesday mornings.
Bernard Ganachaud himself has retired, but nothing in his half rustic, half baroque bakery has changed. Jean Jeudon has taken over and makes the same breads. In addition to the "flûte Gana" (of which the last come out of the oven around 7:30 p.m.), there is an amazing range of special loaves made with leaven and stone-ground flour: *pains de campagne*, multigrains, *tougnoles*, *tordus de Gers*, and the *pain chouan*, a magnificent long loaf weighing 4 pounds baked from a blend of two white flours. People come from all over Paris to buy such delicious loaves, and quite right too.

PARIS SUBURBS

BOULANGERIE DENIVET
7, rue Darnétal, 77100 Meaux.
Tel. 64 34 10 02.
Closed Sundays and Mondays.
This small bakery, with its gray façade, may not look special, but it is. Do not be deceived by the simplicity of the surroundings or the modesty of Jean-Michel Denivet, the son of a baker who started learning his father's trade from the age of ten. The reasons for the excellent quality of the bread are obvious: the flour (classic, or stone-ground organic), most of which comes from the excellent Decollogne-Lecocq mills, situated only a few miles away; authentic craftsmanship, including hand-shaping and manual weighing; long fermentation in wicker *bannetons*, and finally baking in a magnificent authentic wood-fired oven, loaded and unloaded with a peel. In addition to fine ryes, whole-wheats, and multigrains, there are two truly exceptional *baguettes*: the *baguette* "meldoise" (with leaven), made from organic flour, and the *baguette* "denivoise," baked from flours

(including stone-ground) blended on the premises. The latest of Jean-Michel Denivet's specialties is the "petit brie de Meaux," which is not only shaped like the cheese but also actually contains some. This bread is delicious accompanied by a glass of red wine.

BOULANGERIE FIACRE
2, rue Bernard-Flornoy, 77120 Coulommiers.
Tel. 64 03 03 32.
Closed Thursdays.
The baker in this tiny shop, the former butcher Gérard Fiacre also gets his flours from the Decollogne-Lecocq mills. His art can be summed up in three words: time, rigor, and passion. Basically two sorts of bread are sold: the customary white-flour loaves baked with leaven, but also containing a touch of baker's yeast (the *ficelles* and *baguettes* are particularly good), and the *pains de campagne* with leaven baked from the best possible flour, one of which measures more than 3 feet across and weighs more than 25 pounds.

AU PAIN D'ANTAN
4, place du Pas-de-Saint-Cloud,
92210 Saint-Cloud.
Tel. 49 11 12 63.
Closed Tuesdays.
The name of this large and beautiful bakery, located near the town hall in Saint-Cloud, neatly sums up the philosophy of its owner, M. Aubry. There is no excessive sophistication here—just authenticity and tradition, both in terms of the bread and the methods used. Work begins on the *baguettes* at 12.45 a.m. After a short kneading, they are subjected to almost six hours of the various stages of fermentation at room temperature. The first loaves emerge from the oven at 7 a.m. This results in a fine, close-textured *baguette* with a tasty, creamy-white crumb. They are fermented with leaven (though the dough can also contain a touch of baker's yeast, especially in winter). M. Aubry offers a "baguette de campagne" with leaven, which contains bran and is fermented for eight hours. All the other loaves are praiseworthy: the hand-shaped *pains de campagne*, the exquisite *fougasses*, the "rustique" (wheat- and rye-flour round), and the beautiful *couronne-épi*.

LE FOURNIL D'ENGHIEN
21, rue du Général-de-Gaulle,
95880 Enghien-les-Bains.
Tel. 34 17 11 22.
Closed Mondays.
Famous for its casino and its racecourse, Enghien also deserves to be known for its bakery. Bernard Pérot, its talented baker, makes various specialties created by Bernard Ganachaud (*flûte, pavé, flûtine,* and *ficelle*), using an oven built in solid refractory brick. His classic *pain de campagne* with leaven, made

from stone-ground flour, is particularly impressive, but he also makes some more unusual loaves, notably a sandwich loaf with honey recommended with *foie gras*, a seaweed bread for seafood, and a bread flavored with thyme suitable for game.

ALSACE

CHARLES WOERLE
10, rue de la Division-Leclerc,
67000 Strasbourg.
Tel. 88 32 00 88.
Closed Sundays.
At once museum, art gallery, and Ali Baba's cave, Charles Woerlé's bakery first enchants the eye before charming the palate. There are countless sculpture breads exhibited here: the *baguettes, pains de campagne*, ryes, and whole-wheats are excellent, but the regional breads are not to be missed either, notably the *Pumpernickel* and the *pain à la bière*, which will certainly tickle your palate.

L'HARMONIE GOURMANDE D'AUTREFOIS
18, rue Dietrich, 67210 Obernai.
Tel. 88 95 47 36.
Closed Sundays and Mondays.
In this bakery at the foot of the Vosges, Matthieu Scholler sells the magnificent loaves baked by his father, Jean-Pierre Scholler, which are also distributed in large numbers to stores in the region specializing in "natural" and dietary products. Here, stone-ground organic meets gourmet cuisine. *Pumpernickel, sübrot*, aniseed, fennel, and cumin breads, and other varieties abound. The traditional Alsatian breads are baked from stone-ground organic flour, fermented with natural leaven and hand-shaped. Jean-

LE PAIN RAVOUX
The Auberge Ravoux at Auvers-sur-Oise, where Vincent van Gogh lived in 1890, has recently been thoroughly restored and is now listed as a historical monument. The restaurant makes exceptionally good bread to accompany the fine traditional cuisine. The *pain à l'ancienne* is probably similar to that which the painter must have eaten. All the ingredients—a combination of whole-wheat and part whole-wheat flour, together with bran—are organic and the loaf is well fermented before being skillfully shaped. The bread can be savored at the Auberge Ravoux itself (52, rue du Général-de-Gaulle, tel. 34 48 05 47) or else at the bakery: M. Marchand, 5, rue du Général-de-Gaulle, tel. 30 36 70 21 (see p. 10).

Pierre Scholler also makes traditional French breads, that is to say ordinary white loaves, but using methods and recipes with a natural leaven developed by the family's forbears more than a century ago.

HELMSTETTER (photo p. 107)
11-13, rue des Serruriers, 68000 Colmar.
Tel. 89 41 27 78.
Closed Sundays.
This bakery, with its beautiful store sign showing a golden pretzel in a *couronne-épi*, is run by Daniel Helmstetter, the current representative of a family of bakers working in the Upper Rhine since 1776 and in Colmar since 1906. Regional specialties are much in evidence: a poppy seed bread called the "berche" (in the shape of a distaff with three-branched braid at the top); the *sübrot* (called *sousweck* in Upper Rhine dialect); the pretzel; a rye bread with cumin; a maslin bread with walnuts (or with figs); and a muesli bread, using *brioche* dough, with apricots, raisins, and almonds.

AQUITAINE

PAIN MAITRE
25, rue Camille-Sauvageau, 33000 Bordeaux.
Tel. 56 92 28 64.
Closed Sundays.
If I were asked who is the best French baker, I would be tempted to reply . . . a Flemish baker. In 1976, Jan Demaître, a former actor and English teacher, moved with his wife to southwest France, where he discovered a dilapidated baking oven adjoining a ruined château. The discovery prompted him to learn the craft which his grandfather had practiced before him. Twelve years later, already a celebrated artisan (his bread is sold in eight different *départements*), he opened a fabulous bakery designed for him by architect Alain Troussel. With its pure, geometric lines, the bakery brings to mind Japan, Mondrian, and art deco—very different from the run-of-the-mill rustic bread store. Organic stone-ground flour; coarse sea salt; filtered water; fermentation with natural leaven of which the starter was begun eighteen years ago); hand-shaping; and baking in a real wood-fired oven: all result in sublime *pains de campagne*, brown and whole-wheat loaves, ryes, and spelt breads, as well as loaves with almonds, hazelnuts, raisins, and walnuts. Jan Demaître salts his dough rather less than is customary, which brings out marvelously the authentic savor of the leavening.

LE BLE EN HERBE
145, rue Judaïque, 33000 Bordeaux.
Tel. 56 24 53 57.
Closed Saturdays and Sundays.
There is a warm atmosphere at the bakery of Aristide Koné, who previously worked for Jan

Demaître. The large wood-fired oven, visible from the store, probably has something to do with it, but the smile and relaxed demeanor of the baker himself also contribute. The methods and organic ingredients are the same as those used at Demaître's (except for the baking, which here is done in an oven whose chambers are heated indirectly) and the quality, as a result, is guaranteed. Whole-wheat loaves, *pains de campagne*, spelt loaves—all are perfect.

ALVES (photo p. 110)
368, avenue Thiers, 33100 Bordeaux.
Tel. 56 86 35 21.
Closed Sunday afternoons.
A beautiful map of France showing the various regional breads adorns one of the walls of this pleasant bakery. The store sells a *couronne bordelaise* (to order), *fougasses*, and a fine *baguette rustique*.

BOULANGERIE THIBAUD
52, boulevard Tourasse, 64000 Pau.
Tel. 59 30 45 55.
Open every day.
An excellent bakery where you can buy several kinds of *pain de campagne* made from organic, stone-ground brown, or white wheat flour. They are hand-shaped and baked on a refractory stone sole: the crust is splendid, the crumb exquisite, and all the loaves keep well.

LE MOULIN DE BASSILOUR (photo p. 110)
Quartier Bassilour, 64210 Bidart.
Tel. 59 41 94 49.
Closed Tuesdays; open every day in summer.
The Inchaurraga family are both millers and bakers in this 1741 water mill in the heart of the French Basque country. They mill wheat, rye, and cornmeal, turning it into bread and cakes at the bakery. Ancestral methods and a stone oven make for fine *pains de campagne* with leaven in various shapes, as well as a whole-wheat loaf, and a rye. They also make a Basque specialty, the aromatic *méture* (with corn meal). Traditionally toasted or dunked in milk, *méture* is also excellent with *foie gras* or duck rillettes.

AUVERGNE

LA PANETIERE MENULPHIENNE
Place de la Croix, 03210 Saint-Menoux.
Tel. 70 43 96 63.
Closed Sundays.
Michel Prothon provides this small town near Moulins with a fine range of organic-flour breads baked with leaven. Slow kneading, hand-shaping, and the use of good flour testify to his stated aim that everything should be natural. His traditional *pains de campagne*, whole-wheat loaves, and rye loaves, all baked in a wood-fired oven, can also be found in the

markets in Moulins, Nevers, Riom, and Montluçon.

CHRISTIAN DANIAS
12, rue du Collège, 15100 Saint-Flour.
Tel. 71 60 03 53.
Closed Mondays.
A recipient of the title "Meilleur Ouvrier de France," Christian Danias says he is "crazy about nature." Not surprisingly, he specializes in the good traditional breads of his adopted region, the Auvergne (he is from the Périgord). Many of his breads contain rye, notably his walnut loaves, rye *baguettes*, and rye loaves with nuts or raisins. Also available are rolls with bacon pieces, cumin, or poppy seed, as well as the dense rolls with potato-meal which are ideal with Auvergne *charcuterie*.

AMANDIO PIMENTA
4, place Mirabeau,
63100 Clermont-Ferrand.
Tel. 73 25 07 13.
Closed Mondays.
A "Meilleur Ouvrier de France" since 1994, Amandio Pimenta specializes in rye breads. His *pain de seigle à l'ancienne*, dense and rich in leaven, enables one to savor the slightly sour taste of the cereal. The fine *pain de campagne*, like the white breads, incorporates fermented dough added during kneading and is made from a wheat and rye blend.

PIERRE NURY
Combraille, 63410 Loubeyrat.
Tel. 73 86 55 95.
Closed Tuesdays.
In the pretty little village of Combraille, there are signposts pointing the way to the *boulangerie*. Make sure you follow them, because the bakery has turned its back on the village and faces a paddock. Baker Pierre Nury, who was awarded the Rabelais d'Or de la Gastronomie in 1993, specializes in rye bread (80 percent), with wheat flour used solely as a ferment. These are strong-flavored loaves with a dense crumb, sold in the traditional way: by weight. The maslin bread (rye/wheat mix) is both weighed and shaped by hand and fermented without yeast. The *baguette* with leaven, christened "combraille" by Pierre Nury, also contains a little rye, while the "bougnat" is an unmolded loaf (10 percent rye) with a blend of whole-wheat and white flours, fermented using the *poolisch* method (like the other wheat-flour loaves here). The result is a "holey" texture beneath a thick crust, full of the flavor of the flour. This bread is also sold by weight. All of Pierre Nury's other loaves (*flûtes*, *pains*, or 1-pound *couronne*), made from pure wheat, are also fermented using the *poolisch* method, which retains the full flavor of good flour.

BASSE-NORMANDIE

HEIZ-LEGRIX
8, boulevard des Alliés, 14000 Caen.
Tel. 31 85 17 42.
Closed Mondays.
This famous Caen caterer is also a fine baker. Christian Heiz and his team offer thirty different kinds of bread each day, in one hundred different forms. They are all made from excellent flour and are fermented with leaven. They include all the Norman specialties, such as *pain brié* (kneaded with a "brake" to remove the air), "butter bread," cider bread, and bread with apples.

BURGUNDY

AU PAIN D'AUTREFOIS
47, rue du Bourg, 21000 Dijon.
Tel. 80 30 47 92.
Closed Sundays and Mondays.
Régis Weil is a true artist of baking. He makes traditional breads with stone-ground organic flour and natural leaven, and bakes them in a wood-fired oven. His range includes *baguettes de campagne*, farmhouse rounds, an unmolded loaf called a "rustique" and a surprising range of ryes (with honey, olives, almonds, apricots, prunes, etc.). The specialties include a fine bread with Comté cheese, a "marbré" (streaked with rye, whole-wheat, and brown flour). The favorite pastime of this young baker is sculpted fancy breads—elephants, tortoises, crocodiles, and others adorn the shop. He will also provide a loaf up to 7 feet in diameter to order for banquets.

BRITTANY

LA GERBIERE
80, avenue de la France-Libre, 29000 Quimper.
Tel. 98 95 41 20.
Closed Sunday afternoons and Mondays.
Christian Leclerc and his wife Patricia opened this modern, airy bakery in 1995. From the street one can see the baker at work at a wood-fired oven made from light-colored stone. They produce a "flûte Gana," as well as traditional regional loaves such as a *pain plié* (where the dough is folded over), a *pain polka*, and a *pain brié*, as well as a whole range of flavored breads made from rye and wheat, containing, variously, bacon, walnuts, hazelnuts, raisins, chorizo, and almonds.

LES CHAUMIERES
Lanneguy, 29340 Riec-sur-Belon.
Tel. 98 06 48 09.
Open Mondays and Thursdays between 4 and 9 p.m.
In a thatched cottage just outside Riec, surrounded by magnificent Cornouaille scenery, Dominique Chedaine kneads stone-ground

organic flour and bakes loaves with natural leaven in a real wood-fired oven. His is a small but perfect range: white breads and brown, a *semi-complet*, raisin breads, and sesame-seed loaves. All are supplied in round, long, or molded shapes, as well as in two weights (1 and 2 pounds).

BOULANGERIE CANEVET
Coulart, 29410 Saint-Thégonnec.
Tel. 98 78 08 76.
Sale to the public: Mondays, Thursdays, and Fridays, between 4 and 8 p.m.
This bakery specializes in *bara goell toaz* ("bread with leaven" in Breton). Twelve types are on offer at the local markets: authentic white breads, whole-wheat loaves, ryes, and special breads, all from organic flour, without baker's yeast and baked in a wood-fired oven. Philippe Canevet's specialty is called *pain montagne* (the recipe comes from the Ardennes). An excellent mix of rye and wheat, it keeps well.

PATRICE RENOUF
1, rue de la Vieille-Boucherie,
35400 Saint-Malo.
Tel. 99 40 86 76.
Closed Sundays (except in July and August, and public holidays).
This popular bakery is situated in the pedestrian zone of the town and is run by a talented baker, Patrice Renouf. The "flûte Gana" is perfect, as is the *baguette de campagne*, with its tarter flavor. The *pain de campagne* (on a leaven), made with rye and whole-wheat flour, is a bread-lover's dream.

LE FOURNIL DE ROTHENEUF
15, place du Canada, Rothéneuf,
35400 Saint-Malo.
Tel. 99 56 00 91.
Closed Tuesdays (except in July and August). Yann Rocaboy inaugurated his brand-new, authentic, wood-fired oven in March 1995. He typifies the new generation of French bakers, who love good traditional bread and whose stores are filled with eager, quality-conscious customers. He offers excellent everyday loaves which have been well fermented, and others, better still, made from stone-ground flour with leaven (*baguettes*, rounds, and *pains polka*). He also uses an old recipe to make the "gâche de Rothéneuf," a soft bread, enriched with butter and sugar, which keeps particularly well. Coming soon is the "pain rothéien," a recipe Yann Rocaboy devised himself using buckwheat flour.

BOULANGERIE FRETAY
10, rue de l'Eglise, Saint-Enogat,
35800 Dinard.
Tel. 99 46 14 35.
Closed Mondays.
Jacques Frétay is another Breton adept of the "flûte Gana." He is also one of the few French

bakers to filter the water for his dough. He uses organic flour in his loaves and coarse Guérande salt. Regional breads are also in evidence: *pain brié*, a rye with raisins, and even an energy-giving "sports" bread, for those determined to enter the chilly waters nearby.

CO PAIN-GALLO PAIN
Quily, 56800 Ploërmel.
Tel. 97 74 86 43.
To order only; open Tuesdays and Fridays.
Co Pain-Gallo Pain represents a unique phenomenon in France: only members of the bakery's association (subscription, one franc a year) can purchase the admirable organic-flour bread baked in this timber-built bakery. The bread, available twice a week, has to be ordered the day before. Daniel Testard (author of a number of books about bread) uses nothing but organic flours, together with rain water, Guérande salt, short kneads, and a very long fermentation (between twelve and eighteen hours). The *pains de campagne* and maslin breads are made with natural leaven and the white breads are baked with a leaven/yeast mix. Also sold are walnut breads, raisin breads, and decorated showpieces for receptions, all superb.

BREAD IN *BARQUETTES*
Bread baked and sold in baskets has become increasingly popular in France in recent years. The *barquette* turns an attractive brown in the oven and the poplar wood imparts a subtle flavor to the bread. It all started in 1993, following a meeting between a manufacturer of *barquettes*, little baskets made from poplar used for strawberries, and the manager of the roller mill the Minoterie du Coutelet, at Meung-sur-Loire, which specializes in organic flours. The Minoterie du Coutelet now supplies about a hundred bakers in the Centre and Paris regions with poplar containers and organic flour, among which the great Michel Moisan (114, rue Patay, Paris), who offers a flavorful 98 percent whole-wheat loaf weighing about a pound. A number of mills have followed the Minoterie du Coutelet's example. The Moulins de Mézières, at Mézières-en-Drouais (Eure-et-Loire *département*), deliver whole-wheat flour and *barquettes* to several dozen bakers in the Paris region, and the excellent Minoterie Tarascon (at Saint-Saturin-lès-Avignon in Provence), provides whole-wheat or brown flours in containers (called *panetons* in the south) to a number of bakers in the Vaucluse.

CENTRE

HONORE LE BOULANGER
54, rue Nationale, 37000 Tours.
Tel. 47 05 73 94.
Closed Sundays.
Philippe Delaunay provides tasty, crusty, hand-shaped breads, some of which are displayed in their wicker dough-baskets. Lovers of the "flûte Gana" will not be disappointed, while those fond of something more rustic can choose from a whole gamut of *pains de campagne* on a leaven, tender and tasty, as well as a rye round with raisins, walnut breads, and chestnut loaves. Due to the high quality of the bread, this is a highly successful enterprise and Philippe Delaunay has just opened a further bakery (in a shopping center called Les Atalantes, at Saint-Pierre-des-Corps), whose serene atmosphere is not affected by the neighboring supermarket. They say that times are hard for bakeries in France, and yet when the bread is good, the baker prospers.

AU VIEUX FOUR
7, place des Petites-Boucheries, 37000 Tours.
Tel. 47 66 62 33.
Closed Sundays and Mondays.
The Mabous have been bakers since 1620. Jacques (tenth generation and "Meilleur Ouvrier de France") has his bakery behind Saint-Gatien cathedral. He recommends that his *pains d'Auvergne*, based on a rye/bran flour mix, be tried with duck *foie gras*. His range also includes *pains de ferme* (a marvelous *pain de campagne*), unmolded *pains de Lodève*, a loaf with cream cheese in the dough, a *pain russe* (black rye tin), an "Italian" *baguette* (unsugared French Vienna), and *fouée*, a Tours specialty (a flattish roll which is split open to make sandwiches). You will find many other types of bread here, but no ordinary white bread such as the *baguette*. All the loaves are made with organic flour, fermented on a leaven for a long time and baked in a real wood-fired oven. You can also enjoy a fabulous breakfast in this establishment.

CHAMPAGNE-ARDENNES

BOULANGERIE HENRI IV
40, rue du Grand-Cloître, 52200 Langres.
Tel. 25 87 06 03.
Closed Sundays.
The Thiéry family have been bakers for seventy-five years, but the red-brick oven that Philippe Thiéry uses is more venerable still, being two hundred years old. He feeds it with bundles of sticks and loads and unloads the bread with a peel. But there is more to good bread than a good oven: you also need good ingredients and expertise, of which Philippe Thiéry has plenty. Here, the farmhouse rounds baked with leaven and whole-wheat

loaves are baked from an excellent stone-ground organic flour. The white-flour loaf "Belle Epoque" is also baked with leaven: its creamy-white crumb is delicious. The yeast breads are baked in a more modern oven at the bakery on place Diderot, but they too are subtle-tasting, golden-brown, and crunchy.

FRANCHE-COMTE

BOULANGERIE DES CARMES
88, Grand-Rue, 25000 Besançon.
Tel. 81 81 00 85.
Closed Sundays.
Claude Mesnier, "Meilleur Ouvrier de France," has invented a heavenly *baguette*, the "baguette des Carmes" (named after the Carmelite abbey in which the bakery is located), which is a god-send for *baguette*-lovers. Made from classic white flour, organic whole-wheat flour, and a touch of chestnut meal, it is made using the *poolisch* sponge-dough method. This bread has a particularly fine "toasted wheat" taste, and is as good as the "flûte Gana" also sold here. Excellent, too, is the regional *pain de ferme* with Comté cheese and, another of the master's inventions, a bread baked with Arbois red wine. Claude Mesnier, who will advise as to which bread suits which dish, also bakes fabulous loaves with lemon, chives, ham, mushrooms, and others ingredients.

HAUTE-NORMANDIE

JEAN-MARIE VIARD
23, allée Eugène-Delacroix, 76000 Rouen.
Tel. 35 98 28 58.
Closed Sundays.
Like every "Meilleur Ouvrier de France," Jean-Marie Viard can bake anything. He uses an electric oven, making fine breads with leaven from stone-ground flour. His *pain brié*, that Norman specialty, is sumptuously aromatic and flavorsome. He makes a Pas-de-Calais specialty, the *pain de Dieppe*, a white bread which keeps exceptionally well. His loaf with apricots (which contains 50 percent whole-wheat flour) and the black *Pumpernickel*-style ryes are equally successful.

LANGUEDOC-ROUSILLON

LA BOULANGE
2, rue Fondeville,
30170 Saint-Hippolyte-du-Fort.
Tel. 66 77 64 74.
Closed Saturdays and Sundays.
François Pelletier fell in love with good bread at the age of thirty, when he was working as a boilermaker. He learned his new trade on the job and for the past ten years has been providing Saint-Hippolyte and the surrounding region with authentic, no-nonsense bread, baked with leaven using fine organic

flour: wheatens (white, brown, and whole-wheat); ryes; spelt breads; and loaves made with local chestnuts. Few breads, then, but all baked to perfection.

LE MOULIN DU MEUNIER
Allée des Chênes, parc Ducup,
66000 Perpignan.
Tel. 68 54 61 60.
Closed Sunday afternoons and Mondays.
This so-called "miller's mill" is in fact a marvelous bakery run by a baker of genius, Gérard Olivier. It is situated in a park, in what was probably an outbuilding of the adjacent nineteenth-century château. The bread is baked from organic flour, fermented with leaven, and shaped by hand. The multigrain (rye, wheat, and barley) is perfectly balanced and the *benoîtons* (rye and raisins), in their bitter-sweet softness, are divine. The attractive *fougasses* are flavored with pine kernels, tripe snippings, lemon, and cream.

MIDI-PYRENEES

BOULANGERIE DES THERMES
18, avenue de la Paix, 31260 Salles-du-Salat.
Tel. 61 90 66 93.
Closed Tuesdays.
Salles-du-Salat, in addition to its thermal baths with their sulfur-rich waters, also has a fine bakery run by Bernard Pons, a "Meilleur Ouvrier de France." His traditional French bread is fermented using the *poolisch* sponge-dough method, as is revealed by the bread's slight hazelnut taste. The *baguette*, made with yeast and fermented dough, is perfection itself. The *pain de campagne* made with leaven and a mixture of white, whole-wheat, and rye flours has a rich flavor, while many of the other breads, made variously with walnuts, lemon, Roquefort, fennel, and saffron, can be eaten on their own, as a gourmet treat. We should be grateful, too, for the chance to savor two regional breads, the *pain de Lodève* and the *tordu* (shaped into the shape of a wet cloth being wrung out).

ANDRE RIVAL
15, rue François-Mousis, Marcadieu,
65000 Tarbes.
Tel. 62 93 39 31.
Closed Sundays.
André Rival is a fine baker who manages to provide up to fifty different breads on a daily basis without sacrificing traditional methods. He uses prime selected flours and insists on long fermentation, hand-shaping, and baking in a wood-fired oven. The docked crusts of his breads are a magnificent golden-brown, while the crumb is dense and full of flavor. In addition to perfect everyday breads, there are regional offerings, such as the *tignolet*, the *tabatière*, the *pain polka*, and the *gâche*.

BOULANGERIE DU PAYS TOY
Saligos, 65120 Luz-Saint-Sauveur.
Tel. 62 92 90 41.
Store sales: Mondays, Tuesdays, and Fridays, from 5 to 10 p.m.
This bakery in a village high up in the Hautes-Pyrénées is run by Elisabeth and Cyrille Greillier. It is known throughout the region for its traditional methods: fresh-milled, stone-ground organic flours (left to stand after milling for no more than three days); natural leaven without baker's yeast; pure spring water; and, of course, a wood-fired oven. White and brown breads, whole-wheat loaves, ryes, spelt breads, loaves with walnuts, almonds, and raisins—all are perfect. Their breads can also be found at the market in Argelès-Gazost on Tuesdays and at the organic market in Pau (Foirail) on Wednesday mornings and Saturdays.

PAYS DE LOIRE

AU PAIN DE MENAGE
11, rue des Petites-Ecuries, 44000 Nantes.
Tel. 40 47 85 13.
Closed Sundays and Mondays.
This establishment (named after the traditional "household bread" of France) is to be found in the city's pedestrian zone near the château. Exposed beams, wrought-iron counters, and wicker dough-baskets decorate the bakery, where Michel Albésa, a baker for forty years, has kept alive the tradition of a delicious local specialty: *pain sucré*, or sugared bread. In former times, the local farmers used to add sugar, milk, eggs, and butter to a small amount of dough they had kept from a batch and then bake it. Michel Albésa has improved this recipe and sells his sugared bread in the shape of a small coburg, which is delicious at breakfast. His *pains de campagne*, enveloped in a tasty-looking and aromatic floured crust, are just as good. Baked with leaven, they are fermented for twelve hours and shaped by hand.

LA HUCHE A PAIN
23 rue des Carmes, 44000 Nantes.
Tel. 40 47 68 32.
Closed Sundays.
Pierre Gaducheau, "Meilleur Ouvrier de France" and forty years in the trade, is an ace at bread-making. As always, his "flûte Gana" will delight lovers of good *baguettes*. Pierre Gauducheau is a shrewd gastronome, who likes to discover good combinations of breads and dishes, which is why you will find an array of subtly flavored breads in his bakery: lemon; tomato; herbs; fennel; and even glasswort. He also makes the specialty of the region—sugared bread—and a loaf of his own invention, the magnificent *pain tigré* ("tabby bread"). Specially devised to accompany *foie gras*, its dough is subtly enriched with butter and sugar.

BOULANGERIE BRETZEL

2, rue Sainte-Anne, 44290 Guenouvry.
Tel. 40 79 23 91.
Open Mondays, Thursdays, and Fridays, from 4:00 to 7:30 p.m. The bread is also sold in a dozen "bio" (health-food shops) and at the markets in Redon (Mondays), Châteaubriand (Wednesdays), Saint-Nazaire (Tuesday and Friday mornings) and Nantes (Saturday mornings, Petite Hollande).
In this bakery in the village of Guenouvry (near Redon), André Houguet uses solely the most natural ingredients: stone-ground flour; filtered water; Guérande salt; and natural leaven. Naturally, everything is baked in an authentic wood-fired oven. The white breads are divided into *pains de ménage* and *pains de campagne*. There are also brown loaves, whole-wheat loaves, wheat-flour loaves with hazelnuts, walnuts and raisins, and rye breads. The regional *tourton* will give you a whole new concept of bread: it is an astonishingly good, bitter-sweet, wheat-flour round baked with leaven and enriched with eggs and brown sugar. You can also learn how to prepare bread with leaven in a day-course with André Houguet in the bakery.

BIOFOURNIL

1, rue Leppo, 49600 Le Puiset-Doré.
Tel. 41 56 70 74.
Closed Mondays.
This fine store in the heart of Anjou makes organic-flour breads with natural leaven. The range includes *pains de campagne*, brown breads, whole-wheat loaves, multigrains (wheat, buckwheat, oat, and spelt mixes), and loaves with raisins and walnuts. Two unmissable and eminently natural loaves are also available: an exquisite, unblended spelt bread and a pure rye (the only wheat is that used in the leavening). Nature in the raw.

LE FOURNIL D'ALEXIS

L'Huilerie (route de Laval),
53100 Mayenne.
Tel. 43 00 47 85.
Closed Tuesdays.
The stone oven in this bakery run by Bruno Boudin may be a new one, but the baking is traditional. The majority of the breads are wheat-flour loaves with leaven. The dough undergoes a minimal kneading, followed by lengthy fermentation and hand-shaping. This splendid dough is made daily into a delicious range of loaves (from those weighing scarcely 2 ounces to ones weighing 5 pounds, and even up to more than 17 pounds to order). All in all, it is good, simple, real bread.

LA TRESSE DOREE

19, rue Saint-Blaise, 85500 Les Herbiers.
Tel. 51 67 28 30.
Closed Wednesdays.

Here one can discover the "préfou," a regional specialty from the southern part of the Vendée. It is a marvelous, flattish bread, docked in squares, enriched with butter, and strongly flavored with garlic. The *baguettes* and white breads, fermented using the *poolisch* method (the baker, Dominique Planchot, calls them "poulichettes"), are excellent, as is the "grignette" (a *baguette* on a leaven containing 30 percent stone-ground flour). Customers can watch the bread being baked (in wood-fired ovens) on Mondays, Thursdays, Fridays, and Saturdays, between 3 p.m. and 6 p.m. The bread tasting is free!

PICARDIE

LA BOULANGE D'ANTAN

56, rue de la République, 60150 Thourotte.
Tel. 44 76 00 70.
Closed Sunday afternoons and Mondays.
Christian Tivoly opened his bakery in Thourotte, a small town near Compiègne, in 1994, equipping it with a new, traditional,

> ### BREAD STATISTICS
>
> France has 35,000 family and industrial bakeries, which employ in all approximately 100,000 people. They provide almost all of the 3.5 million tons of bread eaten each year (5 ounces a day per head).
> The precise amount consumed varies greatly from one social group to another. Farmers eat $6^1/_2$ ounces per head, while managers, doctors and lawyers manage only around 3. Hence, the average yearly consumption in rural areas is 150 pounds per person, while in Paris it reaches only just over 70.
> The French eat many different kinds of bread and these figures include Vienna breads and *biscottes*. Some 35 percent only eat fresh-baked loaves, 23 percent fresh bread but also sometimes pre-packed loaves and *biscottes*, 14 percent fresh-baked bread and Vienna breads, 9 percent (mostly women) eat only dietary breads and 3.5 percent consume solely pre-packaged bread.
> Contrary to a popularly held belief, the French do not consume more bread than their fellow Europeans. They are sixth in the league after the Greeks, the Portuguese, the Italians, the Germans and the Irish. In the various countries of the European Community there are around 200,000 family and industrial bakeries and Europe's inhabitants consume around 25 million tons of bread a year.

wood-fired oven. The yeast-fermented white breads are given a pinch of leaven and the *pains de campagne* are baked from stone-ground flour. Daily, more than a dozen different special breads are also baked, incorporating ingredients such as Comté cheese, walnuts, and chorizo. Here is another brilliant example of the renaissance of bread-making in France.

POITOU-CHARENTES

AU BON PAIN DE FRANCE

Place du Champ-de-Foire, 17500 Jonzac.
Tel. 46 48 02 26.
Closed Thursdays.
Jean-Louis Mierger is a "Meilleur Ouvrier de France" who bakes everything, from a delicious flour-dusted *baguette* with pointed ends to an organic whole-wheat loaf. Particularly welcome are the loaves flavored with Gruyère, Roquefort, bacon pieces, walnuts and raisins, and walnuts and prunes. Just as tempting is the unmolded *pain de Lodève*, originally from the Hérault. Its exquisite taste is a result of long fermentation. It has a thick crust and keeps for a long time.

PROVENCE
ALPES-COTE D'AZUR

LE PAIN DE THIERRY

Le Vieux Village, 04510 Mallemoisson.
Tel. 92 34 78 34.
To order, except Wednesdays and Saturdays.
Baker Thierry Grand Dufay set up his bakery in an abandoned school in 1991. He produces around three hundred loaves a day, which he sells at markets in neighboring towns such as Digne, Manosque, and Forcalquier, and through stores specializing in natural products. His admirably docked breads are all made from organic flour, fermented with natural leaven (no yeast), hand-shaped, and baked in a stone-built oven. They include *pains de campagne*, brown breads, whole-wheat loaves, maslin bread, loaves with olives, sesame seed, and anchovies, and a *pompe*, a Provençal Christmas treat made with olive oil and orange flower.

BOULANGERIE PAIN ET TRADITION

22, rue Vernier, 06000 Nice.
Tel. 93 88 83 33.
Closed Sundays.
The secret of the fine bread sold by M. and Mme. Ceccarelli may lie in their flour, which comes straight from the Colagne roller-mill in the Lozère. Apart from the *baguette* (enriched with a little dough from a batch made the day before), all the loaves are hand-shaped. There are tasty special breads (with bran, with rye, with leaven, or whole-wheat) and a range of flavored breads (with walnuts, hazelnuts, Roquefort, onions, etc.). The rolls

made with thyme, garlic, and aniseed offer all the savors of Provence. Last but not least are the *fougassettes* (with olives, Roquefort, anchovies, and bacon pieces and orange flower), to be enjoyed while reading a book by Giono or Pagnol.

BOULANGERIE ARTISANALE DES MAURES
Quartier Taurelle-Route Nationale 7, 83340 Le Cannet-des-Maures.
Tel. 94 73 46 42.
Closed Mondays.
This bakery has a reputation for natural and authentic bread, made from organic stoneground flour and natural leaven. Most of the loaves are baked in a wood-fired oven. They are salted with Guérande salt and purified water is used. In addition to traditional breads, such as the *pains de campagne* (from the hefty *miche* weighing 5 pounds to the *ficelle*), and whole-meal, rye, maslin, and spelt loaves, you will find *fougasses*, a great regional specialty, in particular *fougasse* with fine Nyons olives.

BOULANGERIE DE L'HERMITAGE
Route du Repenti, 83590 Gonfaron.
Tel. 94 78 31 66.
Closed Saturdays and Sundays.
In this real artisanal bakery, Eric Dufaye bakes only bread on a natural leaven made with organic flour. There are no *baguettes*, just wholesome, golden rounds made with white, brown, whole-wheat, or maslin flour. Also sold is a bread called "kamut" (ancient Egyptian for "wheat"), the name for a variety of wheat (*Triticum polonium*), some grains of which were apparently discovered in a tomb. The grains were analyzed and chemically reconstituted, and the variety is now being cultivated in the United States. Although it sounds too good to be true, *T. polonium* is far richer in proteins and minerals than ordinary cultivars, and can be baked into a marvelously soft and flavorful bread, tasting somewhat like spelt.

ROGER AUZET
61, cours Bournissac, 84300 Cavaillon.
Tel. 90 78 06 54.
Closed Tuesdays.
Also in Cavaillon: Fournil des Condamines, Centre Commercial des Condamines, avenue du Général-de-Gaulle, tel. 90 71 84 73; closed Tuesdays.
The jovial Roger Auzet, "Meilleur Ouvrier de France," specializes in traditional Mediterranean breads, such as *fougasses* made with fried tripe pieces or anchovies, and bread with garlic cloves, olives, or thyme. M. Auzet describes himself as "a baker, not a breadseller" and this he emphasizes with his fine *pain de Beaucaire*, a white loaf with leaven made from flour from the Colagne mill, and a fine *pain de campagne* crown. He also makes two excellent *baguettes*: one *à l'ancienne*, the other with leaven.

RHONE-ALPES

BOULANGERIE NIVON (MAURIN FILS)
17, avenue de la Gare, 26000 Valence.
Tel. 75 44 03 37.
Closed Mondays.
Denis Maurin represents the third generation of bakers in this firm founded in 1855. The local specialties which have made this bakery world famous are not strictly speaking breads, but sublime Viennese pastries (such as the "pogne de Valence" and the "suisses"). Pic, a famous restaurant in Valence, made the right choice when it selected this bakery to supply its French bread. The white *pains de campagne* with leaven, made from stoneground flour, and the Ardèche rye breads (heavy ryes, and rye with walnuts or with raisins) are all worth tasting. The *pain béarnais* (unmolded and the result of long fermentation) is made from "Florence-Aurore," one of the best French wheat varieties.

DOMINIQUE BRUN
14, rue Gustave-André, 26120 Chabeuil.
Tel. 75 59 01 87.
Closed Mondays.

THE MONKS' BREAD

ARTISANAT MONASTIQUE DE PROVENCE
Abbaye Saint-Madeleine,
84330 Le Barroux.
Tel. 90 62 56 31.
Closed Mondays. Bread is sold from 10.30 a.m. to 12 p.m. and 2.15 to 5.15 p.m.; on Sundays, from 9.15 to 9.45 a.m., 11.45 a.m. to 12.15 p.m., and 2.45 p.m. to 5.15 p.m.
Surrounded by magnificent countryside, the monks of the Saint-Madeleine abbey near Mont Ventoux spend their lives in prayer, study, and manual labor. In 1982, they began to make bread for their own consumption. The following year they decided to sell it in their craft store. One of the monks went up to Paris to take a course with Lionel Poilâne and today their bread is heavenly. The *pains de campagne* with leaven, made from a blend of white flour and organic wholewheat flour, are light, dense, and delicious, while the *pain de Beaucaire* (originally from a town on the nearby Rhone), containing black olives and enriched with olive oil, has all the scents of Provence. The flavorful rye bread with walnuts fills you with an energy, as it were, of divine origin.

Dominique Brun supplies the famous Valence restaurant, Pic, with delicious "griches" (flavored or plain rolls), rolls containing, three vegetables (carrots, spinach, and celery), and others called "triple alliance" (wheat flour combined with rye, sesame, and linseed). But this is not the only distinction of this bakery-cum-tearoom, whose best asset is a legacy of Dominique Brun's father, Jean. The latter had a passion for history and turned this establishment into something of a bread museum. Here you can admire the charming pictures from the past which decorate the walls, while sampling historical breads, such as Greek *melitates* (wheat flour with honey and olive oil) or a "Pompeii" loaf, molded just like those that have been found in the ruins of the city. Dominique Brun, following on from his father, also makes specialty loaves: bread with squash; a wealth of fine *fougasses*; the unmolded *pain de Beaucaire*; and a number of organic-flour loaves baked with leaven.

BOULANGERIE ARTISANALE JACO'PAIN
Le village, 26190 Saint-Thomas-en-Royans.
Tel. 75 47 59 82.
Closed Sunday afternoons and Mondays.
In his bakery in a tiny village at the foot of the Vercors, Sylvain Faure makes loaves from stone-ground organic flour with a lengthy fermentation (without yeast), salted with Guérande salt, hand-molded, and baked in a wood-fired oven. He sells six fine, natural, traditional breads: *pains de campagne* (wheat and rye); multigrain (wheat, rye, barley, soya, buckwheat, and maize); a walnut bread; a whole-wheat bread; a whole rye (only the leaven is made with wheat); and a spelt bread.

LES BLES D'OR
48, Grande-Rue de la Guillotière, 69007 Lyon
Tel. 72 80 07 72.
Closed Sunday afternoons and Mondays.
Luc Mano is one of the two or three finest bakers in France. Born in Bordeaux, he has been involved in the bread-making trade since the age of fourteen. There is one key secret (or almost one) to his success: time. All of the dough that he uses, even that of the *baguettes*, is fermented (at room temperature) for a minimum of twenty hours. That is a record for France. Naturally, all of his breads are made with natural leaven, using a starter begun fifteen years ago, which he refreshes and enriches constantly. The stunning rounds, *baguettes*, and *ficelles* are all made from stone-ground flour. Luc Mano is a brilliant artisan, as is evident from his *pain frappé* (a white round, knocked back a second time during shaping, whose crust is so soft that the baker recommends it for those with delicate teeth), his *pain de campagne* (hardly kneaded and lightly baked), containing practically

double the normal quantity of leaven and yet not at all sour, and his multigrain and flavored breads (one of which is made with walnuts, raisins, and hazelnuts). Another sublime loaf is the spelt bread, which brings out all the mineral flavors of this cereal. Luc Mano also likes working to order: you can request absolutely any sort of loaf and he will find a way of fulfilling your heart's desire.

LA BOULANGERIE SAVOYARDE

Ecole-en-Bauges, 73630 Le Châtelard.
Tel. 79 54 82 74.
Closed Saturdays and Sundays.
Also available in Paris and London, at the Montignac store.
This bakery (which supplies the Bocuse and Orsi restaurants in Lyon) is situated in the center of a village of two hundred inhabitants in the Bauges massif. Patrick Le Port, the excellent baker, uses organic flour, fresh spring water, and coarse sea salt. He favors slow kneading and a five-hour fermentation in wicker *bannetons*, before baking in an extraordinary wood-fired oven with a double crown which can accommodate hundreds of loaves. He bakes whole-wheat loaves, five-grain loaves, ryes, and loaves with sesame seeds, walnuts, and raisins, all of which are equally delicious. Since January 1995, Patrick Le Port has also been baking a truly exceptional loaf, the "kamut" (see Boulangerie de l'Hermitage, p. 172).

JEAN-PIERRE VEYRAT-DUREBEX

74230 Manigod.
Tel. 50 44 92 64.
Closed Wednesdays; open every day during school vacations.
In this little village in Savoie, at an altitude of about 3,500 feet, lives a baker who, as far as I know, is unique in France. Jean-Pierre Veyrat-Durebex bakes his bread in an authentic old wood-fired oven: one where the wood burns in the baking chamber itself, on the spot where, once the stone has become white-hot, the loaves are placed. He is therefore the only baker who can truly claim that wood-burning actually flavors his bread! His oven is more than one hundred and fifty years old and is stoked with bundles of kindling (mostly fir), which suits the *pains de campagne* marvelously (longs, rounds, and *en couronne*). Naturally these are fermented with leaven and hand-shaped. They possess a superb crust and dense crumb, and have a particularly rich taste (much appreciated by those who enjoy the region's *fondue*). At the Auberge de l'Éridan, the restaurant run by the celebrated

Marc Veyrat (no relation), it is this bread that is served: a recommendation indeed.

BELGIUM

BOULANGERIE DEWALQUE

12, rue de l'Abbé-Péters, 4960 Malmédy.
Tel. (080) 33 03 76.
Closed Sunday afternoons, Wednesdays, and Thursdays.
Marc Dewalque is a baker who knows everything about natural, organic-flour bread. He is the publisher of a photocopied quarterly called *Les Miettes de la bio*, packed with information about bread and bread making. In his bakery in Malmédy, a little town in the Ardennes near the German frontier, Marc Dewalque makes solely organic loaves (although he has no right to call them such, as he has refused to pay the high duties imposed on bakers in the Walloon region). His range includes: breads with leaven; whole-wheat loaves; spelt breads; *pains d'Ardenne* (brown flour and rye); a "pain de randonnée" (with hazelnuts to provide energy while on a walk); a multigrain (with whole wheat, rye, barley, and oats); *baguettes*; *ficelles*; and, of course, *pistolets*, Belgian breakfast rolls. Everything is traditional, authentic, and delicious.

GERMANY

HEBERER (WIENER FEINBÄCKEREI) (photo p. 117)

Frankfurt am Main.
This firm, established in 1871, has a number of branches in the city, selling succulent poppy-seed or sesame-seed rolls, which are a delight at breakfast time. They are particularly tasty eaten with cheese, pork meats, or jam.

LOCHNER (photo p. 116)

Kalbächergasse 10,
60313 Frankfurt am Main.
Tel. (69) 9 20 73 20.
This bakery supplies the excellent restaurant in the Hessicher Hof hotel (a favorite meeting place for publishers during the Frankfurt Book Fair). Situated in a street baptized "Fressgasse" (greedy pig), the firm of Lochner is well known for its excellent breads with walnut, sunflower seeds, and whole-grain rye.

KADEWE

Tauentzienstrasse 21, 10789 Berlin.
Tel. (30) 2 12 20.
Perhaps the largest specialist food hall in the world, where both selection and display are

impeccable. Crowds come here to buy all the traditional German breads, as well as loaves supplied by the French company Lenôtre, including a multigrain loaf and several aromatic breads.

SWITZERLAND

BIO ANDREAS (photos p. 121)

Andreasplaz 14, 4051 Basel.
Tel. (61) 261 84 86.
As its name implies, this bakery, with its charming interior, specializes in organic bread. Customers can choose from country wheaten breads, a number of multigrains made with leaven which combine barley, buckwheat, corn, oats, or spelt, and the house specialty, loaves concocted for apéritifs (recommended with white wine). These are made with olives, onions, saffron, and, most ingenious of all, mustard. All these offerings are baked in a wood-fired oven which can be seen from the store. This oven is also used to bake pizzas, as the bakery is also a restaurant serving breakfast and lunch.

BROTHUUS ZOLLER (photos pp. 119, 120)

Rosenstrasse 68, 4058 Basel.
Tel. (61) 691 09 31.
Closed Saturdays and Sundays.
A first-rate Swiss bakery which uses only organic stone-ground whole-wheat flours and natural leaven. They offer excellent rye breads, such as the whole-grain "Traumähri," or the "Walliser" with cracked rye grains, which is also made with prunes and walnuts ("Walliser Zwetschgen"). Another typical Swiss specialty is a multigrain called the *sako*: the Zoller variety has eight different ingredients (rye, wheat, oats, soya, sesame seeds, squash, sunflower seeds, and linseed).

SUTTER (photo p. 120, bottom)

Aeschenvorstadt 6, 4051 Basel.
Tel. (61) 271 49 52.
Also: Rosentalstrasse 28, 4508 Basel.
Tel. (61) 691 10 88.
Yet another excellent establishment in Basel, which upholds the finest Swiss traditions in bread making. Its great specialty is the *Urigsbrot* (puckish bread), a wheat-flour and rye, whose crust has a curiously crumpled appearance. Try the delicious *Walliserbrot* (bread from the Valais)—a rye bread with cracked rye grains, stuck with oats, which is eaten thinly sliced with sausage, smoked meats, or cheese. Customers can also admire the extraordinary festival bread, the *Traubenbrot* (bunch of grapes).

A P P E L L A T I O N S

PROFESSIONAL QUALIFICATIONS AND OFFICIAL TYPES OF FRENCH BREAD

There are a range of classifications and controls—*appellations*—which apply to retail baking in France. They are generally indications either of professional qualifications or of bread quality and are usually displayed in the window or on the wall of the bakery or printed on the wrapper. They can tell the customer a great deal about the quality of the bread sold there. Most of these *appellations* are subject to strict regulation (far stricter than in Britain for the most part), but they can nonetheless prove somewhat misleading. Indeed, some of them seem to have been devised more to encourage the inferior baker than to help customers in search of good bread. Here are some of the more important *appellations*.

ARTISAN BOULANGER. To earn this title, which is often posted in the window, the baker must possess a *certificat d'aptitude professionnelle* (CAP) in baking (at least eighteen weeks' training, an exam, and practical experience) or have practiced his trade for more than six years. The title "Maître artisan boulanger" is reserved for those with a *maîtrise* or equivalent, and for the "Meilleurs Ouvriers de France," providing they have been working for at least two years. However, it can also be conferred on bakers who do not have a diploma but who are particularly renowned.

PAIN MAISON. This regulated *appellation* only applies to those breads which are entirely kneaded, shaped, and baked at the point of sale. This is by no means, therefore, a guarantee of quality, as a *pain maison* can of course be legitimately produced by an inexpert baker. The *appellation* is intended to enable the customer to distinguish a real bakery from a simple "baking terminal," where pre-packed dough arrives deep-frozen and is baked on the premises. *Boulangeries froides* (bread outlets which sell bread made elsewhere, perhaps by hand) are also not entitled to this appellation, although they sometimes supply excellent bread.

PAIN DE TRADITION FRANÇAISE. This *appellation*, reserved, curiously, for wheaten breads, excludes loaves which have been subjected to deep-freezing or those which contain the additives often employed in baking: ascorbic acid (vitamin C, which accelerates the fermentation of the dough) and lecithin (a fat derived for the most part from soya germ, which increases bread volume and improves shelf-life). When such additives and improvers are not used, the dough has to be fermented for longer.

Although long fermentation is a good thing, the *appellation* is not a guarantee of quality, as it allows for the use of other additives (such as bean meal, soya, and malted wheat) that are never used in the best "traditional" breads.

PAIN AU LEVAIN. This *appellation*, which indicates a loaf made with leaven, unfortunately causes confusion between several different methods of fermentation. The *appellation* in fact allows for the supplementary use of yeast (up to 0.2 percent of the weight of the flour) and also permits the use of dehydrated leaven (often already incorporated into the flour at the mill). It therefore makes no distinction between a real leaven (made by using a "starter" which can last for weeks—even years—and produces the most wonderful bread) and a piece of dough which is taken from a batch made one day to be used as leaven the next. The *appellation*, which only excludes bread raised solely by means of baker's yeast, would gain from being made more explicit.

PAIN CUIT AU FEU DE BOIS. (Bread baked in a wood-fired oven.) The wood-fired oven is synonymous with all that is natural and authentic and has as such become an important selling point. As a result, the *appellation* is often incorrectly applied. Theoretically, it should apply only to bread baked on the sole of the oven in the baking chamber where the wood is actually burnt. Apart from a handful of communal ovens in rural areas, there is, to my knowledge, only one baker in all France who bakes his bread in this manner: Jean-Pierre Veyrat in Manigod, Savoie. This *appellation* can, at a pinch, be applied to loaves that have been baked in a baking chamber heated directly, where the heat from a wood-fired hearth beneath the chamber is channeled through a "duct." On the other hand, it is not acceptable to use it to describe bread cooked in wood-fueled ovens heated indirectly, where the baking chamber is not in direct contact with the flames. Some unscrupulous bakers use the expression "bread baked in a wood-fired oven," but if the oven in question is indirectly heated, the wood can have no effect at all on the quality of the bread.

PAIN BIOLOGIQUE. (Organic-flour breads.) Only breads whose ingredients are produced without any artificial chemical additives can be termed *biologique*. This excludes cereals cultivated with the aid of herbicides, pesticides, or chemical fertilizers; flours treated with chemical pesticides during storage; or those combined with various additives, such as preservatives. However, as long as they do not exceed 5 percent of the composition of the bread, certain non-organic ingredients are authorized (such as spices, herbs, sesame seeds, and certain fatty additives). As for the non-organic ingredients of the bread itself, European Community legislation applying to organic products authorizes the use of baker's yeast, refined salt, and "drinking" water. Other, more logical, organic bakers use only natural leaven, unrefined sea salt, and filtered tap or pure spring water. In France, four private organizations regulate and approve organic produce: Écocert, Qualité France, SOCOTEC, and Bio Contact. Numerous bakers provide *bio* breads, as do health food stores (and supermarkets), as well as specialized markets. Here is a list of the main organic French breads, which are baked and sold according to a strict set of specifications and regulations, or distributed in specialized shops and markets:

Borsa. Around a thousand bakers produce "Borsa" bread. It is baked using an organic flour (milled by breakage) and a dehydrated organic leaven derived from milk ferments.

Lima. There are seventy-five outlets for "Lima" bread, which is made with natural leaven.

Lemaire. One thousand five hundred bakers offer this bread baked on a leaven. The specifications allow for the addition of baker's yeast at the kneading stage.

La Vie Claire. The stores with this name sell an organic bread baked with leaven (yeast is authorized).

Nature et Progrès. About forty bakers follow the specification laid down by Nature et Progrès, producing loaves made from organic flour, with no additives, kneaded slowly and salted with unrefined sea salt. Nature et Progrès have created two separate categories of bread: the first applies to bread which is baked solely with natural leaven, while the second applies to bread incorporating the addition of a maximum 0.2 percent of baker's yeast.

PAIN DE SEIGLE. French regulations stipulate that a *pain de seigle* (rye bread) should contain at least 65 percent rye flour. When the percentage is lower, the loaf is not authorized to carry this *appellation*, and should be termed a *pain au seigle* (bread with rye).

PAIN DE SON. This *appellation* is regulated in the same way as that covering rye breads: the bread concerned should contain at least 20 percent bran (the rest should be type 55 wheat flour, 75 percent extraction rate). If the percentage is lower, the loaf must be called a *pain au son*. The legislation also stipulates the quantity of permitted pesticides present in the bran (it should not exceed 1 or 2 milligrams per kilo of flour, depending on the pesticide).

FRENCH CHEFS AND THEIR BREAD SUPPLIERS

Great French chefs have understood for some time that a good restaurant must serve good bread. Offering bread to diners as they arrive is a welcoming gesture that everyone appreciates. Some chefs make their own loaves, while others are supplied by excellent bakers. The following list includes some of the best chefs in France:

JOEL ROBUCHON (Paris) makes his own delicious bread (a divine *pain de campagne* made using flour from the Decollogne-Lecocq mills) and hands samples out to his diners as they leave his restaurant (see p. 150).

PAUL BOCUSE (Collonges-au-Mont-d'Or) is supplied by Philippe Jocteur (Boulangerie de l'Ile Barbe, 5 place Henri-Barbusse, 69009 Lyon, tel. 78 83 98 35). M. Jocteur prepares wonderful part-baked rolls, which are then baked in the restaurant before being served.

MICHEL BRAS (Laguiole) only serves homemade breads: rye; classic wheat flour with leaven; and bread made from a special flour ground by the excellent mill at Chirac in the Lozère, the Minoterie de Colagne.

ALAIN DUCASSE (Le Louis XV, Hôtel de Paris, Monaco) is probably the chef who offers his diners the widest range of breads of all. They can choose from around fifteen kinds of roll, presented on a trolley. The wonderful bread is made by Patrick Roy, the master baker at the Hôtel de Paris and a true baking ace. The Nice *michette* is made with olive oil and goes particularly well with Alain Ducasse's Mediterranean cooking; it is recommended, in particular, with the appetizers. The *fougasse* with *lard de campagne* is recommended with suckling pig, the little olive *baguette* with the young partridge, the chestnut roll with game in general, and the walnut rye loaves with the cheese course. The *feuillantine* is an absolute delight (made with cornmeal, it is shaped into the form of a little fan and served with appetizers and fish), as are the *grissini*, plain or flavored with Parmesan, or even rolled in thin bacon slices. Equally heavenly is the peppered roll made with pickled tomatoes. All these examples represent the very summit of bread gastronomy.

PIERRE GAGNAIRE (Saint-Etienne) is almost as much a baker as a chef, since he makes a number of delicious and original breads, all with natural leaven. They include rye mini-*baguettes*, buckwheat loaves with seaweed, white bread with olives and walnuts, milk breads with fried onions, and admirable crusts of spelt bread to accompany cheese.

The HAEBERLIN family (Auberge de l'Ill, Illhaeusern) makes the most delicious white rolls on *poolisch*, plain or flavored with sesame seed, poppy seed, figs, walnuts and—wonder of wonders—truffles. The firm also obtains its bread from a good Colmar baker, whom we have already had occasion to mention (Daniel Helmstetter, 13 rue des Serruriers, 68000 Colmar, tel. 89 41 27 78; see p. 107).

ÉMILE JUNG (Au Crocodile, Strasbourg) entrusts the preparation of his bread to a master *pâtissier-boulanger*, Alfred Georg. In addition to classic breads with leaven, rye breads, and multigrain loaves, diners can also enjoy a succulent *brioche* with *foie gras*, as well as two regional specialties: ale bread and poppy-seed bread.

GUY LEGAY (L'Espadon, Hôtel Ritz, Paris) joins forces every day with the baker Bernard Burban (named "Meilleur Ouvrier de France") to bewitch diners at the Paris Ritz. Bernard Burban makes a variety of delicious rolls, including one with bacon pieces, and a range of ryes (with walnuts, with cumin, with red wine, or with shallots; see pp. 150–151).

BERNARD LOISEAU (La Côte d'Or, Saulieu) is supplied by a good baker in the local town, who prepares for him a superb *pain gris du Morvan* (special light rye), a *pain de campagne*, and a fig rye loaf (M. Paulizac, rue des Fours, 21210 Saulieu, tel. 80 64 18 92; see pp. 100 and 147).

ALAIN PASSARD (Arpège, Paris) offers two mouth-watering homemade breads: an organic-flour farmhouse *miche de campagne* and a *baguette* of blended wheat and buckwheat flour. He also buys bread from a fine bakery (René Départ, 30 rue du Général-Leclerc, 95320 Saint-Leu-la-Forêt, tel. 39 60 00 18).

PAOLO PETRINI is one of the best Italian chefs in Paris. He makes three or four kinds of loaf himself, including a sublime *focaccia*, marvelous traditional *grissini* (long, thin, and, of course, hand-rolled), and a brown *pain de campagne* made from organic wheat flour, which is served sliced (see p. 113).

LA MAISON PIC (Valence) is supplied by two excellent bakers, mentioned already: Dominique Brun (14, rue Gustave-André, 26120 Chabeuil, tel. 75 59 01 87) and Denis Maurin (17, avenue de la Gare, 26000 Valence, tel. 75 44 03 37).

At the restaurant run by OLIVIER ROELLINGER (Restaurant de Bricourt, Cancale), all the bread is made on the premises (*pain de campagne* with leaven; a rye loaf for seafood; bread with seaweed for fish and shellfish) and baked in a real, direct-heat, wood-burning oven.

ALAIN SENDERENS (Lucas, Paris) makes his excellent bread himself (rolls with leaven; raisin breads; cumin breads).

In the TROIGROS (Roanne) restaurant, all the bread—from the *fougasses*, white rolls, and maslin rolls to the ryes with pistachio nuts or walnuts—comes from two local bakers: Pierre Dubois (98, rue Mulsant, 42300 Roanne, tel. 77 71 47 51) and Dufour & Fils (76, rue Mulsant, tel. 77 71 27 42).

FREDDY VAN DE CASSERIE (La Villa Lorraine, Brussels) proposes a range of delicious breads, which are made in a bakery where the restaurant's former regular supplier was in charge, until his death ten years ago. La Villa Lorraine bought up the bakery, which has since become La Boutique du Grand Cerf (22, rue du Grand-Cerf). The store sells cooked dishes as well as the full range of breads served in the restaurant: white table rolls; sandwich loaves; brown wheat-flour loaves; rye and spelt bread (for oysters); and walnut and raisin bread (for cheese).

ROGER VERGÉ (Le Moulin de Mougins, Mougins) offers his guests whole-grain rye rolls for seafood, fruit-flavored rolls (with figs, quince, or apricot), a walnut, almond and barley blend for *foie gras*, and toasted *ficelles* for salads and *charcuterie*. There are also olive-oil *fougasses* to start the meal, and walnut and raisin breads (for cheese). The restaurant's capable supplier is Yannick Tavolaro (Au Bon Pain Chaud, 85, boulevard Paul-Doumer, 06110 Le Cannet, tel. 93 45 79 30; see p. 153).

MARC VEYRAT (Auberge de l'Eridan, Veyrier-du-Lac) serves his bread on a magnificent Savoyard wooden trolley. His bakery supplier is a man who shares his name, Jean-Pierre Veyrat (see p. 171), the only expert baker I know of who bakes his *pain de campagne* in a real wood-burning oven like those of the past, where the wood is burned on the sole.

F L O U R S

Distinguishing between white, brown, or whole-wheat flours when they are packaged is no easy task. Often the only indication of the type of flour is the letter "T" followed by a number, printed on the bag.

Ordinary flours used by bakers, like those in stores and supermarkets, are distinguished by a number, which corresponds to the degree of sieving. From unbolted whole-wheat flour—containing the whole of the grain and its bran—to the whitest "whites," which have passed through dozens of sieving processes to be rid of as much bran (the seed sheath) as possible, the range is vast.

In France, the figure which indicates the degree to which the flour has been sieved is the "taux de cendres," the ash level. The ash is the mineral residue which comes from the bran and which remains after the flour has passed through an oven heated to a temperature of 900° C (approximately 1600° F). The higher the amount of ash, the higher the bran content of the flour tested. Combustion of 100 grams of normal white baking flour produces around 55 milligrams of ash. This quantity is indicated on the bag by "type 55," or "T 55." Whole-wheat flour, for example, is indicated by "T 150" on the bag.

Another method of calculating—which gives different figures—is prevalent in southern Europe and Britain. It involves comparing the weight of the grist before and after milling. The difference between the two values then gives the extraction rate: the weight of a whole-wheat flour amounts to about 95 percent of the total weight of the grist before milling. Regular white flour rates at 75 percent, the remaining 25 percent consisting of the bran, germ, and other eliminated impurities. It is this extraction rate which one finds on bags. The method is sometimes also used in France for stone-ground flours.

In the United States and Britain, flours are also distinguished by their protein rates. Proteins are found only in the berry. The higher the protein rate, the less bran the flour contains. Other quality control tests include "falling number" (to test for a starch-damaging enzyme), moisture, and "color" grading.

The table on the right will help in recognizing the various types of wheat flour (often blended on the spot by bakers). As for rye, there only four grades in France: 70, 85, 130, and 170. As rye breads nearly always contain a proportion of wheat flour, these grades are used by bakers to make their own individual recipes, as a particular grade is not used to bake a particular bread.

SPECIAL FLOURS

If you make your own bread at home, you should not hesitate to use the best available flours from a local flour merchant. In France, the top bakers—Basile Kamir, Jean-Luc Poujauran, Joël Robuchon—all use the stone-ground, organic flour produced by the Moulins Decollogne-Lecocq. Whole-wheat, wheat-grain, or just slightly branny, it makes for baking of supreme quality. It can be purchased either at the above-mentioned bakers or in the food stores listed below.

Paris: Arc-en-Ciel, 8, rue Rochebrune (11th *arrondissement*); Delannoy, 95, rue Mouffetard (5th); Daniel Dupuy, 13, rue Cadet (9th); Raoul Foyard, 143, boulevard Davout (20th); Ganachaud, 150, rue de Ménilmontant (20th); Moulin de la Vierge, 166, avenue de Suffren (15th), 82, rue Daguerre (14th), and 105, rue Vercingétorix (14th); Olivier Traiteur, at the organic market on the boulevard Raspail, Sunday mornings; Poujauran, 19, rue Jean-Nicot (7th); Tart'Mania, 9, rue Guillaume-Bertrand (11th); Vie Naturelle, 178, avenue Dumesnil (12th).

Outskirts of Paris: Au Naturel, 4, rue Jean-Moulin, 93260 Les Lilas; Country Life, La Grande Paroisse, 77820 Les Écronnes; Denivet, 8, rue Darnetal, 77100 Meaux; Fiacre, 2, rue Bertrand-Flornoy, 77100 Coulommiers; Les Nouveaux Robinsons, 49, rue Raspail, 93100 Montreuil; Olivier Traiteur, at the markets in Boulogne, Joinville-le-Pont, and Pontault-Combault.

French Provinces: Aux Rayons Verts, 9, rue Laurent-Desramez, 51100 Reims; Germinal, 22, rue de Preuilly, 89000 Auxerre.

Type	Extraction Rate	Usage
45	67–70%	pastries
55	approx. 75%	white breads and some *pains de campagne*
65	78–80%	*pains de campagne*
80	82–85%	brown breads
110	88–90%	brown breads
150	90–98%	whole-grain breads

A DAY AT THE MILL

Why not visit a mill—windmill or water mill—while you are in France? Some are still in working order and provide a fascinating trip down memory lane. On the third Sunday of June each year, the Fédération Française des Amis des Moulins (a support group for France's many mills) organizes a "journée nationale des moulins" (national mills' day). All the old mills are opened to the public and those which are still grinding set their water wheels or vanes turning. The day ends with a reception, sundry activities, and midsummer night bonfires. A hundred or so French mills can also be visited throughout the year. For further information contact: **Fédération Française des Amis des Moulins**, 5, chemin de la Fontaine, Saint-Yon, 91650 Breuillet. Tel. (1) 69 94 04 30.

CHIRAC FLOUR

The Minoterie de Colagne, in Chirac in the Massif Central, uses traditional millstones to turn organic cereals into excellent wheat or spelt flour. The flour is so good that it is used by some of the best bakers in southern France (Auzet in Cavaillon and Ceccarelli in Nice, for example), as well as by the reputable Michel Bras in his restaurant at Laguiole. Flour from spelt, an exquisite wheat variety that was common in antiquity, is coming back into favor today thanks to its extraordinary mineral taste. Unfortunately it is impossible to purchase flour from the Minoterie de Colagne in small quantities. But if the prospect of a 25-kilo bag is not too daunting, do not hesitate, as such flour never disappoints.

Minoterie de Colagne, Chirac, 48100 Marvejols. Tel. 66 32 70 03.

ALI BABA'S FLOUR

Opening the door to the firm of Izrael, in the Marais neighborhood of Paris, is like entering Ali Baba's very own grocery store. The store is piled high with the most diverse and exotic foodstuffs. Among the treasures it contains are sacks of flour. One can buy wholesale: wheat flour (patent and whole-grain); rye flour; cornmeal; buckwheat flour; rice meal and multigrain mixes (wheat, rye, barley, rice, oats, etc.). The shop also supplies two kinds of organic flour—spelt and buckwheat—in bags of 1 or 2 pounds. Finally, if grinding your own flour attracts you, you can choose from wheat, barley, spelt and oats.

Izrael, 30, rue François-Miron, 75004 Paris. Tel. 42 72 66 23. Closed Sundays and Mondays.

MILL-SUPPLIED BREAD MIXES

A large number of French bakeries sell breads baked using flour and a special *diagramme de fabrication* (baking guidelines) developed and supplied to bakers by certain mills. These are in general excellent breads, produced entirely in the bakery, although it must be said that some bakers are less good at following instructions than others. A sign in the window usually indicates when such loaves are on sale. Do not hesitate to try them!

BAGUEPI. Launched in 1900 by the Grands Moulins de Pantin et Corbeil (which forms part of the group Française de Meunerie), this *baguette* is made by around 1,500 French bakers. Its principal asset is its bran-rich flour (type 65), which really makes it a *baguette de campagne*, with a fine creamy-white crumb. There is a still more rustic version made from brown wheat flour, rye, and a compressed leaven. Both products are sold in paper bags.

BANETTE. Created by the millers Unimie, the "Banette" is sold by around three hundred French bakers and is without doubt the most famous example of its type. This charming little 7-ounce *baguette*, recognizable by the sharp excrescences on its crust (a guarantee of hand-molding, which also accounts for its good, airy crumb) can be exquisite. Its excellent savor is the result of the addition of a little fermented dough during the relatively short kneading process. "Banette" flour is pure wheat of the highest quality, without improvers. Other flours are prepared by Unimie for a whole range of different products: "Banette bio" (organic); "Banette Briare" (an unmolded bread, sold by weight, made of brown and rye flour); "Banette son" (with bran); "Banette complet" (whole-wheat); "Banette levain" (with leavening).

BOULE BIO (MAGASINS CARREFOUR). Baked and sold in more than a hundred Carrefour supermarkets throughout the country (each has its own bakery), the "Boule bio" is the creation of Michel Montagne, an expert baker at one of the best mills in all France, Decollogne-Lecocq. It is without doubt the best supermarket bread baked and distributed in France, and is even one of the best French breads of any kind. It is a *pain de campagne* on a leaven (not an ounce of baker's yeast), made from stone-ground organic flour. The dough is fermented for five hours, hand-shaped, and cooked on the oven sole. The crust is splendid, the crumb very smooth, and it can be kept for up to ten days. It weighs anything between 1 and 2 pounds.

CAMPAILLOU. The "Campaillou" loaf was developed by the Grands Moulins de Paris. It is a *pain de campagne* baked with leaven and is unmolded (it looks rather like a paving stone). It is baked from a mixture of wheat flour, rye flour, and malted wheat. Dehydrated rye leavening is incorporated into the flour. This light *pain de campagne*, with its airy crumb, is sometimes sold by weight. It is today made by 3,500 bakers throughout the country. The Grands Moulins de Paris have also developed a very fine *baguette*, the "Campaillette" (produced from a flour type 65), which gives the loaf its specific color. It is characterized by the two ridges and the three docking slashes on the crust. The "Campaillette" can be found in 1,200 bakeries. From the same millers comes the "Ciapo," an Italian-style bread which can be used to make excellent *panini*.

COPALINE. The "Copaline" *baguette* has been adopted by a number of bakeries and comes from a pure wheat flour produced by the Inter-Farine mills. It is unusual for being enriched with wheat germ (specially treated so as not to adversely affect shelf life), giving the loaf a marked flavor and making it particularly nutritious. The mill simply delivers the flour, however, without any preparation or baking guidelines, leaving the rest up to the bakery. Consequently, the quality of the "Copaline" depends to a great extent on the quality of the baker.

FESTIVAL. The "Festival" *baguette* is supplied to around a thousand bakers. Les Meuniers de France, the millers who blend this high-quality flour, are very strict as regards its treatment in the bakery. It has to be fermented using the *poolisch* method (this alone requires an initial ferment culture of between twelve and sixteen hours) and hand-shaped. The resulting loaf often approaches perfection. The *baguette* is attractive, tapering towards the ends, with a crust which is very lightly floured and docked with four long slashes. The airy crumb gives off a slight hazelnut aroma, characteristic of bread made using the *poolisch* method. This is a very fine French *baguette*.

FLEURIANE. Only around four hundred bakers sell this *baguette*, made using a flour supplied by mills from the Soufflot group. It is made from pure wheat flour without additives and contains a touch of bran, which gives the crumb a creamy hue. The nicely golden *baguette* is lightly dusted with flour and the crumb has fair-sized, irregular holes. It is always sold in a paper bag.

FLUTE GANA. "Gana" is a contraction of "Ganachaud," and Bernard Ganachaud is not a miller but a baker. This true bread fanatic, an inventive genius, has himself developed the mysterious flour and the *diagramme de fabrication* used today by about forty bakers to make the "flûte Gana." In fact, it is not a real *flûte* at all, but a *baguette*, and a slightly heavier one than average (around 9½ ounces). It is distinguished by its single lengthways slash, but above all by its high quality, a consequence of three basic factors: the two secret ingredients added to its wheat flour; its fermentation using the *poolisch* method (giving it a subtle hazelnut taste); and the hand-shaping, which results in the telltale dense, soft, and well-aerated crumb. The "flûte Gana" is magical: no sooner does a baker taste it than he or she wants to make it. It is a decision they never regret, as customers are soon to be seen queuing up for it.

FRANCILIENNE. Born in September 1994, the "Francilienne" is a tasty *baguette* developed by the Grands Moulins de Brie. Its unusual feature is that it contains some rye, which goes marvelously with its rustic appearance (the crust is matte and slightly floured, and the Grands Moulins de Brie advise that it should be hand-molded). The crust is crunchy and the crumb has a fine density. As its name suggest, the "Francilienne" is only to be found in the Ile-de-France, where forty bakers have already adopted it.

RETRODOR. Created by the excellent Chartres millers, Viron, the "Rétrodor" *baguette* has delighted customers of about one hundred bakeries, mainly in Normandy and the ile-de-France. It is sometimes good enough to win prizes, notably the Grand Prix de la Baguette de la Ville de Paris in 1994 (thanks to René-Gérard Saint-Ouen) and again in 1995 (Jean-Noël Julien). A truly excellent flour, slow kneading, four-hour fermentation time: these are the main secrets of the success of this *baguette à l'ancienne*, which weighs in at around 10 pounds. Its solid crust is a nice golden color and the crumb is perfect, allowing one to savor the full flavor of the wheat flour in the mouth (it contains little yeast).

MAKING YOUR OWN BREAD

Traditional home-baking has become increasingly popular in recent years, but making bread in the home is not quite as easy as it might appear, and results can prove surprising. The addresses below are for those who would like to become proficient home bakers. For those of you who prefer not to have to bother to learn, there exist entirely automated bread-making machines which knead, ferment, and bake the dough. They are sold with a recipe book.

ECOLE DE GASTRONOMIE FRANÇAISE
RITZ-ESCOFFIER

Hôtel Ritz, 15, place Vendôme, 75001 Paris. Tel. 42 60 38 30; fax 40 15 07 65.
This school, situated in the luxurious surroundings of the Hôtel Ritz (where the illustrious Auguste Escoffier was the first *chef de cuisine*), offers baking courses four weeks a year, organized into five afternoon sessions. The Ritz's own excellent baker, Bernard Burban (a "Meilleur Ouvrier de France"), teaches how to make *baguettes*, *pains de campagne*, sandwich and French Vienna loaves, rye loaves, and wholewheat bread (as well as *croissants*, *brioches*, and *pains au chocolat*). Class size is limited to eight students, and English-speakers have an interpreter at their disposal. Each student will be provided with clean cook's jacket and trousers.

LE CORDON BLEU

8, rue Léon-Delhomme, 75015 Paris. Tel: 53 68 22 50; fax 48 56 03 96.

This venerable institution of French gastronomy—founded in 1895—gives practical courses in baking three times a year in four-day sessions (from 9 a.m. to 4.30 p.m.). Students are taught how to use fresh yeast, select flours, and correctly execute all the processes from kneading the dough to baking itself. The syllabus includes: *baguettes*, *pains de campagne*, granary loaves (with added bran), walnut bread, sandwich loaves, *pain brioché*, brioches, and croissants. Each class contains around ten students.

ECOLE DES AMATEURS GASTRONOMES

Lenôtre, 48, avenue Victor-Hugo, 75106 Paris. Tel. 45 01 71 71.
One day a month, from 9 a.m. until 6 p.m., the famous firm of Lenôtre teaches how to make mini-*baguettes* and flavored rolls (with, for example, spinach, raisins, walnuts, prunes, and hazelnuts). The staff, professionals from the Ecole Lenôtre, have all been trained in teaching newcomers to bake. The firm itself serves breakfast and lunch, and provides overalls. On completing the course, students are allowed to take with them the rolls they have made, as well as a present of a chef's hat.

LE FOURNIL BRETZEL

2, rue Saint-Anne, 44290 Guenouvry. Tel. 40 79 23 91.
In his bakery in this little Breton village, the excellent baker André Houguet organizes day courses which teach the bread-lover how to make excellent bread on a leaven at home. The course takes place once a month, although regularity can vary depending on the demand. This enthusiast for fine, organic bread baked in a wood-burning oven also offers free visits of the bakery on Mondays, Thursdays, and Saturdays, and introductory courses for school groups during which the children can make their own rolls.

THE CULINARY INSTITUTE OF AMERICA

433, Albany Post Road, Hyde Park, New York, NY 12538-1499.
Tel. 914-452-9600.
This famous American university for chefs has commissioned Raymond Clavel to do three videocassettes: *Tradition of French Bread Baking*, *Baguettes and Pains de Campagne*, and *Specialty Breads*. The professor explains his guiding principles and methods, which can then be adapted for home use. The video can be ordered by phone: 800-285-8280.

THE VILLAGE BAKERY MELMERBY LTD

Melmerby, Penrith, Cumbria CA10 1HE. Tel. 01768 881515.
This award-winning bakery organizes two-day and five-day bread-making courses, which are given by expert baker Paul Merry in his home near Penrith in the North Pennines. The courses cover many aspects of bread-making and cater for beginners, although some are organized for more advanced students.

BASIC RECIPES

Because you have kneaded it yourself, watched its slow rising and breathed the heavenly aroma that fills the house as it bakes, homemade bread often seems more appetizing than the store-bought variety. But how can a basic bread from your own kitchen compare to that of professional bakers, who have the skills and the tools to produce perfect loaves every time? I asked two of France's top bakers, Marcel Montagne and Dominique Saibron, for their advice on home bread-baking.

Now semi-retired, Marcel Montagne is one of the great figures of French baking. He began his career as a baker and oversaw production in several traditional bakeries before one of France's top flour mills, Decollogne-Lecocq, hired him in 1977 to improve the quality of its stone-ground organic flours. While working

there Montagne perfected his bread-baking techniques, which are ideally suited to this exceptional type of flour. He also taught his art to a series of apprentices who would later become some of the country's top names in baking: Basil Kamir of Le Moulin de la Vierge, Jean-Luc Poujauran and Domique Saibron. In the last week of July every year, to celebrate the harvest festival at Nohant in southwest France, Montagne makes bread in the open air to demonstrate the real meaning of the word "baker." He also appears each year at the bread stand of the European fair Marjolaine in Paris. I can't encourage you strongly enough to attend one of these amazing demonstrations.

After working as a pastry chef and baker in several fine restaurants, Dominique Saibron opened his own boutique in 1988 at the

Place Brancusi in Paris. He quickly grew famous for the quality of his bread and pastries, and now ranks among the top three or four bakers in the city. In 1994, feeling cramped in his small boutique, Saibron put it up for sale and began searching for a larger space. The day it sold, Carrefour supermarkets asked him to supervise the production of all their fresh pastries and a high-quality bread. He accepted, thus beginning a new adventure.

For the home baker, Montagne has perfected recipes for whole wheat and brown breads and Saibron has developed a recipe for white rolls. These simple but delicious breads all call for organic flour, available in health food shops and many major supermarkets. Enjoy them with any dish, or as a gratifying breakfast or snack.

Brown or Whole-Wheat Bread

Makes four brown or whole wheat loaves of 12 oz. (300 g) each

FOR THE BROWN LOAVES:
1 lb. 10 oz. organic stone-ground blended wheat flour (700 g)
OR 13 oz. each organic stone-ground whole-wheat flour and organic white flour (350 g each)

FOR THE WHOLE-WHEAT LOAVES:
1¹/₂ lbs. organic stone-ground whole-wheat flour (650 g)

²/₃ oz. (1¹/₂ tbsp.) unrefined sea salt (18 g)
2 cups flat mineral water (500 mL)
²/₃ oz. (20 g) cake yeast (2 tbsp. fresh yeast, crumbled, or 1¹/₂ tsp dried yeast)
Butter or oil for greasing the tins

TOOLS:
Large mixing bowl
Thermometer (a digital one works well)

Household scale
Four bread tins, 6 inches (15 cm) long and about 3 inches (7–8 cm) wide

Allow 4 hours for the mixing, kneading, rising and baking. This doesn't mean you will be in the kitchen all that time, but the dough needs between 2 and 3 hours to rest, or rather to rise.

Warm the water to 77 F (25 C) in winter or cool it to 60 F (15 C) in summer.

Put the salt, water and flour in a large mixing bowl, then add the yeast.

Mix all these ingredients with your hands until they form a smooth ball.

Place the dough on a lightly floured work surface and knead it with the palms of your hands for 8 minutes.

Put the dough back in the mixing bowl, cover it with a clean cloth and allow it to rise for 1 hour.

Remove the dough on to the work surface and divide it into 4 equal parts.

Form each part into a sausage shape and place it in one of the tins, already greased with butter or oil.

Cover each tin with a cloth and allow the dough to rise for about 1¹/₂ hours. The ideal temperature for the rising is 77 F (25 C). Each loaf should double in volume before baking.

Place a metal pan filled with water in the oven and preheat it to 475 F (240 C) for 15 minutes.

Cook the bread for 20 minutes, leaving the water in the oven and avoiding a variation in heat.

Remove the loaves from the pans at let them cool on racks before serving.

Recipe by Marcel Montagne
Translated by Rosa Jackson

White Bread Rolls

For 16 white rolls of 4 oz. (100 g) each

INGREDIENTS:
2¹/₄ lbs. organic white flour (1 kg)
A little extra flour
³/₄ oz. (1 tbsp. plus 2 tsp.) unrefined sea salt (22 g)
1²/₃ cups flat mineral water (650 mL)
¹/₄ oz. (5 g) cake yeast (1¹/₂ tsp fresh yeast, crumbled, or ¹/₂ tps. dried yeast)

TOOLS:
Large mixing bowl
Thermometer (a digital one works well)
Razor blade
Household scale
Optional: Electric mixer fitted with a dough hook (such as Kenwood or KitchenAid)

Allow at least 5 hours for the mixing, kneading, rising, cooking and cooling.

These rolls can easily be frozen once cooked. Place them in airtight plastic bags before freezing.

Bring the water to 95 F (35 C) in winter or 77 F (25 C) in summer.

Mix all the ingredients except the yeast in the mixing bowl, then knead the dough on a work surface for five minutes.

Add the yeast and continue to knead for five minutes.

Flour the dough lightly, place it back in the bowl, cover it with a cloth and allow it to rise for 30 minutes.

Hit the dough against a lightly floured work surface once or twice to stop the rising. Place it back in the bowl and allow it to rise for 2¹/₂ hours.

Divide it into 16 parts weighing about 4 oz. (100 g) each. Check the weight using a floured scale (remove or add dough until you reach the correct weight) and place the balls of dough on a floured work surface.

With floured hands, roll the portions into smooth balls. Place them on a floured baking sheets and sprinkle them with flour.

Allow them to rise for 30 to 50 minutes depending on the room temperature: 30 minutes might be enough at 73 F (23 C), but if the room is cold it may take longer.

Place a metal pan filled with water in the oven. The steam will improve the rising and browning of the bread. Heat the oven to 475 F (240 C) for 15 minutes.

When the oven is hot, just before putting the rolls in the oven, slit lightly with a razor blade to make a large cross on the surface of the rolls. Bake for 30 minutes.

Remove the rolls from the oven and let them cool.

VARIATION WITH AN ELECTRIC MIXER:
Put the salt, water [95 F (35 C) in winter or 77 F (25 C) in summer] and flour in the bowl of the electric mixer. Mix on slow speed (number 1) for five minutes.

Add the yeast and continue to mix on slow speed for 10 minutes.

Leaving the hook in the dough, cover the bowl with a cloth and allow the dough to rise at room temperature for 30 minutes.

Mix again on slow speed for 10 seconds to stop the rising.

Remove the hook from the dough and cover it with a cloth. Allow it to rise at room temperature for 2¹/₂ hours.

Remove the dough from the bowl and weigh portions of 100 g each. Check the weight using a scale (remove or add dough until you reach the correct weight) and place the portions on a floured work surface.

Continue to shape and cook the dough as indicated in the recipe for hand-mixed rolls.

Recipe by Dominique Saibron
Translated by Rosa Jackson

M U S E U M S

The museums listed below, dedicated to the memory of the most universal of culinary traditions, give the visitor a chance to explore the world of bread more thoroughly. They trace its history, describe the techniques used in the past, and exhibit the tools of this ancient trade.

FRANCE

MUSÉE DES ARTS ET TRADITIONS POPULAIRES
6, avenue du Mahatma-Gandhi, 75116 Paris.
Tel. 44 17 60 00.
Open every day except Tuesdays, from 9:45 a.m. to 5:15 p.m.
One of the rooms in the cultural gallery of this museum (room 224) illustrates the theme "From Wheat to Bread." There are displays of old tools and bread-making equipment (millstones, peels, kneaders, bakery interiors), which show the various steps from the cultivation of wheat to its transformation into bread, as well as models of windmills and water mills, and domestic and communal bread ovens. There is also a slide show. The study gallery (room 422), devoted to "natural and vegetable foodstuffs," contains an old kneader, wicker dough-baskets, and a selection of the marks used to distinguish the different loaves in a communal oven, together with numerous traditional baking tools.

MUSÉE DE LA BOULANGERIE
12, rue de la République, 84400 Bonnieux.
Tel. 90 75 88 34.
Open 10 a.m. to 12 p.m. and 3 p.m. to 6:30 p.m. From 1 June to 30 September, open every day except Tuesdays. From 1 April to 31 May and 1 to 31 October, open Saturdays and Sundays. Closed from 1 November through 31 March.
The Lubéron is a magnificent setting for this delightful museum, located in a large, seventeenth-century edifice. The ground-floor bakery (in use until 1920) has been renovated and contains the original oven and the various tools of the bakery. The two upper stories contain documents relating to wheat cultivation, milling, and baking, as well as the symbolism of bread through the ages. The vaulted cellars contain a fine collection of harvesting tools, including an amazing American harvester-binder dating from the 1920s.

LE FOUR À PAIN
MUSÉE DE LA BOULANGERIE RURALE
27350 La Haye-de-Routot.
Tel. 32 57 07 99 or 35 37 23 16.
In March and from 19 September to 30 November: open Sundays and public holidays, from 2:30 to 6 p.m.; in April and May: open Saturdays, Sundays, and public holidays, from 2 to 6:30 p.m.; in June and until 13 July: open Saturdays, from 2 to 6:30 p.m. and Sundays, from 10 a.m. to 6.:30 p.m.; from 14 July to 18 September: open every day, from 10 a.m. to 6:30 p.m.
This museum is located in a charming little eighteenth-century thatched cottage, which was once the bakery of La Haye-de-Routot, in the Brotonne nature reserve, ten miles from Rouen. It has a one-hundred-and-fifty-year-old wood-fired oven and a small collection of documents and tools tracing the development of the trade, from its origins to the present day. The collection also houses a real kneader from the 1930s and a "parisien" (for storing dough pieces during fermentation) dating from the beginning of the century. It is best to visit it on a Sunday afternoon, as the baker then sets the old oven with faggots and loads it with regional specialties (*pain brié, gâche, pain plié*, and an apple bread named the "demi-douillon"). An hour later, you can purchase some of these breads from the past. Every first Sunday in April, this museum-bakery organizes a celebration of bread. You can spend the whole day watching demonstrations of how to prepare and bake bread, molding your own piece of dough and sampling the finished product.

LA MAISON DU BLÉ ET DU PAIN
Rue du Pont, 71350 Verdun-sur-le-Doubs.
Tel. 85 91 57 09 or 85 76 27 16.
Open from June through September inclusive (and the rest of the year for groups by appointment), every day except Tuesdays, from 3 to 5 p.m.
Housed in the former village hall (from which one can gaze at the confluence of the river Doubs and the river Saône), this small museum traces the history of seventy-five centuries of harvesting and forty of bread-making, through images, old tools, and other artefacts, and a thundering soundtrack. The museum is soon to be renovated and enlarged.

MUSÉE RENÉ-BAUBÉROT
Place Saint-Thyrse, 87290 Châteauponsac.
Tel. 55 76 31 55.
Open every day from 1 August through 15 September; open Sundays and public holidays from 16 September through 30 June.
This charming little museum is housed on the ground floor of a former Benedictine priory founded in 1318 and located to the north of Limoges. It outlines the history of bread, from wheat cultivation to baking. One of its finest exhibits is a splendid cherry-wood kneader. Next door there is a painstaking reconstruction of a late nineteenth-century Limousin interior.

MUSÉE COMMUNAL HISTORIQUE-FOLKLORIQUE
Rue Saint-Nazaire, 84380 Mazan.
Tel. 90 69 70 19.
Open every day in July and August; Sundays and public holidays in June and September. (Low season: visits by appointment.)
Located in a former chapel not far from Mont Ventoux, this museum contains a varied collection of objects relating to the Vaucluse (art, techniques, Neolithic pottery). There is a fine seventeenth-century baker's oven in the garden.

GERMANY

DEUTSCHES BROTMUSEUM ULM
Salzstadelgasse 10, 89073 Ulm.
Tel. (731) 6 99 55.
Open Tuesdays to Sundays, from 10 a.m. to 5 p.m. and until 8:30 p.m. on Wednesdays.
The German Museum of Bread is situated in an old salt depot dating from the end of the sixteenth century. The ground floor houses a fine reconstruction of a 1910 bakery, while a video shows the various stages of modern bread-making. On the first floor, there is a large collection of documents, objects, and tools illustrating six thousand years of bread-making techniques (from wheat cultivation through milling and baking). The second floor is an exploration of the symbolic, religious, and cultural aspects of bread through various statuettes, paintings, and posters.

EUROPÄISCHES BROTMUSEUM
Berlepscher Strasse 27,
37133 Mollenfelde-Friedland.
Tel. (5504) 5 80.
Open every day, from 10 a.m. to 5 p.m.
The European Museum of Bread, with its rich collection of objects and works of art, addresses thirty different themes. "Machine tools for the bread-making trades," "five centuries of wooden molds," "festival breads and pastries," "the history of milling," and "bread in the twentieth century" are just some of the aspects covered. It is a comprehensive and popular museum of considerable size (fourteen rooms in all) covering the art, traditions, and evolution of bread making.

BELGIUM

INTERNATIONAAL MUSEUM VOOR BROOD, BANKET, SUIKERBAKKERIJ EN IJSBEREIDING WALTER PLAETINCK
"Zuidgasthuishoeve," Albert I laan 2,
8630 Furnes.
Tel. (058) 31 38 97.
Open Mondays through Thursdays, 8 a.m. to 6 p.m.

This museum of baking, pastry cooking, confectionery and ice cream is housed in a magnificent seventeenth-century farmhouse near the beautiful town of Furnes (or Veurne, as it is known in French). It has a splendid reconstruction of a turn-of-the-century bakery, together with an extensive collection of tools used in baking and pastry cooking. In an adjoining room, one can taste different breads while admiring the fine, old, wood-fired oven dating from 1880 (and still in working order), or watching a video on turning grain into bread. A further room explores the breads of the world, past and present. Next to the nearby barn there is a garden where a number of the cereals cultivated for bread-making are grown.

THE NETHERLANDS

BAKKERIJMUSEUM

Kapellerweg 15, 5575 BG Luyksgestel.
Tel. (0497) 541314.
Open every day except Sundays and holidays. Baking demonstrations every Wednesday at 1:30 p.m., and every day at 1 p.m. during the school vacations; booking required for groups; demonstrations also possible in the morning by arrangement.
The Museum of Baking is situated not far from the Belgian frontier. It houses a splendid reconstruction of a nineteenth-century bakery, with an oven dating from 1850, an exhibition room (where refreshments are served), and a mill. It is best to visit during the demonstrations of bread-making, when you will be invited to do some kneading or molding yourself.

« HET WARME LAND »
NEDERLANDS BAKKERIJ MUSEUM

Kerkhofstraat 13, 8051 GG Hattem.
Tel. (05206) 41715.
From May through October: open from Monday through Saturday, from 10 a.m. to 5 p.m.; in July and August: also open on Sundays, from 1 p.m. to 5 p.m.; from November through April: open Tuesday through Saturday, from 10 a.m. to 5 p.m. Closed in January and certain holidays.
The fine Dutch Museum of Baking was founded by a baker, Willem Barendsen, and is housed in superb historic buildings in the center of the old town (two medieval town farmholdings, a stable, and a former café). Its exhibits trace the history of Dutch baking. There is a reconstruction of a nineteenth-century bakery, various baking ovens, millstones, and a small industrial mill. Traditional bread is actually baked on the premises.

SWITZERLAND

ALIMENTARIUM – MUSÉE DE L'ALIMENTATION

Quai Perdonnet, rue du Léman, 1800 Vevey.
Tel. (21) 924 41 11.

CELEBRATING BREAD

The Journée Nationale du Pain (national bread day) should be instituted soon in France, taking place on 16 May, which is St. Honoré's day, the patron saint of bakers. In the meantime, there already exist several events which celebrate bread. To begin with, there is the harvest festival, for which decorated breads are often made. Some bread museums also organize cooking demonstrations and tastings.

In a few regions of France, the starting up of the communal oven for the cooking of family batches is sometimes the occasion for beautiful village ceremonies. This is the case in the Hautes-Alpes, in the small village of Villard-d'Arène. Every third weekend in November, the communal wood-fired oven is lit for the baking of the *pain bouilli*, a very large round weighing 15 pounds. The rye flour from which it is made is kneaded with very hot water and boiled for one hour. Five batches, each consisting of one hundred rounds, are made. All the men in the village knead each batch together in a large kneading basin. The magnificent stone wood-fired oven is also used to cook delicious desserts for the feast.

Every year, on the first or second weekend of October, a bread, wine, and cheese fair is held in the Halle in Beaune, in the Côte d'Or. Around fifteen wine estates from different regions in France take part. Several hundred cheeses and some tasty breads prepared specially by the bakers of Beaune are on offer to accompany the wines.

The most exuberant bread festivals, however, take place in Sicily, where bread has always been venerated as a symbol of plenty. In each village, the women make decorative festival bread. The loaves, which are given geometric, vegetable, and animal forms of extraordinary refinement, are taken in a procession through the streets of the village, or occasionally arranged on magnificent reed arches erected in the main street. On occasion, bread competitions are organized in certain neighborhoods. These celebrations reach a peak in Salemi, in the province of Trapani, on 19 March, when St. Joseph is celebrated. A "Joseph altar" with several levels is built and decorated with a multitude of marvelously sculpted breads, together with oranges and flowers. Ritual offerings to Joseph, the "father of Providence," these breads are for everyone a symbol of prosperity and happiness.

Open every day except Mondays, from 10 a.m. to 12 p.m. and 2 to 5 p.m.; from April through October: 10 a.m. to 5 p.m.
Founded by Nestlé, the Museum of Food is situated on the shores of the Lake of Geneva and is concerned with all the scientific, ethnological, and historical aspects of food in general. The section devoted to bread is dominated by a diorama showing the cultivation of cereals and their transformation into bread in an Anatolian village, the use of the ancient *tribulum* (used to separate the grain from the straw), the grinding of wheat in a mill, and the baking of bread and flat cakes. This is a fascinating glimpse of traditional bread-making methods.

LA MAISON DU BLÉ ET DU PAIN

Place de l'Hôtel-de-Ville, 1040 Echallens.
Tel. (21) 881 50 71.
Open every day except Mondays, from 9 a.m. to 6 p.m.
This magnificent museum is housed in a restored eighteenth-century farm. Ideally it should be visited in summer, when it can be reached by the special train from Lausanne to Echallens, which is pulled by an old steam engine and passes through the finest cereal-farming land in Switzerland. This is a "living museum," with an extraordinary collection of equipment, tools, and furniture connected with bread making. Visitors can learn how to knead and mold, and even set the millstones running. Bread is baked on the premises in one of the four working ovens.

MOULINS SOUTERRAINS DU COL-DES-ROCHES

2412 Le Col-des-Roches NE.
Tel. (39) 31 89 89.
From May through October: open every day, from 10 a.m. to 12 p.m. and 2 p.m. to 5:30 p.m. (last guided tour at 5 p.m.).
In the seventeenth century, a Swiss named Jonas Sandoz had the ingenious idea of making use of the water of the underground river Bied by adapting a deep excavation in the rock: the water was harnessed to power an oil mill, a sawmill and two water mills. Since 1973, the association, La Confrérie des Meuniers, has been restoring the main elements of the machinery and has organized an exhibition on the history of hydraulic engineering, mills, and bread-making. Visiting the spectacular galleries and underground wells, with their splendid old machinery, is an impressive experience.

WICK'S BÄCKEREIMUSEUM RAPPERSWILL

Alte Jonastrasse 80, 8640 Rapperswill.
Tel. (55) 27 15 44.
Visit by appointment.
Paul Wick is a baker and also a collector of everything to do with bread- and pastry-making (books, equipment, tools, etc.). This miscellaneous collection bears witness to his unflagging enthusiasm.

BREAD ACCESSORIES

The bread bins and breadbaskets commonplace in the past are today rarely used. A number of stores still sell such objects, however, and a small number of them provide a particularly interesting or wide-ranging choice.

FRANCE

LA CARPE
14, rue Tronchet,
75008 Paris.
Tel. 47 42 73 25.
This temple to the arts of cooking and eating sells numerous bread knives (it is best to avoid serrated edges and go for a long knife with a keen blade), a bread-slicer for cutting up *baguettes*, and wooden breadboards (including one of solid beech) with a built-in tray for removing the crumbs. To keep bread fresh, you can choose between jute bags (adapted for rounds or *baguettes*) and several sorts of bread bin (enameled metal, steel, or solid wood, with built-in slicer). Try also the clever little plastic box for sandwich loaves, whose size can be adjusted depending on the length of the loaf. They also sell an electric bread machine which kneads dough and bakes it, producing all kinds of bread, including *brioches*. I cannot recommend it, however, because I have not tried it.

LA GADGETIERE
1, place Pierre-Brisson,
75116 Paris.
Tel. 47 20 52 20.
As its name implies, this very useful store is full of gadgets: the warming stone (heart- or flower-shaped) is no gadget, however. It is designed to be placed in the breadbasket, after being heated in the oven, in order to keep toast warm. Also available: a toaster for the fireplace, as nothing makes better toast.

POILANE
8, rue Cherche-Midi,
75006 Paris.
Tel. 45 48 42 59.
Closed Sundays.
Also: 49, boulevard de Grenelle,
75015 Paris.
Tel. 45 79 11 49.

The famous baker has designed a clever bread bin of his own. It is an attractive round box made from light ash. When moistened, its linen cover serves as a humidifier. The box also contains a breadbasket which can be used to serve the bread sliced at table. Linen bags, ideal for keeping *pains de campagne* and coburgs fresh, are also available; as they have handles, they are also perfect for transporting loaves.

GREAT BRITAIN

THE CONRAN SHOP
81 Fulham Road,
London SW3.
Tel. 0171-589 7401.
Also: 117, rue du Bac,
75007 Paris.
Tel. 42 84 10 01.
This store specializes in high-quality furniture, interior decoration, and kitchenware. The round breadboards (sycamore is the most popular, followed by ash) are magnificent. The toasters are as impressive as Cadillacs!

DIVERTIMENTI
139 Fulham Road,
London SW3.
Tel. 0171-581 8065.
Also: 45 Wigmore Street,
London W1.
Tel. 0171-935 0689.
This specialist kitchenware shop supplies more than just knives and boards. It also sells enamel and ceramic bins, including a non-stick variety for *baguettes*, boards with built-in crumb trays, and crumb brushes. Toasters and toast-racks complete the range.

GENERAL TRADING COMPANY
44 Sloane Street,
London SW1.
Tel. 0171-730 0411.
Also: 10 Argylle St, Bath, tel. 01225 461507; 2–4 Dyer Street, Cirencester, tel. 01285 652314.
Perhaps the most striking item in this store (for which kitchenware forms just one part of the stock) is a large, shiny, bright red, metal bread bin! The ubiquitous breadboards with crumb trays are also present, as is, more unexpectedly, a hand-kneader with pallets.

DAVID MELLOR
4 Sloane Square,
London SW1.
Tel. 0171-730 4259.
This specialist kitchenware store is well known for its wide-ranging stock of saucepans and knives for the professional. It also supplies earthenware, enamel, and wooden bread bins, and hand-crafted bread boards (some long enough to take a *baguette*).

UNITED STATES

CHEF'S CATALOGUE
3915 Commercial Avenue
Northbrook, IL 60062
Tel. 312-480-9400 or 800-338-3232
The Chef's Catalogue provides a wide selection of professional restaurant equipment and kitchen essentials for the home chef. Equipment for use in bread making includes KitchenAid mixers, baking stones, baker's peels, and professional flour and dough scales.

CHARLES LAMALLE
36 West Twenty-fifth Street
New York, NY 10036
Tel. 212-242-0750
This venerable restaurant supplier with a French accent carries professional-quality kitchen equipment. For the baker, offerings include baguette pans, earthenware molds, French palette knives, ramekins, and many other pieces of equipment. Products are available at the store or through mail order.

WILLIAMS-SONOMA
P.O. Box 7456
San Francisco, CA 94120
Tel. 415-421-4242 or 800-541-2233
For over thirty years Williams-Sonoma has been supplying American home cooks with fine kitchenware, tableware, cookbooks, prepared foods, and gifts. For the baker, it is an excellent source for a variety of hard-to-find specialty flours, as well as baking stones, scales, baking pans, marble rolling pins, copper molds, and more. The attractive stores are located in all major U.S. cities, and the products are also available through a mail order catalogue.

G L O S S A R Y

BAGEL. Round or ring-shaped roll, with a particularly soft crumb, poached before baking. This Jewish specialty has become very popular in the United States.

BAGUETTE. The best-known French loaf, which originated in Paris in the 1920s. More *baguettes* are eaten in France than any other type of loaf. The *baguette* (or "French stick") is usually made from pure white flour and should be fermented with yeast. It weighs around 8 or 9 ounces and is approximately 27 inches long. In France, authentic traditional *baguettes* are called *baguettes de tradition, baguettes à l'ancienne* or *baguettes 1900*.

BAKING CHAMBER. The part of the oven with a door where the loaves are baked.

BANAL OVEN. In the Middle Ages, an oven incorporated into the suzerain's ban, that is to say, essentially his property. Any person using it would have to pay a levy. A similar feudal right was held by the lord over the banal (or bannal) mill.

BANNETON. French term for a small wicker dough-basket of varying shape, which is lined with linen. It is used to ferment the dough pieces. In England, special "dough bowls" are used.

BARLEY. Widely grown cereal crop, often used today for brewing and animal feed. As it is not possible to bake barley into good bread unblended, it is added to mixtures and multigrain breads. For a long time, pure barley—or barley mixed with a little wheat—formed the base of bread eaten by the poorest people. Such were the loaves miraculously multiplied by Christ in the Bible at the feeding of the five thousand.

BARM. A leavening agent derived from the malted liquor used in brewing. It used to be employed before the introduction of compressed yeast.

BATARD. A French wheaten bread, of the same weight but stouter than the *baguette.*

BATCH. A quantity of loaves baked (though not necessarily loaded) at the same time.

BATCH(ED) BREAD. Loaves fermented and baked so close together that the sides touch and join. In Scotland, long, narrow loaves of batch bread are very common.

BERRY. The main farinaceous part of the cereal grain, comprising starch grains contained in a net of protein (the gluten).

BLOOMER. An oval, white-flour or light-rye loaf, deeply docked diagonally on the top. The crust should be crunchy and the crumb dense.

BOLTING, BOULTING. The sifting of the cereal millings (or "break") in the bolter to make pure flour (the "whites," for example).

BRAIDED BREAD. Loaf, often milk-enriched, shaped into the form of a braid. Such breads are traditional in eastern Europe.

BRAN. The outer husk protecting the berry. Bran is eliminated during milling when a white wheat flour is required, but is retained in the production of whole-wheat flour. Breads with added bran are prized for their digestive properties.

BRIÉ, PAIN. A specialty from Normandy, it has a long shelf-life and a very compact crumb. The name comes from the French verb *brier*, meaning to crush the dough with a *brie*— a "brake," or wooden kneading implement— in order to expel the air.

BUCKWHEAT. A cereal crop ("Saracen corn"), formerly common, which used to be made into pancakes, broths, flat cakes, and (whenever wheat and rye were scarce) bread. It is used in certain multigrain breads.

BUN. A small roll, made from "bun dough," often sweetened, eaten at tea-time, especially in Britain. In the United States, buns are rolls used by fast-food restaurants to make hamburgers.

CAMPAGNE, PAIN DE. Type of French loaf. It can have different ingredients and be of various shapes, its main characteristic being its rustic appearance. It has a rather thick, floured crust and a dense and tasty crumb. It can be made from pure wheat flour with a greater or lesser proportion of bran, or else from a mix of rye and wheat flours. It is often fermented with leaven.

CHAPATI. Indian unleavened flat bread of fine-ground whole-wheat flour baked on a griddle, or *tava*, and served warm as a dip.

CIABATTA. Wheat-flour-based Italian bread, from the region around Milan. It is flat and rectangular, has an almost beige, floured crust, and a soft crumb.

COB. A smooth-crusted, oven-bottom loaf, often with a slightly soft crust. It is one of the oldest British bread types.

COBURG. An oven-bottom bread with a cross slash. Popular in Britain, it dates from the nineteenth century and is probably of German origin.

CORN. In most of the United States, Canada, Australia, and New Zealand, the common name for maize. In Britain, "corn" denotes the main crop of a particular region. *See* MAIZE.

COTTAGE. A British white round loaf, made from wheat flour, consisting of a round of dough with another smaller piece placed on top of it. The hole in the middle is commonly made with a spoon handle. The cottage loaf must be baked by hand and is tricky to notch.

COURONNE. A common French fancy bread in the shape of a ring.

CRACKED GRAIN. Cracked wheat bread, with broken grains stuck in the top, is a favorite British and American recipe. Such loaves can be baked in tins or on the oven sole.

CROWN. The top of the baking chamber; in a traditional oven, the "ceiling" of the vault.

DANISH LOAF. In England, a white, cylindrical, wheat-flour loaf with a deep central slash which almost splits the bread in two. Such a loaf has nothing to do with bread from Denmark itself, which tends to be of a light rye.

DIVIDING. Cutting the dough mass into smaller, loaf-sized pieces (rounds). When the operation is performed manually, a dough-cutter is used (today, this is a large plastic blade). In modern bakeries, a machine divider is more often used.

DOCKING. Making a razor-blade cut into the dough piece just before loading it into the oven, to allow the loaf to develop better during baking. This "slashing" (for a large cut) or "notching" (for a smaller one) can also serve as the baker's signature. The cut is known as a *coup de lame* in French.

DOUGH ROUND (OR PIECE). A piece of dough which has been shaped prior to baking.

DRESS, TO. To sharpen the millstones—that is, profile the grooves—with a dressing hammer (*rhabiller la meule* in French).

EXTRACTION RATE. The quantity of flour extracted from the (wheat) grist, expressed as a percentage. A white-flour extraction rate of 72 percent, for example, indicates 28 percent of the grain has been eliminated. The shorter (lower) the extraction rate, the whiter the flour. Longer extraction rates (around 90 percent) would indicate a brown flour including bran.

FANTASIE, PAIN DE. A name given in France to small white loaves fermented with yeast, such as *baguettes* and *bâtards*, as distinct from the traditional large brown loaves made with leaven.

FERMENTATION. Transformation of the dough due to the action of microorganisms contained in the leavening agent, or the baker's yeast. This is evidenced by an increase in volume of the dough as it "rises" due to the production of carbon dioxide. Fermentation is necessary to obtain a full-bodied loaf, with a soft and airy crumb. Fermentation also enhances aroma and taste.

FICELLE. In France, a thin *baguette* weighing around 4 ounces.

FINAL PROOF. The fermentation period (*apprêt* in French) between shaping and baking. At this stage the dough piece attains its final size.

FIRST PROOFING. The first period of fermentation (often synonymous with bulk fermentation) between kneading and dividing. It is essential in order to give strength to the dough and improve taste. Reduction in the duration of first proofing has been at the root of the general decline in bread quality since the 1960s.

FLEURAGE. French term for the dry powder sprinkled onto both peel and dough piece to prevent the latter sticking to the former during loading. It should be tasteless and odorless and easy to brush off after baking. Rice powder, corozo powder (from the corozo nut), crushed olive stones, or else finely ground bran are used. The English term "dusting" is mainly used to describe the decorative process of sprinkling flour on top of the bread.

FLUTE. French loaf similar to a *baguette* and weighing around 7 ounces.

FOUGASSE. A southern French and Mediterranean specialty, the *fougasse* is a flat bread, pierced by little cuts, often molded into the shape of branches or a cogwheel. It is often flavored with ingredients such as anchovies, rosemary, olive oil, or bacon pieces.

FRACTIONS. Different amounts of variously milled grist which come off a roller mill with each successive milling. Also known as "streams" or, when remilled, "tails."

GLUTEN. A plant protein mixture surrounding the starch particles in the wheat grain. Its elasticity and impermeability to fermentation gases allow the dough to rise and the loaf to develop correctly. Only wheat and, to a lesser extent, rye possess sufficient gluten to provide for adequate panification.

GRANARY. Type of British bread made from a combination of fine wheat meal, rye flour, and malted grain, which gives the loaf its distinctive taste. A stronger, whole-wheat variant also exists.

GRIDDLE CAKE. A flat bread or cake, unleavened, which is baked on a griddle, a circular iron plate.

GRISSINI. An Italian specialty from the region around Turin, *grissini* are long, thin bread sticks, made from white flour enriched with olive oil. They are dry and crunchy.

HANDING-UP. The shaping of dough immediately after dividing and scaling. The dough is given a roughly round shape, before assuming its final form during molding.

HEARTH. The part of a wood-burning oven where the fuel is burnt. In present-day wood-fueled ovens, the hearth lies beneath the baking chamber.

HOPPER. Machine for feeding grain to the millstones or, subsequently, for pouring flour into a receptacle.

INTERMEDIATE PROOF. "Rest period" for the dough rounds after being cut from the mass of dough. This enables the dough to recover from the "felling" and to continue fermenting before molding.

KNEADER/KNEADING. Formerly, the kneader was just a wooden trough in which the bread was kneaded by hand. Since the end of the First World War, these old kneaders have been replaced by kneading-machines, complete with electric motors and equipped with strong metal paddles. Kneading is the baker's first task: mixing the various ingredients which go to make up the bread until a smooth and homogeneous dough is obtained. In French, the dough trough is known as the *pétrin*, and the kneading-machine as a *pétrin mécanique*.

KNOCK-BACK. Removing the fermentation gases after first proof to improve bread texture.

LEAVEN. A mixture of flour and water which is left to ferment for a long time, the presence of natural yeasts in the flour serving to ferment the dough. A leaven can also be obtained from a specially made ferment or from a sour "starter." The French term is *levain*.

MAIZE. Cereal crop originating in the Americas, known in the United States as "corn." It was introduced into Europe by Columbus. Corn breads always contain a proportion of wheat flour, as maize on its own cannot provide a good bread. They are eaten in the United States and in Portugal.

MAN TO. Chinese steam-cooked wheat rolls.

MASLIN. A blend of equal quantities of wheat and rye flours. In former times (and occasionally still today) the two crops were grown in the same field.

MICHE. A large round French loaf weighing more than 2 pounds.

MICHETTA. Italian wheat-flour roll, often made into sandwiches.

MILLET. One of the earliest cereals to be consumed by man. East Indian millet, or pearl millet, can be an ingredient in multicereal breads.

MILLSTONE. Either of a pair of thick discs of stone which serve to grind cereals and produce flour. The grist is deposited through a hole in the upper "runner" and is crushed between it and the lower "bedder," which remains immobile. Millstones have largely been replaced by modern roller mills, in which the grain is broken by a series of steel cylinders. Stone-grinding, which conserves the wheat germ better, resulting in a richer and more natural flour, has become increasingly popular recently.

MOLDING (SHAPING). The second fashioning of the dough round before baking, in which the loaf is given the desired shape. The operation is done either manually or, for the easier shapes, by machine (drum-molder). Hand-molding is a guarantee of high quality.

MULTIGRAIN BREADS. A bread comprising a mix of different cereal flours. Combinations of between three and twelve grains are possible, though wheat flour remains the main ingredient.

NAN, OR NAAN. A traditional flat bread from northern India, whose fine wheat-flour dough is enriched with yoghurt. It is flavored in many different ways and served warm.

OATS. A cereal nowadays used above all as livestock feed, but which is also made into certain special breads, in addition to being used for porridge and muesli.

ORGANIC FLOUR AND BREAD. Organic bread should only be so called when it is baked from organic flour, that is flour milled from cereals cultivated and stored without chemical additives (fertilizer, herbicides, pesticides, etc.).

OVEN MASTER. Name sometimes given to the person whose responsibility it is to load and regulate the ovens in the bakery. This task is nowadays often performed by the master baker or store owner himself.

OVEN. The best bread ovens are built of stone or refractory brick (they weigh several tens of tons) and are fired by wood or gas. The flames give out heat which accumulates in the oven body; once the fire is extinguished, the heat diminishes gradually as the bread bakes. Such ovens are often loaded with a peel (they are sometimes called peel-ovens). Other ovens, such as electric traveling, setter, and reel ovens, are used in large-scale plants. In France, the traditional oven is called a *four maçonné*.

OVEN SPRING. The rise of a loaf in the oven.

PAIN PERDU. French name for stale bread soaked in eggs, sugar, and milk, then cooked in butter, and served with jam, etc. It is known as French toast in the United States or "poor knights of Windsor" in Britain.

PANINO. Italian for sandwich. It can be based on almost any kind of bread, including *michetta* and *ciabatta*.

PARISIEN. French white wheaten loaf weighing nearly a pound.

PATENT FLOUR. The purest flour (sometimes called "whites") from the best milling streams of the grist (the "chop" in roller mills). The French term is *farine de gruau*, which is used to make *pain de gruau*, fine wheaten bread.

PEEL. Wooden shovel serving to load and unload loaves when using a traditional peel-oven. Thanks to the advent of modern electric traveling ovens, it has largely been replaced by the conveyor belt.

PISTOLET. Belgian milk roll, round and split down the center.

PITA (OR PITTA) BREAD. The soft, round, wheaten flat bread of Greece. It can be stuffed and served as a sandwich. Variants of *pita* are found throughout the Middle East under different names.

PLAN-SIFTER. A machine used in industrial mills which originated in Hungary in the last century. It consists of a set of superimposed flat sieves of varying grades, which separate and grade the broken grain.

POLKA BREAD. A generally round loaf, the top being docked in a square. It is a specialty of the Loire region.

POOLISCH (OR POOLISH). A method of preparing the dough using a liquid leaven, invented around 1840 in Poland. Similar to the sponge-dough method, the starter consists of yeast and equal parts of flour and water. The leaven is left to ferment for a number of hours before final mixing and kneading.

POST MILL. Form of windmill. The boxlike body containing the mechanism and millstones is mounted on a wooden post fixed to a horizontal beam, enabling it to be turned to face the wind by means of a tailpole.

PROOFER, OR RETARDER PROOFER. A cabinet designed to retard final fermentation of the dough. It permits the baker to control the length of fermentation and bake his or her bread at a convenient time.

PUMPERNICKEL. Rye bread of German origin, also popular in Scandinavia and eastern Europe. Slightly sweet and enriched with fats, its brown crumb is extremely dense and it has a long shelf-life.

QUERN. Pyramidal stone used to grind grain by hand in ancient times.

ROLLER. The cylindrical grooved ("fluted") rollers used in roller mills to mill the grist and produce flour.

RYE. Rye (*seigle* in French) is the only cereal apart from wheat that has sufficient gluten to be made into bread unblended. In France *pain de seigle* must contain at least 65 percent rye (otherwise it is known as *pain au seigle*). In Britain, heavy rye (about 40 percent) and light rye (about 15 percent) breads also contain wheat. Whole-grain rye is a northern specialty.

SANDWICH LOAF, OR TIN LOAF. Anglo-American loaf with a soft crust, ideal for making sandwiches. It is often baked in a tin.

SCALING (UP). The operation of weighing and correcting the weight of the dough rounds after dividing.

SCUFFLE. Baker's mop used to clean the inside and sole of a wood-fired oven before loading the rounds.

SIMIT. A small, crusty roll, garnished with sesame seeds, common throughout the Middle East.

SODA BREAD. Originally a wheat-flour-based Irish specialty made with bicarbonate of soda as a leavening agent. It is often flavored with bacon, caraway seeds, or raisins.

SOLE. The base of the baking chamber of a bread oven, where the loaves are placed for baking. The stone soles of wood-burning ovens bake the best bread.

SOURDOUGH (ACID DOUGH). A piece of dough (sometimes just called the "sour") comprising flour and water (and often juice squeezed from a fruit), which is fermented for a few days and used as a "starter" to prepare the leaven.

SPELT. Variety of wheat (*Triticum spelta*) formerly used to make bread. Spelt flour is particularly suitable for bread making and can be made into a tasty loaf. This cereal, which was neglected for a long time because it was difficult to cultivate mechanically, is gradually coming back into favor.

STOCK. A ledge on the front of the oven on which are placed the various implements (peels, etc.) used to load and unload the oven.

STRAIGHT DOUGH. A procedure for preparing dough, common in England, in which all the ingredients are mixed together in one go. No-time dough is dough which can be divided as soon as it is mixed—not necessarily the same thing.

STRONG. Said of a flour with a high percentage of gluten and consequently best for bread making.

TOWER MILL. "Dutch" windmill generally made of stone, of which the movable top, the "cap," is rotated to face the wind. It is also known as a smock-mill or a frock-mill.

TORTILLA. A flat unleavened bread made from corn originated in Mexico.

TRAMEZZINO. A small triangular sandwich eaten in Italy, often made with a tin loaf.

TRENCHER. A slice of bread used as a plate in the Middle Ages. The trencher would absorb the juices from the meat and was eaten at the end of the meal or given to the servants.

UNLEAVENED BREAD. Bread which does not contain leaven or a leavening agent (that is to say, made with unfermented dough), such as the Jewish *matzo*, eaten during Passover, or the Catholic Host.

VIENNOIS, PAIN. A French wheaten bread, sweetened and enriched with milk and fat, in the form of a small *baguette* or as rolls.

VIENNESE ROLL. Plain light roll with a shiny crust.

WEAK. Said of a flour with a low percentage of gluten, suitable for cookies.

WHEAT. One of the oldest and most important of cereal crops, of the genus *Triticum*. Common or bread wheat (*T. aestivum*) and durum wheat (*T. durum*), which is used for pasta, are the most widely used modern species, divided into many variant cultivars. Early wheats include emmer and einkorn.

WHEAT GERM. The living part of the wheat seed, from which will be born the new plant when sown. The germ is rich in fats and vitamins, but is removed during roller milling. Traditional stone-grinding, however, conserves the wheat germ. Whole-wheat bread contains wheat germ.

WHEAT MEAL. Flour of approximately 85 percent extraction, used for various specialty breads and the normal "brown" loaf.

WHEATSHEAF. A showpiece bread in this shape.

WHOLE-WHEAT (WHOLEMEAL) BREAD. A loaf of varying composition and weight, comprising the entirety of the wheat grain: berry, germ, and bran. It is a bread much appreciated for its nutritional qualities. In French, it is known as *pain complet*.

YEAST. Baker's yeast is composed of the living cells of the yeast strain *Saccaromyces cerevisiae*. It allows for the fast and controllable fermentation of the dough. Most loaves today are fermented using a type of compressed yeast derived from brewer's barm at the beginning of the century.

B E C O M I N G   A   B A K E R

It is not necessary to have a qualification in order to become a baker in France, and many of today's best bakers learned the trade on the job. Nonetheless, in every French *département* there are training centers, many excellent, for apprentice bakers preparing the CAP (*certificat d'aptitude professionnelle*).

Institut National de la Boulangerie-Pâtisserie (address p. 184).
This institute offers eighteen-week training courses for the CAP and the *brevet de maîtrise* (twenty-one weeks).

Ecole Supérieure de Cuisine Française.
11, rue Jean-Ferrandi, 75006 Paris,
tel. 49 54 29 03.
This training center offers courses to people aged between sixteen and twenty-five for the

CAP in baking. The two-year program alternates a week of theory and a week of practical work under a baker. The center also organizes crash courses in bakery for schoolchildren.

Ecole de Boulangerie et de Pâtisserie de Paris.
BP 382, 75624 Paris Cedex 13, tel. 44 24 75 00.
This private school, founded by the Grands Moulins de Paris in 1929 and recognized by the state, offers various preparatory courses for the CAP in baking, the *brevet de maîtrise* and the *bac professionnel alimentation* (majoring in baking and pastry-making).

Les Compagnons du Devoir.
82, rue de l'Hôtel-de-Ville, 75180 Paris Cedex 04, tel: 44 78 22 50.
Before entry to one of the three centers run by the Les Compagnons du Devoir, the young stu-

dent (minimum age sixteen and having completed his or her *3ème*, or eighth grade) has to undergo a week of tests and interviews. If successful, he or she signs a contract of apprenticeship. After the CAP, the apprentice spends a year as a trainee under a baker; they then have to decide whether they want to try to become an "aspirant." If they do, they have to embark on a "tour de France" (three cities over a three-year period), after which they finally apply to become a member (*compagnon*) of the guild. This title is only awarded on acceptance of a *travail de reception* (the equivalent of the "masterpiece" of old). Once a *compagnon*, they continue the "tour de France" for a further two years, after which it is now they who are responsible for training apprentices.

BIBLIOGRAPHY

GENERAL WORKS

Ashley, Sir William. *The Bread of our Forefathers; An Inquiry in Economic History.* London, 1928.

Brothwell, D. and P. *Food in Antiquity: A Survey of the Diet of Early Peoples.* 1969.

Bürher, E.M. and W. Zehr. *La Pain à travers les âges.* Paris, 1985.

Calvel, Raymond, *La Boulangerie Moderne.* Pairs, 1980.

Casson, L. "Grain Trade in the Hellenistic World," in *Transactions of the American Philological Association,* 1954.

Confédération Nationale de la Boulangerie. *Mon Métier Boulanger.* Paris, 1985.

David, Elizabeth. *English Bread and Yeast Cookery.* Harmondsworth, 1979.

Desportes, Françoise. *Le Pain au Moyen Age.* Paris, 1987.

Jacob, H.E. *Histoire du Pain depuis 6000 ans.* Paris, 1985.

Kaplan, Steven L. *Bread, Politics, and Political Economy in the Reign of Louis XV.* 2 vols. The Hague, 1977.

————. *Provisioning Paris: Merchants and Millers in the Grain and Flour Trade in the Eighteenth Century.* Cornell, 1985.

Moritz, L.A. *Grain-mill and Flour in Classical Antiquity.* 1958.

"Nutritional Aspects of Bread and Flour," *Health and Social Subjects Reports.* Department of Health and Social Security. London, 1981.

Paston-Williams, Sara. *The Art of Dining: A History of Cooking and Eating.* London, 1993.

Stear, C.A., ed. *Handbook of Bread Making Technology.* Oxford, 1990.

Storck, J. and Teague, W.D. *Flour for Man's Bread: A History of Milling.* St. Paul, Minnesota, 1952.

Tannahill, Reay. *Food in History.* First published 1973. New and revised edition, Harmondsworth, 1988.

COOKBOOKS

Alford, Jeffrey and Naomi Duguid. *Flatbreads and Flavors: A Baker's Atlas.* New York, 1995.

Bateman, Michael, and Heather Maisner. *The Sunday Times Book of Real Bread.* Aylesbury, 1982.

Beard, James. *Beard on Bread.* New York, 1988.

California Culinary Academy. *Breads at the Academy.* Sant Rosa, California, 1985, 1993.

Clayton, Bernard Jr. *Bernard Clayton's New Complete Book of Bread.* Revised and expanded edition, New York, 1995.

Collister, Linda and Anthony Blake. Photography by Anthony Blake. *The Bread Book.* London, 1993.

Dannenberg, Linda. Photographs by Guy Bouchet. *Paris Boulangerie Patisserie: Recipes from Thirteen Outstanding French Bakers.* New York, 1994.

Duff, Gail. *Bread: 150 Traditional Recipes from around the World.* New York, 1993.

————. *The Complete Bread Book.* London, 1993.

Field, Carol. *The Italian Baker.* New York, 1985.

————. Photography by Joyce Oudkerk Pool. *Foccacia: Simple Breads from the Italian Oven.* San Francisco, 1994.

Hensperger, Beth. Photography by Joyce Oudkerk Pool. *The Art of Quick Breads: Simple, Everyday Baking.* San Francisco, 1994.

————. *Bread for all Seasons: Delicious and Distinctive Recipes for Year-Round Baking.* San Francisco, 1995.

Harlow, Jay. Photography by Viktor Budnik. *The Art of the Sandwich.* San Francisco, 1990.

Jaine, Tom. Photographs by Jacqui Hurst. *Making Bread at Home: 50 Recipes from Around the World.* London, 1995.

Johnson, Ellen Foscue. *The Bread Book: A Baker's Almanac.* Pownal, Vermont, 1994.

Kelly, Sarah. *Festive Baking in Austria, Germany, and Switzerland.* Harmondsworth, 1985.

Martin, Carolyn. *Our Daily Bread: Secrets from the Bakers of Cornwall.* Padstow, Cornwall, 1993.

Neal, Bill. *Biscuits, Spoonbread, and Sweet Potato Pie: 300 Recipes that Celebrate the Glories of Southern Baking.* New York, 1996.

Romer, Elizabeth. *Italian Pizza and Hearth Breads.* New York, 1987.

Shulman, Barbara Rose. Photography by Steven Mark Neetham. *Great Breads: Home-baked Favorites from Europe, the British Isles, and North America.* Sherbourne, Vermont, 1995.

Sokolov, Raymond. *With the Grain.* New York, 1996.

Steele, Louise. *The Book of Sandwiches.* London–New York, 1989.

Willian, Anne. *Look and Cook: Classic Breads.* London, 1995.

BREAD IN LITERATURE

Bosco, Henri. *Tante Martine.* Paris, 1972.

Daudet, Alphonse. *Lettres de mon Moulin.* Paris. 1994.

Giono, Jean. *Jean le Bleu.* Paris, 1932.

Gómez-Arcos, Agustin. *L'Enfant du Pain.* Paris, 1983.

Le Clézio, J.-M. G. *L'Inconnu sur la Terre.* Paris, 1978.

Lentéric, Bernard. *Les Maîtres du Pain.* Paris, 1993.

Pagnol, Marcel. *La Femme du Boulanger.* Paris, 1989.

Ponge, Francis. *La Partie Prise des Choses.* Paris, 1942.

HISTORICAL SOURCES

Diderot, Denis and Jean Le Rond d'Alembert. *L'Encyclopédie ou Dictionnaire raisonné des sciences, des arts et des métiers,* 1768.

Edlin, A. *A Treatise on the Art of Bread-Making.* London, 1805, reprinted 1992.

Kirkland, John. *The Modern Baker, Confectioner, and Caterer.* London, 1907.

Malouin, Paul-Jacques. *Description et détails des arts du Meunier, du vermicelier et du boulanger,* 1767. Reprinted Bayac, 1995.

Parmentier, Antoine Auguste. *Le Parfait Boulanger.* Paris, 1788. Reprinted Marseille, 1981.

Pliny the Elder. *Natural History,* First century A.D [Book XVIII, 27–29, bread]. Translated from the Latin by H. Rackman. Cambridge, Mass., 1950.

PICTURE CREDITS

P. 1 Nicolas Bruant; p. 2 Flammarion; p. 3 Guy Bouchet; p. 4 Flammarion; p. 5 Flammarion; p. 6 Willy Ronis/Rapho; p. 8-9 F. Kollar/AFDPP © Ministère de la Culture; pp. 10, 11, 13, 14 and 15 Pierre Ginet; pp. 16 and 17 Prunin/Rapho; p. 18 Heudorfer/Deutsches Brotmuseum, Ulm; p. 19 Roger-Viollet; p. 21 Photo Lensini/Opera del Duomo, Siena; p. 22 Artephot/Oronoz/Escorial, Madrid; p. 24 Dagli Orti/Archaeological Museum, Naples; p. 25 Dagli Orti/National Gallery of Antique Art, Rome; p. 26 Bibliothèque Municipale, Lyon; p. 27 Réunion des Musées Nationaux/Musée du Louvre, Paris; p. 28 Rijksmuseum, Amsterdam; pp. 29 and 30 Réunion des Musées Nationaux/Musées du Louvre, Paris; p. 31 Jean-Loup Charmet/Bibliothèque Nationale de France, Paris; p. 33 Réunion des Musées Nationaux/Musée du Louvre, Paris; p. 34 Bulloz; p. 35 top Dagli Orti/Rome Museum; p. 35 bottom Roger-Viollet/Museuo Civico, Merano; p. 36 top Bildarchiv Preussischer Kulturbesitz/Museum für Deutsche Volkskunde, Berlin; p. 36 bottom Jean-Loup Charmet/Musée Carnavalet, Paris; p. 37 Roger-Viollet; p. 38 top Edimedia; p. 38 bottom Réunion des Musées Nationaux/Palais du Tau, Reims; p. 39 Heudorfer/Deutsches Brotmuseum, Ulm; p. 40 Roger-Viollet; p. 41 Bibliothèque Nationale de France; p. 42 top Jean-Loup Charmet; p. 42 bottom Bettmann Archive, New York; p. 43 top Archiv für Kunst, Berlin; p. 43 bottom Harrods Archive, London; p. 44 Scala/Germanisches Nationalmuseum, Nuremberg; p. 45 top Réunion des Musées Nationaux/Musée National du Château de Fontainebleau; p. 45 bottom Scala/Antella; p. 46 Scala/Odessa Museum; p. 47 Dagli Orti, Paris; p. 49 Jean-Bernard Laffitte; p. 50 top Véron-Skinner, Paris; p. 50 bottom Jean-Bernard Laffitte; p. 51 Véron-Skinner; p. 52 B. Veysset/Explorer, Vanves; p. 53 Bridgeman Art Library, London; p. 54 H. Silvester/Rapho; p. 55 top Jean-Bernard Laffitte; p. 55 bottom H. Silvester/Rapho; p. 57 Réunion des Musées Nationaux/Musée du Louvre, Paris; p. 58 top Philippe Giraud/Terres du Sud, Venasque; P. 58 bottom Roger-Viollet; p. 59 J. N. Reichel/Top, Paris; p. 60 bottom Philippe Giraud/Terres du Sud; p. 61 P. Plisson/Explorer, Vanves; pp. 62-63 Bulloz/Musée du Petit Palais, Paris; pp. 65, 66-67 Pierre Ginet; p. 68 top Régis Weil, Dijon; p. 69 Philippe Giraud/Terres du Sud, Venasque; p. 70 Bridgeman Art Library/ Museo Pohjanmaan, Oulu; p. 71 top Bildarchiv Preussischer Kulturbesitz/Museum für Deutsche Volkskunde, Berlin; p. 71 bottom W. Louvet/Visa, Vanves; pp. 72 and 73 F. Kollar/AFDPP © Ministère de la Culture; p. 74 Jean-Loup Charmet/Bibliothèque des Arts Décoratifs, Paris; p. 75 Bildarchiv Preussischer Kulturbesitz, Berlin; p. 76 bottom Pierre Ginet; pp. 78 and 79 Nicolas Bruant; p. 80 F. Kollar/AFDPP © Ministère de la Culture; p. 81 Guy Bouchet; p. 82 top F. Kollar/ARDPP © Ministère de la Culture; p. 83 bottom Pierre Ginet; pp. 84-85 Nicolas Bruant; p. 86 Véron-Skinner; p. 87 Cinestar, Paris; pp. 88 and 89 Nicolas Bruant; p. 90 top F. Perri/Cosmos, Paris; p. 90 bottom Jean Gaumy/Magnum; p. 91 Nicolas Bruant; p. 92 C.N.M.H.S./© Spadem 1996; p. 93 top Pierre Ginet; p. 93 bottom Edimédia; p. 94 Roger-Viollet; p. 95 top Photothèque des Musées de la Ville de Paris/© Spadem 1996; p. 96 Roger-Viollet; p. 97 Bridgeman Art Library/Giraudon, London; pp. 98-99 Nicolas Bruant; p. 100 top Jérôme Darblay; p. 100 bottom J.-P. Terrillon; p. 101 top Pierre Ginet; p. 101 bottom Nicolas Bruant; p. 102 Pierre Ginet; p. 103 Flammarion/Deduisson collection; pp. 104 and 105 top Pierre Hussenot/Top; p. 105 bottom Réunion des Musées Nationaux/Musées des Arts et Traditions Populaires, Paris; p. 106 Véron-Skinner; p. 107 Pierre Ginet; p. 108 top Atelier photo Francis Holveck/Le Chasse Marée, Douarnenez; p. 108 bottom Soazig/Explorer, Vanves; p. 109 Pierre Ginet; pp. 110 and 111 Pierre Ginet; p. 112 Pierre Hussenot; p. 113 Pierre Ginet; p. 114 Museum of Advertising and Packaging, Gloucester; p. 115 bottom Pierre Ginet; p. 116 Pierre Ginet; p. 117 top Archiv für Kunst, Berlin; p. 117 bottom La Phothothèque Culinaire, Courbevoie; pp. 118, 119, 120, 121 Pierre Ginet; p. 122 top Jérôme Darblay; p. 122 bottom Marc Walter; p. 123 Bruno Barbey/Magnum; pp. 124 and 125 Pierre Hussenot; pp. 126 and 127 Pierre Ginet; pp. 128 and 129 H. Silvester/ Rapho; p. 130 top Deville/Gamma, Vanves; pp. 130 bottom and 131 Swanson/Gamma; p. 132 Pierre Ginet; p. 133 © Jean Gabanou/ DIAF, Paris; p. 134 top Burt Glinn/Magnum; p. 134 bottom Dubois/Explorer, Vanves; p. 135 Pierre Hussenot/Top; p. 136 top Robert Harding, London; p. 136 bottom Pierre Hussenot/Top; p. 137 Jérôme Darblay; p. 138 Roland Michaud/Rapho; p. 139 Franken/ Explorer, Vanves; p. 140 Eric Lawrie/ Hutchinson Library, London; p. 141 Dannemiller/Saba-Rea; p.142 Bettmann Archive; p. 143 Bettmann Archive; p. 144 left Michael London; p. 144 right Flammarion; p. 145 left Berenice Abbott/Commerce Graphics Ltd, East Rutherford; p. 145 right Robert Harding Picture Library, London; p. 146 Pierre Hussenot; p. 147 top J. P. Terrillon; p. 147 bottom G. Bavoillot; p. 148 Pierre Ginet p. 150 Hervé Amiard/Top; p. 151 Pierre Ginet; pp. 152 and 153 Pierre Ginet; p. 154 Hulton Deutsch, London; p. 155 Pierre Ginet; p. 156 Mary Evans Picture Library, London; p. 157 Pierre Ginet; p. 158 Keystone/Sygma, Paris; p. 159 Photographer's Gallery/Len De Pas, Washington; p. 160 Pierre Ginet; p. 161 Flammarion.

Abendbrot (evening bread) 118
aesh 136
Alembert, Jean Le Rond d' 31, 35
Apfelnussbrot 118, 120
Apollinaire, Guillaume 96
apple bread 152

bagel 132, 144–145
baguette 8, 12, 14, 16–17, 37, 41, 74–75, 77, 82, 86–87, 90, 93–96, 105–106, 111, 114, 140, 144–145, 148–150, 153–158
baguette viennoise 101
bakeries: Acme Bread 144; Autre Boulange (L') 10; Boulangerie Azrak 100; Cheasapeake Bagel Bakery 144; Harrods Food Hall 43, 114; Galli's 128; Lionel's Poilâne 78, 81, 89–90, 106; Max Poilâne's 81; Moulin de la Vierge (Le) 78, 89, 91; Rock Hill Bakehouse (The) 144
Balcaen, Georges 72–73
bängeli 119
baps 114
barbari 137
Barbier, Edgar 56, 60, 61, 64
Bard, William W. 42
bâtard 12, 17, 41, 96, 105, 108, 145, 149, 156
bauerruch 121
Belgium 119
benoîton 101
Béraud, Henri 10
berches 106
biova 126
black bread 130–132
blinis 130
Bosco, Henri 17
Boucherès, Laurent 86, 91
Bouscarel, M. 154
braided bread 106, 132, 144
brioche 10, 114, 150
Britain 14, 115, 156
broa de milho 122–123
bun 114, 140, 145
Burban, Bernard 150–152, 155

Cahier 38
Calvel, Raymond 103, 149
Canada 142–144
carasàu or *carta de musica* 113, 126

Cato Censorius 23
cereals: barley 32, 41, 46, 103; black weat 55; buckweat (saracen corn) 46, 55, 64; corn 46, 53–54; durum 64; linseed 64; millet 46, 54, 64; oats 54; rye 46, 52, 64, 114, 117; sesame 64; spelt 64; wheat 48–50, 64
Cervantès 56
challa 132
chapati 139
chapeau (hat) 93, 110
charleston 106
chernyi khilb 130
Chesapeake Bagel Bakery 144
China 139
ciabatta 126–128, 144
Cipriani, Arrigo 126
ciriola 126
Continental Baking Corporation 42
cordon (cord) 93, 107
corn bread 142
corn pone 142
cottonseed bread 103
couronne 103, 105
couronne bordelaise 111
couronne de Bugey 106
Cousin, Michel 10
cramique 119
cressene 72
croissant 96, 119
Czech Republic 132

Daudet, Alphonse 55, 58
Daumard, Marie 8
Denmark 118
Derécourt, Guy 64–69
Diderot, Denis 31, 35, 93
Du Cange 26
Ducasse, Alain 64
Dupaigne, Bernard 134

Egypt 136
Epicurus 12, 14
Eurysaces, Vergilius 23
Evans, Oliver 37

faluche 108
fer à cheval (horseshoe) 107
fermentation 76, 83, 101, 149
ficelle 12, 41, 75, 96, 150, 155–156
flatbrod 118
flûte 96
flûte Gana 74, 86

flûtine 14
focaccia 126–128, 144
fouée 110
fougasse 94, 105–106, 137
francala 137
France 14, 93–110, 142
francesine 126
French Vienna bread 34, 95, 101, 157
fruit breads 107, 153
Furstenberg, Mark 158

gâche 108
Ganachaud, Bernard 74, 82, 86–87, 89
Ganachaud, Isabelle 82
Ganachaud, Valérie 82
Gauducheau, Pierre 150
Genet, Jean 53
Germany 117
gingerbread 115
Giono, Jean 95, 105
Gluten bread 103
gluten bread 103
Goethe, J. W. 117
Gómez-Arcos, Agustín 124
Greece 128, 137
Grimm, Brothers 23, 118
grissini (sticks) 113, 126, 144

Halladay, Daniel 58
Helsmetter, Daniel 106
Herodotus 23
Homer 23
Hooper, Stephen 58
Hugo, Victor 45, 48
Huysmans, J.K. 154

Ireland 115
Italy 126, 140, 156

Japan 139
Jeudon, Jean 14, 55, 64, 86
Juvenal 25

Kamir, Basil 64, 77, 83
kesret 136
khoubz 137
kneading 34, 36, 72, 74, 77, 81–82, 85, 100–101, 149
Körnlipicker 121

La Fontaine, Jean de 25
La Reynière, Grimod de 96
Landbrot 117
Latin America 140
lavash 137
Le Clézio, J.-M.G. 78, 83

Lecocq, Pascal 64–69
Lecocq, Pierre 64
Lee, Edmund 58
Legay, Guy 150
linenseed bread 103
Loiseau, Bernard 100, 147
London, family 144

Mahou, Jacques 150
main de Nice (Nice Hand) 105
maniode 106
matzos 22
Maurice, Xavier 68
Mayer, Louie 114
maza 23
Meikle, Andrew. 58
mella 23
Mendel, Gregor 37
Mesnier, Claude 150–152
méture 111, 156
mezza luna (half-moon) 128
michetta, or *rosetta* 126–128
Middle East 136–137
Miller, Henry 142
mills: Bassilour 56, 111; at Chesnay 56–64; Decollogne–Lecocq 64, 68–69; Giraud 68; du Rat 56; Saint–Pierre 58
mini-baguette 150
mischbrot 117
moricette 106
Müller 37
naan 139

Necker, Jacques 32
Netherlands 117

orange-flavored rolls 152
organic bread 159
ovens 8, 12, 37, 87–90, 135–136

Pagnol, Marcel 93, 95, 105
pagnotta 126
pain à l'ail (bread with garlic) 101
pain à la bière (beer bread) 107
pain à la pomme de terre (potato bread) 101, 142
pain à la Reine (Queen's bread) 32
pain au fenouil (bread with fennel) 101, 152
pain au fromage (cheese bread) 101, 153
pain au lait (milk bread) 96

pain au lard (with bacon pieces) 101, 150
pain au seigle (with rye) 100, 150
pain au thym (thyme bread) 101
pain au vin (wine-flavored) 150, 152
pain aux figues (with figs) 101, 152
pain aux noix (with walnuts) 101, 107, 150–153
pain aux oignons (with onions) 101
pain aux olives (with olives) 101, 152
pain ballé 31
pain bis (with bran) 32
pain bouli 106
pain boulot (sandwich bread) 108
pain brié or *au cumin* 101, 108, 150–152
pain chapelet (rosary bread) 31
pain coiffé 106
pain collier (necklace) 111
pain complet (whole-wheat bread) 52, 100, 159
pain coquille (shell loaf) 28
pain cornu 93
pain d'Aix 105
pain de Beaucaire 106
pain de Brane 32
pain de brode 28
pain de campagne 10–17, 77, 83, 89, 93, 100, 148–150, 153, 156–158
pain de Chailly 28
pain de deux-couleurs 31
pain de fantaisie (fancy bread) 41, 95
pain de Gonesse 26–28, 32
pain de gruau 101
pain de Lodève 106
pain de méteil (maslin bread) 106, 150

pain de seigle (rye bread) 100, 103, 117, 150–153, 155
pain épi 103, 108
pain fendu (split loaf) 93, 106
pain gris du Morvan 147–148
pain ménage (household bread) 94
pain mollet 31–32, 93
pain or *pain parisien* 83, 87, 90, 96, 106
pain perdu (French toast) 142, 156–157
pain platine 108
pain plié (folded loaf) 93, 110
pain Poilâne 43, 84–85, 145
pain polka (chequerboard loaf) 93, 96, 110–111
pain ravoux 10
pain rennais 110
pain rousset 31
pain-égalité (equality bread) 32
pains aux céréales (multigrain bread) 55, 103
pains de festin (festival breads) 32, 133
pane de Trani 126
pane sciapo 126
paratha 139
Parmentier, Augustin Antoine 31
Péguy, Charles 56
petit pain (roll) 12, 31, 76, 83, 96, 154
Petrini, Paolo 113
pide 137
pioneer bread 142
pistolet 119
pita 128, 137, 154
Pliny the Elder 23
Poilâne, Lionel 43, 60, 75–84, 87–90, 96, 106, 145, 152, 156–157
Poilâne, Max 64, 77–81, 87, 89
Poland 130
pompette 94
Ponge, Francis 16

poolish 34, 36, 77–78, 101
poppy-seed bread 107, 118, 152
porte-manteau (coat hanger) 111
Portugal 122
Poujauran, Jean-Luc 64, 96, 150
pretzel 35, 38, 106, 107, 117
Proust, Marcel 90
Prunier, Jean-Pierre 153
Pumpernickel 107, 117–118, 130, 144
raisin bread 115, 152–153

Rebuchon, Joël 64, 150
Restaurants: Côte d'Or (La) 100, 147; Espadon (L') 150, 155–156; Harry's Bar 126; Hôtel de Paris 64; Joël Robuchon 64, 150; Lucas-Carton 64, 152; McDonald's 145; Tartine (La) 154
Rimbaud, Arthur 71
Roggenbrot 117
rollermills 37
rolls 114
rugbrød 118
Russia 130

saffron bread 156
Saibron, Dominique 140
Saint-Exupéry, Antoine de 16
sako 55, 119
Sandwich, Lord 154
sandwich loaf 100, 114, 154, 157
sandwiches: 126, 140, 148, 154–155; *bruschetta* 140, 156; *crouston* 156; *croque-monsieur* 158; *jambon-beurre* 154; *pa amb tomàquets* 156; *pan-bagnat* 154; *panini* 126, 140; *pizza* 140; *pita* 154; *tacos* 140; *tortino* 140; *tramenzzini* 126, 154
Sauserbrot 120

Scandinavia 117–118
Schwarzwalder Bauerbrot (Black forest peasant bread) 117
scones 114
Senderens, Alain 64, 152–153
Seneca 12
simits 137
smørrebrød (butter bread) 118
soda bread 114–115, 144
sorghum bread 103
soufflâme 110
soya bread 103
Spain 123–124, 140
spelt bread 103
spoon bread 142
stone-ground bread 159
Sübrot 106–107
Sulzberger, Jacob 37
Switzerland 118–120

Tabu, Thierry 78, 86, 89–91
Tebbenhof 34
tignolet 111
tordu 106, 111
tortilla 54, 140
tourton 110
Traubenbrot 158

United States 14, 142, 144, 156
Urigsbrot (puckish bread) 120

Verneuil, Henri 87
Veyrat, Jean-Pierre 87
Vietnam 139
Virgil 23

Watt, James 37
Woolf, Virginia 114
yeast 32–34, 76–77, 96

Zang, baron 34
Zola, Émile 48
Zürich bread 118
Zwetochgenbrot 120

ACKNOWLEDGMENTS

The author would like to express his sincere gratitude to the following people who provided invaluable assistance during the preparation and writing of this volume: Georges Balcaen, Edgar Barbier, Jean-Luc Bourny, Jean Charbonnier, Bruno Denis, Guy Derécourt, Jacques Duhesme, Patrick Ferrand, Mark Furstenberg, Bernard Ganachaud, Jean-Marie Jaudon, Basile Kamir, Corby Kummer, François L'Yvonnet, Patricia Menay, Marcel Montagne, Luciana Mottola-Colban, Lionel Poilâne, Max Poilâne, Tina Rakoto, Philippe Roussel, Dominique Saibron, Thierry Tabu, Leda Vegliardi Paravia . . . and all the bakers who graciously invited him into their bakeries.

He would also like to thank Ghislaine Bavoillot and the editorial team who worked on this book: Sophie Alibert, Nathalie Bailleux, Claire Lamotte, Véronique Manssy, Caroline Regnaut-Labord, Marc Walter, and particularly Béatrice Petit for her admirable picture research.

The publishers would like to thank in particular Robert Faivre, who worked as a baker for many years in Clairegoutte (Haute-Saône); from fascinating anecdotes to valuable technical information, he communicated his love of good bread and desire to create this book.

The publishers also thank all the people who provided assistance and advice during the preparation of this volume: Cecilia Abert, Leslie J. Barr (United States), Madame Baudon, Anna Bini (Florence and the Casa Bini restaurant in Paris), Yvonne Courtney (London), Joe Fitchett, Madame Gantois of the École de boulangerie, Madame Ursel Gerner of the Hotel Nizza in Frankfurt, Urs Hunziker (Switzerland), Amanda James, Mr. D. C. Janssens of the Maison de Van Gogh (Auvers-sur-Oise), Jean-Marie Jaudon, Régine Kopp, Corby Kummer (United States), Magali Le Gall, Sandra Livingstone, and Sabine Möbius (Bakery Department, Harrods, London) Marie-Line Madou, Pierre-André Masteau, Janet Pilch (London), François-Xavier de Wouters.

Grateful acknowledgments also go out to the restaurant owners, chefs, bakers, and millers who allowed us to taste the thousand-and-one breads sampled during the preparation of this book: the Alves bakery (Bordeaux), the Maures artisanal bakery, Roger Auzet, Gwenith Bassetti of Grand Central Bakery, the Bio Andreas bakery (Basel), Michel Bourdin of the Connaught Hotel (London), Jean Bouscarel, Bernard Burban of the Ritz Hotel in Paris, Antonio Carluccio of the Neal Street Restaurant (London), Arrigo Cipriani of Harry's Bar (Venice), Michel Cousin, Michel Dobbs of the Tom Cat Bakery (Long Island), Mr. Engström of the Flora Danica restaurant (Paris), Mr. de Troze of the Au Vatel Jourdan restaurant (Brussels), Mark Furstenberg of the Marvelous Market (Washington, D.C.), Bernard Ganachaud, Paul and Marc Haeberlin of the Auberge de l'Ill, the Heberer restaurant (Frankfurt), Christian Heiz of the Heiz-Legris bakery (Caen), the Helmstetter bakery (Colmar), Monique and Emile Jung as well as Alfred Georg of the Au Crocodile restaurant, Lydie Kromwel of Baguépi, Gaston Lenôtre, Mr. Lhuillier of the Moulin de Bassilour, the Lochner bakery (Frankfurt), Michael and Wendy London of the Rock Hill Bakehouse (Greenwich, New York), Marcel Montagne, Jean-Louis Palladin (Washington, D.C.), Jean-Luc Poujauran, Paolo Petrini, the Sutter bakery (Basel), Mr. Henri Tarascon, of the Zoller bakery (Basel).

Finally, the publishers would like to thank Pierre Ginet and Christine Drin, who photographed with great talent the breads of France and the world, and whose extreme flexibility allowed them to photograph the breads at their freshest; Olivier Canaveso and Barbara Kekus (Octavo); Margarita Mariano; and Murielle Vaux, who were responsible for the production of this volume.